Kafka and the Universal

Interdisciplinary German Cultural Studies

Edited by
Irene Kacandes

Volume 21

Kafka and the Universal

Edited by
Arthur Cools and Vivian Liska

DE GRUYTER

ISBN 978-3-11-045532-8
e-ISBN (PDF) 978-3-11-045811-4
e-ISBN (EPUB) 978-3-11-045743-8
ISSN 1861-8030

Library of Congress Cataloging-in-Publication Data
A CIP catalog record for this book has been applied for at the Library of Congress.

Bibliographic information published by the Deutsche Nationalbibliothek
The Deutsche Nationalbibliothek lists this publication in the Deutsche Nationalbibliografie;
detailed bibliographic data are available on the Internet at http://dnb.dnb.de.

© 2016 Walter de Gruyter GmbH, Berlin/Boston
Cover image: Franz Kafka, 1917. © akg-images / Archiv K. Wagenbach
Printing and binding: CPI books GmbH, Leck
♾ Printed on acid-free paper
Printed in Germany

www.degruyter.com

Table of Contents

Arthur Cools and Vivian Liska
Kafka and the Universal: Introduction

Jean-Paul Sartre's saying that "Kafka's testimony is all the more universal as it is profoundly singular"[1] is indicative of a key paradox in the reception of Kafka during the twentieth century, a paradox that has wide-reaching implications for our understanding of the interface between literature and philosophy. It is characteristic of the philosophical reception of Kafka's work that it is repeatedly invoked in the context of attempts to escape from universal notions that have been inherited from a modern foundational thinking; these notions include the subject, thinking, and existence. Of paramount importance in this context is the concept of *singularity*, which is at odds with philosophy's ambitions, which have traditionally been expressed in terms of the universal and the essential. Philosophical attempts to counter this tradition frequently turn to modern literature in search of an experience of *singularity* that involves a sense of alienation that cannot be encapsulated by concepts. The striking frequency of references to Kafka in this endeavor (more so even than to other modernist writers such as Beckett, Mallarmé, Proust, or Joyce) is surprising, given that Kafka's prose is characterized by rather indeterminate spatio-temporal representations and seemingly uninterrupted realistic descriptions. His writing has thus been widely praised for its rendering of a universal *condition humaine*. Kafka is indeed often regarded as the ultimate witness to the human condition in the twentieth century and, like Dante, Shakespeare, and Goethe in their times, is attributed universal significance. Why is it, then, that Kafka can nevertheless be considered to have given the ultimate voice to the experience of the singular?

The paradox between the universal significance attributed to Kafka's work and the references to it as a paradigmatic expression of a singularity that cannot be subsumed under any generalization engenders questions not only regarding Kafka's specificity, but also about philosophy's approach to his work. These questions require attention to how Kafka's writings introduce singularity at both the semantic and the formal level in a radically inconspicuous manner, and to philosophy's "double bind," especially as concerns philosophy's attempt to articulate the singular while inevitably resorting to its traditional tendency of conceptualizing its object of investigation. The contributions to this volume address, in a

---

1 Jean-Paul Sartre, "La Demilitarisation de la culture" ("The Demilitarization of Culture"), excerpted in *Situations VII*, Gallimard, Paris 1962, 322–331, 326.

variety of ways, the interplay between literature and philosophy that is at stake in this paradox.

An interdisciplinary approach is essential for a volume dedicated to clarifying the ways in which philosophy and literature are related to each other in Kafka. The contributions to this volume approach the paradox of the universal and the singular from a variety of perspectives and points of departure. While some treat the topic in straightforward philosophical terms and regard the universal in an ontological, epistemological, or phenomenological sense, others focus on it through more cultural and religious terms. The latter is particularly true for those essays in which Kafka's Jewishness, and Judaism more generally, plays a central role. Some of the essays in this volume are devoted to showing a philosophical position or clarification of concepts in Kafka's writings and their reception; others explore individual literary stories in order to show how they challenge pre-established concepts of the universal and invite us to reconsider the meanings of the universal. We did not wish to separate these two approaches into different sections, as this would suggest a dichotomy between a philosophical and a literary approach to the paradox of the universal and the singular in Kafka. Such a clear demarcation would resolve the paradox rather than expose it. Instead, we opted to structure the volume according to recurrent themes in the contributions: these include ambiguity as a tool of deconstructing the pre-established philosophical meanings of the universal, the concept of the law as a major symbol for the universal meaning of Kafka's writings, the presence of animals which, in Kafka's scenes and stories, blurs the divide between the singular and the universal, the modernist mode of writing as challenge of philosophical concepts of the universal, and the social and political meaning of the universal in contemporary Kafka reception. These themes constitute the five sections of the volume. In each, the interplay between philosophy and literature is illuminated in light of new approaches to the question of the universal.

In the first section, entitled "The Ambiguity of the Singular," the meaning of Kafka's literary work is reconsidered in relation to the philosophical discourse on the universal. The opening chapter, Stanley Corngold's "The Singular Accident in a Universe of Risk: An Approach to Kafka and the Paradox of the Universal," formulates concisely the main problem of the universal and the singular in relation to the work of Kafka: in short, do we submit this work to philosophical examination if we attribute to it a universal meaning or, on the contrary, do we read Kafka's writings and learn from this reading in order to reconsider the meaning of the universal? In the former case, we apply pre-established concepts of the universal and the singular to Kafka's work; in the latter we discover in Kafka's writings new meanings of the singular and the universal. Corngold shows that one cannot separate these two directions of research and explains why: Kafka, on several occasions, refers to a philosophical legacy of the universal, especially to "the pure, the true, the immutable."[2] Hence, Corngold initiates an inquiry on the philosophical *in* Kafka's work while simultaneously declaring the primacy of his fiction for the confessional. Consequently, Corngold's approach combines a clarification of the philosophical legacy in Kafka with a particular attention to the specific linguistic features and images of Kafka's sentences.

In his "Philosophy and Ambiguity in Benjamin's Kafka," Brendan Moran examines the role of ambiguity in the manifestation of the paradox. He argues that not paradox but ambiguity is the philosophical element in literature. The paradox creates a straightforward opposition to the mythical, whereas philosophy reveals the intrusion of ambiguity in myth and opens a dimension of polyvalence (*Mehrdeutigkeit*). Moran focuses on ambiguity in Walter Benjamin's interpretation of Kafka's writings and shows that Benjamin implicitly regards Kafka's literary work as "a victory over Kierkegaard's paradox,"[3] according to which the individual stands in an absolute relation to the absolute.

Starting from a remark by Theodor Adorno on Benjamin's approach to Kafka, Søren Rosendal brings to the fore an astonishing relation between Kafka and Hegel in his contribution, "The Logic of the 'Swamp World': Hegel with Kafka on the Contradiction of Freedom." In a traditional interpretation, this relation has been described as a radical opposition: Kafka expresses the singular experience of the individual exposed to and victimized by a universal, impenetrable system. Hegel, in contrast, develops a systematic logic in which the experience of the individual disappears. Rosendal, however, points to an intersection between Hegel and Kafka, which is the inescapability of contradiction within the structure of freedom: the possibility of a free act depends on the outer, objective space of action which is not empty but a "swamp world." In order to demonstrate that Kafka and Hegel share a secret affinity, the author is particularly attentive both to the movement and fluidity in Hegel's logic of contradiction and to the ambiguous ways of describing the protagonist's actions in Kafka's writings.

In the third chapter of this section, "The Necessary Revision of the Concept of the Universal: Kafka's 'Singularity,'" Arnaud Villani presents Kafka's work as the starting point of a new thinking that facilitates questioning the ontological tradition of philosophy as a whole. In this tradition, the universal is thought conceptually by separating (abstracting) the meaning of all things from any marks of

---

2 Franz Kafka, *The Diaries 1910–1923*, ed. Max Brod, trans. Joseph Kresh and Martin Greenberg with cooperation of Hannah Arendt, Schocken Books, New York 1976, 387.
3 Walter Benjamin, *Gesammelte Schriften* [*Collected Writings*], Vol. II:3, eds. Rolf Tiedemann and Hermann Schweppenhauser, Suhrkamp Verlag, Frankfurt/M. 1977, 1268.

the singular event from which it arises. The power of this thought results from the possibility to grasp (*be-greifen*, *con-cipere*) the essence of things. Kafka, however, restores the resistance of the singular via a thought that the author calls "abrupt," because it cannot separate the specificity of each singular phenomenon from the presence of the whole. A thick, detailed, unstable writing that is able to undo evident conceptual relations or to realize unexpected conceptual cross-overs follows from this transformation of thought.

The volume's second section, entitled "Before the Law," collects three original approaches to the parable "Before the Law." It is interesting to note that this text remains a major reference in reflection on the universal in Kafka, not least because of the concept and the figuration of law that it implies. In this short parable, which constitutes one of the central literary texts of modernity, the universal meets the singular in a paradoxical way. As noted in the story, "the law should be accessible for everyone at any time"; nevertheless the door through which one could gain admittance to the law is "only intended for you." This contradiction, involving the concise settings of the law, challenges the reader to interpret the narrative's most minute signs and details.

In "*Am-ha'aretz*: The Law of the Singular. Kafka's Hidden Knowledge," Eli Schonfeld finds in a Talmudic passage the source that may have inspired Kafka for this short story. The protagonist of the story, the man from the country who comes to the doorkeeper and requests admittance to the law, is, according to Schonfeld, the Talmudic figure of the *am-ha'retz*, who was associated in rabbinic literature with those who were ignorant of the law and opposed to the *talmid chacham*, the scholar of the law. From this starting point, the author recalls Benjamin's distinction between law and *Lehre* and Benjamin's preference, in his reflections on Kafka, for the latter. Interpreting the doorkeeper in the story as a figure of the *talmid chacham*, Schonfeld shows how Benjamin's distinction functions in "Before the Law" and argues that this story reveals the place *before* the law as the place of predilection with regard to the law. This is contrary to contemporary interpretations according to which Kafka's story expresses the idea of a fulfilment of the law – an access to the law – or the idea of a suspension or *difference* of the law.

From a different perspective, Arthur Cools, in his contribution, "Desire and Responsibility: The Case of K.," joins in his interpretation of Kafka's parable the idea that "before the law" *is* the law. However, his main focus is the protagonist Josef K. of *The Trial*, the novel in which the parable of "Before the Law" is told. Cools argues that the story "Before the Law" can be understood as a kind of abstract symbol of the narrative of *The Trial*, but he searches in the singular chain of images in this narrative for the signs that can reveal something about the nature of the law and the demand of having access to the law. In order to approach the enigmatic meanings of Kafka's parable, the author examines whether, how, and to what extent it is possible to embed the narrative of *The Trial* into the Greek legacy of the tragic model. The opening scene of the tragic model is indeed the problem of being chosen or accused by a demand that is addressed only to the individual and to which she or he has no access, as is the case in *The Trial*. However, the examination reveals fundamental differences, in particular as concerns the concept of law: in Greek tragedy, the law is clear, but in default; in *The Trial*, however, the law is omnipresent, but not transparent. As such, Cools argues (against Zygmunt Bauman's interpretation, according to which Kafka's parable calls for a new approach to justice and responsibility) that the law in Kafka's narrative is not the expression of a universal idea of justice, responsibility, or freedom according to which the protagonist claims his innocence. In interpreting the chain of images in *The Trial*, he shows that the reverse is the case: the law and the demand to have access to the law are the expression of and are bound by the ambiguities of the protagonist's erotic desires.

Michal Ben-Naftali's contribution, "Derrida-Reads-Kafka," deals with the presence of Kafka's "Before the Law" in Derrida's readings. She shows how the transcendence of the law, as figured in Kafka's parable and which Derrida avoids identifying in Jewish terms of the Tora, is a basic structure in Derrida's thought and operates in his reflections on the fictional moment of foundation, whether it is political, as is the case of his essay "Force de Loi: le 'fondement mystique de l'autorité'" ("Force of Law: The 'Mystical Foundation of Authority'"),[4] or moral, as for instance in his interpretation of Freud's account of the origin of moral law. This basic structure is revealed in Derrida's approach to literature, in particular in what he calls the Biblical origins of literature. The main figure of this origin is Abraham, who keeps his secret and remains silent when he commences to prepare the sacrifice of his son Isaac. This secret and this silence delineates a scene and a space where the law remains inaccessible, where father and son are related to each other through the secret of the father, and where the son witnesses the silence of the father. In this way, Ben-Naftali points at an astonishing continuity in Derrida's readings of literary texts which relates the Biblical narrative of Abraham to Kafka's parable "Before the Law" through a reading of Kafka's "Letter to His Father." In light of this continuity, she argues, Kafka's parable "Before the Law" becomes a kind of symbol for the nature of the literary work as such.

The animal is the central issue in the volume's third section, entitled "Animals." There are unquestionably many animal figures in Kafka's writing. They seem to express each time an experience of singularity *par excellence* not

---

4 Jacques Derrida, "Force de Loi: le 'fondement mystique de l'autorité,'" Galilé, Paris 2005.

only because they do not fit into the concepts and categories of human existence, but moreover because they are related to an experience of a unique event, as is the case in the story of the giant mole and in "The Metamorphosis." However, in Kafka's narratives, these events influence human interactions and disturb the apparently evident concepts of human understandings.

Rodolphe Gasché's contribution, "Of Mammoth Smallness: Franz Kafka's 'The Village Schoolmaster,'" is a close reading of Kafka's story "The Village Schoolmaster [The Giant Mole]" and a fascinating examination of the struggle in this story between the schoolmaster of the country and the narrator, the businessman of the city. Gasché brings to the fore the meanings of the giant mole as a key element of his interpretation of this narration although the presence of the mole is most elusive in the story. In establishing a surprising similarity with the structure of the singular and the universal in the story "Before the Law," the author carefully shows how the unique (in)significance of the giant mole determines the protagonists' interactions and transforms the traditional concepts of the universal. In this way, he demonstrates why a widespread assumption in Kafka scholarship – that Kafka's heroes are the victims of an oppressive bureaucratic system – is in fact mistaken.

In his contribution, "Irreducible Pluralities: The Jewish Legacy of Franz Kafka," David Suchoff addresses the question of the universal from a different perspective, that of Kafka's humour. Laughter is the capacity of obtaining pleasure from the failure of matching universal categories. Kafka, according to Suchoff, finds a specific Jewish way to express this capacity. Suchoff thus addresses particular attention to Kafka's multiple languages: his interest in Yiddish theatre, his rewritings of the story of Abraham, his attitude towards the German language. In this reflection, the presence of the animal figures in Kafka's writings, as is the case in "Report to an Academy" and "Investigations of a Dog," plays a major role because the animals encourage one to de-identify with the German language or to undermine the authority of the relation to the father or to discover the gaps in the legacy of the past. In this way, Kafka invites us to the experience of laughter, "that animal in us all."

Kafka's bestiary is the central core of Anna Glazova's original approach in her contribution, "Kafka's Cat-Lamb: The Hybridization of Genesis and Taxonomy." Glazova is interested in the phenomenon of hybridization in Kafka's writings which undermines and resists conceptualization. In her approach, this phenomenon is not limited to the imagination of the figure of a hybrid, but includes a linguistic aspect: a cross-over between proper names and animal figures. In this respect, hybridization transforms the signifying function of general terms. Glazova examines in particular the hybrid figure of the cat-lamb in Kafka's story "A Crossbred," showing a genealogy from two conflicting names from Kafka's paternal and maternal bloodlines: Kafka means "jackdaw" in Czech; Loewy derives from "Löwe," or "lion." Being a child of both means to be a bird and a cat, a prey and a predator. In a fascinating deepening of Kafka's Jewish taxonomy of animals, Glazova shows that the hybridization is not just a linguistic tool to express the singular: in fact, it still conceals a logic, the logic of sacrifice, as in the story of Abraham and Isaac.

The chapters of the fourth section, entitled "Modernism," resituate and reconsider certain features of modernism in Kafka's work in light of the question of the universal. How does the attention to the specific conditions of literary production concern and transform the universalist concept of literature that is traditionally based upon the ethical function attributed to literature? This is the central question in Jean-Michel Rabaté's contribution, "Kafka's Anti-Epiphanies." He calls attention to Kafka's aphorisms, especially the Zürau aphorisms, which are, according to the author, the ultimate expressive form of Kafka's modernism. In order to understand how this fragmentary form mediates between the universal and the particular, Rabaté compares Kafkan aphorism to the Joycean epiphanies. He details an interesting similarity between them with regard to the concept of truth, which is not destroyed but plays a role as a decentering tool in discourse. Yet he also mentions an important difference: whereas Kafka continues to refer to the Jewish framework of messianic promise, Joyce contents himself with the promise of a text to come.

In "Modernism's Particulars, Oscillating Universals, and Josefine's Singular Singing," Lorraine Markotic situates Kafka's modernism into the broader field of modernity. Focussing on Kafka's short narratives, she analyses different stylistic and semantic strategies that Kafka invents in order to destabilize the dialectic connection between the universal and the particular: the universal loses its function of comprehension and is neutralized as something meaninglessness; the particular is not temporally located or individualized but is instead permeated by abstract, undefinable power relations. Kafka did not intend, the author concludes, to grasp the universal through the particular; on the contrary, in his writings they become indistinguishable. Markotic shows how this is at stake in Kafka's short story "Josefine, the Singer." Commenting on Derrida's reflections on the gift and the reciprocity that follows from it, she notes that in Kafka's story one cannot even be certain about who is giving and who is receiving. In this respect, the story does not afford any means to clarify whether Josefine's singing can be considered as something particular or as something universal.

The last chapter of this section, Galili Shahar's "The Alarm Clock: The Times of Gregor Samsa," is devoted to the different dimensions of temporality in Kafka's story "The Metamorphosis." Shahar examines the complex time structures of the modernist narrative. Here, the universal is represented by the mechanical time of the alarm clock in Samsa's room, which introduces the mechanization of human existence and the return of the creaturely body with its gestures, noises, and cries. Shahar confronts this mechanical time with another time in the story, one that is revealed by the writing desk in Samsa's room, namely, the time of the student and the years of childhood, the time of writing. This time escapes the mechanized time of the alarm clock, because it is a condensed time. The author describes the tensions, inversions, and distortions of these time structures in order to define the event of literary writing.

A volume dedicated to Kafka and the universal must contend with contemporary Kafka reception and assess in particular the social and political meanings that Kafka's work evokes. The contributions collected in the final section, entitled "After Kafka," discuss three main positions in the Kafka reception. In "Reading Kafka: A Personal Story," Shimon Sandbank retraces his readings of Kafka from Walter Benjamin to Gilles Deleuze to Jacques Derrida. At the beginning and the end of this line of explication, the author refers to what he calls Kafka's "cancellation technique": the different linguistic modalities of retreating and negating what has just been said. This technique destabilizes the establishment of any fixed general meaning. Benjamin's distinction between doctrine and fiction was an eye-opener for the elusive traces of transcendence yet it was unable to account for the singular negativity in Kafka's writings. This also applies to Deleuze and Guattari: they were the first to state the immanence of law, which is, however, incompatible with Kafka's negativity. For this reason, Derrida replaced the others: deconstruction, according to Sandbank, is quite close to Kafka's cancellation technique. However, Sandbank underscores an important difference: whereas the deferral of meaning is an effect of language, according to Derrida, in Kafka it is not language but the writer who doubts, negates assumptions, and undermines the meanings of what has been written.

In "*Kafka, Pro and Contra*: Günther Anders's Holocaust Book," Kata Gellen traces a completely different position in the reception of Kafka, that of Günther Anders. Anders was sharply critical of Kafka. He considered that Kafka helped to absolve a generation of Nazi sympathizers from their guilt through his having invented a world in which guilt and punishment are uncoupled. Gellen draws particular attention to Anders's interpretation of Kafka's Jewishness, which he claimed was infected by a secular, universalist theology that is actually Christian. For this reason, Anders considers that Kafka's view of guilt is not Jewish, since it is based upon a conception of original sin and redemption. In this respect, one understands better the central core of Anders's critique – that Kafka betrays his Jewishness – and Anders's diagnosis of the resurgence of interest in Kafka in post-war Germany. Gellen does not hesitate to discuss the main problems of Anders's position in the contemporary reception of Kafka. However, for her, the importance of Anders's Kafka book lies in the possibility to reread Kafka in relation to the Holocaust without ascribing to Kafka's descriptions of suffering and loss a predictive value.

"The position in which thought finds itself after 1945 forces Hannah Arendt to leave the realm of philosophy and turn to literature [to Kafka]": this sentence, at the beginning of the final contribution, Birgit R. Erdle's "Dis/Placing Thought: Franz Kafka and Hannah Arendt," summarizes one of the central ideas to which this volume is dedicated. For Arendt, who refers to the fragments "He" in Kafka's journals, the grounds of reality (*der Boden der Tatsachen*) have changed and this change is marked by the fact that thinking and reality are no longer linked with one another. It immediately reveals the philosophical condition of the significance of Kafka's work to which Arendt refers in order to shed light on this gap between thinking and reality, which is also a "gap between past and future." According to Arendt's readings, Kafka enables a prolongation of the struggle between the two extremes of the gap without searching to bridge the abyss or to jump into the timeless sphere of metaphysics. According to Erdle, however, Arendt is too much in search for a metaphor in Kafka's "He" fragments to name the new place of thinking. Erdle detects yet another meaning in these fragments, namely, that of the outside of the law and the specific Jewish experience of time.

This volume is the result of a fruitful collaboration, not only between the editors but also among many colleagues, primarily the participants of two different conferences, one on "Kafka and His Readers," held at the Hebrew University of Jerusalem in 2012, the other on "Kafka and the Paradox of the Universal," organized at the University of Antwerp in 2013. We invited several scholars to write additional papers for the volume. We thank them for accepting this invitation and enriching the scope of this book, and the participants of the two conferences for lively and enlightening discussions and for their contributions to this volume. The publication of this book would not have been possible without the support of a number of people and institutions: the Institute of Jewish Studies at the University of Antwerp, the Ministry of Education of the Flemish Community, the FWO (Fonds for Wetenschappelijk Onderzoek, Flanders), and the Hebrew University of Jerusalem. We thank Jeremy Schreiber for his careful editing of the manuscript; his attentiveness to the nuances of the English language greatly improved the volume. We are deeply grateful to Manuela Gerlof of De Gruyter for her encouragement throughout the production of this book, and last but not least to Irene Kacandes, the editor of the series "Interdisciplinary German Cultural Studies," for her inspiring guidance. We hope the readers of this book will share our sense that this volume participates in important ways in exploring the interface between literature and philosophy and Kafka's role in this relationship.

Section 1: **The Ambiguity of the Singular**

Stanley Corngold

The Singular Accident in a Universe of Risk: An Approach to Kafka and the Paradox of the Universal

Kafka's testimony is all the more universal as it is profoundly singular.
– Jean-Paul Sartre, "The Demilitarization of Culture"

The subject *qua* "self-consciousness" [...] participates in the universal precisely and only in so far as his identity is truncated, marked by a lack; in so far as he is not fully "what he is."
– Slavoj Žižek, *Metastases of Enjoyment*

The more authentic the works, the more they follow what is objectively required, the object's consistency, and this is always universal.
– Theodor Adorno, *Aesthetic Theory*

I mean of course my mother whose image, blunted for some time past, was beginning now to harrow me again.
– Samuel Beckett, *Molloy*

This golden Hades is no place to be blowing one another to bits. It's a place to come and think, [...] to study the molten vignettes in mirages.
– Paul West, *The Very Rich Hours of Count von Stauffenberg*

This essay examines Kafka's works in the perspective of disciplinary philosophy, a perspective that immediately involves "the paradox of the universal." For what Kafka and philosophy have in common is the effort to represent what is universally the case ("truth") in propositions that are irreducibly singular – singular in the sense of being linguistically specific, constrained by their materiality (their sound-look) and the contingent connotation of their diction. (I exempt symbolic and formal logic.)

Kafka's plangent appeal strengthens this idea: "I can still get fleeting satisfaction from works like 'A Country Doctor' [...]. But happiness only in case I can raise the world into purity, truth, immutability."[1] *Das Reine, Wahre, Unveränderliche* – purity, truth, immutability – is a good enough indicator of what we might

---

1 Franz Kafka, diary entry of 25 September 1917, in *Kafka's Selected Stories: New Translations, Backgrounds and Contexts, Criticism*, ed. and trans. Stanley Corngold, Norton Critical Edition, Norton, New York 2007, 205. ("Zeitweilige Befriedigung kann ich von Arbeiten wie 'Landarzt' noch haben, [...] Glück aber nur, falls ich die Welt ins Reine, Wahre, Unveränderliche heben

call "the universal" – and hence an ideal that *prima facie* can never be more than approximated by the sentences we write, which are specific and singular by virtue of their rhetorical and material character. For Jean-Paul Sartre, however, this ideal is realized to an exemplary degree in Kafka's stories and fictions, "Kafka's testimony [being] all the more universal as it is profoundly singular."[2]

Such universalist intentions are not strange to other modernist writers contemporary with Kafka: they inform the specifically anchored aperçus of Marcel, the fictive narrator in Marcel Proust's À la *recherche du temps perdu* [*In Search of Lost Time*]; and James Joyce is said to have remarked, about his insistent focus on the city of Dublin, "In the particular is contained the universal." True, Joyce had a special idea of "universality" when he made the singular heart of Dublin the heart of "all the cities in the world."[3] It might be interesting to substitute Prague for Dublin in Joyce's formula, narrowing Kafka's singularity to a focus on Prague and concluding that the outcome of this focus is also the universality of "all the cities in the world." This claim actually figures in a popular text, broadcast by Radio Bremen in 2010:

> Only a few writers are so persistently identified with a city as Franz Kafka with Prague. Almost his entire life ran its course here, and this city on the Moldau left conspicuous traces in his work. From the perspective of the Altstädter Ring, the historical center of Prague, Kafka himself once said, "Here was my high school, there the university, and a bit further to the left my office. My entire life is confined to this circle."[4]

Yet, on reflection, Kafka's singularity requires more than this focus, although it is by no means irrelevant, *ex negativo*, to his deepest concerns. Near the end of his

---

kann." See Franz Kafka, *Tagebücher in der Fassung der Handschrift* [*Diary in the Manuscript Version*], ed. Michael Müller, S. Fischer, Frankfurt/M. 1990, 838.)

2 Jean-Paul Sartre, "La Démilitarisation de la culture" ("The Demilitarization of Culture"), excerpted in *Situations VII*, Gallimard, Paris 1962, 322–331, 326.

3 Richard Ellmann, *James Joyce*, Oxford University Press, Oxford 1959, 505. Ellmann is citing Arthur Power, *From the Old Waterford House: Recollections of a Soldier and Artist*, Ballylough Books, London 1940, 64.

4 Radio Bremen, "Porträt: Franz Kafka: Auf Spurensuche in Prag" ("Portrait: Franz Kafka: Searching for Traces in Prague"), 7 July 2010, http://www.radiobremen.de/kultur/portraets/kafka/kafka108.html. My translation. (Original German transcript: "Nur wenige Schriftsteller werden so nachhaltig mit einer Stadt identifiziert wie Franz Kafka mit Prag. Fast sein gesamtes Leben hat sich hier abgespielt und in seinem Werk hat die Stadt an der Moldau unübersehbare Spuren hinterlassen. Aus dem Blickwinkel des Altstädter Rings, dem historischen Zentrum Prags, hat Kafka selbst einmal gesagt: 'Hier war mein Gymnasium, dort die Universität und ein Stückchen weiter links mein Büro. In diesem kleinen Kreis ist mein ganzes Leben eingeschlossen.'")

short life Kafka spoke to Dora Diamant about his sordid immersion in Prague and hence of the disposability of all his works from before 1923, owing to their having been written in a condition of unfreedom.[5] The essence of Prague was, for Kafka, not at all universal; Berlin, for one thing, was freer.

The writer Louis Begley, in his rather nasty little monograph on Kafka, scolds Kafka for knowing so little of such modernist literature as Joyce's *Dubliners*.[6] Let it be agreed for the moment that additional immersion in the life of a provincial city, represented in a style of what Joyce called "scrupulous meanness," would have neither enriched Kafka's focus nor excited his interest in getting to the heart of all the cities in the world. Kafka's singularity lies, at least on the surface, in taking for his heroes creatures never before seen on earth (or on the seas), such as the metamorphosed Gregor Samsa, or Odradek, or Josephine the songstress, or Poseidon the marine bureaucrat; these images have the peculiar singularity of dreams, in that they are at once exceedingly vivid in detail (*apollinisch*, or "Apollonian," according to Nietzsche) yet are also touched by a mood, an aura chiefly troubling, and hence are like nightmares or disturbing hallucinations. These images do not actually envisage anything one ordinarily experiences in the daylight of cities (leaving aside the Satanic light of the media circus). They belong to another order of the world – or, one could say, "cosmos," in the spirit of Walter Benjamin's injunction to himself as a critic of Kafka: "Den Funken zwischen Prag und dem Kosmos überspringen lassen" – "Have the spark jump over, between Prague and the cosmos."[7]

Gregor Samsa will occupy this discussion in due course. For now, I will proceed to literature's handmaiden, philosophy, keeping in mind Roberto Calasso's caveat from his afterward to an English translation of Kafka's Zürau aphorisms: "If there is a theology [and a philosophy, I would add] in Kafka, [the collection of Zürau aphorisms] is the only place where he himself comes close to declaring it. But even in these aphorisms abstraction is rarely permitted to break free of the image to live its own life, as if it has to serve time [read: be incarcerated] for having been autonomous and capricious for too long, in that remote and reckless age where philosophers and theologians still existed."[8]

---

5 Nicholas Murray, *Kafka*, Yale University Press, New Haven 2004, 371–372.
6 Louis Begley, *The Tremendous World I Have Inside My Head: Franz Kafka: A Biographical Essay*, Atlas & Co., New York 2008.
7 Walter Benjamin, *Benjamin über Kafka* [*Benjamin on Kafka*], ed. Hermann Schweppenhäuser, Suhrkamp, Frankfurt/M. 1981, 157. My translation.
8 Roberto Calasso, "Veiled Splendor" (Afterward), trans. Geoffrey Brock, in *Franz Kafka, The Zürau* [sic] *Aphorisms*, trans. Michael Hofmann, ed. Roberto Calasso, Schocken Books, New York 2006, 109–134, 119.

We do not have the privilege, however, of disregarding this fabulous "remote and reckless age where philosophers and theologians still existed" – for this age is once again our own. Peter Thompson, a scholar of Ernst Bloch, offers a sober comment in this matter: "Religion and Kafka have come back as themes precisely because we are once again living in an eschatological and apocalyptic era in which it is easier to imagine the end of the world than it is to imagine a different and better one."[9]

The concurrence of singular and universal that Joyce speaks of, and which I will impute to Kafka as his intention, is also the goal of the "extraordinarily exciting power" of *philosophy* – this is provable in at least one special modern case. This power is found in the work of Jacques Derrida, whose prowess, according to Jonathan Culler, consists in his "reading texts in their singularity [...] while also identifying ubiquitous logics on which they relied and pervasive systems to which they contributed."[10] It is hardly surprising that even when philosophical discourse addresses the singular objects of its concern (for example, when Derrida addresses Kafka's parable "Before the Law" ("Vor dem Gesetz"), he notes the guard's abundant nasal hair and that in psychoanalytic circles *ante portas* – literally, "before the gates" – means premature ejaculation), philosophy aims to produce results of universal validity.[11] Philosophy, as deconstruction, may thereafter proceed to identify the "logics" that these results employ, the "pervasive system" to which they contribute, with a view to putting the claim to such universally valid templates "under erasure." (Note, though, that Derrida's erasure of the claim to a logic having universal validity is meant to be universally valid only so long as the action of erasure goes on and on.) But more suggestive than the singularity of its objects, as in this mention of Derrida's thought and the texts he reads with unusual acuity, is the singularity of much modern philosophical discourse as such: I am referring to Derrida's own story of the "white mythology," the unique pattern of subcutaneous images and tropes and story elements informing this discourse in each individual case. Such patterns are altogether vivid in Derrida's essays, as well as in the work of other modern philosophers, such as Heidegger, Wittgenstein, and Žižek – a singularity evident in their distinctive styles.

---

9 Peter Thompson, "Kafka, Bloch, Religion and the Metaphysics of Contingency," in *Kafka, Religion, and Modernity*, Oxford Kafka Studies III, eds. Manfred Engel and Ritchie Robertson, Königshausen und Neumann, Würzburg 2014, 177–187, 178.
10 Jonathan Culler, "Forum: The Legacy of Jacques Derrida," in *PMLA* 120.2 (2005): 472–473, 472.
11 Jacques Derrida, "Before the Law" ("Devant la loi"), trans. Avital Ronell and Christine Roulston, in *Acts of Literature*, ed. Derek Attridge, Routledge, New York and London 1992, 183–220.

Nonetheless, having invoked the mutuality of Kafka's literature, and philosophy, I will insist on the former's distinctive charm – its *Zauber* ("magic") leaving aside its *Logik* ("logic") – and treat this charm as an incentive to our friendship with Franz Kafka.[12] Roland Barthes wrote, "All criticism is affectionate. [...] This should be carried even further, almost to the postulation of a theory of affect as the motive force of criticism."[13] It is such affection that now guides our thought-adventure – a "friendship," too, that, like any *ship*, needs to know where it is heading. And so we must reflect: Are we to study Kafka with the tools of a philosophically well-grounded position on the universal and the singular – in a word, submit Kafka to *philosophical* examination? Then the aim would be to see how well Kafka's work conforms to that position, and to this end we would employ tools such as, say, Hegel's analysis that "the being as such of finite things is to have the germ of this transgression in their in-itselfness: the hour of their birth is the hour of their death."[14] The accumulation of mere particulars – such finite things – leads, as in Hegel's *Logik*, not to "das Ganze" ("the whole") but to a "schlechte Unendlichkeit" ("bad infinity"). Proceeding in this way, and thereby addressing Kafka's conformity with – or calculable disparity from – Hegel's (or some other's) philosophical position, we would then try to discern how Kafka's work negates, nuances, or enlarges that position – and then, with such riches in tow, return sail to a port in the Empire of Philosophy. That is one way to navigate. Or ought we to have the opposite direction in mind, such that the intention is to perform an *epoché* – that is, to bracket everything that might have been learned from philosophy about the singular and universal, and then, affecting naïveté, sail anew into these strange seas of thought, our progress fueled only by the warmth of our friendship with Kafka and whatever has been learned from him, as if *nous avions "lu tous les livres" [et maintenant] "ô mon coeur, entend[on]s le*

---

12 The full title of Thomas Mann's great novel reads: *Doctor Faustus: The Life of the German Composer Adrian Leverkühn, As Told By a Friend* [*Doktor Faustus: Das Leben des deutschen Tonsetzers Adrian Leverkühn, erzählt von einem Freunde*] and it is this introit that I want to apply. (Mann, who greatly admired Kafka, would not object, I think, nor would Kafka, who greatly admired Mann.) For "Zauber" and "Logik," see Dieter Hasselblatt, *Zauber und Logik. Eine Kafka Studie* [*Magic and Logic: A Kafka Study*], Wissenschaft und Politik, Wiesbaden 1964.
13 Roland Barthes, *The Grain of the Voice: Interviews 1962–1980*, trans. Linda Coverdale, Hill and Wang, New York 1985, 331.
14 Georg Wilhelm Friedrich Hegel, *The Science of Logic*, ed. and trans. George di Giovanni, Cambridge University Press, Cambridge 2010, 101. ("[D]as Sein der endlichen Dinge, [welches] als solches ist, den Keim des Vergehens als ihr Insichsein zu haben; die Stunde ihrer Geburt ist die Stunde ihres Todes." Georg Wilhelm Friedrich Hegel, *Wissenschaft der Logik*, I:1:1:2:B.c "Die Endlichkeit" ("The Finitude"), Hofenberg, Berlin 2013, 99.)

chant des matelots!" – of sailor Gracchus ("we have 'read all the books' [and now] 'oh my heart, hear the song of the sailors'").[15]

At first glance, the first direction seems obviously the more persuasive: we wish to submit Kafka's work to a philosophical examination based on pre-established concepts of singularity and universality – or, to put such concepts into more cogent literary terms: to address Kafka with intuitions as to image and law. The second, opposite direction would seem rather limited and abstruse: to address a problem embedded in the philosophical tradition, from the standpoint of what has been learned uniquely from our friendship with Kafka. And yet it is bemusing to realize that the latter approach is exactly what has been done, for decades and the world over, under the heading of the "Kafkaesque." For when learned judges speak of the "Kafkaesque" character of the cases before them, they are, of course, doing the philosophy of law as inspired by their understanding of Kafka – and in many instances it is an impressively accurate understanding. In particular cases, culled from the online casebook Westlaw, the sufferings of the accused appear to have leapt from the pages of *The Trial* [*Der Process*] and are identified as such. There have been trials in American courts conducted in a language that the accused literally could not understand; in others, the condemned was not present when his sentence was read. In one such case, counsel alludes plainly to the penultimate paragraph of *The Trial*, which includes the sentence "Where was the Judge whom he had never seen?"[16] Similarly, the case of *O'Brien v. Henderson*, heard before the U.S. District Court for the Northern District of Georgia, in 1973, presents a scenario I find poignantly relevant to life at American universities in the wake of the Civil Rights Act of 1964 (read: political correctness):

> the petitioner claimed that the Board of Parole had violated his due process rights by revoking his parole *without the proper explanation* that was constitutionally required [...] Commenting on the unusual volume and vagueness of the *petitioner's pleadings*, Circuit Judge Edenfield noted "that not even the most skilled of counsel, finding himself in the Kafkaesque situation of being deprived of his liberty by a tribunal which will adduce no reasons for its decision, can complain concisely and clearly of his objections to such a decision [...] [Such a situation] leaves the prisoner no recourse but to approach the court with an attempted rebuttal of all real, feared, or imagined justifications for his confinement."[17]

---

15 My translation.
16 Franz Kafka, *The Trial*, in *The Penguin Complete Novels of Franz Kafka*, trans. Willa and Edwin Muir, Penguin Books, Harmondsworth 1983, 5–176, 172. ("Wo war der Richter, den er nie gesehen hatte?" Franz Kafka, *Der Proceß*, ed. Malcom Pasley, S. Fischer, Frankfurt/M. 1990, 312.)
17 Cited in Amanda Torres, "Kafka and the Common Law: The Roots of the 'Kafkaesque' in *The Trial*," an unpublished seminar paper for the conference "Kafka and the Law," held at the Columbia Law School (7 May 2007), 10–11.

And so one sees Joseph K., in *The Trial*, offering the Court police his bicycle license in an attempt to excuse his imagined offense.

In this matter of doing the philosophy of the singular and the universal whenever the term "Kafkaesque" is applied to some set of affairs, we might consider another sort of litigious example. In Woody Allen's film *Annie Hall*, the character Pam says to Alvy (played by Allen), "Sex with you is really a Kafkaesque experience." Then, realizing that her lover is upset by this remark, she hastens to add: "I mean that as a compliment."[18] What she is saying, for our purposes, is that these dimensions of lived experience – sex, a universal – with Alvy – a singular self – having concurred under a Kafkan coverlet, so to speak, are a fortuitous event, a happy thing. This is a fact that would actually encourage us to sail, per the second proposed mode of navigating Kafka, away from him and towards that philosophy which means to situate the great world of real contingencies by placing it under categories of universal law. Like so many other investigators these past decades, the character Pam – not unlike Judge Edenfield – is doing philosophy – here, the philosophy of sex – with its fabled concurrence of a universal drive and its particular concretion – as she sails under Kafkan skies. One might compliment her with the phrase that Goethe used to describe the optimal sort of procedure in classifying singular phenomena under general ideas – for she is, after all, practicing, with undercover Kafkaesque guidance, just such a *zarte Empirie*, or "tender empiricism."

It merits noting that Allen has staged here a genuine Lacanian tableau. In Lacan's profiling of Freud, the psychoanalytic situation is not the familiar one of the anguished, repressed *homme moyen sensuel* who is required to read a paper on the paradox of the universal in the works of an obscure Prague writer while secretly, unconsciously fantasizing a midsummer night of sex. No, as Žižek, would say, no!: the real psychoanalytic situation deals with our *homme moyen intellectuel* who, in the sexual embrace of his beloved, fantasizes cracking open the pages of a crisp, new volume from De Gruyter devoted to discussion of the singular and universal in the works of Franz Kafka... "and so on."[19]

At this point, even having carefully considered the alternative route (involving Judge Edenfield and Pam), I will reverse course and tack more directly toward my thesis to read Kafka philosophically, though with the same Goethean caveat

---

18 *Annie Hall*. Dir. Woody Allen. United Artists, 1977.
19 The mention of Slavoj Žižek is not, I think, *mal apropos*, since, along with Mladen Dolar, he is the leading representative of the Slovenian school of literary and psychoanalytical criticism, which has produced eye-opening and altogether respectful Lacanian studies of Kafka, frequently concentrating on the concept of the undead.

in mind: to handle him with care, so as to leave him – he who is more than the object of study, he who is our friend – in a state no more tormented than the one we found him in, that is, to leave him neither wriggling upon a pin nor twisted to our purposes, but instead accompanied by a sisterly shape, so to speak, a *conceptual* model (of the concurrence in his work of aspects both singular and universal) having the same genetic structure.

Where, then, are the necessary guides to the philosophical reading of Kafka? I will take first directions from a book that, though written by a young professor of philosophy a half-century ago, has shaped this field of study immeasurably: Arthur Danto's 1965 book *Nietzsche as Philosopher*, which established Nietzsche, for the first time in America (at least, in the years following the Second World War), as a source of analytic philosophical inquiry. To do this, Danto had to conjure – under the heading of "the main philosophical tradition"[20] – the kinds of questions to which a source-author allegedly suited to philosophical inquiry provides answers; such questions that include: What is the self? What can we know? What can we will? There is not a question of this type that does not involve a concurrence of the two dimensions under scrutiny here: a radical singularity and a principal universal intelligibility.[21] Our task is to narrow the field of inquiry to the phenomena in Kafka's story-world that display this concurrence most clearly.

It is tempting to focus on the question of the self, for this self-thing is at once an ontic singularity and an ontological universal[22]; and it recommends itself especially to the Kafkan perspective as a meeting place of law (superego) and image (ego).[23] Kafka's confessional writings contribute abundantly to this topic – despite his occasional disavowal of it, as in the familiar refrain first articulated

---

20 Arthur Danto, *Nietzsche as Philosopher: An Original Study*, Columbia University Press, New York 1965, 22.
21 Add to this Robert Conquest's poem "Philosophy Department," which begins:
    Such knotty problems! Check your lists:
    How come the universe exists?
    How does consciousness, free will,
    Match up with brain cells? – Harder still [...].
See: http://bookhaven.stanford.edu/2009/11/conquest/.
22 Consider "das Selbst" – "the self" – of Heidegger's *Being and Time* [*Sein und Zeit*], a fundamental structure of so-called *Existentialien* ("existentials").
23 This is where a good deal of the current interest in Kafka lies, to judge from a recent paper by Matthew T. Powell, who writes: "In his use of animal protagonists, Kafka locates an opportunity to explore the tension between human and non-human – the same tension that exists between self and other. By playing off this tension between what is 'the self' and what is 'not the self,' Kafka is able to explore the ontology of otherness. He enlists animal stories in order to clarify the space between self and other that is critical to maintaining notions of identity." See Matthew

in his meditation on his Jewish identity: "What have I in common with Jews? I have hardly anything in common with myself [...]."[24] The poet W.H. Auden, who afforded Kafka a sublime status in the history of great poets, whose ranks include Shakespeare and Dante, titled his finest essay on Kafka "The I Without a Self."[25]

But the question of the self – oneself! – is not so easily set aside; and so we have Kafka's more refined discussion of self-abnegation in the crucial distinction "Not shaking off the self, but consuming the self,"[26] a burning off of all the particular hurts, longings, opaque places of the self for the sake of the work of art and its feint toward universality: we recall Kafka's imagined happiness "only in case I can raise the world into purity, truth, immutability."[27] It is evident that the concurrence of singular and universal that is imputed to Kafka is the very thing he sought as his chief predilection, as his goal. And here, in a critical enterprise, I will promptly assert the primacy of Kafka's fiction to the confessional, to the diary entry, which always means to invoke the god or demon of fiction, by whom Kafka wishes to be possessed.[28] "In German," he noted, "the word *sein* stands both for the verb *to be* and for the possessive pronoun *his*."[29] A *Schriftstellersein* ("the being-of-a-writer") that wrote while unpossessed would be the great, surviving shame if such work were ever published.

A number of striking correlations between the three philosophical questions mentioned earlier and the dominant strain of individual works of Kafka are evident. Think: What is the self? *The Metamorphosis* [*Die Verwandlung*]. What

---

T. Powell, "Bestial Representations of Otherness: Kafka's Animal Stories," in *Journal of Modern Literature* 32.1 (2008): 129–142, 129.

24 Franz Kafka, diary entry of 8 January 1914, in *The Diaries of Franz Kafka, 1914–1923*, ed. Max Brod, trans. Martin Greenberg (with the assistance of Hannah Arendt), Schocken Books, New York 1949, 11. ("Was habe ich mit Juden gemeinsam? Ich habe kaum etwas mit mir gemeinsam [...]." Kafka, *Tagebücher*, 622.)

25 W.H. Auden, "The I Without a Self," in *The Dyer's Hand and Other Essays*, Vintage, New York 1989, 159–167.

26 Franz Kafka, *The Blue Octavo Notebooks*, trans. Ernst Kaiser and Eithne Wilkins, ed. Max Brod, Cambridge, Exact Change 1991, 39. ("Nicht Selbstabschüttelung sondern Selbstaufzehrung." Franz Kafka, *Nachgelassene Schriften und Fragmente II* [*Posthumous Writings and Fragments II*], ed. Jost Schillemeit, S. Fischer, Frankfurt/M. 1992, 77.)

27 See footnote 1.

28 To abide by these concerns, however, requires that a particular methodological point be made clear: that this is not a combing of Kafka's notebooks for propositions of a philosophical character (as tempting as they might be, as helpful to our task they may be, by simplifying it).

29 Kafka, *The Blue Octavo Notebooks*, 90. ("Das wort sein bedeutet im Deutschen beides: Dasein und Ihm-gehören." Franz Kafka, *Nachgelassene Schriften und Fragmente I* [*Posthumous Writings and Fragments I*], ed. Malcolm Pasley, S. Fischer, Frankfurt/M. 1990, 123.)

can I know? *The Trial*: "The Scriptures are unalterable and the comments often enough merely express the commentator's bewilderment."[30] What can I will (on the strength of what do I desire)? *The Castle [Das Schloss]*.[31]

1 Image and Law[32]

I want to consider the concurrence of the singular and the universal in Kafka's stories as the meeting of image and law. I hardly need to note that the word "law" (*Gesetz*) in Kafka's writings is many-sided to a fault. What this means for Gershom Scholem, say, is not what it means for Jacques Derrida, for one; indeed, the very opacity of Kafka's emphasis on the law prompted Walter Benjamin to write to Scholem that "I do not wish to go into explicit detail on this concept."[33]

So, in evoking Kafka's law, one must speak of a single, distinctive sense of the concept. The law, as it comes to the fore in Kafka's stories, is the law of the unfolding of a beginning image, and it is to this law that the main character is *subject*. In this light, the law, for Kafka – being (viz. Derrida) neither a natural thing nor an institution – is "literature" in its active unfolding.[34] At the end of a day in 1910, having written nothing, Kafka noted in his diaries: "What excuse do I have for not yet having written anything today? None. [...] An invocation sounds continually in my ear, 'If you would come, invisible judge [*Gericht*: also, 'court']!"[35] The identification of law and literature in Kafka's universe was never plainer. Derrida's

---

30 Kafka, *The Trial*, 164. ("[Denn] die Schrift ist unveränderlich und die Meinungen sind oft nur ein Ausdruck der Verzweiflung darüber." Kafka, *Der Proceß*, 298.)

31 See my "Ritardando in *Das Schloß*," in *From Kafka to Sebald: Modernism and Narrative Form*, ed. Sabine Wilke, Continuum, London 2012, 11–26.

32 Section II of this essay is extracted, with some changes and additions, from my article "Kafka's Law in a Universe of Risk," in *The American Reader* 1.3 (2013): 110–119.

33 Walter Benjamin and Gerhard Scholem, *The Correspondence of Walter Benjamin and Gershom Scholem, 1932–1940*, trans. Gary Smith and Andre Lefever, ed. Gershom Scholem, Harvard University Press, Cambridge 1992, 136. ("Mit diesem Begriff will ich mich in der Tat explizit nicht einlassen." Benjamin, *Benjamin über Kafka*, 79.)

34 In her article "Doing Justice to Kafka's *The Trial*: Literature and Jurisprudential Innovation," Jill Scott reiterates a point that has often been made: for Kafka, the law is "literature." She stresses the claim in Derrida's commentary on "Before the Law" that the law is neither natural nor an institution. See http://www.queensu.ca/german/undergraduate/courseinfo/ints/322/Doing_Justice_To_Kafkas_The_Trial_Jill_Scott_2011.pdf.

35 Kafka, diary entry of 20 December 1910, in *Kafka's Selected Stories*, 194. ("Womit entschuldige ich, daß ich heute noch nichts geschrieben habe? Mit nichts. [...] Ich habe immerfort eine Anrufung im Ohr: Kämest du doch, unsichtbares Gericht!" Kafka, *Tagebücher*, 135.)

exclusions – the law being neither nature nor a positive institution – are helpful, as far as they go.[36] But I will attempt to give the law a local – a fictional – habitation as the concrete realization of the possibilities of literature in every individual case. In his 2005 Nobel Prize Lecture, Harold Pinter remarks of one of his plays: "I allow a whole range of options to operate in a dense forest of possibility before finally focusing on an act of subjugation."[37] This is the sort of effortful focusing set in motion by Kafka's beginning images, a focusing which, *in media res*, aims to guide his protagonists through a series of what Beatrice Sandberg has termed "hypothetical alternatives, relativizations, and constrictions toward a solution."[38] On this matter of the constriction, the subjugation to law of narrative possibilities, Nietzsche, Kafka's best dialogist, is informative: "Every artist knows how far from any feeling of letting himself go his 'most natural' state is – the free ordering, placing, disposing, giving form in the moment of 'inspiration' – and how strictly and subtly he obeys thousandfold laws precisely then, laws that precisely on account of their hardness and determination defy all formulation through concepts.[39] Or, if one prefers, Proust: "Writers, when they are bound hand and foot by the tyranny of a monarch or a school of poetry, by the constraints of prosodic laws or of a state religion, often attain a power of concentration from which they would have been dispensed under a system of political liberty or literary anarchy."[40]

Kafka's major works begin with a striking, capacious image; these images are "initiofugal," and the law – better: "a" law – comes to light as its narrative unfolding. The singularity of the opening image of K. in *The Trial* is to his "process" what Kafka's singularity is to Kafka's universality: Kafka's opening image is the nucleus of Kafka's law. Roberto Calasso has detected the same movement in Kafka's Zürau

---

36 And yet a critic as incisive as Erich Heller, addressing the question of the meaning of *The Trial*, throws up his hands in the end, asking: "What is [K.'s] guilt? What is the Law?" See Erich Heller, *Franz Kafka*, The Viking Press, New York 1974, 82.

37 Harold Pinter, "Nobel Lecture 2005: Art, Truth & Politics," in *PMLA* 121.3 (2006): 811–818, 812.

38 See Beatrice Sandberg, "Starting in the Middle? Complications of Narrative Beginnings and Progression in Kafka," in *Franz Kafka: Narration, Rhetoric, and Reading*, eds. Jakob Lothe, Beatrice Sandberg, and Ronald Speirs, The Ohio State University Press, Columbus 2011, 123–148, 136.

39 Friedrich Nietzsche, *Beyond Good and Evil: Prelude to a Philosophy of the Future* [*Jenseits von Gut und Böse: Vorspiel einer Philosophie der Zukunft*] (1886), Aphorism 188. See http://www.thenietzschechannel.com/works-pub/bge/bge5-dual.htm. ("Jeder Künstler weiss, wie fern vom Gefühl des Sichgehen-lassens sein 'natürlichster' Zustand ist, das freie Ordnen, Setzen, Verfügen, Gestalten in den Augenblicken der 'Inspiration,' – und wie streng und fein er gerade da tausendfältigen Gesetzen gehorcht, die aller Formulirung durch Begriffe gerade auf Grund ihrer Härte und Bestimmtheit spotten.")

40 Marcel Proust, *In Search of Lost Time*, trans. C.K. Scott Moncrieff, T. Kilmartin, and D.J. Enright, Modern Library, New York 2003, 491.

aphorisms: "Each of those sentences presents itself as if the greatest possible generality were intrinsic to it. And at the same time each seems to emerge from vast deposits of dark matter."[41]

The law of the subject/self is unfolded from the dark matter of the *ungeheueres Ungeziefer* – the monstrous vermin – of *The Metamorphosis*; the law governing possible cognition is unfolded from the dark matter of Joseph K.'s arrest in his bed; the law governing desire – and the will to enact desire – unfolds from the dark matter of the *scheinbare Leere*, or illusory emptiness, of *The Castle*...[42] There are countless other such correlations throughout Kafka's oeuvre. *The Trial*, for one, describes just that, a trial as a process, where, as the priest explains, "The verdict is not so suddenly arrived at, the proceedings only gradually merge into the verdict."[43] The verdict that retroactively proves the effectiveness of the law is produced by the *Verfahren* – the process set in motion with Joseph K.'s arrest. The verdict proves the effectiveness of the law, though it neither posits nor identifies the law, which remains implicit in the proceedings.

The concept of universality is commonly cast in terms of an intensive and extensive totality. The first is a claim of totality based on a single principle or property distinctive for its depth (or altitude or intensity): Theodor Adorno, for example, asserts that Kafka's universe is a hermetically sealed representation of the substance of late capitalism and its attendant mood of alienation, that of being *in grosser Verlegenheit*, or "completely at a loss."[44] *Verlegenheit* is the state of mind (read: *absence* of mind) that makes the subject most vulnerable to damage.[45]

---

41 Calasso, *Franz Kafka, The Zurau* [sic] *Aphorisms*, 123.

42 Franz Kafka, *Das Schloß*, ed. Malcolm Pasley, S. Fischer, Frankfurt/M. 1982, 7.

43 Kafka, *The Trial*, 160. ("'Das Urteil kommt nicht plötzlich, das Verfahren geht allmählich ins Urteil über.'" Kafka, *Der Proceß*, 289.)

44 Theodor W. Adorno, "Aufzeichnungen zu Kafka" ("Notes on Kafka"), in *Gesammelte Schriften* [*Collected Works*] 10.1, Suhrkamp, Frankfurt/M. 2003, 254–287, 265.

45 This phrase opens Kafka's "A Country Doctor" ("Ein Landarzt"): "I was completely at a loss" ("Ich war in grosser Verlegenheit"). "See Franz Kafka, "A Country Doctor," in *Kafka's Selected Stories*, 60–69, 60; and Franz Kafka, "Ein Landarzt," in *Drucke zu Lebzeiten* [*Works Published During His Lifetime*], eds. Wolf Kittler, Hans-Gerd Koch, and Gerhard Neumann S. Fischer, Frankfurt/M. 1994, 252–261, 252. This phrase appears in more than one crucial place in Kafka's published work: for example, the officer from "In the Penal Colony" ("In der Strafkolonie"), who, while recalling the radiance on the prisoner's face as the latter endured his sixth hour of torment, "had evidently forgotten who was standing before him; he had embraced the traveler and laid his head on his shoulder. The traveler was completely at a loss" ["hatte offenbar vergessen, wer vor ihm stand; er hatte den Reisenden umarmt und den Kopf auf seine Schulter gelegt. Der Reisende war in großer Verlegenheit"]. See Franz Kafka, "In the Penal Colony," in *Kafka's Select-*

This is the essential mood of the beginnings of Kafka's narratives; it is a mood of risk, the felt exposure to damage, the affective anticipation of a law whose violation is at stake. As the famous deleted passage from the beginning of *The Trial* has it: "That is why the moment of waking up was the riskiest moment of the day."[46] In this light, Kafka's work exhibits a universally intelligible immersion in anxiety.[47]

My aim is to bring Kafka's signature anxiety, his *existential* anxiety, to bear on his task as a writer: I am concerned with the specific *anxiety of narration*, where a false decision risks violating the law immanent to the opening image. Here, Aristotle's *Rhetoric* is perfectly apt; according to Aristotle, in the words of the sage Peter Thompson, "the unavoidable and potentially unmanageable presence of multiple possibilities – or the complex nature of decisions – creates and invites rhetoric."[48]

I am alluding to the anxiety that might be dispelled by writing – or, better, displaced by writing – and there is also the very anxiety of writing, where one could err badly. According to Max Brod, Kafka "often spoke of the 'false hands that reach out toward you in the midst of writing'" ["die falschen Hände, die sich einem während des Schreibens entgegenstrecken"].[49] At other times Kafka said

---

ed Stories, 35–60, 48; and Kafka, *Drucke zu Lebzeiten*, 226. The artist in "A Dream" ("Ein Traum") is at one point completely at a loss; his distress unnerves the hero, Joseph K. (Kafka, *Drucke zu Lebzeiten*, 297).

46 Franz Kafka, *The Trial*, trans. Willa and Edwin Muir, Schocken, New York 1968, 257–258. ("Darum sei auch der Augenblick des Erwachens der riskanteste Augenblick im Tag." Franz Kafka, *Der Proceß. Apparatband*, ed. Malcolm Pasley, S. Fischer, Frankfurt/M. 1990, 168.)

47 "All his books," wrote Milena, "depict the horrors of mysterious misunderstandings and of undeserved human guilt. He was a man and a writer with such a sensitive conscience that he heard things where others were deaf and felt safe." See Jana Cerna, *Kafka's Milena*, trans. A.G. Brain, Northwestern University Press, Evanston 1993, 180. "Alle seine Bücher schildern das Grauen geheimnisvollen Unverständnisses, unverschuldeter Schuld unter den Menschen. Er war ein Künstler und Mensch von derart feinfühligem Gewissen, daß er auch dorthin hörte, wo andere, taub, sich in Sicherheit wähnten." Milena Jesenská, "Nekrolog auf Franz Kafka," in Franz Kafka, *Briefe an Milena* [*Letters to Milena*], eds. Jürgen Born and Michael Müller, S. Fischer, Frankfurt/M. 1991, 379.

48 Thompson, "Kafka, Bloch, Religion and the Metaphysics of Contingency," 183. In this matter of the relation of the rhetoric of narration to law, of the rhetoric of narration as law, in the Jewish tradition, as exemplified by Kafka, readers will profit from Vivian Liska's article "'Before the Law stands a doorkeeper. To this doorkeeper comes a man...': Kafka, Narrative and the Law," in *Naharaim* 6/2 (June 2013): 175–194. Also see my "On Scholem's Gnostically-Minded View of Kafka," in *Kafka, Religion, and Modernity*, 135–153.

49 Cited in *Kafka's Selected Stories*, 213. German text cited in Franz Kafka, *Über das Schreiben* [*Franz Kafka, On Writing*], eds. Erich Heller and Joachim Beug, Fischer, Frankfurt/M. 1983, 160.

that what he had written – and especially what he had published – had "led him astray" (*beirrten*) in his attempt to write new things. Kafka's final, brief diary entry begins: "More and more fearful as I write. It is understandable. Every word twisted in the hand of the spirits – this twist of the hand is their characteristic gesture – becomes a spear turned against the speaker."[50]

With this distribution of anxiety, I am turning away from an intensive totality of Kafka's work (and personality) to an extensive totality, even while retaining the concept of anxiety in relation to a law. For anxiety always exists in relation to an unspecified law as the risk of its violation. I once tried to render this relation in terms of space and text: Kafka "is the writer who brings to light a depth or hiddenness of background – the irreducible strangeness of that other law. His dialogical partner Nietzsche responds to this matter: 'Can it be,' he wrote, 'that all our so-called consciousness is a more or less fantastic commentary on an unknown, perhaps unknowable, but felt text?'"[51] This so-called consciousness is a necessarily anxious consciousness, haunted by a sense of bad faith, of being "dans l'erreur." In this light, Kafka's stories comprise a "more or less fantastic" commentary on the text of the law. Kafka's object as a writer is the felt text supporting the phantasmagoric singularity of its surface, like the truth that Benjamin saw not as spread out in a fan but as lodged in its folds. Kafka's writing means to strip away the phenomenal skin of the living letter of the law. His great parable reads:

> Before setting foot in the Holiest of Holies, you must take off your shoes, but not only your shoes but everything, traveling clothes and luggage, and under that, your nakedness and everything that is under the nakedness and everything that hides beneath that, and then the core and the core of the core, then the remainder and then the residue and then even the gleam of the imperishable fire. Only the fire itself is absorbed by the Holiest of Holies and lets itself be absorbed by it; neither can resist the other.[52]

---

50 Kafka, diary entry of 12 June 1923, in *Kafka's Selected Stories*, 212–213. ("Immer ängstlicher im Niederschreiben. Es ist begreiflich. Jedes Wort, gewendet in der Hand der Geister – dieser Schwung der Hand ist ihre charakteristische Bewegung – wird zum Spieß, gekehrt gegen den Sprecher." Kafka, *Tagebücher*, 926.)

51 Stanley Corngold, *Franz Kafka: The Necessity of Form*, Cornell University Press, Ithaca 1988, 4. For the Nietzsche reference, see Friedrich Nietzsche, *Morgenröte, Kritische Studienausgabe* [*Dawn, Critical Study Edition*], eds. Giorgio Colli and Mazzino Montinari, dtv/De Gruyter, Munich 1988, 113.

52 Kafka, Notebook "G," in *Kafka's Selected Stories*, 213. ("Vor dem Betreten des Allerheiligsten mußt Du die Schuhe ausziehn, aber nicht nur die Schuhe, sondern alles, Reisekleid und Gepäck, und darunter die Nacktheit, und alles, was unter der Nacktheit ist, und alles, was sich unter diesem verbirgt, und dann den Kern und den Kern des Kerns, dann das Übrige und dann den Rest und dann noch den Schein des unvergänglichen Feuers. Erst das Feuer selbst wird vom

What I am stressing now, apropos of Kafka's work, is this wider distribution of this anxiety, its lodgement in many folds. While anxiety always exists in relation to one "nameless" law, this law acquires many facets, however phantasmal, by virtue of the responses to it – the plurality of its felt implications: its history, the narrative of its precedents. Like the text (*Schrift*: scripture, writing) of the parable "Before the Law," "the scriptures are unalterable and the comments often enough merely express the commentator's bewilderment" ("die Schrift ist unveränderlich und die Meinungen [aber] sind oft nur ein Ausdruck der Verzweiflung darüber").[53] The anxiety of the literary genius is productive of such commentary. And the commentator's work, to borrow Benjamin's image for Goethe's *Dichtung* (poem) *Elective Affinities* [*Die Wahlverwandtschaften*], "remains turned toward the interior in the veiled light refracted through multi-colored panes."[54]

And so the model of Kafka's universality is an extensive totality, based finally on Kafka's own experience of (and devotion to) – and here is the jump – principles of actuarial insurance: a worldly perspective on anxiety, or risk. Kafka's "universe" – what lends his images and scenes a universal reference – is the actuarial totality of the risk of damage and the attendant assignation of fault, which is to say, too, that the law of the unfolding of the initial image, initiofugal, is intelligible only through an extensive totality of interpretations, both inside and outside the text, each of which, in falling short, is to some degree at fault and responsible for damages done to the immutable text of the law. As the prison chaplain states to Joseph K., "You have not enough respect for the written word."[55] This written word (*Schrift*) is reminiscent of Nietzsche's previously noted "unknown, perhaps unknowable, but felt text" ("ungewußter, vielleicht unwißbarer, aber gefühlter Text"). The parties who are responsible, each one at risk, constitute an insurance community – what François Ewald calls "l'état providence" ("the welfare state")[56]: they include the author, the narrator, the afflicted hero, and their readers, all "choristers of lies" – in which, according to Kafka, a possible truth

---

Allerheiligsten aufgesogen und läßt sich von ihm aufsaugen, keines von beiden kann dem widerstehen." Kafka, *Nachgelassene Schriften II*, 77.)

53 Kafka, *The Trial*, 164; Kafka, *Der Proceß*, 298.

54 Walter Benjamin, "Goethe's *Elective Affinities*" ("Goethes Wahlverwandtschaften"), in *Selected Writings, Volume 1: 1913–1926*, eds. Marcus Bullock and Michael Jennings, Harvard University Press, Cambridge 1996, 297–360, 352. ("[B]leibt dem Innenraum im verschleierten Lichte zugewendet, das in bunten Scheiben sich bricht." Walter Benjamin, *Gesammelte Schriften* [*Collected Works*], eds. Rolf Tiedemannn and Hermann Schweppenhäuser, Suhrkamp, Frankfurt/M. 1990, 123–201, 195.)

55 Kafka, *The Trial*, 163. ("Du hast nicht genug Achtung vor der Schrift." Kafka, *Der Proceß*, 295.)

56 François Ewald, *L'état providence*, Édition Grasset & Fasquelle, Paris 1986.

is contained, for "mitteilen kann man nur das was man nicht ist, also die Lüge. Erst im Chor mag eine gewisse Wahrheit liegen" – "one can communicate only what one is not, ergo: the lie. It is only in the chorus that a certain truth might be found."[57] Each chorister is a fold in the fan, as it were.

Kafka's heroes, and no less their author and their interpreters, run the gamut of risky situations, a project not unfamiliar to the risk assessor. One can see Kafka's entire literature as a widening outward of the focus he employed in the Workmen's Accident Insurance Institute of the Kingdom of Bohemia in Prague.

Danger confronts the heroes at every turn: Karl Rossmann, who is cast adrift in rough America; Joseph K., who opens doors only to find himself embedded in scenes of perversity, abjection, and horror (in the case of his visit to Titorelli the artist, he finds himself literally "embedded" in such a scene); and K., in *The Castle*, is continually repulsed, threatened, and insulted, though he is the bravest – or perhaps least prudent – of the lot. These dangers are objective correlatives, the concretions, of Kafka's anxiety. The law of the story illuminates the world of things and concerns that come to light for a hero concretized in an initial image of a man or woman or animal *in grosser Verlegenheit*, completely at a loss, absent of mind.

Added to this gamut of embodied risks, as suggested earlier, is the risk every interpreter takes in proposing his or her own inevitably inadequate and misleading interpretation. The truth *lies in* the work – but will never be evident as a totalizing proposition – such as the judgment *Sei gerecht* – be just. (Note how that proposition fails to become inscribed in the body of the officer in "In the Penal Colony.") In the material life it represents, the literary work bundles together as concrete damages the risk of pure loss, factored as the loss of hope, of possessions, of love, of life. What compensation is there for so much loss? Answer: The truth of the work, which no hero – or reader – attains to. But the risk of the failure of interpretation is compensated for by the supportive totality of interpretations – the chorus of valuable lies.

Consider the steady denuding, the steady impoverishment, of the heroes of Kafka's three novels, whose correlative is the steady denuding, the disturbing impoverishment, of narrative opportunities. This process of unfolding is rarely a march toward the combustion of anxiety in a perfect contact with the law; I say "rarely," and not "never," because Kafka felt such an ecstasy at the conclusion of writing "The Judgment" ("Das Urteil"), though this was an ecstasy he would never again realize, a moment "im Litterarischen" ("in the literary field") "in which I

---

57 Kafka, *Nachgelassene Schriften II*, 348. My translation.

dwelled completely in every idea but also fulfilled every idea and in which I not only felt myself at my boundaries but at the boundaries of the human as such."[58]

2 A Model Case[59]

In concluding, I want to point to the wide gamut of interpretative possibilities – the riskiest interpretations – of *The Metamorphosis*. In doing so, let us keep in mind a chief aspect of the image that assails Kafka at the outset: "When Gregor Samsa woke up one morning from unsettling dreams, he found himself changed in his bed into a monstrous vermin."[60] This poetry of rich beginnings is dense, compact, pregnant with possibility. It contains literally endless possibilities of story development.

"How everything can be risked, how great a fire is ready for everything, for the strangest inspirations," Kafka wrote, "and they disappear in this fire and rise up again."[61] Images that leap out, even from dreams or somnambulistic states, can be immersed in the destructive element – the process, *writing*, that Walter Benjamin called the "burning of the dream" ("die Verbrennung des Traumes").[62] In the course of the story, they unfold according to an "unknown, perhaps unknowable but felt" law, and there they survive.[63]

---

58 Kafka, diary entry of 28 March 1911, in *Kafka's Selected Stories*, 195. ("[I]n welchen ich ganz und gar in jedem Einfall wohnte, aber jeden Einfall auch erfüllte und in welchen ich mich nicht nur an meinen Grenzen fühlte, sondern an den Grenzen des Menschlichen überhaupt." Kafka, *Tagebücher*, 34.)

59 This section (III) of this essay is extracted, with some changes and additions, from the introduction to Franz Kafka, *The Metamorphosis*, trans. and ed. Stanley Corngold, The Modern Library, New York 2013, v–xliii, xxvi–xxxv.

60 Franz Kafka, *The Metamorphosis: Translation, Background and Contexts, Criticism*, trans. and ed. Stanley Corngold, Norton Critical Edition, Norton, New York 1996, 3. ("Als Gregor Samsa eines Morgens aus unruhigen Träumen erwachte, fand er sich in seinem Bett zu einem ungeheueren Ungeziefer verwandelt." Kafka, *Drucke zu Lebzeiten*, 115.)

61 Kafka, diary entry of 23 September 1912, in *Kafka's Selected Stories*, 197. ("Wie alles gewagt werden kann, wie für alle, für die fremdesten Einfälle ein großes Feuer bereitet ist, in dem sie vergehn und auferstehn." Kafka, *Tagebücher*, 460.)

62 Walter Benjamin, *One-Way Street and Other Writings*, trans. J.A. Underwood, Penguin, London 2009, 47; Walter Benjamin, *Einbahnstraße*, Rowohlt, Berlin,1928, 6.

63 It was soon after writing this and other sublime diary entries that Kafka wrote *The Metamorphosis*, the "süße Seiten" ("sweet pages") of which he liked well enough but which finally dissatisfied him on account of what he considered its botched ending. He made this judgment in a letter to Felice Bauer written (presumably) around midnight of 5–6 September 1912. It is

In allowing his stories to develop *in just one way*, has Kafka wasted the power of his dream, drained it of creative possibilities – condemned it, "subjugated" it, to a *bad singularity*?[64]

Consider, then, in this perspective, *The Metamorphosis* and how the story unfolds. After the initial shock, Gregor struggles to regain his equilibrium. The family, failing to call either a locksmith or a doctor, open their door to the office manager. Grete Samsa assumes the care of her unfortunate brother, but then, growing bored, becomes bratty and impatient. His father, who abhors his son, takes revenge, bombarding him with small apples. Gregor crawls back into his room and meekly, tenderly, dies, whereupon the family celebrates their liberation by going on a picnic.

Every single such plot element actually realized implies the death of other possibilities. And this narrowing down of narrative choices does not occur simply or innocently. Gregor's speech sputters; his eyesight grows dim; we hear of his deprivation with dismay; it will crush the life chances of this almost-human being. We read on, with fading hope, perhaps, that Gregor might be rescued, liberated; like Gregor, we are "eager to see how today's fantasy would gradually fade away" ("gespannt, wie sich seine heutigen Vorstellungen allmählich auflösen würden"),[65] and yet we must suffer his depletion all along – and hence the whole story's depletion – for this is Gregor's story only, narrated from a standpoint virtually congruent with Gregor's own. His world of misery is the Samsas' only world.[66]

At the same time, this dwindling away of Gregor's life chances does not exclude a *richness* that we readers can realize. It is like a consolation for the lost variety of plot possibilities: the "variousness and complexity" *of interpreta-*

---

suggestive that Kafka criticized the *ending* of the story but never its *beginning* – that first rush of images – which leads one to think that he was quite satisfied with his initial impulse until a business trip prevented him from developing to the end its fullest implications.

64 "The tremendous world," he wrote, "that I have inside my head. But how free myself and free it without being torn to pieces. And a thousand times rather be torn to pieces than retain it in me or bury it. That is why I am here, that is quite clear to me." Franz Kafka, *The Diaries of Franz Kafka, 1910–1913*, ed. Max Brod, trans. Joseph Kresh, Schocken, New York 1948, 288. ("Die ungeheuere Welt die ich im Kopfe habe. Aber wie mich befreien und sie befreien ohne zu zerreißen. Und tausendmal lieber zerreißen, als sie in mir zurückhalten oder begraben. Dazu bin ich ja hier, das ist mir ganz klar." Kafka, *Tagebücher*, 562.) The tremendous world – the "worlds" he had inside his head – this extensive totality, this universal.

65 Kafka, *The Metamorphosis*, 6; Kafka, *Drucke zu Lebzeiten*, 121.

66 This narrowing-down has a spatial, an architectural, correlative: the narrow room, the door slammed shut, then opened just a chink.

tions we can bring to bear on the one storyline we have.[67] Every single sentence marches in a line, a straight line, leading through Gregor's steady diminishment to his starving away to death. But each of these so-to-speak discrete or confined moments on the plotline is trembling with virtual lunacy. This is what we feel; and it invites *our* lunacy or, let us say, our widest imagination of interpretation of that moment. And so the loss of extravagant plot possibilities is compensated for by the richness of interpretation that the reading collective has produced over the years.

This is Kafka's genius: from his openings he conjures the one storyline that will invite interpretation through all the discourses of his time and times to come. For Gershom Scholem, an eminent reader of his work, nothing compares with the attraction of working out an incisive interpretation of a text. But here the word "attraction" is too casual, certainly, in Adorno's view. The reader's attempt at an incisive interpretation is not optional. Kafka's sentences come at us with the force of an onrushing locomotive: "Through the power with which Kafka commands interpretation, he collapses aesthetic distance. He demands a desperate effort from the allegedly 'disinterested' spectator of an earlier time, overwhelms you, suggesting that far more than your intellectual equilibrium depends on whether you truly understand; life and death are at stake."[68]

Explanatory religious concepts (Christian, Jewish, mystic, other) might come to help. Kafka's contemporary William Butler Yeats wrote a story entitled "The Crucifixion of the Outcast," a phrase that casts a suggestive light on Gregor. Consider his cruciform position at the end of Part I, when he is being tormented, with his father's willing cooperation:

> [...] Gregor forced himself – come what may – into the doorway. One side of his body rose up, he lay lop-sided in the opening, *one of his flanks was scraped raw*, ugly blotches marred the white door, soon he got stuck and could not have budged anymore by himself, his little legs on one side dangled tremblingly in midair, those on the other were painfully crushed against the floor – *when from behind his father gave him a hard shove, which was truly his*

---

67 This phrase is from Lionel Trilling's *The Liberal Imagination*, viz. "[...] literature is the human activity that takes the fullest and most precise account of variousness, possibility, complexity, and difficulty." See Lionel Trilling, *The Liberal Imagination: Essays on Literature and Society*, Viking, New York 1950, xii.

68 Theodor W. Adorno, "Notes on Kafka," in *Prisms*, trans. Samuel Weber and Shierry Weber, Spearman, London 1967, 243–271, 246. ("Durch die Gewalt, mit der Kafka Deutung gebietet, zieht er die ästhetische Distanz ein. Er mutet dem angeblich interesselosen Betrachter von einst verzweifelte Anstrengung zu, springt ihn an und suggeriert ihm, daß weit mehr als sein geistiges Gleichgewicht davon abhänge, ob er richtig versteht, Leben oder Tod." Adorno, "Aufzeichnungen zu Kafka," 256.)

2

salvation, and bleeding profusely, he flew far into his room. The door was slammed shut with the cane, then at last everything was quiet. [Emphasis added.][69]

Such is Gregor's crucifixion, as it were. Consider, too, his manner of dying: "He remained in this state of empty and peaceful reflection until the tower clock struck three in the morning. He still saw that outside the window everything was beginning to grow light. Then, without his consent, his head sank down to the floor, and from his nostrils streamed his last weak breath."[70]

This image recalls the Gospel of John (19:30) – "When Jesus therefore had received the vinegar, he said, It is finished: and he bowed his head, and gave up the ghost." The three o' clock may have been suggested by the Gospel of Matthew (27:40), where the scoffing multitude says, "Thou that destroyest the temple, and buildest it in three days, save thyself. If thou be the Son of God, come down from the cross," or by the last three hours of the agony: "Now from the sixth hour there was darkness over all the land unto the ninth hour" (Matthew 27:45).[71]

One scholar, Kurt Weinberg, writing in an adventurous Jewish tradition, interprets Gregor's early failure to catch the five o'clock train as an allegory of spiritual failure, for Kafka has coded into the five o'clock train (recall the Five Books of Moses) the train of redemption, the train of the sacramental time that brings the Jewish Messiah: Gregor is thus literally the *stiff-necked* unbeliever.[72] For the aforementioned Gershom Scholem, it is the very gloomy dereliction of the scene, the radical absence of divine justice, that, by an effort of the concep-

---

69 Kafka, *The Metamorphosis*, 15. ("Gregor drängte sich – geschehe was wolle – in die Tür. Die eine Seite seines Körpers hob sich, er lag schief in der Türöffnung, seine *eine Flanke war ganz wundgerieben,* an der weißen Tür blieben häßliche Flecken, bald steckte er fest und hätte sich allein nicht mehr rühren können, die Beinchen auf der einen Seite hingen zitternd oben in der Luft, die auf der anderen waren schmerzhaft zu Boden gedrückt – *da gab ihm der Vater von hinten einen jetzt wahrhaftig erlösenden starken Stoß,* und er flog, heftig blutend, weit in sein Zimmer hinein. Die Tür wurde noch mit dem Stock zugeschlagen, dann war es endlich still" (emphasis added). Kafka, *Drucke zu Lebzeiten*, 142.)

70 Kafka, *The Metamorphosis*, 39. ("In diesem Zustand leeren und friedlichen Nachdenkens blieb er, bis die Turmuhr die dritte Morgenstunde schlug. Den Anfang des allgemeinen Hellerwerdens draußen vor dem Fenster erlebte er noch. Dann sank sein Kopf ohne seinen Willen gänzlich nieder, und aus seinen Nüstern strömte sein letzter Atem schwach hervor." Kafka, *Drucke zu Lebzeiten*, 193.)

71 Gregor's death is nevertheless unlike Christ's, according to Mark (15:37) or Luke (23:46), since Gregor's last moment is silent and painless.

72 Kurt Weinberg, *Kafkas Dichtungen: Die Travestien des Mythos* [*Kafka's Fictions: The Travesties of Myth*], Francke, Berne 1963.

tual will called "dialectical theology," affirms the necessary existence of a higher order that promises redemption.

Then there is the Eastern mystic reader, who connects Samsa's transubstantiation to an esoteric tradition called, in Sanskrit, "saṃsāra," "[which] refers to the cycle of reincarnation or rebirth in Hinduism, Buddhism, Jainism, Sikhism and [...] related religions."[73] Since the word "Verwandlung" also means "transfiguration," we see that the gates to every sort of religious reading are open – leaving only the question of whether that gate leads to an apprehension of what Kafka called "the imperishable fire" ("den Schein des unvergänglichen Feuers") – the light of the law that fashions this story.[74]

Such is the discourse of religion. Closely following is the discourse of economics, which the story takes no pains to hide and which has produced an abundance of critical essays all more or less titled "Marx and Metamorphosis." Gregor's parents are indebted to Gregor's employer – debts that Gregor feels obliged to repay. The German word for these debts, "Schulden," also refers to one's guilt. Can we speculate that Gregor's horrible appearance is the external expression of the guilt he bears, a dream-like, symptomatic expression of the unclean relation to the debts he has assumed, to something falsely messianic in his nature?

There is a second, striking metamorphosis of the economy of money and music in this story. From the description of Gregor's pre-metamorphic years, we learn two important facts about his money and his musical culture. On one hand, owing to his parents' debts (his decision to pay off the debts accumulated by his ancestors!), Gregor needs to earn money – a lot of money! How everyone rejoiced when "his successes on the job were transformed, by means of commission, into hard cash that could be plunked down on the table at home in front his astonished and delighted family" ("[seine] Arbeitserfolge sich sofort in Form der Provision zu Bargeld verwandelten, das der erstaunten und beglückten Familie zu Hause auf den Tisch gelegt werden konnte").[75] But being made of more sensitive metal, Gregor is interested in something finer, something that money can buy: a ticket of admission for his sister to enter the conservatory of music. So, at the end of the rainbow, there is something more than an escape from poverty and social disgrace for his family; Gregor harbors a notion of cultural improvement – and, hence, of implicit social advancement for his family – though his enjoyment of actual music is only vicarious: for, "it was his secret plan that she, who, unlike

---

73 See Michael J. Ryan, "Samsa and saṃsāra: Suffering, Death, and Rebirth in 'The Metamorphosis,'" in *German Quarterly* 72.2 (1999): 133–152.
74 Kafka, Notebook "G," in *Kafka's Selected Stories*, 213; Kafka, *Nachgelassene Schriften II*, 77.
75 Kafka, *The Metamorphosis*, 20; Kafka, *Drucke zu Lebzeiten*, 152.

him, loved music and could play the violin movingly, should be sent next year to the Conservatory" ("es war sein geheimer Plan, sie, die zum Unterschied von Gregor Musik sehr liebte und rührend Violine zu spielen verstand, nächstes Jahr [...] auf das Konservatorium zu schicken").[76] The exact definition of this cultural attitude, which seeks to acquire social distinction by publicly trafficking in the institutions of art, is philistinism. As long as Gregor is at work earning money, he is this philistine. But something interesting happens to him after his metamorphosis, which, in the economic sense, means becoming unemployable. Gregor becomes enthralled by the music of his sister's violin, so enthralled, it turns out, that he risks – and loses – his life for it. "Was he an animal, that music could move him so?" ("War er ein Tier, da ihn Musik so ergriff?") the narrator asks.[77]

At this point we will conjure a rival to the economist-reader – the sentimentalist reader, who interprets Gregor's question as a mere rhetorical question, meaning, "Oh, of course he cannot be an animal. Look how fine his responses are!" Gregor's newfound love of music, the sentimentalist-reader thinks, signals his ascent to a higher plane of aesthetic enjoyment. He is on his way to acquiring the dignity of a higher kind, in the sense of Schopenhauer and Nietzsche. But our economist-reader disagrees and will not read Gregor's question as a mere rhetorical one. He considers the question to be a real question and supplies an informed answer. "Was Gregor an animal?" Of course, he is. He is unemployable! He stands outside the society of market exchange, what Kafka calls the world of "property and its connections" ("Besitz und seine Beziehungen").[78]

As a consequence of the music Gregor hears, he never ceases to be at least animal-like: fiddle playing strikes a licentious chord in him. It conjures his sister's naked neck, which he means to kiss after making certain, by hissing and spitting at intruders, that henceforth she will play her music for him alone. Our economist's point is that we may understand the metamorphosis as inverting Gregor's relation to capital: with money, as a man, he is a philistine; without money, as a "vermin," he is a music lover of sorts – or, more accurately, the debased lover of a musician. Here, some readers may suddenly understand the moment as a wild parody of the final scene of Thomas Mann's story "Wälsungenblut" (1905)

---

76 Kafka, *The Metamorphosis*, 20; Kafka, *Drucke zu Lebzeiten*, 152.

77 Kafka, *The Metamorphosis*, 36; Kafka, *Drucke zu Lebzeiten*, 185.

78 *Nachgelassene Schriften II*, 59. I agree with the answer of our economist-reader, and I will risk offering a personal proof of the correctness of this position. I do not judge Gregor's fascination with sound to be a mark of his higher nature; I consider him to be in the same league with my wife's brother-in-law's Siamese cat Nino, who is so captivated by my wife's voice, it seems, that he springs for the telephone receiver and bites it and moans whenever she is on the phone. (My wife's explanation: "He wants to stay in touch.")

(translated into English as *The Blood of the Walsungs*), which tells of incestuous lovemaking between brother and sister after they have been enthralled by the music of Wagner's "The Valkyrie" ("Die Walküre").[79]

Readers alert to the gutter ideologies of Kafka's time will not fail to recognize the racist, biopolitical dimension of Gregor's metamorphosis: Austro-Hungarian cranks and crackpots were eager to attack their Jewish neighbors by vilifying them with low comparisons; and the dictionary of anti-Semitic insults included qualities that are found, by analogy, in Gregor's appearance and in his behavior. It is unpleasant to repeat such epithets: he is "a parasite," he is "low," he "scuttles" about on his business, he is unmusical, he is licentious, etc. But soon the

---

79 Mann's story was composed in 1905 and due for publication that year in the *Neue Rundschau*. It was already typeset when Mann suddenly withdrew it, realizing that its anti-Semitic tenor would give grievous offense to his wife and her Jewish family. He finally published it privately in 1921. How, then, can Kafka have known of it? In 1906, Mann had sent copies of the story to Arthur Schnitzler and Jakob Wassermann, among others. The story then circulated in samizdat, and news of the scandal was bruited about in Vienna and thereafter, it might well be supposed, in Prague. Kafka was a devoted reader of the *Neue Rundschau* and of the works of Schnitzler and Wassermann and would have perked up at any mention of writings coming from their desk. (Wassermann was one of the several authors whom Kafka declares he was "thinking of" apropos of writing "The Judgment." See Kafka, diary entry of 12 September 1912, in *Kafka's Selected Stories*, 197; Kafka, *Tagebücher*, 461.)

One benefit as to method arises at this point, where one may have noticed how hard it is to stay within the boundaries of any single interpretative framework. We can think of Kafka's stories as constructions of a sort – like monads (they are self-enclosed). Like the scripture in the Cathedral scene in *The Trial*, these stories are, as the priest says, "unalterable" (*unveränderlich*). At the same time, these stories are equipped with windows; they are "windowed monads," so to speak (with apologies to Leibniz – and thanks to Whitehead), built of scintillating perspectives, which take in the light of interpretative minds and give out that light at an angle of refraction.

Hence, no such window is entirely transparent; the gaze of no spectator, no reader, is focused enough not to glance off its glassy surface. And because each of Kafka's stories has *many* windows, a glance at one will communicate with another. The windows catch one another's light: perspectives scintillate.

This conceit is Kafka's, who was not able to see the gaze as a single ray of light. "One can disintegrate the world by means of very strong light" – "Mit stärkstem Licht kann man die Welt auflösen" – he wrote, meaning by "auflösen" to "break its hold." For the word "world" (*Welt*) in our context write: "the world of the story" – the world of *The Metamorphosis*. However, Kafka continues, "For weak eyes the world becomes solid, for still weaker eyes it seems to develop fists, for eyes weaker still it becomes shamefaced and smashes anyone who dares to gaze upon it." Kafka, *The Blue Octavo Notebooks*, 91. ("Vor schwachen Augen wird sie fest, vor noch schwächeren bekommt sie Fäuste, vor noch schwächeren wird sie schamhaft und zerschmettert den, der sie anzuschauen wagt." *Nachgelassene Schriften und Fragmente II*, 125.) Never mind. We will dare to approach a few more windows onto *The Metamorphosis*. The one I now have in mind is a dirty window.

comparison breaks off, and its truth-value is compromised, for Gregor also enjoys an acrobatic lightness of being and dies with the desire to please his family – almost. Kafka also takes pains to write that "[Gregor's] conviction that he would have to disappear was, if possible, even firmer than his sister's" ("seine Meinung darüber, daß er verschwinden müsse, war womöglich noch entschiedener, als die seiner Schwester"),[80] which makes her the agent of his disappearance and leaves him as something less than saintly leper – though a good deal more than abject scum. What Gregor is, is not readily answerable except as the distillation of the totality of answers that has been posed and will continue to be posed to the question of his being.

Are there other readings? Indeed there are. There is the medicinal: Gregor's predicament is a replica of Kafka's intuitive forecast of his own tuberculosis, which would lay him low. "Of course Gregor had to admit," we recall, "that he would not be able to keep up even this running for long, for whenever his father took one step, Gregor had to execute countless movements. He was already beginning to feel winded, just as in the old days he had not had very reliable lungs."[81] There is the biographical reading: Gregor is the family invalid; he punishes the family with his odium by assuming a cripple's or pariah's existence. True, he is himself punished by his sick body and by his dependency, but he thereby achieves the covert, doubly aggressive expressiveness of the tyrant invalid and the family idiot.

Another biographical reading summons the plight of the artist, the writer, who, in Kafka's family, is a changeling, a negative miracle, an outsider. For one moment we have plain evidence of Kafka's taste for such semi-private games. As the narrator explains: "Well, in a pinch Gregor could do without the chest, but the [writing] desk had to stay" ("Nun, den Kasten konnte Gregor im Notfall noch entbehren, aber schon der Schreibtisch mußte bleiben").[82] Here Samsa becomes an alias of Kafka, a notion given support in an (unfortunately) unreliable book by a young friend of Kafka's, Gustav Janouch. He claims to recall one of their conversations, which now borders on the cryptogrammatic:

---

80 Kafka, *The Metamorphosis*, 39; Kafka, *Drucke zu Lebzeiten*, 193.
81 Kafka, *The Metamorphosis*, 28. ("Allerdings mußte sich Gregor sagen, daß er sogar dieses Laufen nicht lange aushalten würde, denn während der Vater einen Schritt machte, mußte er eine Unzahl von Bewegungen ausführen. Atemnot begann sich schon bemerkbar zu machen, wie er ja auch in seiner früheren Zeit keine ganz vertrauenswürdige Lunge besessen hatte." Kafka, *Drucke zu Lebzeiten*, 170.)
82 Kafka, *The Metamorphosis*, 25; Kafka, *Drucke zu Lebzeiten*, 163.

"The hero of the story is called Samsa," I [Janouch] said. "It sounds like a cryptogram for Kafka. Five letters in each word. The S in the word Samsa has the same position as the K in the word Kafka. The A..."

Kafka interrupted me.

"It is not a cryptogram. Samsa is not merely Kafka, and nothing else. *The Metamorphosis* is not a confession, although it is – in a certain sense – an indiscretion."

"I know nothing about that."

"Is it perhaps delicate and discreet to talk about the bugs [*Wanzen*] in one's own family?"[83]

There is the etymological reading, which I have discussed in detail elsewhere and to which I am partial: Gregor, in the lines of his being, is a distorted metaphor.[84] But this *etymological* reading should not be confused with the *entomological* reading, which will briefly occupy us. Vladimir Nabokov, who greatly admired the story, considered it, as did Elias Canetti, a literary work that nothing could surpass – one of the few great, perfect poetic works of the twentieth century. Nabokov believed that Gregor's melancholy and feelings of alienation might be cured with a bit of scientific enlightenment. He could have been spared all his desolation, Nabokov wrote, if only he had recognized that he is "a domed beetle, a scarab beetle with wing-sheaths." His promise of happiness lies in his flying out the window and joining all "the other happy dung beetles rolling the dung balls on rural paths."[85]

But there is a good objection to this reading. Interestingly, the phrase "dung beetle" – *Mistkäfer* – does appear in the story, quite as if Kafka had been forewarned about Nabokov's reading of his hero's predicament. "Come over here for a minute, you old dung beetle!" ("Komm mal herüber, alter Mistkäfer!") says the gigantic, bony cleaning woman, who presides over Gregor's end. But then, significantly, we read: "To forms of address like these Gregor would not respond but remained immobile where he was, as if the door had not been opened" ("Auf solche Ansprachen antwortete Gregor mit nichts, sondern blieb unbeweglich auf seinem Platz, als sei die Tür gar nicht geöffnet worden").[86] He is not a dung beetle; he is "a monstrous vermin" – a proper English epithet that has an exact precedent in the language of a pamphlet written in 1581 by an English Protestant, Walter

---

83 Gustave Janouch, *Conversations with Kafka*, trans. Goronwy Rees, New Directions, New York 1971, 32.

84 Corngold, *Franz Kafka: The Necessity of Form*, 47–89.

85 Alfred Appel Jr., "An Interview with Vladimir Nabokov," in *Nabokov: The Man and His Work*, ed. L.S. Dembo, University of Wisconsin Press, Madison 1967, 19–44, 43.

86 Kafka, *The Metamorphosis*, 33; Kafka, *Drucke zu Lebzeiten*, 179.

Haddon, against the Portuguese bishop Jerome Osorio de Fonseca, in a theological dispute about papal authority: "O monstruous vermine: did I ever speake or think any such matter?"[87] Gregor is a "monstruous vermine" – an *ungeheures Ungeziefer* – and not an insect of a specifiable kind. Moreover, it may not be irrelevant that the modifying word *ungeheuer*, which Kafka chose, traces to a Middle High German word (Latin: *infamiliaris*) meaning a creature having no place at the hearth, a creature outside all human family; and that the word for vermin, *Ungeziefer*, goes back to a Middle High German word meaning a creature unacceptable as sacrifice to the gods and hence outside the world order altogether. (Kafka studied Middle High German at his university before taking his degree in law.) At this point, we might recall our economic reading, where the post-metamorphic – hence unemployable Gregor – has become unsuited to sacrifice to the gods of capitalism.

There appears to be no end to these discussions, which have taken the place of theological dispute, often retaining the same angry language. But the language of this discussion can also be of the whimsical sort; and so, we have Philip Roth imagining Kafka, despite Kafka's real death in 1924, fleeing the Central European concentration camp of the 1930s and surfacing in Newark as a Hebrew teacher and romancer of the young Philip's Aunt Rhoda.[88] "In poetry," writes John Coetzee, "the metaphoric spark is always one jump ahead of the decoding function: [...] another unforeseen reading is always possible."[89]

With respect, then, to our original question as to the power of Kafka's images: we now know that these images are surreal (brilliantly incisive, but contrary to fact); more than that, they are *super*real. Once they have originated a plot, they

---

[87] "Perhaps the most famous religious dispute of the latter half of the sixteenth century was that between Walter Haddon (1516–1572), the distinguished English Latinist, and Jerome Osorio de Fonseca (1506–1580), Portuguese bishop and eminent Ciceronian. [...] Though neither participant was primarily a theologian, the affair attracted a great deal of attention in its time because of the commanding reputations of both men as Latin stylists. By his fellow Englishmen, Haddon was regarded as the best Latin orator, poet, and epistolist of his generation; and on the Continent Osorio was widely admired not only for his skill in Scriptural studies but also for his excellent Ciceronianism. [...]

"The result was *Contra Hieron. Osorium ... Responsio Apologetica* (1577), dedicated to Sebastian, King of Portugal. [...] In the prefatory epistle, Haddon expresses regret at having to re-enter the controversy in such sharp language as Osorio had forced him to employ." Lawrence V. Ryan, "The Haddon–Osorio Controversy (1563–1583)," in *Church History* 22.2 (1953): 142–154, 142, 151.

[88] Philip Roth, "'I Always Wanted You to Admire My Fasting'; or, Looking at Kafka," in *Reading Myself and Others*, Farrar, Straus and Giroux, New York 1975, 247–270.

[89] John Coetzee, *Diary of a Bad Year*, Viking Adult, New York 2007, 23.

invite a seemingly endless variety of perspectives, types of explanation, which draw on all the conceptual resources of Kafka's time – and all times to come.

And here the word "invite" is too casual – at least, we recall, in the view of Theodor Adorno. For Adorno, the reader's appeal to one or more of these discourses or types of explanation (to which, on reflection, we can add the bureaucratic, the cinematic, the fantastic, the familial) is not optional: Kafka's sentences, Adorno writes, come at the reader with the force of an onrushing locomotive: each sentence of Kafka's says "interpret me": "Through the power with which Kafka commands interpretation, he collapses aesthetic distance. He demands a desperate effort from the allegedly 'disinterested' spectator of an earlier time, overwhelms you, suggesting that far more than your intellectual equilibrium depends on whether you truly understand; life and death are at stake."[90] Kafka's work *demands* interpretation: it is the desperate demand of the incisive image, the individual sentence – laid on a "chorus" of readers – to raise their singularity into a probable universe of "purity, truth, and immutability."[91]

Works Cited

Adorno, Theodor W., "Aufzeichnungen zu Kafka," in *Gesammelte Schriften* 10.1 (Frankfurt/M.: Suhrkamp, 2003), 254–287.
Adorno, Theodor W., "Notes on Kafka," in *Prisms*. Trans. Samuel Weber and Shierry Weber (London: Spearman, 1967), 243–271.
Appel Jr., Alfred, "An Interview with Vladimir Nabokov," in *Nabokov: The Man and His Work*. Ed. L.S. Dembo (Madison: University of Wisconsin Press, 1967), 19–44.
Auden, W.H., "The I Without a Self," in *The Dyer's Hand and Other Essays* (New York: Vintage, 1989), 159–167.

---

90 Adorno, "Notes on Kafka," 246. ("Durch die Gewalt, mit der Kafka Deutung gebietet, zieht er die ästhetische Distanz ein. Er mutet dem angeblich interesselosen Betrachter von einst verzweifelte Anstrengung zu, springt ihn an und suggeriert ihm, daß weit mehr als sein geistiges Gleichgewicht davon abhänge, ob er richtig versteht, Leben oder Tod." Adorno, "Aufzeichnungen zu Kafka," 256.)
91 Ulrich Gaier's account of the way to understand the goal hinted at in Kafka's parable "The Departure" ("Der Aufbruch") has a similar thrust: "The way to reach this goal – from here, to everywhere, to 'away-from-here'– is exactly mirrored in the movement of the concepts – from specific, to general, to pure privative motion. [...] [T]imeless and away from everything, [the goal] can be reached only through an integration and totalization of all moments and all communicable things." Ulrich Gaier, "Chorus of Lies – On Interpreting Kafka," in *German Life and Letters* 22.4 (1969): 283–296, 293.

Barthes, Roland, *The Grain of the Voice: Interviews 1962–1980*. Trans. Linda Coverdale (New York: Hill and Wang, 1985).

Begley, Louis, *The Tremendous World I Have Inside My Head: Franz Kafka: A Biographical Essay* (New York: Atlas & Co., 2008).

Benjamin, Walter, *Benjamin über Kafka*. Ed. Hermann Schweppenhäuser (Frankfurt/M.: Suhrkamp, 1981).

Benjamin, Walter, *Einbahnstraße* (Berlin: Rowohlt, 1928).

Benjamin, Walter, *Gesammelte Schriften*. Eds. Rolf Tiedemannn and Hermann Schweppenhäuser (Frankfurt/M.: Suhrkamp, 1990).

Benjamin, Walter, "Goethe's *Elective Affinities*," in *Selected Writings, Volume 1: 1913–1926*. Eds. Marcus Bullock and Michael Jennings (Cambridge: Harvard University Press, 1996), 297–360.

Benjamin, Walter, *One-Way Street and Other Writings*. Trans. J.A. Underwood (London: Penguin, London 2009).

Benjamin, Walter and Gerhard Scholem, *The Correspondence of Walter Benjamin and Gershom Scholem, 1932–1940*. Ed. Gershom Scholem. Trans. Gary Smith and Andre Lefever (Cambridge: Harvard University Press, 1992).

Calasso, Roberto, "Veiled Splendor" (Afterward), trans. Geoffrey Brock, in *Franz Kafka, The Zurau* [sic] *Aphorisms*. Trans. Michael Hofmann. Ed. Roberto Calasso (New York: Schocken Books, 2006), 109–134.

Cerna, Jana, *Kafka's Milena*. Trans. A.G. Brain (Evanston: Northwestern University Press, 1993).

Coetzee, John, *Diary of a Bad Year* (New York: Viking Adult, 2007).

Corngold, Stanley, *Franz Kafka: The Necessity of Form* (Ithaca: Cornell University Press, 1988).

Corngold, Stanley, "Kafka's Law in a Universe of Risk," in *The American Reader* 1.3 (2013): 110–119.

Corngold, Stanley, "Ritardando in *Das Schloß*," in *From Kafka to Sebald: Modernism and Narrative Form*. Ed. Sabine Wilke (London: Continuum, 2012), 11–26.

Culler, Jonathan, "Forum: The Legacy of Jacques Derrida," in *PMLA* 120.2 (2005): 472–473.

Danto, Arthur, *Nietzsche as Philosopher: An Original Study* (New York: Columbia University, 1965).

Derrida, Jacques, "Before the Law," trans. Avital Ronell and Christine Roulston, in *Acts of Literature*. Ed. Derek Attridge (New York and London: Routledge, 1992), 183–220.

Ellmann, Richard, *James Joyce* (Oxford: Oxford University Press, 1959).

Gaier, Ulrich, "'Chorus of Lies' – On Interpreting Kafka," in *German Life and Letters* 22.4 (1969): 283–296.

Hasselblatt, Dieter, *Zauber und Logik. Eine Kafka Studie* (Wiesbaden: Wissenschaft und Politik, 1964).

Hegel, Georg Wilhelm Friedrich, *The Science of Logic*. Ed. and trans. George di Giovanni (Cambridge: Cambridge University Press, 2010).

Hegel, Georg Wilhelm Friedrich, *Wissenschaft der Logik* (Berlin: Hofenberg, 2013).

Heller, Erich, *Franz Kafka* (New York: The Viking Press 1974).

Janouch, Gustave, *Conversations with Kafka*. Trans. Goronwy Rees (New York: New Directions, 1971).

Kafka, Franz, *The Blue Octavo Notebooks*. Ed. Max Brod. Trans. Ernst Kaiser and Eithne Wilkins (Cambridge: Exact Change 1991).

Kafka, Franz, *Briefe an Milena*. Eds. Jürgen Born and Michael Müller (Frankfurt/M.: S. Fischer, 1991).

Kafka, Franz, *The Diaries of Franz Kafka, 1910–1913*. Ed. Max Brod. Trans. Joseph Kresh (New York: Schocken, 1948).
Kafka, Franz, *The Diaries of Franz Kafka, 1914–1923*. Ed. Max Brod. Trans. Martin Greenberg (with the assistance of Hannah Arendt) (New York: Schocken Books, 1949).
Kafka, Franz, *Drucke zu Lebzeiten*. Eds. Wolf Kittler, Hans-Gerd Koch, and Gerhard Neumann (Frankfurt/M.: S. Fischer, 1994).
Kafka, Franz, *Kafka's Selected Stories: New Translations, Backgrounds and Contexts, Criticism*. Ed. and trans. Stanley Corngold, Norton Critical Edition (New York: Norton, 2007).
Kafka, Franz, *The Metamorphosis: Translation, Background and Contexts, Criticism*. Ed. and trans. Stanley Corngold, Norton Critical Edition (New York: Norton, 1996).
Kafka, Franz, *Nachgelassene Schriften und Fragmente I*. Ed. Malcolm Pasley (Frankfurt/M.: S. Fischer, 1990).
Kafka, Franz, *Nachgelassene Schriften und Fragmente II*. Ed. Jost Schillemeit (Frankfurt/M.: S. Fischer, 1992).
Kafka, Franz, *Der Proceß*. Ed. Malcom Pasley (Frankfurt/M.: S. Fischer, 1990).
Kafka, Franz, *Der Proceß. Apparatband*. Ed. Malcolm Pasley (Frankfurt/M.: S. Fischer, 1990).
Kafka, Franz, *Das Schloß*. Ed. Malcolm Pasley (Frankfurt/M.: S. Fischer, 1982).
Kafka, Franz, *Tagebücher in der Fassung der Handschrift*. Ed. Michael Müller (Frankfurt/M.: S. Fischer, 1990).
Kafka, Franz, *The Trial*, in *The Penguin Complete Novels of Franz Kafka*, trans. Willa and Edwin Muir (Harmondsworth: Penguin Books, 1983), 5–176.
Kafka, Franz, *The Trial*, trans. Willa and Edwin Muir (New York: Schocken, 1968).
Kafka, Franz, *Über das Schreiben*. Eds. Erich Heller and Joachim Beug (Frankfurt/M.: Fischer, 1983).
Liska, Vivian, "'Before the Law stands a doorkeeper. To this doorkeeper comes a man…': Kafka, Narrative and the Law," in *Naharaim* 6/2 (2013): 175–194.
Murray, Nicholas, *Kafka* (New Haven: Yale University Press, 2004).
Nietzsche, Friedrich, *Beyond Good and Evil: Prelude to a Philosophy of the Future* (1886), http://www.thenietzschechannel.com/works-pub/bge/bge5-dual.htm.
Nietzsche, Friedrich, *Morgenröte, Kritische Studienausgabe*. Eds. Giorgio Colli and Mazzino Montinari (Munich: dtv/De Gruyter, 1988).
Pinter, Harold, "Nobel Lecture 2005: Art, Truth & Politics," in *PMLA* 121.3 (2006): 811–818.
Proust, Marcel, *In Search of Lost Time*. Trans. C.K. Scott Moncrieff, T. Kilmartin, and D.J. Enright (New York: Modern Library, 2003).
Powell, Matthew T., "Bestial Representations of Otherness: Kafka's Animal Stories," in *Journal of Modern Literature* 32.1 (2008): 129–142.
Radio Bremen, "Porträt: Franz Kafka: Auf Spurensuche in Prag," 7 July 2010, http://www.radiobremen.de/kultur/portraets/kafka/kafka108.html.
Roth, Philip, "'I Always Wanted You to Admire My Fasting'; or, Looking at Kafka," in *Reading Myself and Others* (New York: Farrar, Straus and Giroux, 1975), 247–270.
Ryan, Lawrence V., "The Haddon–Osorio Controversy (1563–1583)," in *Church History* 22.2 (1953): 142–154.
Ryan, Michael J., "Samsa and saṃsāra: Suffering, Death, and Rebirth in 'The Metamorphosis,'" in *German Quarterly* 72.2 (1999): 133–152.
Sandberg, Beatrice, "Starting in the Middle? Complications of Narrative Beginnings and Progression in Kafka," in *Franz Kafka: Narration, Rhetoric, and Reading*. Eds. Jakob Lothe,

Beatrice Sandberg, and Ronald Speirs (Columbus: The Ohio State University Press, 2011), 123–148.

Sartre, Jean-Paul, "La Démilitarisation de la culture," excerpted in *Situations VII* (Paris: Gallimard, 1962), 322–331.

Scott, Jill, "Doing Justice to Kafka's *The Trial*: Literature and Jurisprudential Innovation," http://www.queensu.ca/german/undergraduate/courseinfo/ints/322/Doing_Justice_To_Kafkas_The_Trial_Jill_Scott_2011.pdf.

Thompson, Peter, "Kafka, Bloch, Religion and the Metaphysics of Contingency," in *Kafka, Religion, and Modernity*, Oxford Kafka Studies III. Eds. Manfred Engel and Ritchie Robertson (Würzburg: Königshausen und Neumann, 2014), 177–187.

Torres, Amanda, "Kafka and the Common Law: The Roots of the 'Kafkaesque' in *The Trial*." Unpublished seminar paper for the conference "Kafka and the Law," held at the Columbia Law School (7 May 2007).

Trilling, Lionel, *The Liberal Imagination: Essays on Literature and Society* (New York: Viking, 1950).

Weinberg, Kurt, *Kafkas Dichtungen: Die Travestien des Mythos* (Berne: Francke, 1963).

Brendan Moran
Philosophy and Ambiguity in Benjamin's Kafka

> We are sinful, not only because we have eaten of the Tree of Knowledge, but also because we
> have not yet eaten of the Tree of Life.
> – Franz Kafka, *The Blue Octavo Notebooks*[1]

For Walter Benjamin, there is a complementary relationship of art and philosophy. Philosophy exercises a persistence of discourse against any ostensibly concluded gesture of an artwork. Philosophy is not a fragment to be treated as inviolably apart; nor can it treat anything else – including the artwork – as inviolably apart. There is no final gesture. The gestural element remains, nonetheless, integral to philosophy; the gestural element openly performs beyond the discursive – beyond the denotative (and any connoted denotations). In the encounter with artworks, philosophy is kept attentive to the resistance of particularity to discursive rendering. Such unyielding is the philosophic element in the artwork. Attentiveness to this element of the artwork is integral to the possibility of criticism being philosophy. The alliance with literature is distinct from any view of philosophy as that which ultimately overcomes the particularity conveyed by literature. As a discourse about truth, philosophy is indeed distinct from the emphatic particularity of literature. Yet the artwork, in conveying particularity as inexpungible from life, offers philosophy a truth that the latter might be inclined to disregard. This attentiveness to particularity can be more philosophic than can a "philosophy" devoted to eliminating particularity.[2]

For Benjamin, the philosophic – whether it happens in an exercise of philosophy per se, in an artwork, or somewhere else – is a disruption of closure. He characterizes closure as "myth" and develops the philosophic as an ongoing exercise of engaging life against discernibly mythic efforts to contain it.

It might seem to follow that the philosophic is an exercise of rendering closures ambiguous. This will indeed be a claim of the following essay; however,

1 Franz Kafka, *The Blue Octavo Notebooks*, ed. Max Brod, trans. Ernst Kaiser and Eithne Wilkins, Exact Change, Cambridge 2004, 37. The German reads: "Wir sind nicht nur deshalb sündig weil wir vom Baum der Erkenntnis gegessen haben, sondern auch deshalb weil wir vom Baum des Lebens noch nicht gegessen haben." See Franz Kafka, *Nachgelassene Schriften und Fragmente II* [*Unpublished Writings and Fragments II*], ed. Jost Schillemeit, Fischer, Frankfurt/M. 1992, 72.
2 For more extensive discussion of this topic, see Brendan Moran, "An Inhumanly Wise Shame," in *Philosophy as a Literary Art*, ed. Costica Bradatan, Routledge, London 2014, 63–75.

this claim is made somewhat counter to Benjamin's tendency to present the philosophic as simply an exercise of creating paradox rather than ambiguity. Benjamin does not present a sustained treatment of philosophy as paradox, although he occasionally mentions the topic. Not far from Benjamin's outlook in this respect is Gilles Deleuze, who claims that philosophy "is revealed not by good sense but by paradox. Paradox is the pathos or the passion of philosophy." Philosophic paradox is opposed to the "complementary forms of orthodoxy – namely, good sense and common sense."[3] Karl Kraus remarks more broadly: "A paradox originates when a knowledge developed prematurely collides with the hogwash [Unsinn] of its time."[4] Benjamin is close to these conceptions of paradox, and he regards such paradoxes as specifically philosophic. The following essay will be an endeavour to indicate that ambiguity can be a *philosophical* element in paradox. Literature can, moreover, particularly accentuate this philosophic ambiguity, which is in turn articulated in philosophic criticism. This essay will provide an indication, principally on the basis of Benjamin's writings on Franz Kafka, of this dynamic of literature and philosophy. Towards the close of the essay, an outline will accordingly be provided of how ambiguity might be integral to Benjamin's own expressly Kafkan objection to Søren Kierkegaard's absolute paradox.

1 A Challenge

An obvious challenge faces this essay. At various points in his works, Benjamin associates, if not identifies, ambiguity with myth. Careful readers have sometimes followed him in this respect or even stated the association more emphatically. What is this ambiguity of myth? For Benjamin, it is above all that myth simultaneously has a claim or presumption to encompass or reassure but cannot actually fulfil this claim or presumption. A formulation of this ambiguity is given in Benjamin's *The Origin of the German Mourning Play* [*Ursprung des deutschen Trauerspiels*] (rejected in 1925 as a habilitation thesis; published in 1928). The anti-mythic, philosophic tendency both recovered and exercised in the *Trauerspiel* book is to turn the ambiguity (Zweideutigkeit) into paradox – to show that the exercise of control by myth ("the demonic world-order") involves simulta-

---

3 Gilles Deleuze, *Difference and Repetition*, trans. Paul Patton, Columbia University Press, New York 1994, 227; Gilles Deleuze, *Différence et répetition*, Universitaires de France, Paris 1968, 293.
4 Karl Kraus, *Aphorismen* [*Aphorisms*], *Schriften* [*Writings*], Vol. 8, ed. Christian Wagenknecht, Suhrkamp, Frankfurt/M. 1986, 164. Cited (somewhat differently) in Paul North, *The Problem of Distraction*, Stanford University Press, Stanford 2012, 144.

neously an experience of resistance to this control.[5] Benjamin's preference for "paradox" over ambiguity seems to arise from a sense that the word "paradox" better conveys contradiction to prevailing opinion (doxa); there is a *para-dox*.[6] The paradox is to transform the ambiguity – bring it "to decline [Absterben]" – so that there is something other than "fate" (Schicksal), something other than an alleged necessity requiring submission and "retribution" (Sühne). There can thus be a "sacrifice" (Opfer), which – while suffering defeat by the old order – also contributes, even if the sacrifice is fatal, to a "victory" of the residual, "historico-philosophic [geschichtsphilosophische] signature" that prophesies the decline of the order.[7] The historico-philosophic impetus, the impetus para-doxical rather than mythic in history, can contribute to the decline of an order that has only an ambiguous claim to commandeer history. The historico-philosophic impetus brings to decline the not entirely credible – and therefore ambiguous – claim or presumption of this order to control or reassure.

There are other such passages in Benjamin's writings, and some of these will be discussed below. Somewhat against the grain of such passages, however, an argument of this essay will be that the aforementioned historico-philosophic paradox always remains ambiguous, for it too arises from a condition in which any contradiction against myth will itself be imbued with mythic closures, conscious or not. The historico-philosophic paradox will, moreover, be an opening to another ambiguity, a philosophic ambiguity that must be respected in all philosophic momentum: this is the ambiguity that may summarily be characterized as "Mehrdeutigkeit," a condition open to various readings.

This opening beyond closed interpretation is a corrective to much that goes by the name "philosophy." Even traditional "philosophic" paradoxes are subject to this correction. No paradox eliminates ambiguity entirely. The correction can involve consideration of words not just in light of predicates associated with them

---

5 Walter Benjamin, *The Origin of the German Tragic Drama*, trans. John Osborne, Verso, London, 1977 (translation modified), 109; Walter Benjamin, *Gesammelte Schriften* [*Collected Writings*], Vol. I:1, eds. Rolf Tiedemann and Hermann Schweppenhäuser, Suhrkamp, Frankfurt/M. 1974, 288.

6 Although it does not refer to relevant texts by Benjamin, a helpful account of this notion of paradox (from Heraclitus to the twentieth century) is David Schur, *The Way of Oblivion. Heraclitus and Kafka*, Harvard University Press, Cambridge 1998.

7 Benjamin, *The Origin of the German Tragic Drama*, 109 (translation modified); Benjamin, *Gesammelte Schriften*, Vol. I:1, 288. For justification of the usage of the term "myth" here, where it is not actually used by Benjamin, see the description of death in the *Trauerspiel* as, in contrast with death in tragedy, signifying historically "the end of myth" (Benjamin, *The Origin of the German Tragic Drama*, 135; Benjamin, *Gesammelte Schriften*, Vol. I:1, 315).

but also in concern for the *linguistic* element that is independent of predication. Benjamin thus criticizes Bertrand Russell for determining paradox entirely on the basis of predicates for the words used. For Benjamin, Russell neglects that words have "meaning" (Bedeutung) and give "indication" (Bezeichnung) in ways that are not identifiable as predicates.[8] With regard to the so-called Cretan paradox (Epimenides the Cretan says all Cretans are liars), Benjamin insists that the statement be taken beyond the logic in which its paradox is obvious (if Epimenides is being truthful, he is lying; if he is lying, he is being truthful). On an "ontological" level, the statement might not be "meaningless [unsinnig] or nonsensical [widersinnig] in itself. This outlook frees up the paradox from its logical contradiction." For instance, the statement is contradictory if uttered by the person to whom it applies. Yet if it is said of anyone else that every judgement made by the latter person predicates the opposite of truth, the statement does not have "contradictory results." Accordingly, the statement "is not a contradiction in *every* sense." In "metaphysics," it is recognized that the logical contradiction of the Cretan's statement is dependent on the "I-form of the judgment." "Its logical semblance is constituted in its subjectivity," which creates the "anti-logical" condition of the proposition. In Benjamin's view, a metaphysical rather than strictly logical approach is thus needed to examine the paradox. In short, "[m]etaphysics" is needed to "ground" (begründen) the statement.[9] With regard to Benjamin's discussion, it has been noted that the Cretan paradox has an untidiness by virtue of the commencement of the paradox by a specific figure – in this case, Epimenides. Unlike W.V. Quine and others, who restate the paradox in less personal terms ("I am lying" or, even more impersonally, "This sentence is false"), Benjamin does not seek to eradicate this untidiness. He brings the untidy condition to the fore.[10] In one of his texts dealing with Russell, Benjamin suggests that confinement of meaning to logical tidiness neglects the "linguistic" element in which words are beyond such confinement.[11]

---

8 Walter Benjamin, *Gesammelte Schriften*, Vol. VI, eds. Rolf Tiedemann and Hermann Schweppenhäuser, Suhrkamp, Frankfurt/M. 1985, 9–11. For criticism of Benjamin's reading of Russell, see Alexei Procyshyn, "Walter Benjamin's Philosophy of Language," in *Philosophy Compass* 9.6 (2014), 368–381.
9 Walter Benjamin, *Selected Writings, Volume 1: 1913–1926*, eds. Marcus Bullock and Michael W. Jennings, The Belknap Press of Harvard University Press, Cambridge 1996, 210–212 (translation modified); Benjamin, *Gesammelte Schriften*, Vol. VI, 57–59.
10 James F. McFarland, *Constellation. Friedrich Nietzsche and Walter Benjamin in the Now-Time of History*, Fordham University Press, New York 2013, 103–107. See W.V. Quine, *The Ways of Paradox and Other Essays*, Harvard University Press, Cambridge 1976 [revised edition], 6–7.
11 Benjamin, *Gesammelte Schriften*, Vol. VI, 10–11.

Benjamin stresses this in his 1916 essay on language (as well as elsewhere). Linguistic being cannot be reduced to spiritual being (meaning circumscribed by humans). Nonetheless, "the deep and incomparable paradox" of identifying spiritual being and linguistic being has an important and warranted application. This paradox and its justifiable application is expressed in "the ambiguity [Doppelsinn]," the *double meaning*, "of the word 'logos.'" The word "logos" serves to keep spiritual being and linguistic being from conflation into one another, and yet also presupposes their contact (admittedly, an indeterminate contact) with one another. The paradox of the contact – the paradox of the identity – of spiritual being and linguistic being is a solution in "the centre" of linguistic theory but "remains a paradox, and insoluble, if placed at the beginning."[12] To begin with the distinction of spiritual being and linguistic being – the distinction making philosophical method an exercise of always beginning anew – is to emphasize that there is communication *in*, not *through*, language. It is to emphasize that linguistic being does not let itself be used exhaustively by humanly conceived meaning. The spiritual being communicated is neither demarcation nor delimitation of linguistic being. "Spiritual being communicates itself in a language and not through a language – that is to say: it is not outwardly [von aussen] identical with linguistic being."[13] Into the paradox of identifying spiritual being and linguistic being, there comes the ambiguity, the *Doppelsinn*, of logos that keeps language free from complete identification with spiritual being and yet maintains their fluctuating contact with one another.

This ambiguity entails an independence of words from meanings given to them; it also entails a constant contact of words and such meanings. Ambiguity ensues for paradoxes, perhaps in a jarring way for paradoxes dependent on highly insistent conceptions of meaning in them. It would be unphilosophic, a denial of logos and its dynamic of language and meaning, if the ambiguity in the contact of language and meaning were unacknowledged. In the aforementioned myth (discussed in the *Trauerspiel* book), the ambiguity – the lack of control or certainty accompanying any notion of control – is actually denied, disregarded, or suppressed. This denial, disregard, or suppression is pierced by the philosophic motion that exposes the ambiguity. Along with this first philosophic

---

12 Benjamin, *Selected Writings, Volume 1*, 63; Walter Benjamin, *Gesammelte Schriften*, Vol. II:1, eds. Rolf Tiedemann and Hermann Schweppenhäuser, Suhrkamp, Frankfurt/M. 1977, 141–142.
13 Benjamin, *Selected Writings, Volume 1*, 63 (translation modified); Benjamin, *Gesammelte Schriften*, Vol. II:1, 142. Also see: under "Fortsetzungsnotizen zu Arbeit über die Sprache" ("Follow-up Notes to Work on Language"), in Walter Benjamin, *Gesammelte Schriften*, Vol. VII:2, eds. Rolf Tiedemann and Hermann Schweppenhäuser, Suhrkamp, Frankfurt/M. 1989, 786–788.

movement that does not quite let myth deny, disregard, or suppress the ambiguity (its claim or presumption versus its lack of credibility), there is a second correlative philosophic ambiguity that is (in German) "Mehrdeutigkeit," which has also long been lexically established as one meaning of the previously noted term "Zweideutigkeit" (ambiguity) and which obviously pertains to a possibility for multiple interpretations.

2 Mythic Ambiguity and Philosophic Ambiguity

Benjamin's writings on Kafka include motifs in which the two aforementioned ambiguities come into mutual play. The first ambiguity may be called mythic ambiguity. It arises when there is a claim to control or to encompass that can be shown to be fraudulent. The work of the philosophic in Kafka's literature, and in Benjamin's criticism, is to show this ambiguity that is otherwise denied by its perpetrators. Philosophy thereby becomes a momentum of paradox in the sense outlined at the outset of this essay: it opposes *doxa* that claims to be truth. The philosophic momentum of paradox is not, however, entirely independent of ambiguity. First of all, it emerges from contexts that are themselves always imbued with mythic ambiguity (devices and orders exercised as though they are true); it does not completely transcend all such contexts, even if it is impelled by an impetus to do so. Second, the philosophic momentum opens to another ambiguity, the one inherent in the contact of language and meaning; this is the ambiguity referred to previously as "Mehrdeutigkeit." Kafka's literature keeps Benjamin's philosophic criticism attentive to all these fluctuations of ambiguity; Benjamin's criticism responds accordingly. As a discourse about truth, philosophy distinguishes itself from the accent placed by literature on particularity. The philosophic in literature, and in turn in criticism, prevents literature from simply absolutizing – mythifying – its particularities, as perhaps do some versions of religion. In conveying ambiguous particularity as inexpungible from life, the artwork is philosophic in presenting to philosophy a pervasive ambiguity (in all the foregoing senses of "ambiguity") that philosophic discourse may otherwise be inclined to disregard. This attentiveness to ambiguity can be more philosophic than is a "philosophy" claiming to eliminate ambiguity entirely. The latter claim exposes itself to the risk of becoming myth in denial of ambiguity.

Although the association of ambiguity with philosophy may seem unique, there have been other attempts to relate ambiguity with the philosophic. Maurice Merleau-Ponty bases the phenomenology of perception significantly on "ambiguous life" (la vie ambiguë).[14] Simone de Beauvoir offers an ethics (morale) of ambiguity, in which she indicts the tendency of most "philosophers" to mask the ambiguity of the human condition.[15] As intimated already, moreover, the etymology of "Zweideutigkeit" is not entirely unfavourable to an association of ambiguity and the philosophic.

The term *zweideutig* (ambiguous) developed in the seventeenth century as a translation of the Latin *aequivocus*, meaning *doppelsinnig* (ambiguous) or *mehrdeutig* (ambiguous, equivocal, conducive to a plurality of interpretations). In the eighteenth century, however, *zweideutig* indeed came to mean *absichtlich unklar* (purposely unclear), which pertains of course to the mythic ambiguity that Benjamin has been shown above to describe. Even so, this "purposely unclear" could refer to a denial, disregard, or suppression of *Doppelsinnigkeit* or *Mehrdeutigkeit*. At the very least, the (admittedly quite incomplete) etymology given here suggests that the term *zweideutig* is *mehrdeutig*.[16] This *Mehrdeutigkeit* – indeed, any *Mehrdeutigkeit* – is, moreover, not necessarily indicative of a mythic swindle, a wilful or semi-conscious unclarity that serves a dominating purpose.[17]

---

14 Maurice Merleau-Ponty, *Phenomenology of Perception*, trans. Donald A. Landes, Routledge, London 2013, 382; Maurice Merleau-Ponty, *Phénoménologie de la perception*, Gallimard, Paris 1945, 418.

15 Simone de Beauvoir, *The Ethics of Ambiguity*, trans. Bernard Frechtman, The Citadel Press, New York 1964, 7; Simone de Beauvoir, *Pour une morale de l'ambiguïté*, Gallimard, Paris 1947, 12.

16 For very succinctly given detail on *zweideutig*, see under "deuten" in *Das Herkunftswörterbuch, Etymologie der deutschen Sprache* [*The Dictionary of Provenance: Etymology of the German Language*], Dudenverlag, Mannheim 2001, 142. The Grimm brothers more elaborately address "zwiedeutig" and "Zweideutigkeit" in a quite similar way, but many of the meanings given are the mentioned or other pejorative senses. Exceptions are the first recorded meanings of "zweideutig" and "Zweideutigkeit," which are somewhat more neutral, pertaining to the simple possibility that words or sense-contexts may have double, often antagonistic, meanings. Such notions of "zweideutig" and "Zweideutigkeit" do, nonetheless, persist. Also noteworthy is that under "Zweideutigkeit" the Grimm brothers include reference to "the undecided double possibility" to which "philosophic language" might refer (see Jacob and Wilhelm Grimm, reworked by Gustav Rosenhagen and others, *Deutsches Wörterbuch* [*German Dictionary*], Vol. 16, Verlag von S. Hirzel, Leipzig 1954, 984–988).

17 There are, of course, other meanings of "zweideutig" and "Zweideutigkeit," that could very well seem relevant to Kafka's writings and Benjamin's reading of them. These include the characterizations *schlüpfrig* (slippery, suggestive, lewd, risqué) or *zotig* (dirty, filthy, smutty) (*Das Herkunftswörterbuch*, 142; *Deutsches Wörterbuch*, Vol. 16, 985, 987) – meanings that could easily be used to characterize some of what Benjamin detects in writings by Kafka, although it might not always be clear whether the lewdness and smuttiness is reinforcing the mythic or pointing to deviance from it.

Nevertheless, careful readers have contended that ambiguity is strictly opposed in Benjamin's readings of Kafka.[18] This claim may seem to find corroboration in Benjamin's Kafka essay, as well as in an earlier, related passage of his "Towards the Critique of Violence" ("Zur Kritik der Gewalt"). In the latter essay, which appeared in 1921, Benjamin discusses the ancient notion of a "retribution" that is provoked by an offense against "unwritten and unknown [unbekannten] law." He explains that the occurrence of such retribution is – "in the sense of the law" (im Sinne des Rechts) – "not coincidence, but fate [Schicksal] showing itself once again in its *deliberate ambiguity* [seiner *planvollen Zweideutigkeit*]."[19] In his Kafka essay of 1934, Benjamin writes something quite similar, albeit with reference to unwritten and unknown laws in Kafka's works: he notes that the human being can "unsuspectingly transgress" those laws and "thus become subject to retribution. But no matter how hard the retribution may hit the unsuspecting, the retribution in the sense of the law is not coincidence but fate that presents itself here in its ambiguity [Zweideutigkeit]."[20]

Noteworthy right away is that Benjamin is referring in these passages to "its" ambiguity – the ambiguity of fateful necessity in law. In other words, there could conceivably be other kinds of ambiguity. This will be discussed shortly.

What is the fateful ambiguity that is mentioned in both the essay on violence and the essay on Kafka? In the former essay, Benjamin – using terminology close to the previously mentioned passage from the *Trauerspiel* book – comments on the "demonic-ambiguous way [dämonisch-zweideutige Weise]" in which all are treated as "'equal'" before the law, so that, for instance, poor and rich alike are prohibited from sleeping under bridges. He surmises that such "mythic ambiguity of laws [...] may not be 'infringed' [übertreten]."[21] It may not be *broken* or *violated*

---

18 Rodolphe Gasché, "Kafka's Law: In the Field of Forces Between Judaism and Hellenism," in *The Stelliferous Fold. Toward a Virtual Law of Literature's Self-Formation*, 269–297, 279; and Dimitris Vardoulakis, *The Doppelgänger: Literature's Philosophy*, Fordham University Press, New York 2011, 209.

19 Benjamin, *Selected Writings, Volume 1*, 249 (translation modified); Benjamin, *Gesammelte Schriften*, Vol. II:1, 199. Italics added.

20 Walter Benjamin, *Selected Writings, Volume 2: 1931–1934*, eds. Michael W. Jennings, Howard Eiland, and Gary Smith, The Belknap Press of Harvard University Press, Cambridge 1999, 797 (translation modified); Benjamin, *Gesammelte Schriften*, Vol. II:2, 412.

21 Benjamin, *Selected Writings, Volume 1*, 249; Benjamin, *Gesammelte Schriften*, Vol. II:1, 198. Benjamin's example is borrowed from Anatole France's *Le Lys rouge* [*The Red Lily*], in which a character remarks on how the poor must "support and [...] conserve the rich in their power and their idleness. They must work [...] before the majestic equality of the law that prohibits rich and poor alike from sleeping under bridges, begging in the streets, and stealing bread" (Anatole France, *Le Lys rouge*, Éditions Gallimard, Paris 1992, 129).

(übertreten). The mythic ambiguity is that the law must be heeded as though it is necessity itself and equal for all, even though it is not fate and patently involves inequality: the rich are less likely than the poor to need shelter under bridges.

Even for these passages from the essay on Kafka and the essay on violence, however, the ambiguity exists in myth and yet is basically ignored or denied by myth. If the ambiguity were instead explored, it could become a variation of the historico-philosophic paradox mentioned in the *Trauerspiel* book: an ambiguity in which domination or indeed justice is presumed or claimed but *demonstrably* unaccomplished. The paradox and detection of ambiguity are complementary rather than opposed. Recognition of the ambiguity leads the ambiguity into a paradox – a scene of conflict rather than complacency and denial.

Such ambiguity recurs (and is never transcended entirely by paradox), however, for mythic closure does not desist even if a specific mythic closure is overcome. No specific exercise of the philosophic rises above all mythic ambiguity; it too emerges from life that is inundated by such taken-for-granted closures. In his essay on violence, Benjamin – in a paraphrasing of Georges Sorel – remarks that the prerogative of the mighty ensures, for instance, the following: any offer of rights accorded in law by the mighty will simply ensure – "in a demonically ambiguous way" – that these "'equal' rights" are mythic.[22] More broadly, mythic ambiguity will persist as long as there is no entirely open-ended exploration of it. It is difficult to imagine that a human life could sustain such exploration; survival alone depends on living with certain closures in and about life, and, indeed, living them as though they are true, which – philosophically considered – they are not. Beyond the imperative of survival, moreover, all sorts of expediencies require that the ambiguities in our lived truths not be addressed as such.

Pressure for the open-ended exploration is, nonetheless, the conceivably ongoing motion of, and for, philosophic acknowledgement of mythic ambiguity. The expressly philosophic in Benjamin's readings of Kafka accordingly includes presentations of ambiguity that myth – closure – ignores. Despite their starkly contradictory statements about the *Vorwelt* (statements that have been examined in detail elsewhere), Benjamin's analyses of Kafka include remarks for which the *Vorwelt* (literally, "pre-world," often translated as "prehistory") is a realm withstanding myth, a realm always preceding and disturbing mythic containment.[23]

---

22 Benjamin, *Selected Writings, Volume 1*, 249; Benjamin, *Gesammelte Schriften*, Vol. II:1, 198.
23 A rudimentary analysis may be found in Brendan Moran, "The 'Forgotten' as Epic *Vorwelt*," in *Layering: Rethinking Contact, Historicity and Critique Across the Humanities*, eds. Maria Margaroni, Apostolos Lampropoulos, and Christos Hadjichristos, Lexington Books, Lanham forthcoming. This essay was written several years ago, and has been extensively revised and corrected as

The containment is ambiguous; its claims may be exposed by philosophic scrutiny to be belied by history that does not let itself be contained. The *Vorwelt* is, therefore, "Kafka's secret present [geheime Gegenwart]" that – as "historico-philosophical index [der geschichtsphilosophische Index]" – facilitates shame, for instance, about any measures indicating presumption somehow to overcome entirely the *Vorwelt*.[24] This emergence of the philosophic presents an ambiguity – that the claim to containment is belied by uncontainable history. This is an ambiguity that myth perpetrates, or simply embodies, but does not acknowledge.

This initial conflict of philosophic impetus and mythic closure exemplifies the first of the two kinds of ambiguity mentioned earlier. In notes towards a revision of the 1934 essay on Kafka (and touching on this first ambiguity), Benjamin refers to how Kafka's gestures are affected by tendencies towards both liberation and subordination. Benjamin claims: "There is no gesture in Kafka's works that is not affected [betroffen] by this ambiguity [Zweideutigkeit] before [moral-legal] decision."[25] "The gesture thereby acquires something enormously dramatic."[26] In the 1934 essay, Benjamin states: "Each gesture is an event – one might even say a drama – in itself."[27] If there is no gesture unaffected by this drama of ambiguity (this drama of liberation and subordination in the face of moral-legal decision), the historico-philosophic gesture of shame about myth – the gesture that Benjamin considers prevalent in Kafka's work – is not independent of the drama.[28] This gesture is simply integral to the ambiguity becoming philosophically dramatic. It shows the ambiguity in which there is a claim to closure and the closure is not

---

chapter 13 of Brendan Moran, *Philosophy as Renegade. Benjamin's "Kafkan" Politics* (forthcoming).

24 Walter Benjamin, letter of 11 August 1934, in *The Correspondence of Walter Benjamin*, eds. Gershom Scholem and Theodor W. Adorno, trans. Manfred R. Jacobson and Evelyn M. Jacobson, University of Chicago Press, Chicago 1994, 453; Walter Benjamin, *Gesammelte Briefe [Collected Letters]*, Vol. IV, eds. Christoph Gödde and Henri Lonitz, Suhrkamp, Frankfurt/M. 1998, 478. To get a sense of the variegated references by Benjamin to "Vorwelt," see Benjamin, *Selected Writings, Volume 2*, 797, 807, 809; Benjamin, *Gesammelte Schriften*, Vol. II:2, 412, 426–427, 429; Walter Benjamin, *Selected Writings, Volume 3: 1935–1938*, eds. Howard Eiland and Michael W. Jennings, The Belknap Press of Harvard University Press, Cambridge 2002, 326; Walter Benjamin, *Gesammelte Briefe*, Vol. VI, eds. Christoph Gödde and Henri Lonitz, Suhrkamp, Frankfurt/M. 2000, 112; Benjamin, *Gesammelte Schriften*, Vol. II:3, 1165, 1213, 1246.

25 Benjamin, *Gesammelte Schriften* Vol. II:3, 1261, 1263.

26 Benjamin, *Gesammelte Schriften*, Vol. II:3, 1263.

27 Benjamin, *Selected Writings, Volume 2*, 802; Benjamin, *Gesammelte Schriften*, Vol. II:2, 419.

28 Benjamin, *Selected Writings, Volume 2*, 808–815; Benjamin, *Gesammelte Schriften*, Vol. II:2, 428–437; Benjamin, *The Correspondence of Walter Benjamin*, 453; Benjamin, *Gesammelte Briefe*, Vol. IV, 478.

complete. The gesture could conceivably break complacency about any claim or presumption to dominate or contain. It can do this, however, by underscoring ambiguity, not by claiming to transcend or escape it entirely. In an apparent objection to the existentialism of Jean-Paul Sartre and Simone de Beauvoir, Maurice Blanchot remarks on the ambiguity that is accompanied by a "subterfuge" seizing "the shifting, changing truth."[29] In elaborating on Kafka, Blanchot states that "Literature is language turning into ambiguity [ambiguïté]."[30] For Benjamin, it seems the ambiguity of literature – the ambiguity of Kafka's literature – arises so that what myth conceals may be exposed: myth conceals its ambiguity; literature – in its philosophic impetus – exposes the ambiguity in order to exercise the paradox, the conflict between the philosophic and the mythic. Philosophic criticism makes explicit both this exposure of ambiguity and the ensuing paradox.

Unlike Sartre and Beauvoir (as Blanchot depicts them), Benjamin's Kafka usually does not claim to seize truth, though his characters sometimes do. Benjamin's Kafka is concerned above all with the failure of such seizing.[31] In this Kafka, the drama of ambiguity – the drama of liberatory and submissive tendencies – is mostly inherent in the philosophic gesture. Even if the philosophic impetus opposes a specific ambiguity by letting a liberatory element prevail against a subordinate one, there will be no shortage of further such ambiguities that permeate our mythic lives. The Kafkan drama is indeed the *para-doxical* confrontation of philosophic impulse and mythic life, but precisely the philosophic must admit the continued ambiguity of liberation: it must acknowledge the ambiguities – not always conscious – whereby we live our lives according to semblances of truth that are, after all, no more than semblances. Any specific philosophic liberation does not annul all such ambiguities, even if Benjamin's writings – including his writings on Kafka – involve a messianism that might seem oriented to eventual elimination of such ambiguities.[32]

---

29 Maurice Blanchot, "Reading Kafka," in *The Work of Fire*, trans. Charlotte Mandell, Stanford University Press, 1995, 1–11, 5; Maurice Blanchot, "La lecture de Kafka," in *La Part du Feu*, Gallimard, Paris 1949, 9–19, 13.
30 Maurice Blanchot, "Literature and the Right to Death," trans. Lydia Davis, in *The Work of Fire*, 300–344, 341; Maurice Blanchot, "La littérature et le droit à la mort," in *La Part du Feu*, 291–331, 328. Blanchot refers to "an ultimate ambiguity whose strange effect is to attract literature to an unstable point where it can indiscriminately change both its meaning and its sign" (342/329).
31 Benjamin, *Selected Writings, Volume 2*, 804, 808; Benjamin, *Gesammelte Schriften*, Vol. II:2, 422, 427–428; Benjamin, *Gesammelte Schriften*, Vol. II:3, 1249; letter of 12 November 1934 to Werner Kraft, in Benjamin, *The Correspondence of Walter Benjamin*, 463; Benjamin, *Gesammelte Briefe*, Vol. IV, 525–526.
32 Benjamin, *Selected Writings, Volume 2*, 811; Benjamin, *Gesammelte Schriften*, Vol. II:2, 432.

This brings us again to the second ambiguity, the philosophic ambiguity as distinct from the mythic ambiguity that is exposed by the philosophic impetus in art and by philosophic criticism. The second ambiguity, the strictly philosophic ambiguity, is that to which the philosophic opens (at least until the Messiah comes). This philosophic ambiguity is the ambiguity that is *Mehrdeutigkeit*. It is not, however, a celebration of all uncertainty of interpretation. In his essay on violence, Benjamin refers to the condition, particularly prevalent in "democracies," whereby policing is facilitated not simply as an exercise in application of the law but as an exploitation of a power that enables police authorities to administer even where there is no clear guideline. Benjamin suggests that this is especially a problem in democracies, for the leeway given to police to exploit such "formless [gestaltlos]," ungraspable, yet pervasive power is greater in democracies than in states where absolute monarchy unites legislative and executive supremacy in the ruler.[33] The ambiguity in "democratic" police power is mythic ambiguity, for the police exercise power that is (falsely) treated as though it is sanctioned legally. Philosophic scrutiny can show this ambiguity in policing. Philosophy also opens, however, the second ambiguity – the philosophic ambiguity of *Mehrdeutigkeit*. It does so, for instance, against the policing that would assert its interpretation against any possibility for *Mehrdeutigkeit*.

In Benjamin's writings on Kafka (as in his reflections on violence), the ambiguity as *Mehrdeutigkeit* is already suggested by the historico-philosophic or critical approach to an ultimate lack in myth of a certain kind of *Mehrdeutigkeit*. Perhaps particularly the latter ambiguity, which prevents mythic identifications, makes questionable the view that ambiguity is fairly straightforwardly supposed to be overcome or transcended (not simply by the Messiah but already) by Benjamin's philosophic critique.[34] In his writings and notes on Kafka, he refers to an unlocking of the ambiguity that is *Mehrdeutigkeit* – in Benjamin's words, a "folie d'interpretation,"[35] a potential for "reflections [Überlegungen] that reach no

---

33 Benjamin, *Selected Writings, Volume* 1, 242–243; Benjamin, *Gesammelte Schriften*, Vol. II:1,189–190.
34 For this view that Benjamin conceives of philosophy as transcending ambiguity, see Eli Friedlander, *Walter Benjamin: A Philosophical Portrait*, Harvard University Press, Cambridge 2012, 21–22, 117–120. As noted above, Benjamin sometimes encourages this view of philosophy; even so, it seems a confusion to consider all multiplicity of meaning as something that Benjamin always identifies with mythic ambiguity. See Friedlander, but also Alison Ross, "The Distinction between Mythic Violence and Divine Violence: Walter Benjamin's 'Critique of Violence' from the Perspective of 'Goethe's *Elective Affinities*,'" in *New German Critique* 41.1 (2014): 93–120, 112, 113, 118, 120.
35 Benjamin, *Gesammelte Schriften*, Vol. II:3, 1229 Ms. 297,

end."[36] In a preparatory note towards his Kafka essay, Benjamin writes in point form: "The gestural/ambiguity [Vieldeutigkeit]/renunciation of rationalizability."[37] For instance, when he considers shame to be the prevailing historico-philosophic gesture of Kafka's writings, it is shame about myth and its would-be resolutions – rationalizations – of life. The latter sort of resolution is conveyed in the *Elective Affinities* essay, which includes not just reference to ambiguity (Doppelsinn, Zweideutigkeit) that mythically seals against philosophic investigation,[38] but also an identification of the mythic spell as panarchic – as a claim to all-encompassing authority.[39] Philosophic ambiguity renders such panarchism questionable, and Benjamin's Kafka presents such potential for questioning, as does in turn Benjamin's criticism.

In this context, Kafka's "ambiguity" (Zweideutigkeit) of gesture becomes important, as Theodor Adorno recognizes in his first response to Benjamin's Kafka essay of 1934. For Adorno, the "ambiguity" (Zweideutigkeit) is between, on one hand, "sinking into muteness" and, on the other, sound – "music." Kafka's expression does not rise entirely above the sinking into muteness that indicates "the destruction of language" in modernity.[40] Adorno's terminology is not entirely Benjaminian, and it is concerned simply with the tension of an antithetically twofold pressure (the conflict of muteness and sound), but it might also indicate Adorno's sense that ambiguity of a sort is central to Benjamin's reading of Kafka and to Kafka's writings themselves. This ambiguity – this conflict of muteness and the will to expression – is not simply mythic. The mythic would end or somehow cloak the conflict; to emphasize the ambiguous conflict would be philosophic.

At least for those aspects of Benjamin's work that have been stressed here, to claim to accomplish something entirely beyond ambiguity would be a forced closure; it would be mythic. As indicated in the previous remarks on mythic ambiguity, the latter serves to cloak or to assert dominance. There is the first kind of ambiguity mentioned previously: a myth seeks to enclose but cannot; it may even, in specific cases, find itself well opposed by philosophic momentum. Inte-

---

36 Benjamin, *Selected Writings, Volume 2*, 802 (translation modified); Benjamin, *Gesammelte Schriften*, Vol. II:2, 420.
37 Benjamin, *Gesammelte Schriften*, Vol. II:3, 1207.
38 Benjamin, *Selected Writings, Volume 1*, 314, 335; Benjamin, *Gesammelte Schriften*, Vol. I:1, 147, 174–175.
39 Benjamin, *Selected Writings, Volume 1*, 317; Benjamin, *Gesammelte Schriften*, Vol. II:1, 151.
40 Theodor W. Adorno, letter of 17 December 1934, in Theodor W. Adorno and Walter Benjamin, *The Complete Correspondence 1928–1940*, trans. Nicholas Walker, Harvard University Press, Cambridge 1999, 70; Theodor W. Adorno and Walter Benjamin, *Briefwechsel 1928–1940* [*Correspondence 1928–1940*], ed. Henri Lonitz, Suhrkamp, Frankfurt/M. 1994, 95.

gral to this historico-philosophic – anti-mythic – momentum must be, however, that it not presume to transcend all ambiguity. To do so would be to succumb to the kind of resolution that Benjamin identifies as mythic. It would be to succumb to the kind of resolution that Benjamin criticizes in certain "'theological'" outlooks, such as Max Brod's, regarding Kafka's writings: outlooks in which Kafka is portrayed as terribly certain, to the point that Benjamin refers to the attempt to cast Kafka's works into a "Weltanschauung."[41] The philosophic is no *Weltanschauung*. Part of the ongoing crisis of philosophy is the ongoing ambiguity of life – including the *Mehrdeutigkeit* of life – in its confrontation with the *court* that would deny, disregard, or suppress such ambiguity.

The ambiguity is twofold, and philosophy is an exercise in showing this. First, there is the ambiguity of myth: myth asserts control, or all-encompassing truth, but this assertion is more ambiguous than is admitted. Philosophy exposes this ambiguity of myth; it makes clear that myth's self-acclamations are practices of concealment. Second, there is the ambiguity that is philosophic: the "Mehrdeutigkeit" that myth discounts or denies. The philosophic impetus demonstrates that myth is not all-encompassing (this is the first presented ambiguity); the impetus thereby opens the situation to *Mehrdeutigkeit* (the second ambiguity). Although Benjamin does not always concede this, the second ambiguity persists even where – in the name of philosophy or something else – it is thought that a paradox, a straightforward opposition to the mythic, has been attained. In his writings on Kafka, Benjamin seems close to admitting the intrusion of ambiguity upon paradox.

3 Ambiguity Intrudes upon Absolute Paradox

There are many different kinds of paradox, and it may not be claimed that ambiguity in paradox always works in the manner stated here. In Benjamin's work, however, at least some paradoxes are addressed along these lines. In the *Trauerspiel* book, he discusses the theological "paradox" of the "unity of the sensory

---

41 Walter Benjamin, review of Brod's *Franz Kafka*, in Benjamin, *Selected Writings, Volume 3*, 317–319; Walter Benjamin, *Kritiken und Rezensionen* [*Criticism and Reviews*], ed. Heinrich Kaulen, Volume 13 of *Werke und Nachlaß, Kritische Gesamtausgabe* [*Works and Posthumous Writings, Critical Edition*], eds. Christoph Gödde and Henri Lonitz with the Walter Benjamin Archive, Suhrkamp, Berlin 2011, 569–573. See too: letter of 12 June 1938 to Scholem, in Benjamin, *The Correspondence of Walter Benjamin*, 560–566; Benjamin, *Gesammelte Briefe*, Vol. VI, 106–114.

and the supersensory object,"[42] but even this unity entails ambiguity. Whereas Hermann Cohen is scandalized by ambiguity (*Zweideutigkeit* and *Mehrdeutigkeit* alike) in baroque allegory, Benjamin opposes Cohen's expectation of "'purity and unity of meaning.'"[43] In Benjamin's *Trauerspiel* book and other writings, there are other references to paradox, which likely have many different implications. These references cannot all be addressed here. No paradox figures, however, as explicitly in Benjamin's material on Kafka as does Kierkegaard's absolute paradox. Thus, at least aspects of the topic of ambiguity in paradox may perhaps be illustrated by discussing some of Benjamin's reservations about Kierkegaard's absolute paradox.

The confluence of the absolute (God) and the particular is an absolute paradox for Kierkegaard. If one "is to receive any true knowledge about the Unknown (the God)," Kierkegaard claims, one "must be made to know that it is unlike" oneself, "absolutely unlike" oneself. True knowledge requires knowing the Unknown as absolutely different from anything one knows.[44] The paradox is that "the individual as particular can," nonetheless, "stand in an absolute relation to the absolute."[45]

In response, one version of Benjamin's Kafka essay includes the claim that each of Kafka's novels and stories is "a victory over Kierkegaard's paradox."[46] In a draft, Benjamin refers simply to "[t]he victory over paradox."[47] In part this claim is based on Benjamin's Adorno-inspired rejection of the "mythological" substrates in Kierkegaard's paradox.[48] These substrates enable Kierkegaard to envision, and to urge, an unmediated relation with the absolute. Benjamin finds in Kafka's writings a tacit rebuttal of Kierkegaard's quest. Part of this rebuttal involves discussion of Abraham in much more profane terms than is proposed in

---

42 Benjamin, *The Origin of the German Tragic Drama*, 160 (translation modified); Benjamin, *Gesammelte Schriften*, Vol. I:1, 336.

43 Benjamin, *The Origin of the German Tragic Drama*, 176–177; Benjamin, *Gesammelte Schriften*, Vol. I:1, 353. Cf. Hermann Cohen, Ästhetik *des reinen Gefühls* [*Aesthetics of Pure Feeling*], Vol. 2, eds. Hermann-Cohen-Archiv under Helmut Holzhey, Georg Olms Verlag, Hildesheim 1982, 305.

44 Søren Kierkegaard, *Philosophical Fragments* [*Philosophiske Smuler eller En Smule Philosophi*], trans. David Swenson and Howard V. Hong, Princeton University Press, Princeton 1974, 57.

45 Kierkegaard, *Fear and Trembling* [*Frygt og Bæven*], trans. Alastair Hannay, Penguin Books, London 1985, 137.

46 Benjamin, *Gesammelte Schriften*, Vol. II:3, 1268.

47 Benjamin, *Gesammelte Schriften*, Vol. II:3, 1210.

48 Benjamin, *Gesammelte Schriften*, Vol. II:3, 1268.

the bible or by Kierkegaard.[49] An attempt has been made elsewhere to examine this.[50] The following discussion will therefore simply outline ways in which Benjamin's "Kafkan" critique of Kierkegaard's paradox takes impetus from Adorno but transforms this impetus into quite distinct conceptions of ambiguity and paradox, and thereby into quite distinct conceptions of literature and philosophy.

In Adorno's book on Kierkegaard (published in 1931), which influenced Benjamin's views on Kierkegaard, it is argued that Kierkegaard's paradox is "ambiguous" (zweideutig). Ambiguous nature is not redeemed or transcended but is always intruding.[51] Adorno adds that "truth becomes ambiguous [zweideutig] as the quintessence [Inbegriff] of the dialectical movement without becoming its measure [Maß]."[52] As is known, Adorno greatly wished that Benjamin would write in a more thoroughly dialectical way.[53] For some of Benjamin's writing, the absolute and the non-absolute exist, in relation to each other, in thorough ambiguity; this may render ambiguity even more a measure in philosophy than Adorno would concede.[54] For Benjamin, this possibility is conveyed in Kafka's literature and articulated in Benjamin's own philosophic criticism.

---

49 Benjamin, *Gesammelte Schriften*, Vol. II:3, 1268–1269; Benjamin, *Selected Writings, Volume 2*, 807–808; Benjamin, *Gesammelte Schriften*, Vol. II:2, 427. See Franz Kafka, *Briefe. 1902–1924* [*Letters. 1902–1924*], ed. Max Brod, Fischer, Frankfurt/M. 1983, 333–334.

50 For remarks on Abraham in relation to Kafka, Kierkegaard, and Benjamin, see Brendan Moran, "Anxiety and Attention," in *Philosophy and Kafka*, eds. Brendan Moran and Carlo Salzani, Lexington Books, Lanham 2013, 201–227, especially 208–213.

51 Theodor W. Adorno, *Kierkegaard: Construction of the Aesthetic*, trans. Robert Hullot-Kentor, University of Minnesota Press, Minneapolis 1989, 72–73; Theodor W. Adorno, *Kierkegaard: Konstruktion des Ästhetischen*, Suhrkamp, Frankfurt/M. 1974, 130–133.

52 Adorno, *Kierkegaaard*, 73/132.

53 Adorno, letter of 17 December 1934, in *The Complete Correspondence*, 69; Adorno, *Briefwechsel*, 93. This is a variation of a criticism of Benjamin's writings that Adorno continued to make for decades after Benjamin's death. See: Theodor W. Adorno, "Introduction to Benjamin's *Schriften*," trans. Robert Hullot-Kentor, in *On Walter Benjamin. Critical Essays and Recollections*, ed. Gary Smith, The MIT Press, Cambridge 1988, 7; Theodor W. Adorno, *Über Walter Benjamin*, ed. Rolf Tiedemann, Suhrkamp, Frankfurt/M. 1990, 39. Also see Theodor W. Adorno, *Negative Dialectics*, trans. E.B. Ashton, Continuum, New York 1973, 53; Theodor W. Adorno, *Negative Dialektik*, Suhrkamp, Frankfurt/M. 1966, 62.

54 Even Adorno remarks on the paradox of Benjamin's impossible quest to have enlightenment and mysticism entirely unite. This impossibility leads to an immersion in multiplicity: "It was nothing other than the explication and elucidation of this paradox, with the only means which philosophy has at its disposal, concepts, that drove Benjamin to immerse himself without reserve in multiplicity [ins Mannigfalte]" (Theodor W. Adorno, "A Portrait of Walter Benjamin" [1950], in *Prisms: Cultural Criticism and Society*, trans. Samuel and Shierry Weber, The MIT Press,

In his Kafka essay of 1934, Benjamin takes issue with various Kierkegaard-ian readings of Kafka. Willy Haas claims that "the upper power, the realm of grace" is depicted by Kafka in *The Castle* [*Das Schloss*], and that "the power below, the realm of the court and of damnation" is addressed in *The Trial*. In *Amerika* (now known as *The Missing Person*), Kafka tries to convey "[t]he earth between the two, [...] earthly fate and its arduous demands." Haas contends that Kafka's writings are fundamentally religious, and that works such as *The Castle* are concerned with God's "awful" playing with the human being. For Haas, the latter motif is a Kierkegaardian-Pascalian one in which the human is somehow generically "always wrong" before an ultimately benign "God."[55] Benjamin thinks Max Brod is the spur for such a reading. Also following this Brodian train of thought, he contends, is Bernard Rang, who refers to the Castle as "the seat of grace" making "the vain efforts and attempts mean, theologically speaking, that God's grace cannot be attained or forced by the human willfully and delib-erately. Unrest and impatience only impede and confound the exalted stillness of the divine."[56] Expressly against Haas's theological reading, however, Benjamin stresses that *The Castle* provides no indication of a forgiving, omnipotent author-ity; rather, *The Castle* suggests the lack of such authority. "'For is an individual official capable of granting pardon?' we read in *The Castle*. 'At most this might be a matter for the administration as a whole, but even it can probably not grant forgiveness, but only judge.'"[57] These judgements are ambiguous in the mythic – the first – sense outlined above: their claims to all-encompassing authority are patently questionable. In the context of Kierkegaard's paradox, it might be said that the particulars do not imply a stillness of the divine to which the particulars can open. Permeating the paradox – permeating the opposition to the prevailing *doxa* – is, moreover, the second ambiguity, the *Mehrdeutigkeit*, that cannot be expunged from experience.

In a preparatory note, Benjamin writes that Kafka's "monstrosities" have their "origin" in "ambiguous [(z)weideutige] connections," which emerge in "the forgotten" (das Vergessene).[58] This "forgotten" is not simply something we forgot

---

Cambridge 1997, 227–241 241; Theodor W. Adorno, "Charakteristik Walter Benjamins," in *Prismen. Kulturkritik und Gesellschaft*, Suhrkamp, Frankfurt/M. 1987, 248–249).

55 Willy Haas, *Gestalten der Zeit* [*Figures of the Age*], Kiepenheuer, Berlin 1930, 175–177.

56 Bernard Rang, "Franz Kafka. Versuch eines Hinweises" ("Franz Kafka. Attempt at a Sugges-tion"), in *Die Schildgenossen* 12 (1932): 115–116, 107–119.

57 Benjamin, *Selected Writings, Volume 2*, 806–807; Benjamin, *Gesammelte Schriften*, Vol. II:1, 425–426. See Franz Kafka, *The Castle*, trans. Mark Harman, Schocken Books, New York 1998, 216; Franz Kafka, *Das Schloß*, ed. Malcolm Pasley, Fischer, Frankfurt/M. 2002, 339–340.

58 Benjamin, *Gesammelte Schriften*, Vol. II:3, 1240.

and could conceivably remember; rather, it is above all something that can be remembered only as forgotten, as irretrievable for consciousness. This element in Benjamin's reading of Kafka has provoked many conflicting accounts, and (as noted) attempts have been made to elaborate why (notwithstanding Benjamin's own contradictory statements about it) there is at least occasional basis in Benjamin's writings on Kafka for reading "the forgotten" as an epic *Vorwelt* that pierces, prevails over, and remains unsubmissive to the world-encompassing claims of myth.[59] This *Vorwelt* is with us but eludes us; it offers no panarchy. It renders ambiguous everything we might perceive or conceive about anything. Kafka's monstrosities emerging from ambiguity are not anathema to the philosophic in literature; instead, they indicate what is essential for it. They demonstrate that myth is not all-encompassing (the first ambiguity), and they thereby open to *Mehrdeutigkeit* (the second ambiguity).

There is no opening by freedom to a divine Nothing (Kierkegaard's God). This element in Kierkegaard's absolute paradox is especially refused by Benjamin. In a note to the 1934 essay, he even claims that the word "God" does not appear in Kafka's writings[60] – an exaggeration, of course.[61] Benjamin does not consider anxiety in Kafka's texts to be the Kierkegaardian catalyst to fearless freedom for the divine. He acknowledges that Kafkan anxiety is not, like fear, simply "a reaction." He also refers, however, to the *Doppelgesichtigkeit*, the ambivalence or two-sidedness, of "the Kafkan anxiety." This might suggest that the Kafkan anxiety is not quite able to be transformed into Kierkegaardian anxiety, which potentially opens to resolute freedom from aesthetic-sensuous or moral constraints.[62] The two-sidedness of Kafkan anxiety seems to be that it may have moti-

---

59 See note 23 above.

60 Benjamin, *Gesammelte Schriften*, Vol. II:3, 1214.

61 In "The Metamorphosis" ("Die Verwandlung"), for instance, Gregor's father greets the news that Gregor is dead with the remark: "Now [...] we can thank God" (Franz Kafka, *The Metamorphosis*, trans. and ed. Stanley Corngold, Norton Critical Edition, Norton, New York 1996, 40; Franz Kafka, "Die Verwandlung," in *Drucke zu Lebzeiten* [*Works Published During His Lifetime*], eds. Wolf Kittler, Hans-Gerd Koch, and Gerhard Neumann, Fischer, Frankfurt/M. 2002, 113–200, 195). In the writings by Kafka that Benjamin had read, there are various such references to God.

62 Benjamin, *Gesammelte Schriften*, Vol. II:3, 1196. For this view of the two-sidedness of anxiety, Benjamin claims to be following Willy Haas's interpretation of the Kafkan anxiety. Benjamin wrote for *Die Literarische Welt*, which Haas edited, so perhaps he is referring to a conversation with Haas, whom he saw regularly in the late 1920s and early 1930s (Howard Eiland and Michael W. Jennings, *Walter Benjamin. A Critical Life*, Harvard University Press, Cambridge 2014, 323, 368). There is, however, no such characterization of Kafka's *Angst* in Haas's *Gestalten der Zeit*, which is the work by Haas mentioned in Benjamin's writings and notes on Kafka. See Haas, *Gestalten der Zeit*, 172–199, where Haas – as noted – interprets Kafka through Kierkegaard. The only

vation to such freedom yet simultaneously may be somewhat embroiled in fears associated with demands of the senses and of the moral order.[63] In Benjamin's Kafka, there tends indeed to be anxiety on behalf of the nothing that eludes but also constitutes all particulars; however, this anxiety is so intermingled with very particular fears that it remains insurmountably ambiguous. For instance, Kafka expresses the wish to unite mundane activity – such as hammering – with the nothing that is the possibility for something to be useful. This wish is portrayed by Kafka, and in turn by Benjamin, as "'only a defense, an embourgeoisement of the nothing, an air of cheerfulness [Munterkeit], that he wants to give the nothing.'"[64] For Kierkegaard, too, the "relation of anxiety to its object, to something that is nothing [...] is altogether ambiguous."[65] Anxiety does not, as unambiguous freedom might, entirely surmount pressures of physicality, customs, laws, and morals.[66] Yet this anxiety can, for Kierkegaard, awaken us to unambiguous freedom, to "freedom's possibility."[67] In contrast, Benjamin's Kafkan anxiety is so ambiguous that it does not open to freedom entirely transcending physicality or legal-moral influences.[68] The interpenetration of absolute and particular – the

---

other work by Haas mentioned in Benjamin's Kafka materials is a contribution to a *Festschrift* for Max Brod's fiftieth birthday; the contribution is a discussion of the friendship between Brod and Kafka, and does not address *Angst* (Willy Haas, "Auslegung eines Aktes der Freundschaft" ("Interpretation of an Act of Friendship"), in *Dichter, Denker, Helfer: Max Brod zum 50. Geburtstag [Poet, Thinker, Helper: On the Occasion of Max Brod's Fiftieth Birthday]*, ed. Felix Weltsch, Verlag von Julius Kittls Nachfolger, Keller & Co., Mähr.-Ostrau 1934, 67–73). In a short "Bibliography on Kafka," Benjamin informally lists this essay by Haas (Benjamin, *Gesammelte Schriften*, Vol. II:3, 1247).

63 For elaboration, see Brendan Moran, "Anxiety and Attention," 201–227.

64 Benjamin, *Selected Writings, Volume 2*, 813–814; Benjamin, *Gesammelte Schriften*, Vol. II:2, 434–436; Benjamin, *Gesammelte Schriften*, Vol. II:3, 1243. Quoting Franz Kafka, *Tagebücher [Diaries]*, eds. Hans-Gerd Koch, Michael Müller, and Malcolm Pasley, Fischer, Frankfurt/M. 1992, 855. Concerning the role of "the nothing" in Benjamin's Kafka writings, see the section on "Use of nothing" in Brendan Moran, "Foolish Wisdom in Benjamin's Kafka," in *Lachen – Ost und West / Laughter – Eastern and Western Philosophies*, eds. Hans-Georg Möller and Günter Wohlfart, Verlag Karl Alber, Freiburg and Munich 2010, 175–192, 183–187.

65 Søren Kierkegaard, *The Concept of Anxiety [Begrebet Angest]*, trans. and ed. Reider Thomte with Albert B. Anderson, Princeton University Press, Princeton 1981, 42–43.

66 Kierkegaard, *The Concept of Anxiety*, 109; Søren Kierkegaard, *The Sickness unto Death [Sygdommen til Døden]*, trans. Alistair Hannay, Penguin Books, London 1989, 60.

67 Kierkegaard, *The Concept of Anxiety*, 42–43.

68 For elaboration, see Moran, "Anxiety and Attention."

Nothing and the something – is such that Kafka enters into ambiguity that undermines the absolute paradox.[69]

This interpenetration is a philosophic movement of the two ambiguities: it shows mythic claims to transcendence to be ambiguous (in not accomplishing what they claim), and thereby unlocks ambiguity as *Mehrdeutigkeit*. In many respects, Benjamin's work is an effort to revitalize this philosophic motion, this complementarity of literature and philosophy. In this complementarity, literature provides openly singular cases that break through mythic denial of ambiguity. Literature shows myth unable to conceal the ambiguity whereby its claims to closure and resolution are rebuffed. With this rebuffing of closure and resolution comes an opening to another ambiguity: the *Mehrdeutigkeit* that figures so prominently in Kafka. In the reception of the literary work, philosophy revitalizes this two-fold engagement with ambiguity and is itself reminded of the inextinguishable singularity that literature brings to the fore.

4 Concluding Words

Against aspects of Benjamin's outlook, and in disagreement with some of his readers, this essay has drawn upon features of his work to note a distinct complementarity of ambiguity and the philosophic. As opposition to prevailing opinion (doxa), Benjaminian philosophic paradox involves at least two kinds of ambiguity: it points to life as embroiled in myths that have only ambiguous claims to closure or transcendence; and it opens to the ensuing ambiguity as *Mehrdeutigkeit* – the lack of a credibly all-encompassing interpretation. This two-fold ambiguity seems to be a basis for Benjamin's disagreement with Kierkegaard's absolute paradox. And this disagreement may extend further. Perhaps other kinds of paradox, including some of Benjamin's own, are permeated by the two kinds of ambiguity discussed in this essay. At least as the confrontation of the universal – that is, philosophic – impetus with myth itself, philosophy involves a paradox – a

---

69 Several decades ago, Heinz Politzer remarked that Kafka's works may be full of paradoxes of many sorts, but precisely these often depend on an "abundance" of ambiguities (Heinz Politzer, *Franz Kafka: Parable and Paradox*, Cornell University Press, Cornell 1966, 22). In an essay from the 1970s in *American Imago*, Stanley Hopper provides an assessment that might be even closer to Benjamin's: "Kierkegaard wants to re*solve* [...] ambiguity by way of [...] the Great *Contradiction*, or 'Paradox,'" "whereas Kafka leads us into the place where we see that everything that lies before us is ambiguous" (Stanley Romaine Hopper, "Kafka and Kierkegaard: The Function of Ambiguity," in *American Imago* 35:1/2 (1978): 92–105, 102).

para-dox – that, *on one hand*, reveals the ambiguity unacknowledged by myth: the ambiguity of a claim to all-encompassing truth, the ambiguity that shows this claim not to be all-encompassing. *On the other hand*, the paradox – as confrontation that would be an assertion of universality against mythic constraint – finds itself confronted with the second ambiguity: the *Mehrdeutigkeit* that cannot be entirely expunged from the attempt at paradox. In a way, the *Mehrdeutigkeit* recalls the oblique singularity that no claim to universality can entirely eradicate. Philosophy must acknowledge, and thereby recognize, its own literary character: the singularity that rebuffs mythic containment by recognizing the ambiguity of such containment, and that thereby conveys life as *mehrdeutig*.

Works Cited

Adorno, Theodor W., "Charakteristik Walter Benjamins," *Prismen. Kulturkritik und Gesellschaft* (Frankfurt/M.: Suhrkamp, 1987), 234–249.

Adorno, Theodor W., "Introduction to Benjamin's *Schriften*," trans. Robert Hullot-Kentor, in *On Walter Benjamin. Critical Essays and Recollections*. Ed. Gary Smith (Cambridge: The MIT Press, 1988), 2–17.

Adorno, Theodor W., *Kierkegaard: Construction of the Aesthetic*. Trans. Robert Hullot-Kentor (Minneapolis: University of Minnesota Press, 1989).

Adorno, Theodor W., *Kierkegaard: Konstruktion des Ästhetischen* (Frankfurt/M.; Suhrkamp, 1974).

Adorno, Theodor W., *Negative Dialectics*. Trans. E.B. Ashton (New York: Continuum, 1973).

Adorno, Theodor W., *Negative Dialektik* (Frankfurt/M.: Suhrkamp, 1966).

Adorno, Theodor W., "A Portrait of Walter Benjamin," in *Prisms: Cultural Criticism and Society*. Trans. Samuel and Shierry Weber (Cambridge: The MIT Press, 1997), 227–241.

Adorno, Theodor W., *Über Walter Benjamin*. Ed. Rolf Tiedemann. Revised and expanded edition (Frankfurt/M.: Suhrkamp, 1990).

Adorno, Theodor W., *Briefwechsel 1928–1940*. Ed. Henri Lonitz (Frankfurt/M.: Suhrkamp, 1994).

Adorno, Theodor W. and Walter Benjamin, *The Complete Correspondence 1928–1940*. Ed. Henri Lonitz. Trans. Nicholas Walker (Cambridge: Harvard University Press, 1999).

Benjamin, Walter, *The Correspondence of Walter Benjamin*. Eds. Gershom Scholem and Theodor W. Adorno. Trans. Manfred R. Jacobson and Evelyn M. Jacobson (Chicago: University of Chicago Press, 1994).

Benjamin, Walter, *Gesammelte Briefe*, Volumes I–VI. Eds. Christoph Gödde and Henri Lonitz (Frankfurt/M.: Suhrkamp, 1995–2000).

Benjamin, Walter, *Gesammelte Schriften*, Volumes I–VII. Eds. Rolf Tiedemann and Hermann Schweppenhäuser et al. (Frankfurt/M.: Suhrkamp, 1974–1999).

Benjamin, Walter, *Kritiken und Rezensionen*, ed. Heinrich Kaulen, Volume 13 of *Werke und Nachlaß, Kritische Gesamtausgabe*. Eds. Christoph Gödde and Henri Lonitz with the Walter Benjamin Archive (Berlin: Suhrkamp, 2011).

Benjamin, Walter, *The Origin of the German Tragic Drama*. Trans. John Osborne (London: Verso, 1977).

Benjamin, Walter, *Selected Writings, Volumes 1–4*. Eds. Michael W. Jennings et al. (Cambridge: The Belknap Press of Harvard University Press, 1996, 1999, 2002, 2003).

Blanchot, Maurice, "La lecture de Kafka," in *La Part du Feu* (Paris: Gallimard, 1949), 9–19.

Blanchot, Maurice, "Literature and the Right to Death," trans. Lydia Davis, in *The Work of Fire*. Trans. Charlotte Mandell (Stanford: Stanford University Press, 1995), 300–344.

Blanchot, Maurice, "La littérature et le droit à la mort," in *La Part du Feu* (Paris: Gallimard, 1949), 291–331.

Blanchot, Maurice, "Reading Kafka," in *The Work of Fire*. Trans. Charlotte Mandell (Stanford: Stanford University Press, 1995), 1–11.

Cohen, Hermann, *Ästhetik des reinen Gefühls*, Vol. 2, Werke, Vol. 9. Eds. Hermann-Cohen-Archiv under Helmut Holzhey (Hildesheim: Georg Olms Verlag, 1982).

de Beauvoir, Simone, *The Ethics of Ambiguity*. Trans. Bernard Frechtman (New York: The Citadel Press, 1964).

de Beauvoir, Simone, *Pour une morale de l'ambiguïté* (Paris: Gallimard, 1947).

Deleuze, Gilles, *Difference and Repetition*. Trans. Paul Patton (New York: Columbia University Press, 1994).

Deleuze, Gilles, *Différence et repetition* (Paris: Presses Universitaires de France, 1968).

Eiland, Howard and Michael W. Jennings, *Walter Benjamin. A Critical Life* (Cambridge: Harvard University Press, 2014).

France, Anatole, *Le Lys rouge* (Paris: Éditions Gallimard, 1992).

Friedlander, Eli, *Walter Benjamin: A Philosophical Portrait* (Cambridge: Harvard University Press, 2012).

Gasché, Rodolphe, "Kafka's Law: In the Field of Forces Between Judaism and Hellenism," in *The Stelliferous Fold. Toward a Virtual Law of Literature's Self-Formation* (Stanford: Stanford University Press, 2011), 269–297.

Grimm, Jacob and Wilhelm, reworked by Gustav Rosenhagen and others, *Deutsches Wörterbuch*, Vol. 16 (Leipzig: Verlag von S. Hirzel, 1954).

Haas, Willy, "Auslegung eines Aktes der Freundschaft," in *Dichter, Denker, Helfer: Max Brod zum 50. Geburtstag*. Ed. Felix Weltsch (Mähr.-Ostrau: Verlag von Julius Kittls Nachfolger, Keller & Co., 1934), 67–73.

Haas, Willy, *Gestalten der Zeit* (Berlin: Kiepenheuer, 1930).

Das Herkunftswörterbuch. Etymologie der deutschen Sprache (Mannheim: Dudenverlag, 2001).

Hopper, Stanley Romaine, "Kafka and Kierkegaard: The Function of Ambiguity," in *American Imago* 35:1/2 (1978): 92–105.

Kafka, Franz, *The Blue Octavo Notebooks*. Ed. Max Brod. Trans. Ernst Kaiser and Eithne Wilkins (Cambridge: Exact Change, 2004).

Kafka, Franz, *Briefe. 1902–1924*. Ed. Max Brod (Frankfurt/M.: Fischer, 1983).

Kafka, Franz, *The Castle*. Trans. Mark Harman (New York: Schocken Books, 1998).

Kafka, Franz, *The Metamorphosis*. Trans. and ed. Stanley Corngold. Norton Critical Edition (New York and London: Norton, 1996).

Kafka, Franz, *Nachgelassene Schriften und Fragmente II*. Ed. Jost Schillemeit (Frankfurt/M.: Fischer, 1992).

Kafka, Franz, *Das Schloß*. Ed. Malcolm Pasley (Frankfurt/M.: Fischer, 2002).

Kafka, Franz, *Tagebücher*. Eds. Hans-Gerd Koch, Michael Müller, and Malcolm Pasley (Frankfurt/M.: Fischer, 1992).

Kafka, Franz, "Die Verwandlung," in *Drucke zu Lebzeiten*. Eds. Wolf Kittler, Hans-Gerd Koch, and Gerhard Neumann (Frankfurt/M.: Fischer, 1992), 113–200.

Kierkegaard, Søren, *The Concept of Anxiety*. Trans. and ed. Reider Thomte with Albert B. Anderson (Princeton: Princeton University Press, 1981).

Kierkegaard, Søren, *Fear and Trembling*. Trans. Alastair Hannay (London: Penguin Books, 1985).

Kierkegaard, Søren, *Philosophical Fragments*. Trans. David Swenson and Howard V. Hong (Princeton: Princeton University Press, 1974).

Kierkegaard, Søren, *The Sickness unto Death*. Trans. Alistair Hannay (London: Penguin Books, 1989).

Kraus, Karl, *Aphorismen*, *Schriften*, Vol. 8. Ed. Christian Wagenknecht (Frankfurt/M.: Suhrkamp, 1986).

McFarland, James F., *Constellation. Friedrich Nietzsche and Walter Benjamin in the Now-Time of History* (New York: Fordham University Press, 2013).

Merleau-Ponty, Maurice, *Phénoménologie de la perception* (Paris: Gallimard, 1945).

Merleau-Ponty, Maurice, *Phenomenology of Perception*. Trans. Donald A. Landes (London: Routledge, 2013).

Moran, Brendan, "Anxiety and Attention: Benjamin and Others," in *Philosophy and Kafka*. Eds. Brendan Moran and Carlo Salzani (Lanham: Lexington Books, 2013), 201–227.

Moran, Brendan, "Foolish Wisdom in Benjamin's Kafka," in *Lachen – Ost und West / Laughter – Eastern and Western Philosophies*. Eds. Hans-Georg Möller and Günter Wohlfart (Freiburg and Munich: Verlag Karl Alber, 2010), 175–192.

Moran, Brendan, "The 'Forgotten' as Epic *Vorwelt*," in *Layering: Rethinking Contact, Historicity and Critique Across the Humanities*. Eds. Maria Margaroni, Apostolos Lampropoulos, and Christos Hadjichristos (Lanham: Lexington Books, forthcoming).

Moran, Brendan, "An Inhumanly Wise Shame," in *Philosophy as a Literary Art*. Ed. Costica Bradatan (London: Routledge, 2014), 63–75.

North, Paul, *The Problem of Distraction* (Stanford: Stanford University Press, 2012).

Politzer, Heinz, *Franz Kafka: Parable and Paradox* (Ithaca: Cornell University Press, 1966).

Procyshyn, Alexei, "Walter Benjamin's Philosophy of Language," in *Philosophy Compass* 9.6 (2014): 368–381.

Quine, W.V., *The Ways of Paradox and Other Essays* (Cambridge: Harvard University Press, 1976 [revised edition]).

Rang, Bernard, "Franz Kafka. Versuch eines Hinweises," in *Die Schildgenossen* 12 (1932): 107–119.

Ross, Alison, "The Distinction between Mythic Violence and Divine Violence: Walter Benjamin's 'Critique of Violence' from the Perspective of 'Goethe's *Elective Affinities*,'" in *New German Critique* 41.1 (2014), 93–120.

Schur, David, *The Way of Oblivion. Heraclitus and Kafka* (Cambridge: Harvard University Press, 1998).

Vardoulakis, Dimitris, *The Doppelgänger: Literature's Philosophy* (New York: Fordham University Press, 2011).

Søren Rosendal

The Logic of the "Swamp World": Hegel with Kafka on the Contradiction of Freedom

1 Introduction: A Shared Contradiction

What could Hegel and Kafka possibly have in common except for the fact that they have nothing in common? Is Kafka not the literary custodian of the last dying breaths of the singular subject faced with an impenetrable and inhuman system; and is not Hegel exactly the philosophical architect who composes this impenetrable and inhuman system whose rigid universality always threatens to "swallow up" the singular subject? I want to argue, in the course of this article, that nothing could be further from the truth.

In a highly enthusiastic letter to Walter Benjamin dated 11 December 1934 Theodor Adorno comments at length on Benjamin's reading of Kafka. Within a surprising parenthesis Adorno notes: "though you are probably not aware of it, there are some astonishingly close connections between Hegel and this work [Benjamin's manuscript on Franz Kafka]."[1] This is – to my knowledge – one of the only places where Hegel and Kafka have been uttered positively in the same passage. But even here the connection is, as Adorno notes, not consciously made.

In the present text I will try to bring the connection between Kafka and Hegel out of the dark. Of course, many connections cannot be drawn here or explored in full,[2] so I will limit myself to some notes on the point where they intersect.

---

1 Theodor W. Adorno and Walter Benjamin, *The Complete Correspondence 1928–1940*, ed. Henri Lonitz, trans. Nicholas Walker, Polity Press, Cambridge 1999, 68.
2 I hope to have the occasion to remedy this in a planned future monograph tentatively and allusively called *Hegel with Kafka*.

I would like to thank Frank Ruda for his many sharp comments and helpful suggestions for this article. Unfortunately, I could do justice to only some of his comments; otherwise the article would have been at least twice as long. Also many thanks to the Antwerp editors – Professor Vivian Liska and Jeremy Schreiber – for their careful reading of the draft of the article. Last but not least thanks to the organizers and participants of the wonderful 2012 conference *Kafka and the Paradox of the Universal* at the University of Antwerp for all the comments on a much different and earlier manuscript of this article that I presented there. The comments by Stanley Corngold and Vivian Liska on Kafka especially echoed in my mind while writing this article.

The point of what could be called their "underground" affinity is, maybe surprisingly, the problem of *freedom*. This affinity takes the form of a contradiction around which this text will revolve. Of course, on their respective textual surfaces the style and temperament of each offer little common ground, but paradoxically what they share is also indicative of their difference. Kafka is to Hegel as the inside of a mask is to the face of the mask: the face within looks nothing like the one outside, and there are hardly any recognizable features; yet without this "distorted" negative interior the positive exterior would not be able to show itself. Formulated otherwise: what seems like a distortion, i.e., the inside of the mask, is also the very possibility of the face of the mask.

I will approach the question of freedom in a "phenomenological" way, *using this word in its strict Hegelian sense*, meaning to unfold the experience of a necessary logic or structure of possibility *via negativa*, i.e., by its absence or distortion or breakdown. Hegel himself often used literary allusions, from Sophocles to Diderot to the Romantics, to show how these negative moments are played out; thus, drawing on Kafka is more in Hegel's spirit than it might *prima facie* appear. For Hegel the positive emerges from the negative. Hegel's way to show how something is possible is to show informative failed attempts of realizing this possibility. The same approach could be applied to Kafka: despite initial appearances, his aporetic worlds do not end in nothing, but, perhaps not evident to Kafka himself, they negatively outline a logic of possibility. However, this logic remains in a state of perpetual tension as a kind of irresolvable contradiction. This is where Hegel enters the scene, since his logic exactly endeavors to hold fast to contradiction, and by holding it fast he thereby extrapolates the *necessity* at the heart of the contradiction. This happens by the "sublation" (*Aufhebung*) of contradiction, meaning to surpass, to preserve, and to bring our comprehension of the contradiction to a new level. In short: to see the contradiction as productive. It means that the negative contradiction is itself a positive structure of reality. In Kafka, as mentioned, these contradictions are held in suspense; they are not sublated but perpetuated. The point of the inherent inescapability of the contradiction is where Kafka and Hegel intersect, and this will therefore be our point of departure. What is needed for the transition from Kafka to Hegel is to see in impossibility the (negatively traced) outline of a possibility.[3]

---

3 This kind of formulation is reminiscent of (and indebted to) Derrida's notion of *conditions of possibility as conditions of impossibility*. What distinguishes my approach from the Derridean one is that I reject the ideal of purity implied with the "impossibility." Instead, all possibility is double-edged: the structure that makes X *possible* also *depends on* non-X (instead of: what makes X *possible* also makes X [as pure, ideal, in itself] *impossible*). The Hegelian approach is

Simply stated, the contradiction is that the structure of freedom is the same as the structure of non-freedom. What will be presented here is the same *virtual structure*,[4] but seen simultaneously from both the perspective of its negative expression in Kafka and its more positive expression in Hegel. Stating the matter in the most simple way we can say that the fault line in this contradiction is between the subject and the object, where the object is the space of actions and the subject the agent. It is a contradiction because the subject is only a subject if it is also an object; it *is* also what it *is not*.[5] The meaning of this "is" and "is not" will be the topic of this article.

The structure of the free subject *includes* the "space" wherein she is and acts. There is no subjectivity without an objective space ("objective" here does not necessarily mean true, but simply what is the opposite of the subject – including other subjects). These two sides cannot be held in abstract separation. They co-emerge, so to speak, but irreducibly so, neither completely *embedded in* nor completely *isolated from* each other. Any action is not just an action exclusively because of the agent, but equally because of *the space of action*. The world where the subject finds herself is more than an empty space inhabited by objects and other subjects. It is a space of possible and impossible actions, a space that "responds," and the status of an action depends on this "response." This space is *both* necessary for the production of any action *and also* the possibility of the destruction of any action. In Kafka, this space is never clearly structured, and the objective side of the action is never symmetrical to its subjective agent. The symmetry between inner (subjective) and outer (objective) is constantly suspended and distorted, and yet it is by this very distortion and tension that we see their mutual and original connection.

I have termed the negative side of this tension, via Benjamin, the "swamp world." But it must be remembered that this negative side is also the condition for

---

to think the irreducible interpenetration of X and non-X without abstraction (or negatively: to show the collapse of abstraction into concretion, i.e. interpenetration). There is no impossible transcendent ideal, only the real immanent tension. The impossible ideal is an ideology produced by adherence to a purist *idée fixe* that this interpenetration is a compromise of a pure transcendent X-in-itself.

4 I borrow this term from Gilles Deleuze's 1967 text "How Do We Recognize Structuralism?" ("À quoi reconnaît-on le structuralisme") in *Desert Islands and Other Texts 1953–1974* [*L'île deserte et autres texts, textes et entretiens*], ed. David Lapoujade, trans. Michael Taormina, Semiotext(e), Los Angeles 2004, 170–192.

5 Note that for Hegel this is only a contradiction within the discourse of what he calls *Verstand* (understanding) whereas the discourse of *Vernunft* (reason) is precisely characterized by the feature that it can *think through* apparent contradictions.

the positive side. This is the main argument presented here. In his "Franz Kafka: On the Tenth Anniversary of His Death" ("Franz Kafka: Zur zehnten Wiederkehr seines Todestages") – the essay that Adorno had read with such enthusiasm – Benjamin notes that

> Kafka did not consider the age in which he lived as an advance over the beginnings of time. His novels are set in a *swamp world*. [...] The fact that it is now forgotten does not mean that it does not extend into the present. On the contrary: it is actual by virtue of this very oblivion. An experience deeper than that of an average person can make contact with it. "I have experience," we read in one of Kafka's earliest notes, "and I am not joking when I say that it is a seasickness on dry land."[6] (Emphasis added.)

In the present text I hope to bring to light and out of forgetfulness the *logic* of the "swamp world" from "the beginnings of time" as something that outlines the negative structure of freedom, and as something that is, as Benjamin says, hidden in its very actualization.

There is also a "swamp world" in Hegel, a primordial natural world whose fundamental concepts extend to the present world. It is a world where both the preservation and destruction of an enduring discontinuous "shape" of a living being depends on the continuity or "fluidity" of this shape with its environment. The argument I present will be that the move from Kafka to Hegel requires only a slight shift in perspective, and that performing this shift will illuminate essential aspects of each figure that are otherwise easily overlooked. In reading Hegel, there is often excessive emphasis on the "resolution" of contradiction, such that it is forgotten that in the "resolution" the contradiction is preserved (remembering the threefold meaning of "sublation"). Conversely, readings of Kafka typically overemphasize the aporetic "absurdity" of irresolvable contradictions. The Kafka presented in this article is not "absurd"; rather, he systematically outlines a logic, sometimes inadvertently, that Hegel can help extract. Kafka also brings out the precariousness or fragility inherent in the contradictory structure of Hegel's conceptions of freedom. It is not a matter of a dot-connecting comparison but rather of the effect of disclosure that both figures can exert on each other.

Starting from the level of the swamp world, I argue against the stale opposition between Hegel as a representative of universality and Kafka as a representative of singularity. In the swamp, the universal grows into and out of the singular, and the singular into and out of the universal.

---

6 Walter Benjamin, "Franz Kafka: On the Tenth Anniversary of His Death," in *Illuminations*, ed. Hannah Arendt, trans. Harry Zohn, Schocken Books, New York 1968, 111–140, 130.

A final semantic clarification before entering the main text: when "freedom" is juxtaposed with "un-freedom," the latter is *not* equivalent with imprisonment, incarceration, confinement, slavery, etc. I take the relation between un-freedom and freedom to mean the same as the relation between inhuman and human, or *unheimlich* and *heimlich*, or undead and dead. "Un-freedom" is defined as the negative that is immanent to freedom as the very condition for actualizing positive freedom. Un-freedom is the distorted internal side of the mask, an underground without depth; freedom is the external side, the surface that hides the underground in its actualization.

2 Shape and Fluidity: The Hegelian Swamp World

Before what is arguably the most famous part of Hegel's *Phenomenology of Spirit* [*Phänomenologie des Geistes*] – namely, the section on lordship and bondage – there are some strange pages that initially seem difficult to place. The overall chapter, the fourth of the book, is titled "The Truth of Self-Certainty" and is divided into two parts[7]; after the heading and before the first part proper begins, one finds some seemingly obscure preliminary pages. These pages describe what I will term the Hegelian Swamp World, for they concern a pre-human natural world reduced to its most basic constituents,[8] what Hegel calls "shapes" (*Gestalten*) and "flux" or "fluidity" (*Flüssigkeit* or *Fluidität*). These concepts are repeated in various guises throughout Hegel's work; in more *logical* terms, they represent important aspects of individuality or singularity (*Einzelheit*) and of universality (*Allgemeinheit*), respectively. Shape and fluidity are also reminiscent of Bataille's distinction, in his seminal conceptualization of the erotic, between the *discontinuous* and the *continuous*.[9] In reviewing this intersection in Hegel's *Phenomenology* I wish to keep in mind both the logical and the erotic aspects while foreshadowing their relevance for reading Kafka. In short, this chapter of

---

7 Part A is called "Independence and Dependence of Self-Consciousness: Lordship and Bondage" and part B is called "Freedom of Self-Consciousness: Stoicism, Scepticism, and the Unhappy Consciousness."

8 Indeed, this corresponds roughly to what – in a much more unfolded version – will be Hegel's philosophy of nature, especially the part on organic nature (see Hegel's *Enzyklopädie der philosophischen Wissenschaften im Grundrisse II: Die Philosophie der Natur*, §§ 337–376, Werke in zwanzig Bänden, Bd. 9; G.W.F. Hegel, *Philosophy of Nature, Vol. I–III*, trans. M.J. Petry, Unwin Brothers Limited, London 1970).

9 George Bataille, *Eroticism* [*L'Erotisme*], trans. Mary Dalwood, Penguin Modern Classics, London 2012.

the *Phenomenology*, and arguably a large part of the overall work, addresses the difficulty of establishing a *self*.[10] A recurring trope of Hegel's examination is the following: when the "self" experiences a loss of self (because its discontinuity has in some way been breached, and so has become fluid, relational, infected, penetrated by otherness, etc.), it is actually experiencing a necessary structure of its selfhood. What the "self" misperceives as a negative impediment is actually *also*[11] a positive condition of it being itself.[12]

Let us turn to the text. In this intersection what is staged is the difficulty of establishing a self within the framework of organic nature. Hegel does not start with individuality as a given fact; instead, he recounts its emergence from this primordial "idealized"[13] swamp world.

Perceived most broadly, organic life can be conceptualized as that which Hegel calls "universal fluidity." Everything is devouring everything: a spectacle of an endless circular orgiastic motion of pure continuity that breaks down any discrete shape into an amorphous flux of excessive life into death and death into life (an organism stays alive by eating another, etc.). It is "the supersession of all distinctions, the pure movement of axial rotation, its self-repose being an absolutely restless infinity."[14] In this sense there is no enduring individual shape in organic nature but only a continuous destruction of shapes. Life is the flux of life. It is a world where no shape can assume a lasting shape, because every shape is superseded by another at all times. This is the flux aspect. But how do individual shapes come about if they are constantly "liquidated"? The answer is already in the question: there can be no continuous flux if there are no distinct shapes. The flux is thus *a flux of distinctive shapes breaking down other distinctive shapes*, wherefore flux necessarily implies its apparent opposite, namely distinctions or differences: "The differences, however, are just as much present as differences in this simple universal medium; for this universal flux has its negative nature only in being the supersession of them; but it cannot supersede the different moments

---

10 This is of course but one aspect of the *Phenomenology* and cannot be reduced to this summation. It is also at the same time a "ladder" to Hegel's philosophy proper, namely, the *Logic* and the *Encyclopedia*.

11 This "also" is very important, as will hopefully become clear in the remainder of the article.

12 In my thesis I have called this the *logic of irreducible complicity*. I cannot expand upon it here, due to space considerations, yet this logic is ubiquitous in the present article.

13 "Idealized" here not in an evaluative sense, but a reduction of a broad range of phenomena to its fundamental structural constituents and dynamics, in short: its essence.

14 G.W.F. Hegel, *Phänomenologie des Geistes*, Werke in zwanzig Bänden, Bd. 3, Suhrkampf Verlag, Frankfurt/M. 1970, 140; G.W.F. Hegel, *Phenomenology of Spirit*, trans. A.V. Miller, Oxford University Press, Oxford 1971, 106.

if they do not have an enduring existence [*Bestehen*]."[15] There is no universal flux if there are no individual shapes by which the flux flows. If nothing endures, then nothing breaks down. What seemed an opposition is actually part of a more complicated whole that makes both sides of the opposition (namely, flux and distinct shape) possible.

The same is also true from the other side: the singular or individual shapes are not self-sufficient or pre-given, but are themselves necessarily constituted *within* the flux of life. The continued subsistence (*Bestehen*) of the particular shapes depends on the fluid breaking down of other shapes. To resist entropy, an organism must "extract" the negative entropy of another organism. To continue its survival it must "assimilate" another organism. To remain closed, as an enduring "shape," it must be open, that is, "fluid." For each shape to be, it must be in a constant metabolism – the shape is a shape only if it is permeable, a membrane. This is also clear from sexual activities that always involve some transgression of bodily discontinuity, whether inwards or outwards. Generally speaking, a "shape" is a closed singular system only as a function of being open and becoming locally de-singularized (*qua* open to otherness).

This tensional unity between shape and flux – at this early point in Hegel's text – outlines the beginning of the contradictory structure of possibility for any individuality as such. In nature, a shape can affirm itself only through the negation of another shape, paradigmatically by consuming it, thereby perpetuating the flux of life. Because of this flux the shape cannot sustain a stable individuality, yet this individuality-destroying flux is also the condition for individuality, since the subsistence of one depends on the destruction of another. Not just meaning that one organism must die to give energy to another organism's survival. But the surviving organism must make itself fluid or continuous with something other which is not itself proper in order to be itself: "This independence of the shape appears as something *determinate, for an other*, for the shape is divided within itself; and the *supersession* [*das Aufheben*] of this dividedness accordingly takes place through an other. But this supersession is just as much within the shape itself, for it is just that flux that is the substance of the independent shapes."[16] At this level the independence of one shape depends on the shape negating the independence of another. What Hegel is trying to show is that any kind of independence *depends* on otherness, even at this primitive stage where independence means (1) dependence on the other through the destructive assimilation of the other, and (2) the transgression of the very boundary of the self that

---

15 Hegel, *Phänomenologie des Geistes*, 140; Hegel, *Phenomenology of Spirit*, 106.
16 Hegel, *Phänomenologie des Geistes*, 140–141; Hegel, *Phenomenology of Spirit*, 107.

is paradoxically perpetuated by this very transgression. This complex logic Hegel extracts from the apparently simple phenomena of living organisms eating other living organisms.

The contradiction at this point can be stated simply: that which breaks down an individual shape – namely, fluidity – is *also* what sustains it: "Its self-given unity with itself is just that fluidity of the differences or their general dissolution. But, conversely, the supersession of individual existence is equally the production of it."[17] The point is that the individuality of the shape is produced *in* the universal fluidity itself and *not* in opposition to it: "this dividedness of the differenceless fluid medium is just what establishes individuality [...] and the dissolution of the splitting-up is just as much a splitting-up and a forming of members [Glieder]."[18] The individual shape is the condition for the universal flux and the universal flux is the condition for the individual shape. The process of this tension is what Hegel terms "desire."

This logic of the tensions in the Hegelian "swamp world" also gets to the heart of the Kafkan "swamp world." In each, the world is foreign or alien to the individual yet at the same time essential and necessary. What is characteristic at this point in Hegel is that individuality is *abstract*: it sees all that is *not it* as being fundamentally *opposed to it*. There can be no continuity between "it" and what is "not it" (which is, broadly speaking, the others and the world, or the *Umwelt*). It can thus affirm itself only by negating what is *not* itself. But this negation, as noted earlier, is also a *continuity* with the other, albeit a destructive one; it must consume, internalize, the other for its own proper subsistence, and therefore it is fundamentally dependent on the other. For a discontinuous living being there is thus no way to "escape" continuity; it is only through continuity that discontinuity is possible, and only through discontinuity that continuity is possible.

Before Hegel finally proceeds to the famous chapter on lordship and bondage, there is a transitional passage that foreshadows what will emerge in the later developments. Due to restrictions in scope I will select only a few points from the argumentations and expand on their significance. In this passage, Hegel writes the famous "contradictory" proposition[19]: "'I' that is 'We' and 'We' that is 'I.'"[20]

---

17 Hegel, *Phänomenologie des Geistes*, 142–143; Hegel, *Phenomenology of Spirit*, 108.

18 Hegel, *Phänomenologie des Geistes*, 142; Hegel, *Phenomenology of Spirit*, 108. (*Glieder* could also, perhaps more appropriately in this local context, be translated as *sections*, *divisions*, or *parts*.)

19 These are called *infinite proposition*, in the sense that they breach the finitude of each term and that the subject and predicate circularly reverse places; they flow into and out of each other, and there is no point of either beginning or end: both are primordial.

20 Hegel, *Phänomenologie des Geistes*, 145; Hegel, *Phenomenology of Spirit*, 111.

This is meant to express, in a compressed proposition, the necessary continuity of the discontinuous "I" – not as a compromise to its being, but as a necessary aspect of it being *itself*.[21] This is also why Hegel's minimal "definition" of freedom is *being-oneself-in-otherness*,[22] that is, the other is not a hindrance to my freedom, but an essential aspect of my freedom: "the freedom of the spirit is not just a being outside of the other, but rather an independence from the other achieved in the other."[23]

The grasping of this requires what Hegel calls a *double sense*,[24] where individuality is not *reduced* but rather *produced* with the other, not *only* in discontinuous opposition but *also and primarily* in its fluid continuity with the other. The double sense is meant to keep both sides in play at once without isolating them, without conflating them, and, importantly, without giving priority to one over the other. The singular "I" is constituted in the tension between the *isolation* (or abstraction) from the "We," and the *participation* (or concretion) in the "We," which results in the *individuation through* the "We." For Hegel, to hold fast to the double sense is to affirm the irreducibility of the tension,[25] and what I term "the space of action" is exactly opened by this irreducible tension. What is so remarkable in Kafka's work is that this tension is brought to its highest negative intensity.

Fast-forwarding through the struggle for life and death between two self-consciousnesses and the subsequent hierarchization into lord and bondsman, I wish to highlight two aspects that can be termed "the insights of the bondsman." The

---

21 A formulation of this point would be that the individual is universal and the universal individual.

22 See "die Freiheit ist eben dies, in seinem Anderen bei sich selbst zu sein" (G.W.F. Hegel, *Enzyklopädie der philosophischen Wissenschaften im Grundrisse I: Die Wissenschaft der Logik*, Werke in zwanzig Bänden, Bd. 8, Suhrkampf Verlag, Frankfurt/M. 1970, 84; G.W.F. Hegel, *The Encyclopedia Logic*, trans. T.F. Gereats, W.A. Suchting, and H.S. Harris, Hackett Publishing Company, Indianapolis 1991, 58).

23 G.W.F. Hegel, *Enzyklopädie der philosophischen Wissenschaften im Grundrisse III: Die Philosophie des Geistes*, Werke in zwanzig Bänden, Bd. 10, Suhrkampf Verlag, Frankfurt/M. 1970, 26; G.W.F. Hegel, *Philosophy of Mind*, trans. A.V. Miller, The Clarendon Press, Oxford 1971, 15. Translation completely altered. The original is as follows: "Die Freiheit des Geistes ist aber nicht bloß eine außerhalb des Anderen, sondern eine im Anderen errungene Unabhängigkeit vom Anderen [...]"

24 See "*die Doppelsinnigkeit*" (Hegel, *Phänomenologie des Geistes*, 145; Hegel, *Phenomenology of Spirit*, 111).

25 "The Concept of this its [self-consciousness's] unity in its duplication embraces many and varied meanings. Its moments, then, must on the one hand be held strictly apart, and on the other hand must in this differentiation at the same time also be taken and known as not being different, or in their opposite significance" (Hegel, *Phänomenologie des Geistes*, 145; Hegel, *Phenomenology of Spirit*, 111).

cause of this struggle is that each part perceives otherness as inherently in opposition to itself. Any continuity is perceived as a loss of self. Neither can grasp that *it can be itself only by also being outside of itself, in the other*. Therefore it thinks that it must destroy this other side of itself: "its essential being is present to it in the form of an 'other,' it is outside of itself and must rid itself of its self-externality."[26] The first step beyond this abstract negation of each other is that one of them, succumbing to the fear of death, submits to the other. But, paradoxically, in the long run it is the submissive bondsman who comes out on top, because he has learned an important practical "philosophical" lesson that is lost on the lord (because the latter is, in some sense, still within nature and only able to negate and enjoy, or consume, objects). These lessons of the bondsman are lessons in fluidity. First, in surrendering to the fear of death the bondsman has lost his hard, abstract self-certainty, as being *only* a discrete and discontinuous being. He has seen himself from the perspective of the non-self, as potentially part of fluidity[27]: "[the bondsman] has experienced the fear of death, the absolute Lord. In that experience it has been internally dissolved, has trembled in every fiber of its being, and everything solid and stable has been shaken to its foundations;" he has experienced "the absolute fluidity of all subsistent beings [*Bestehens*]."[28] Yet in the terror of fluidity, there is a positive and essential lesson. He is not made completely fluid nor is he killed, but he has overcome his hard discontinuity; in a sense he has become *open* towards the non-self instead of trying to negate it. He has learned to see the "bigger picture" – his perspective has become complex and more concrete, beyond mere abstract negation. Thus, he has achieved a middle ground, or a unity, between continuity and discontinuity, and on this level new possibilities emerge.

The second lesson concerns his relation and continuity towards the non-self, the object. Because he is forced to *work* for the lord he must withhold gratification (consumption or negation of the object), and since he cannot *enjoy* directly he must *form* the object, preparing it for enjoyment by the lord. This opens the realm of *formation* (*Bildung*) through work with the object, instead of simply negating it: "It is in this way, therefore, that consciousness, qua worker, comes to see in the independent being [of the object] its own independence [zur Anschauung

---

26 Hegel, *Phänomenologie des Geistes*, 149, Hegel, *Phenomenology of Spirit*, 113.
27 The knowledge of death without the actual experience of death is what allows for a self-reflexivity, to think of one's being from the perspective of one's own non-being. This is why, for Hegel, the knowledge of death is also the beginning of philosophy.
28 Hegel, *Phänomenologie des Geistes*, 153; Hegel, *Phenomenology of Spirit*, 117.

des selbständigen Seins *als seiner selbst*]."[29] Through formation of the world the bondsman turns it into a world of his own, a space of action that, in some way, corresponds to himself. Instead of seeing the world as constitutively foreign, he now sees the possibility of positive continuity across the negative divide between self and non-self, or, rather, he sees the necessity of non-self for the self, the concrete unity of the two. The slave gives permanency to his individuality not by destroying an alien world but by creating a space that *reflects* his individuality.[30]

What has been experienced is that fluidity – the continuity beyond the bonds of bodily or individual integrity – does not entails a necessary loss of self, but is *also* the very possibility of the self, of self-expression. What is important is that, because of this double-edged structure, fluidity can always go both ways. If the externalizing, fluid "loss" of self is the only way to be an actual self, then there is no pre-given self that is automatically actualized. Because *otherness*, or negativity, is essential in a positive way for the (expression of) *self* its being is always *given over* to a precarious yet irreducible tension between the two: I always express myself together with a world that is not myself (therefore it can be both hostile and responsive).

In Hegel, we have the double sense of going *both ways* at the same time, thus outlining the productivity of the tension, whereas in Kafka it is a sense of going *no way*, of being stuck in the pure potentiality of the tension.[31] The universal fluidity of "the swamp world" also exhibits the minimal logic of individual self-subsistence. The power of Kafka is that he is constantly "looking the negative in the face."[32] But Kafka loses himself in tarrying with the negative, remaining in what I would call an *animated suspension*. This results in an experience of utter powerlessness (what Hegel calls *despair*). The infusion of Hegel in Kafka allows for a novel rendition of this powerlessness as something more than simply the last

---

29 Hegel, *Phänomenologie des Geistes*, 154; Hegel, *Phenomenology of Spirit*, 118.

30 Or, more correctly, he has learned about the *potential* for it, since at this point he is still restricted by his position of bondage.

31 The "pure potentiality" should not be confused with Giorgio Agamben's extremely interesting treatment of pure potentiality (or impotentiality). Whereas he has a bivalent notion of possibility designating two states: the *potential to be* and the *potential not to be*, he does not seem interested in the question of *how* potentiality is actualized (rather, his whole project is exploring the potential of non-actualization, of impotentiality). Hegel would surely call Agamben a Beautiful Soul (which is meant critically). The pure potentiality that I mention here is the (always ambiguous) conditions of actualization either minus actualization, or rather minus *effective* actualization. For more on Agamben, see his *Potentialities: Collected Essays in Philosophy*, ed. and trans. Daniel Heller-Roazen, Stanford University Press, Stanford 1999.

32 Hegel, *Phänomenologie des Geistes*, 36; Hegel, *Phenomenology of Spirit*, 19.

word to be said on Kafka, for we can extricate the condition of freedom from the logic of the swamp.

3 Un-freedom in Kafka as the Condition for Freedom

The Kafkan un-freedom, which reveals the very conditions of freedom, is not, or is very rarely, intended to be thought of as imprisonment, incarceration, physical restraint, or brute force. In a note from 1920 Kafka makes this eminently clear: "the prisoner was actually free, he could participate in everything, nothing outside was lost for him, he could even leave his cage, as a matter of fact the bars were several meters apart, he wasn't even captive."[33] What Kafka is noting is that there is a form of captivity that is constituted not by bars but by the very space wherein one lives, acts and thinks. A prisoner in an "open" space. And the same applies to freedom: it, too, is dependent on a specific form of space. There is a captivity that is constituted not by enclosure but by a failure in the identity between the subject and object, the agent and the space of action. The logic of this failure is what I have termed *un-freedom*. This logic is suspended out between two extremes, namely, a resigned *rejection of all immanent space*, as if the world *as such* is not conducive to freedom, and a *belief in some transcendent space* of pure freedom, that is impossible to reach.

In Kafka's unfinished novels, especially *The Trial* [*Der Prozeß*] and *The Castle* [*Das Schloß*], the protagonists (respectively, Josef K. and K.) are slowly being *exhausted*, in the literal sense of "being emptied out," because each is unable to actualize any action in the world wherein he finds himself. This is not to say that neither participates in the world around him; on the contrary, this is all they do, but their participation lacks any proper efficacy. Each is in a state of animated suspension. Either nothing happens, in the sense that all that is done dissipates into nothing, or whatever happens is deformed, such that K. cannot recognize himself in the effect of his actions. It is not that there is no correspondence between the hero and the others, but that it is never adequate or symmetrical. It is even difficult to pinpoint this textually, since it is expressed only in the continuous circular frustration of both *being* in the world and yet *not having one's being* in the world.

---

33 Franz Kafka, *Hochzeitsvorbereitungen auf dem Lande und andere Prosa aus dem Nachlass* [*Wedding Preparations in the Country and Other Prose from the Estate*], Fischer Taschenbuch Verlag, Frankfurt/M. 1983, 216 (my translation).

Throughout the unfinished novels the reader experiences this tension, mainly in the form of various dissociations between cause and effect. This tension is not only about causes without effects and effects without causes; it is also about dissymmetry between causes and effects, belated causes, and, most importantly, about *distortive symmetries* between cause and effect ("distortive" like a face in a broken mirror or house of mirror-type distortions). If successful free actions occur within a space that structures the significance of actions, then Kafka's world is one where it is not clear *how* or *if* the space is structured. This world, rather, seems to be completely disordered, a "swamp world [*Sumpfwelt*]," as Benjamin describes it.[34] Thus, it is never clear what exactly an action means, and so there is no ground for K. to recognize himself in the objectivity of his actions (there is no stable objectivity of his actions, they are *less* than actions). This is why he is constantly in search of some (ultimately unreachable) space, be it the High Court or the Castle, where his words and actions would have undistorted symmetrical efficacy.

The Trial presents various representative parts in this respect. In the second chapter, K. is unable to find the examination room, which is purportedly located in a large, confusing housing complex for poor people. The locality itself shows that the space of action is unsettled. Why would juridical affairs take place in *that* place? The space of placements[35] is unhinged from the outset. In order not to reveal that he is there for a legal hearing, or examination, K. fabricates a story that he is in fact looking for a carpenter called Lanz and starts going door to door in hope of finding the examination room. Suddenly, as if from out of nowhere, a washwoman pulls him into the examination room: it is a small room, packed with people, both on the floor and in a gallery above. The air is thick, stale, leaving K. almost unable to breath; the room is so crowded that he almost cannot move: a veritable space of non-action. The examining magistrates reproach him for being too late; when K. indifferently dismisses this, his words are, strangely, met with a roar of applause from half of the room. Moreover, when the magistrate mistakenly assumes that K. is a painter by trade, K.'s scornful correction of the magistrate is met by heartfelt laughter from the same half of the crowd. These effects give K. the impression that he is confronted with symmetry in a space of sympathetic others who recognize him as a valid agent: "When K. now started to speak, he was

---

34 Benjamin, "Franz Kafka: On the Tenth Anniversary of His Death," 130.
35 I borrow this term, though not its complete meaning, from Alain Badiou's *Theory of the Subject* [*Théorie du sujet*], trans. Bruno Bosteels, Continuum, London 2009.

convinced he was speaking for them [*in ihrem Sinne zu sprechen*]."[36] Overeagerly and unsolicited, K. begins speaking from a small podium, expressing both deep disdain for the court system and outrage at his treatment during his arrest. His exalted talk is met with tense awaiting silence. At one point someone bizarrely screams: "Bravo! Why not? Bravo! I say bravo!"[37] K. misinterprets the silence during his talk as evidence that his speech is holding his audience captive in deep interest. At the end the silence is broken by unspecified but noisy sexual activity between the washwoman and a man.[38] K. attempts to re-establish some degree of order and earnestness, but nobody seems interested. Most likely, there had never been order to begin with; the responses from the audience had no actual significance. K. jumps from the podium and is caught in the crowd around him; seeing them face to face, he now completely doubts the efficacy of his speech: "Had he overestimated the effect of his speech?"[39] Up close, he notices that the people of the crowd all carry badges (*Abzeichen*) of the same type. Outraged that they are all part of the court, K. makes his way out, thinking he has achieved nothing. The inconsistent, ambiguous, and senseless responses from the crowd testify to the fluid lack of structure of this space. Because of this de-structured space, the symmetrical tension between cause and effect (talk and response) breaks down into blind causes with senseless effects. It is a swampy space, where things interpenetrate senselessly and without consistency; K. finds himself amidst a juridical orgy, a "hearing" where nothing is heard, or, rather, where it is never certain what is heard and what is not heard, and to what effect.

K.'s mistake is that he assumes or believes that he is not in a "swamp" but in an ordered setting. He talks, assuming both that his words are heard and that they are heard because they stem from him. What becomes apparent, however, is that the response from the "floor" is completely aleatory. It is not that the intended audience is unresponsive, but that its response is unstructured and asymmetrical. It is thus never clear in what space K. really finds himself. At the end, the space shows itself to be without any clear order, to be more interested in some sordid interruption than in K.'s words, to be driven by some primordial sexual "swamp" drive. The arrogance, or idiocy, that K. exhibits, lies in his belief that he is an individual agent abstractly independent of the space wherein he acts.

---

36 Franz Kafka, *Der Prozeß*, Fischer Taschenbuch Verlag, Frankfurt/M. 1983, 39; Franz Kafka, *The Trial*, trans. Mike Mitchell, Oxford University Press, Oxford 2009, 33.
37 Kafka, *Der Prozeß*, 41; Kafka, *The Trial*, 35.
38 The sexual nature of the act is specified in more detail in a passage crossed out by Kafka in his manuscript.
39 Kafka, *Der Prozeß*, 43–44; Kafka, *The Trial*, 38.

He does not examine the space, but instead interrupts the magistrates; he does not enquire into their intentions, nor consider that he might even be in the wrong room, standing before the wrong crowd. Yet none of this seems to present itself as a problem for him. He is certain of himself, and affirms this by negating (uttering his spite for) the court. And yet: he believes in the court, for throughout the novel he continues searching for it, its true symmetrical core.[40]

Later, in the chapter titled "The Thrasher" ("Der Prügler"), K. is confronted with an *exaggerated effect* of which he is supposed to be the cause. He discovers the two guards who harassed him during his arrest and who were among the main targets of his apparently failed speech in the examination room. He finds them at his office in a small lumber-room, where they are about to be whipped by a man in a leather outfit. The space is again completely out of place. They claim that K. was the cause of this punishment: "Sir! We're going to be given a thrashing because you complained about us to the examining magistrate."[41] Despite K.'s pleas and attempts at bribing him, the thrasher will not cease to inflict the physical punishment that K. has apparently caused.

It is important to note that not only can the impotence of actions be alienating, but also too *strong* effects of action, akin to what Freud called "the uncanny effects associated with the omnipotence of thoughts, instantaneous wish-fulfillment."[42] I might silently wish that my neighbor drops dead, but if it materially happens shortly thereafter then this would make the space of action appear *too* responsive, even to my darkest thoughts, as if by some magical power I had circumvented the strictures of "civilization," like some telekinetic version of a wild animal unhindered in following its initial deadly instinct. The space becomes uncanny, unhomely (*unheimlich*): the familiarity of cause and effect breaks down, yet it is also homely, for it realizes the wish and corresponds to who you are (but is *too* homely, darkly and alienatingly homely, so to speak). The world becomes uncanny, unhomely, when our actions have no material effect, but also when our thoughts and actions have overly direct material effect. The logic of this swamp world is to be *too* continuous, *too* fluid, when it was expected to be discontinuous and discrete, and *too* isolating, when it was expected to be continuous.

---

40 For more on this and the problem of Kafka's adherence to or counterfactual belief in the purity of (especially paternal) authority in general see Walter Sokel's excellent essay "Freedom and Authority in the Fiction of Franz Kafka," in *The Myth and Power of the Self: Essays on Franz Kafka*, Wayne State University Press, Detroit 2002, 311–324.

41 Kafka, *Der Prozeß*, 74; Kafka, *The Trial*, 58.

42 Sigmund Freud, *The Uncanny* [*Das Unheimliche*], trans. David McLintock, Penguin Books, London 2003, 154.

These are examples of the absence of the balance between cause (intention) and effect (reception, recognition), the relation of which is essential in establishing actual free agency. The problem with Kafka's world is not the excess of bureaucratic order that stifles the free spontaneity of the individual. Rather, it is *the very lack of order* that obfuscates the possibility of action for the individual. This lack of order – there is no fixture or structure that gives an action a stable meaning – is what makes the world swampy. In some sense Kafka's world is not just a world of infinite limits, but also one of infinite permeability. Yet this permeability cannot support any actions, for there is no way to know if and how the space will react – sometimes it is barring without any bars, sometime open without any sense or direction.

Because K. only encounters spaces of non-action, defined as unstructured space that lends no clear significance and thus no objectivity to his action, he tries to exploit this very lack of structure, this orgiastic disorder of "the swamp world," by resorting to sex and sexuality as the basest instance of a structuring principle: "Women have great power. If I could persuade some women I know to work together for me, I would be bound to get through. Especially with this court, that consists almost entirely of skirt-chasers."[43] Within this swampy non-structure, women function as the very instrument of access to the court, or at least K. believes so.[44] They become a means of agency that K. lacks on his own accord. The paradox is that K. *actually believes* in the *validity* of the court (or the castle), all the while trying to employ *invalid* means to access this "pure" court-in-itself. What we can actually learn from Kafka (something he perhaps never learned himself) is that there is nothing behind the surface, that the manifestation is the level of truth and not "mere" appearances.[45]

Thus, there are no real *actions* in Kafka's work, only *pre-actions* trying to access the very space of action itself. But these never objectify into more than empty gestures in the antechamber of non-action. What K. is seeking to establish by these pre-actions is a connection to the absent addressee of his actions. Yet his actions never reach this addressee who would give him an adequate response. Instead, he is confronted only with ineffective or unwilling intermediaries, and

---

43 Kafka, *Der Prozeß*, 180; Kafka, *The Trial*, 152.
44 Benjamin notes: "It is from the swampy soil of such experiences that Kafka's female characters rise. They are swamp creatures like Leni [from *The Trial*], 'who stretches out the middle and ring fingers of her right hand between which the connecting web of skin reached almost to the top joint, short as the fingers were.'" See Benjamin, "Franz Kafka: On the Tenth Anniversary of His Death," 130–131.
45 I explore this is more detail in the yet unpublished "epilogue" to this article: "Abstraction, or Four Kafkan Strategies of Spacelessness."

thus never attains the actuality he was striving for. It is not that there is only discontinuity between K. and the world; rather, there is an "inverting" continuity alienating K. from the world the more he participates in it. This inverting or distorting continuity is exactly the logic of the swamp in its most negative aspect. All the reactions that K. receives serve only to stall indefinitely his position in the intermediary state. He finds himself trapped between constantly being active and yet never performing an action. It is this Kafkan tension between incessant naked *activity* and absent meaningful *action* that constitutes the swampy quality of his world. What makes his world alienating is exactly that K. is *never* restrained but is allowed seemingly free movement; of course, this "freedom" is futile, since the very space wherein it is performed precludes freedom. One could imagine the alienating quality vanishing if K. actually *were* restrained, since then it would be just a matter of breaking free, a straightforward negative act of self-assertion. It is not difficult to trace a certain wish for confinement and isolation in Kafka's work. There would be a clear structure, a simple, physical difference between being restrained and not being restrained. But, alas, it is a much more subtle restraint that is the source of alienation. This restraint could be called *ambient restraint*, where the space of action and the space of sense is unreceptive or distortive vis-à-vis the individual in question. This is the kind of restraint that is at work in Kafka. Focus is often drawn to it in light of two common features in his writing: the incessant references to the *air* of the spaces where the protagonist find himself; and the focus on *pure gestures*, where the meaning of the gesture seems unspecified.

I will begin by examining the pure gesture: In the very short story "The Knock on the Courtyard Gate" ("Der Schlag ans Hoftor") the significance of an act, namely, the knocking on a gate, is at stake. The story is told from the perspective of a brother whose sister – while they are passing the eponymous gate – does *something*. He is not sure if she simply raised her fist or whether she actually knocked, and, if so, why she would have done so. This gesture without a clear sense avalanches into extreme effects. In short, this is the dissymmetry between cause (act) and effect (reception). Suddenly, horsemen come riding in surrounded by great clouds of dust. The brother tries to explain the misunderstanding and to clarify the situation; however, as he sends his sister back home (to dress herself appropriately before she appears in front of the judge), he himself unwittingly has to face the judgment. For the brother the matter seems quite simple, and he is confident that he can explain it in no time. But as soon as he enters the farmhouse parlor that serves as a court,[46] it becomes clear that he holds no power over the question of the sense of his sister's gesture. The naked act itself no longer even

---

46 Again, the court is not in its "proper" place, the space of placement is misplaced.

seems relevant, and it is far outweighed by the judging reception of the others. The makeshift "courtroom," itself an unstructured space as such, has a strange bed-like object (half plank bed, half operating table) awaiting the brother. This peculiar "bed" is the "place" of his complete passive reduction to the judgment of others.[47] The story ends with a change in the air and the impossibility of escape: "Could I still sense any other air than that of a prison? That is the great question – or rather, it would be the question if I had any prospect of being released."[48] There is an extreme disproportion here between the gesture by the individual and the question of the gesture's sense as interpreted by others. Owing to the extreme imbalance in favor of the interpretation by the others, the singular gesture itself becomes almost irrelevant. Moreover, it is not the agent herself but rather her brother who must account for it, a condition that further dissociates the intention, the gesture, and the interpretation from each other. What this expresses is the excess of ascription of significance from others. The brother is caught between the *ambiguity* of the gesture and being the *patient* of the judgment of others as to the sense of the naked gesture. The problem here is that the space of action swallows the singular action itself in a responsive distortion blown out of proportion, thereby precluding the independence of the agent.

The protagonist is *swamped* by the judgment of the others. But this swamping is a distorted, de-structured version of the structure that also positively gives sense to an action and establishes it in the world. Without the responsiveness to the action it would be not an action but an empty or naked gesture devoid of sense. Sense is not hidden in the singular gesture; the gesture only achieves sense depending on the space wherein it occurs. Kafka's short text intensifies *ad absurdum* the tension between the responsive space and the naked gesture, each being "inflated" without either coming into mutual communion or contact. These are the two sides of the necessary tension (action and reaction) brought, by Kafka, to their highest negative intensity. The continuity between the two serves only to separate them into two discontinuous abstractions: a *pure* senseless judgment, and a *naked* senseless gesture. Any sense of an action, if it is possible, resides in their interpenetration.[49]

---

47 This object is reminiscent of the apparatus from "In the Penal Colony" ("In der Strafkolonie") that inscribes the judgment into the flesh of the condemned until he dies from the wounds of the inscriptions.

48 Kafka, *Hochzeitsvorbereitungen auf dem Lande*, 80; Franz Kafka, *Kafka's Selected Stories: New Translations, Backgrounds and Contexts, Criticism*, ed. and trans. Stanley Corngold, Norton Critical Edition, Norton, New York 2007, 125.

49 An action, for Hegel, is always "public," always interpenetrating with the others, a "lonely" action is thus always also the *result* of the interaction with other: "in merely doing something

What is formidable in both Kafka and Hegel is their respective abilities to tarry with the negative, as Hegel terms it,[50] that is, to *resist* this interpenetration to the highest intensity, exactly *in order to show its necessity*. The difference is that, for Hegel, this is *also* the point of finding oneself "in utter dismemberment,"[51] whereas for Kafka it is the point of misrecognition and ultimately of death and disappearance into nothing, the animated suspension moving towards suspended animation.

I now turn to the problem of air. This is the "universal element," the immediate medium of continuity between the inside and the outside; it is also the space of openness, the outside as such. The problem with the structure of possibility is that, like air, it is transparent and ambient; it is experienced only when it is absent. It is a kind of dependence that is not experienced *as* dependence. Who would say that it is a burden to breathe, except someone approaching death? The alienating quality of Kafka's world is created not because of a lack of direct independence, but, inversely, because of a lack of any *positive* kind of dependence.

This is presented most explicitly in *The Castle*, when the protagonist, K., wants to convince the castle – the unseen yet ubiquitous instance that ascribes sense and significance to the village inhabitants – that he is indeed who he claims to be, namely, a land surveyor hired by the castle. Here, the central issue is not about the question of guilt or innocence, as in *The Trial*, but about *the very person himself*, about the establishment of his very being, the establishment, or continuity, of his subjective (claim to) being in objectivity.[52] Throughout *The Castle* K. is

---

[*Allein indem sie etwas tun*], and thus bringing themselves out into the light of day, they directly contradict by their deed their presence of wanting to exclude the glare of publicity and participation by all and sundry. Actualization is, on the contrary, a display of what is one's own in the element of universality where it becomes and should become the affair of everyone" (Hegel, *Phänomenologie des Geistes*, 309; Hegel, *Phenomenology of Spirit*, 251, translation modified). "A consciousness that opens up a subject-matter soon learns that others hurry along like flies to freshly poured-out milk, and want to busy themselves with it" (Hegel, *Phänomenologie des Geistes*, 309; Hegel, *Phenomenology of Spirit*, 251). Even when we act alone, we implicitly expect others to understand our actions to mean what we take them to mean, which might also be the very reason why we try to do them *alone*; or we do them alone in fear that they will be taken wrongly, judged prematurely, misunderstood, etc. Robert Pippin deals partly with this problem, under many qualifications and restraints, in his excellent and detailed study *Hegel's Practical Philosophy: Rational Agency as Ethical Life*, Cambridge University Press, Cambridge 2008.

50 "bei [dem Negativen] verweilen" (Hegel, *Phänomenologie des Geistes*, 36; Hegel, *Phenomenology of Spirit*, 19).

51 Hegel, *Phänomenologie des Geistes*, 36; Hegel, *Phenomenology of Spirit*, 19.

52 Indeed, perhaps K. is not who he takes himself to be. There are many elements in the novel that indicate this: for example, the fact that his "assistants" who were supposed to come with

constantly trying to establish himself as who he takes himself to be, to be at home within the world: once again, however, it is a world that has, literally, no space for him. He *is there*, and yet he *is not there*.

For example: After seducing Frieda – who, being a woman, he hopes will serve as his access to the castle – K., in his coital reveries, begins reflecting on the foreign nature of the air: he "kept feeling that he had lost himself, or was further away in a strange land [*in die Fremde*] than anyone had ever been before, a strange land where even the air was unlike the air at home, where you were likely to stifle in the strangeness of it, yet such were its senseless lures that you could only go on, losing your way even more."[53] Whenever air is evoked as a medium of suffocation, one can be sure of having entered a space of non-action. There is no guarantee in the medium of continuity. It is not just that the air might turn thick and stale and viscous, but also that its continuity is distorting like a mirage. The externalization of the subject can be a distortion of the subject if the medium of externalization is alien or hostile to him. This is the logic of the swamp, that is, that there is no structured space but just a swampy space (that negatively shows the necessity of the structure of the space of action for any action as such). The closer one is to the swamp, the more impenetrable becomes the air. Within the swamp, senseless shifts in continuity and discontinuity allow for no stable action to be actualized. The "senseless lures" is not simply a reference to something sexual, for here sexuality is merely an instrument of accessibility; rather, I would argue, it is a reference to the fact that K. confusingly believes that there is a possibility of complete affirmation of his being within the swampy space of the castle, as if it contained a pure core of symmetry. Despite the swampy perversity and obscurity of the castle, K. cannot resist going through the swamp in search of symmetry, of having his being affirmed instead of remaining a vague foreign body. But the more he approaches the swamp the more distortive is the "symmetry"; in a sense, however, he cannot stop "hoping" – he is stubbornly attached[54] – hence the "senseless lures" that he cannot resist.

---

his "surveying instruments" (the objective proof of K. being who he claims to be) never arrive, or that he is not even sure what village he finds himself in. Of course, and more importantly, the constant ambiguity of K. being arbitrarily recognized and dismissed as being a land surveyor expresses the tension inherent in the objective establishment of the subjective. In the end it does not even seem important if he is a land surveyor or not: he simply desires to have his bare existence objectively affirmed by the castle.

53 Franz Kafka, *Das Schloß*, Fischer Taschenbuch Verlag, Frankfurt/M. 1983, 43–44; Franz Kafka, *The Castle*, trans. Anthea Bell, Oxford University Press, Oxford 2009, 40 (translation modified).
54 I borrow this term from Judith Butler's *The Psychic Life of Power*, Stanford University Press, Stanford 1997.

The paradox is that K. is an empty character; his sole content is his reluctant attempts to have his being positively affirmed by the castle that, in turn, consistently refuses him any stable ascription. Indeed, there is nothing binding him to either the castle or the village where he finds himself, and he could freely depart; he faces no accusation, no conviction, no possible guilt, just a rejection of his person beyond his bare, minimal presence. He has bound himself to the castle in hope that it will affirm his being.[55] Thus, on the one hand, K. is completely on his own; in this sense he is *independent*, a singularity, yet this independence is completely ineffective and abstract, for it cannot establish any universal actuality for others. All that is constant in his actions is their asymmetry, their failure. On the other hand, K. is completely *dependent* on the castle, for he believes it to be the instance that objectively establishes his being, even as he is oblivious to the fact that he is in a universal swamp devoid of proper symmetry, where the objective actuality of his actions is distorted in their very actualization. The castle is a dark distillation of all that goes wrong in the space of non-action; nonetheless, K. harbors a senseless belief in some pure core. But if there is a core to the castle it is even more rotten than its manifestations. This is evident by the fact that the closer K. comes to the castle (as well as the closer Josef K. comes to the court) the more it becomes dirty, disorganized, unstructured, bedridden, sickly, lewd, decadent, obscure, perverted, etc. Of course, it is no coincidence that K. is (supposedly) a land surveyor in a foreign space that seems impossible to survey. Even if he were to be recognized as a land surveyor, he would be unable to survey the land, since the land itself is incoherent, unstructured – another testament to the fact that it is not a space of action. There is no way to survey a swamp; each part continuously flows into another. Yet, there is nonetheless a logic to this swamp world, because besides its destructive potential it is this unstable seasickness-inducing ground that makes freedom possible.

---

55 Hence K.'s strange dismissal of Frieda's equally strange (in light of the non-locality of the story) geographically localizable suggestion of emigration (again, notice the "lure" that binds him, not to Frieda, but to the castle): "He slowly removed his arm from her waist, and they sat for a while in silence, until Frieda, as if K.'s arm had given her a warmth that was essential to her now, said: 'I won't endure this life here any more. If you want to keep me we must go away, emigrate, go anywhere, to the south of France, to Spain.' 'I can't emigrate,' said K. 'I came to this place meaning to stay here, and stay I will.' And in a spirit of contradiction which he didn't even try to explain he added, as if to himself: 'What could have lured me to this desolate part of the country but a longing to stay here?'" (Kafka, *The Castle* 121–122).

4 Conclusion: The Concrete Universality of the Swamp

"Concrete" literally means "to be grown together." Hegel vigorously argues for a "concrete universal," which means that it is *grown together* with "singularity." It would be wrong to assume that either term had an independent existence *before* their concrete unity (this is what Hegel diagnoses as abstract thinking). Rather, the universal is universal only in and through the singular, and the singular only in and through the universal. In a famous example, Hegel recounts a joke about a man who goes to the market and asks for fruit; when the man is offered pears, apples, cherries, etc. he declines, since he had asked for fruit, *not* pears, apples, cherries, etc. This is a clear case of abstract thinking, where universality (fruit) is held strictly apart from singularities (pears, apples, etc.). However, we should not be led to think that Hegel is "against" abstraction as such, for it is an essential part of his logical procedure: "we must pay due respect to the infinite force of the understanding in splitting the concrete into abstract determinacies and plumbing the depth of the difference – this force which alone is at the same time the mighty power causing the transition of the determinacies."[56] Hegel always uses the force of abstraction to show that it is unsustainable and that it must transition into the concrete; by holding it apart in abstract difference, bringing it into tension and eventual collapse, he shows the necessity of their concrete unity. In Kafka's world, we are placed in the infinite tension between the abstract and the concrete, suspended over "the depths of difference." Or, to be more precise, we also receive the concrete, but it is always distorted, swampy, grown together in monstrous ways. This distortion is not something external; rather, it is inscribed (as a necessary possibility) within the nature of the concrete universal. If freedom is to be by oneself in the other, as Hegel defines it, then the possibility of this equally entails the possibility of being alienated from oneself in the other. What "the swamp" entails is the necessary openness and complicity between the two sides, the singular and the universal, but in an always potentially destabilized way. More precisely, this means that the concrete universal is both *necessary and unstable*: it is necessary that both extremes are grown together, yet by their being grown together the concrete universal also becomes unstable, open, both to production and to destruction. It is, paradoxically, this necessity of the concrete that

---

56 G.W.F. Hegel, *Wissenschaft der Logik*, Werke in zwanzig Bänden, Bd. 6, Suhrkampf Verlag, Frankfurt/M.: 1970, 286; G.W.F. Hegel, *The Science of Logic*, trans. George di Giovanni, Cambridge University Press, Cambridge 538–539.

opens a world of possibility – and possibility is, of course, always double-edged, stable and unstable, for both ways are opened: un-freedom and freedom are two sides of the same structure (just as the structure of consciousness is also the possibility of insanity, not some external state). Kafka's characters are un-free but *not* because there is no relation to the space where they act (this would be something bordering on absolute imprisonment in one's own body), but because of the specific stifling relation that ensues from a de-structured space. In Kafka's "swamp world" there are interpenetrations, relations, communications: it is erotically charged, but always only to the effect of stripping the protagonist of the efficacy of his proper agency, reducing him to a dog or a bug, a faithful outcast caught in the same world that has cast him out, never within, never without. But, and this is the important positive point, it is the same swampy structure of never-within-never-without that opens the space of freedom, and this necessary openness means that freedom is never guaranteed because it is fundamentally complicit with un-freedom. The contradictory ground of possibility is seasickness on dry land. The "infinite force" of Kafka is that in taking the abstraction and suspension to its highest intensity, he necessarily, albeit almost reluctantly, shows the distorted "inner face" of freedom.

Works Cited

Adorno, Theodor W. and Walter Benjamin, *The Complete Correspondence, 1928–1940*. Ed. Henri Lonitz. Trans. Nicholas Walker (Cambridge: Polity Press, 1999).

Agamben, Giorgio, *Potentialities: Collected Essays in Philosophy* (Stanford: Stanford University Press, 1999).

Badiou, Alain, *Theory of the Subject*. Trans. Bruno Bosteels (London: Continuum, 2009).

Bataille, George, *Eroticism*. Trans. Mary Dalwood (London: Penguin Modern Classics, 2012).

Benjamin, Walter, *Benjamin Über Kafka: Texte, Briefzeugnisse, Aufzeichnungen* (Frankfurt/M.: Suhrkamp Verlag, 1981).

Benjamin, Walter, *Illuminations*. Ed. Hannah Arendt. Trans. Harry Zohn (New York: Schocken Books, 1969).

Butler, Judith, *The Psychic Life of Power* (Stanford: Stanford University Press, 1997).

Deleuze, Gilles, *Desert Islands and Other Texts 1953–1974*. Ed. David Lapoujade. Trans. Michael Taormina (Los Angeles: Semiotext(e), 2004).

Freud, Sigmund, *The Uncanny*. Trans. David McLintock (London: Penguin Books, 2003).

Hegel, G.W.F., *Enzyklopädie der philosophischen Wissenschaften im Grundrisse I: Die Wissenschaft der Logik* [Werke in zwanzig Bänden, Bd. 8] (Frankfurt/M.: Suhrkampf Verlag, 1970).

Hegel, G.W.F., *Enzyklopädie der philosophischen Wissenschaften im Grundrisse III: Die Philosophie des Geistes* [Werke in zwanzig Bänden, Bd. 10] (Frankfurt/M.: Suhrkampf Verlag, 1970).

Hegel, G.W.F., *Phänomenologie des Geistes* [Werke in zwanzig Bänden, Bd. 3] (Frankfurt/M.: Suhrkampf Verlag, 1970).

Hegel, G.W.F., *Phenomenology of Spirit*, trans. A.V. Miller (Oxford: Oxford University Press, 1971).

Hegel, G.W.F., *Philosophy of Mind*. Trans. A.V. Miller (Oxford: The Clarendon Press, 1971).

Hegel, G.W.F., *Philosophy of Nature, Vol. I–III*. Trans. M.J. Petry (London: Unwin Brothers Limited, 1970).

Hegel, G.W.F., *The Science of Logic*. Trans. George di Giovanni (Cambridge: Cambridge University Press, 2010).

Hegel, G.W.F., *Wissenschaft der Logic* [Werke in zwanzig Bänden, Bd. 6] (Frankfurt/M.: Suhrkampf Verlag, 1970).

Kafka for the Twenty-First Century. Eds. Stanley Corngold and Ruth V. Gross (New York: Camden House, 2011).

Kafka, Franz, *The Castle*. Trans. Anthea Bell (Oxford: Oxford University Press, 2009).

Kafka, Franz, *Erzählungen* (Frankfurt/M.: Fischer Taschenbuch Verlag, 1992).

Kafka, Franz, *Hochzeitszvorbereitungen auf dem Lande und andere Prosa aus dem Nachlass* (Frankfurt/M.: Fischer Taschenbuch Verlag, 1983).

Kafka, Franz, *Kafka's Selected Stories: New Translations, Backgrounds and Contexts, Criticism*. Ed. and trans. Stanley Corngold, Norton Critical Edition (New York: Norton, 2007).

Kafka, Franz, *The Metamorpohis and Other Stories*. Trans. Willa and Edwin Muir (New York: Schocken Books, 1995).

Kafka, Franz, *Der Prozeß* (Frankfurt/M.: Fischer Taschenbuch Verlag, 1983).

Kafka, Franz, *Das Schloß* (Frankfurt/M.: Fischer Taschenbuch Verlag, 1983).

Kafka, Franz, *The Trial*. Trans. Mike Mitchell (Oxford: Oxford University Press, 2009).

Kafka, Franz, *The Zürau Aphorisms*. Trans. Michael Hofmann (London: Harvill Secker, 2006).

Pippin, Robert, *Hegel's Practical Philosophy: Rational Agency as Ethical Life* (Cambridge: Cambrige University Press, 2008).

Sokel, Walter, *The Myth and Power of the Self: Essays on Franz Kafka* (Detroit: Wayne State University Press, 2002).

Arnaud Villani
The Necessary Revision of the Concept of the Universal: Kafka's "Singularity"

A harmful habit, which includes the argument of authority (*Magister dixit!*), consists in understanding words as they occur in language, without questioning their semantic make-up afresh. Doing so risks making a serious mistake in the interpretation of Parmenides's *Poem* if one maintains that here the verb *echein* indicates possession ("to have"), although in fact it designates a "firm hold," and if, in political philosophy in general, one inherits the term *kratos* from the tradition without detecting another meaning in it besides that of "dominant power." Philology is a highly cautious discipline and aims to achieve all required scientificity, but at least it has the audacity to assume that behind every word is a semantic, and thus noetic, evolution.

This semantic evolution, which often proceeds by derivation, manifests what is at work in words, this "intangible mist" that the Stoics called *lekton*, or "meaning." Yet any particular meaning derives from a general meaning. Hegel gives an account of this meaning and of its evolution over time when he writes, in *The Phenomenology of the Spirit* [*Die Phänomenologie des Geistes*],

> Time was when man had a heaven, decked and fitted out with endless wealth of thoughts and pictures. The significance of all that is, lay in the thread of light by which it was attached to heaven; instead of dwelling in the present as it is here and now, the eye glided away over the present to the Divine, away, so to say, to a present that lies beyond. [...] Now [...] man's mind and interest are so deeply rooted in the earthly that we require a like power to get them raised above that level. His spirit [...] seems to long for the mere pitiful feeling of the divine in the abstract, and to get refreshment from that.[1]

Here already meaning clearly appears as a global way of seeing things, an intuition linked to the *Everything of things*. An example: So long as what was essential for the traditional community rested on the idea that *reciprocal exchange* creates what is shared – an idea clearly manifested in the *potlatch*, in exogamy, and more

---

1 Georg Wilhelm Friedrich Hegel, *The Phenomenology of Mind, Volume 1*, trans. James Black Baillie, Routledge, New York 2014 [1910], 8.

A previous version of this chapter appeared as "Kafka et la conscience de l'abîme," in *Cahiers de l'Herne* 108: "Kafka," eds. Jean-Pierre Morel and Wolfgang Asholt, Paris Éditions de l'Herne, Paris 2014, 194–199.

generally in the "ceremonial gift"[2] – a festive banquet where each person benefitted from "equal parts" (the *daîs eisê*, the *daps*) was welcomed as a great benefit to the group. As the meaning of this practice has weakened, the calculation of the operation's cost has emerged, and then of the ruin that it would entail. According to "the era of the conception of the world" and the passing of time, the same root, *+dap–*, thus aims to express a "festive banquet to seal the community" (*daps*) in a very positive sense, and an "extravagant expenditure" (*dapané*) and "ruinous damage" (*dam-num* in Latin) in a very negative sense. This demonstrates that the world is forms which are at once recognizable: moreover, these forms are *reproduced by the senses* and *instituted by meaning* from an ideational whole; this whole corresponds to the concrete reality of the *thought* of this era, which the *semantic-noetic evolution* translates.

Meaning determines everything, yet in a *Wechselwirkung* ("interaction") its opposite occurs as well. As Medieval thinkers claimed of the Being and the One, meaning and the whole are exchangeable. In the seemingly obvious and transparent term "universal," one must therefore suspect the thickness of a semantic make-up that affects the couple "universal/singular." As we know, this pair resonates with another pair: "general/particular." One might think that all has been said in repeating that the universal is not the general and the singular not the particular. Yet I do not consider this division as anything but a *trompe-l'oeil*. The real break divides between a way of grasping "all things" in a link that is *polemical* and yet also bound up with a whole that does not overshadow, and an entirely different way of "seeing things," one that assumes the conceptual and "intelligible" universality of the transcendent, while singularity would be the pitiful trace of the body.

Indeed, "rational" thought, which comes to encompass and dominate all of Occidental thought under the name of *logos*, constitutes a prerequisite to any serious conception of the real: the universal *dominates and overshadows* the real. This implies a disjunction between the things that surround us and the One-Whole, which, simply through the force of what is intelligible, presents itself as inalterable majesty, beyond the sensory world. Such logic is disjunctive and exclusive, since the universal and the particular, the Whole as One and all multiple things, natural consorts, are considered direct adversaries: "either ... or." Joining the camp of the multiple, the particular and the singular will no longer be able to rid themselves of this suspicion of divergent organization, where everything

---

2 This major ethnographic concept was brought up anew and explained masterfully in Marcel Hénaff, *The Price of Truth: Gift, Money, and Philosophy* [*Le Prix de la vérité: Le Don, l'argent, la philosophie*], trans. Jean-Louis Morhange, Stanford University Press, Stanford 2010.

tends to scatter itself in countless directions, awaiting the astringent power of the One. Whether they wish to or not, the particular and the singular incline towards unthinkable chaos. Plato insists on this: they are on the side of the *alogos*, the unsayable, the unthinkable, the irrational, the "too much."[3]

This *noetic* decision (since everything occurs in thought, and, as Gustave Guillaume puts it, is "thought-enveloped") fractures the world. For, inversely, every community's principles of reciprocity are encapsulated in Heraclitus's oxymoronic formula *hen panta*, from which the first German Romantics took their rallying cry *Hen kai pan*. Does this expression offer a wise aphorism? Does it summarize the thought of Heraclitus, under the name of the "unity of opposites," or, to speak with Nicolas de Cusa, of "*coïncidentia oppositorum*"? Is it a colorful period of the history of philosophy? No. It summarizes the strong thought that precedes the great "rationalism." Yet, in my opinion, that this thought precedes the great current of Occidental logocentrism does not mean that it is inferior; indeed, I would consider it in certain ways superior, subtler.

One must explain why the expressions "*hen panta*" and "*hen kai pan*," with their variant "*hen diapheromenon heautôi*," from the beginning of Hölderlin's novel *Hyperion* – all expressions revered by Hölderlin, the two Schlegel brothers, Schelling, Novalis, and Nietzsche – would be "noetic" in this very way. For it is clear that for a long time we no longer understood either their import or their stakes. Reading Kafka's works, notably the diaries, letters, and *Reflections on Sin, Suffering, Hope and the True Way* [*Betrachtungen über Sünde, Hoffnung, Leid und den wahren Weg*], reveals the character strangely "displaced" from his work and offers irrefutable evidence that *he does not think like us*. And I would willingly believe that he shares with traditional communities certain portions of thought on what is essential, an issue the German Romantics and Nietzsche attempted to rethink, shaped as they were by pre-Socratic and heterodox mystical culture (via Böhme). We do not wish to admit it, because we continue to feel that they thought incorrectly, that they *stammered thought* during this era, and that, luckily, progress has done its work from the Primitives to us. Yet let us recall the insistence and the precision with which Lévi-Strauss showed that the "savage mind" knew how to *look at* the surrounding world incomparably better than we do, for it did so with the eyes as well as the spirit.

We thus begin to define the problem of the universal and of its necessary revision. *Hen panta* means "an entire world in the energizing tension of opposites." The textual form of this expression, the oxymoron (think of the simple word *deinon*, meaning marvelous and terrifying at once) confronts two completely

---

3 See Plato's *Philebus*, 21d.

concrete elements, with the promise of *resisting* as long as necessary. One could demonstrate that *hen* is totalizing Unity,[4] neither presupposed nor all-encompassing nor transcendent, which *creates itself* at the same time as the resistance of its opposite continues. This opposite is *Panta*, "everything" in its immense, incalculable diversity, brought together in "a living, a thousand times divided, inward whole."[5] Instead of ridiculously opposing multiplicity, as though it was a *poikilos* – that is, on one hand a variegation responsible for the ills of the city-state, and, on the other, an ethereal Unity of perfect order and idyllic essence, always situated beyond, in that inaccessible, other place which preserves it from encroaching time, yet in fact immediately a *dead unity*[6] – the thought of the Pre-Socratics (and it is significant that one finds an identical notion in the work of the Chinese Lao Tseu and Confucius, during a comparable period) "stands firm" and maintains the principle of this paradoxical union, seemingly impossible yet nonetheless vibrant and alive, the *One-in-All-Things*.

So we understand why pairs were *invented*: "universal/singular" and "general/particular." Through their difference that has no stakes they are destined to create a diversion, to hide the Platonic operation that has effaced from thought the possibility of a "symbolic" confrontation, leaving neither dead nor vanquished nor slave nor inferior. We now know enough about this venerable way of thinking, which compels us to redefine the term of the universal, and thus, of the singular. Kafka understood, at least intuitively, what I have just evoked, and this is why he is a *step ahead* of us. His replies in *Conversations with Janouch* [*Gespräche mit Kafka*] bear witness to this, even if the renderings of the conversations are not always reliable.[7] For what a cross and what bewilderment the originality of Kafka's thought represents, particularly for those of us who, at the end of a propagandistic bimillennium, believed Plato and followed his disjunction

---

4 I tried to do so in *Parménide, le Poème* [*Parmenides, the Poem*], text and translation, in collaboration with Pierre Holzerny, followed by *Parménide et la dénomination* [*Parmenides and the Denomination*] (Hermann, Paris 2008), and in *Parménide* (Sils–Maria, "Cinq Concepts" series, 2013).

5 Friedrich Hölderlin, "Letter No. 172: To his Brother," in *Essays and Letters on Theory*, ed. and trans. Thomas Pfau, SUNY Press, Albany 1988, 139. See my study "Figures de dualité: Hölderlin et la tragédie grecque" ("Figures of Duality: Hölderlin and Greek Tragedy"), in *Cahier de l'Herne Hölderlin*, Éditions de l'Herne, Paris 1989, 277–296.

6 One must remember that Aristophanes, mocking Socrates, whom he considers ridiculous in a straw basket in mid-air, named this beyond "the clouds." Schopenhauer made of this the *uedäh* (an invented, and untranslatable, term) and Master of the Absolute, and Nietzsche the "field-dispensary of the soul" and the "telephone from the beyond."

7 See Gustav Janouch, *Gespräche mit Kafka*, Fischer Verlag, Berlin 1968, published in English as *Conversations with Kafka*, trans. Goronwy Rees, New Directions, New York 2012 [1971].

unconditionally, not stopping to exclude, to judge, to exterminate without noticing.

It is vital to understand the implications of this forgotten noetic. We see that the simple foundation of Occidental logic, the "principle of identity," in the form of "non-contradiction" and the "excluded middle," is the *machine of war* that overcame the type of thought that makes use of "both ... and" as an "immanent disjunctive synthesis."[8] We see that the *discriminating* principle – exciting for the concept, rich in innumerable scientific triumphs, yet deadly for the "living whole" – enters thought, owing to what appears to be the base of all logic. Adding to the classical descriptions of the failures of dichotomy, Deleuzian reflection associates disjunction with that which motivates it. I separate the fluxes: I block one; the other I let pass. To what end? In order to manifest the exercise of *domination*, to *capitalize* on an income, to make us aware of the presence of an *End*.

If A cannot be B, at the same time and from the same perspective, this unquestionably distances the *possibility of metamorphosis*. One could imagine Plato very busy with this task, once he considered himself the nomothete of his new city-state. For in ostracizing the poets, he excluded their tales of metamorphosis. But above all, disjunction, when overshadowed by a transcendence (the Deleuzian name derives from this: "transcendent disjunctive synthesis": "either this or that, not both"), disseminates everywhere the contagion of a spirit of domination, hidden by its final End. It is in the name of glorious tomorrows, of Paradise regained, of final Reconciliation, that the *domination* of person over person and of the whole over the all of the earth's resources can be exerted. The Universal is the name that covers these wrongdoings.

Less obviously, on the level at which Kafka works, this *spirit of domination* – which logic exerts or instrumentalizes for its own ends – insinuates itself into language so as to be used in every sentence, in every thought. We see how, since the Greeks, the spirit of hegemony deposits itself in the furrows of language. Benveniste has shown the link between powerful desire (*oregô* in Greek: "to aspire to something with all one's might") and the organization of territory and of the city-state in the *Imperium* (+*reg*–, the same root, is present in *regula, regio* – in the double sense of straight line and of region – and in *rex, directus*, and *Recht*, the Law). More particularly, the respective vocabularies of the concept and of practice converge on one point: *taking charge in a purely dominant way*. How can one be

---

8 It is this "both ... and" that comes into play to the fullest in *The Castle* [*Das Schloss*] and turns K. into a person who is at once guilty and innocent, the Helpers into entities that change before our eyes, intimates into strangers, inaccessible Klamm into a sleepwalking beer drinker. See my *Lectures du Château de Kafka* [*Readings of Kafka's Castle*], Belin, Paris 1984, 18, 34, 53, and 54.

astonished, then, by the constant presence of curving roads or of crookedness (*Krumm*), of this proximity of the fall, physically present in the Helpers?

It is not coincidence that the same image – of leading herds or of men become cattle – runs through language. In Greek, *epagô* – precisely the verb that constitutes the concept in Socrates's "epactic discourse" – means "to lead the herd to line up, in order to pass, one by one, through the bottleneck of the enclosure." There we find the origin of *arithmetic* counting. The verb *reducere* shares the same nature: "to lead the herds back toward the enclosure," from which "reduce" derives. And one can follow with the aggressiveness that Levinas noticed in *der Begriff*, or in *concipere*, which he translates as "the grasp of the concept" (*la griffe du concept*). We encounter the same thing, in Roman law, in the symmetry of *aikhmalôtos* ("caught at the spear's tip," in order to designate the slave) – and *mancipere* ("to take control of a slave, designating him as such by the gesture of putting one's hand (*man–*) on his shoulder").

Thus, we can appreciate the concealed intentions contained in the post-Platonic concept *katholou* (literally: *kata holou*, "according to the point of view of all") and the Latin concept *universus*, "turned towards the one." The "all" of the universal, dedicated to concept and to logic, therefore no longer has any connection with the "mark of everything in the singular." We know that "*singulus*" is formed from +*sin–* (*ein–*, in German), the same word as *heis*, *(s)mia*, *hen* in Greek ("that which presents itself one by one, as a single unit, *singulatim*") and +*gulus* ("marking a power of rebellious life"; in German, *–zeln*). Even placed along the linguistic and grammatical thread that assigns it to be nothing but the "straight man" of the universal, the singular rebels: it is a "wild boar" (well named: *loner*) at bay. But we will utilize precisely this resistance of the singular to make of it what must, at all costs, be tamed: repetition of the Platonic gesture that designates the sphere of the *sensoripathic* sensibility as responsible for all drift towards chaos, itself a true challenge for Reason, which dreams of nothing but order. From this comes the topos of "mastering" the passions.

"Turned towards the One," then, like the gaze of the people raised "unanimously" towards the face of the Monarch in the frontispiece of Hobbes's *Leviathan*. The "general" still carries with it something blurry and alive, that is to say, turbulent, won from a symbolic and hard-fought struggle that does not kill (the slave is put to death during his lifetime). In fact, the "general" carries with it the notion of species (*genos*, *genus*) and of natural filiation; above all, it represents the translation of the Greek *koinon*, which is fundamental to politics. *Ta koina*, the equivalent of *ta dêmosia*, or public affairs (*res publica*), the "common good": this still concerns a *concrete* community. Its opposite, the "particular," is precisely the "private" sphere (*ta idia*), which the Greeks find so hardly incompatible with the common good that they braid and connect one sphere with the other in order to construct political man, the citizen.

In the same way, such a particular conception of an interweaving of religion and politics preserves something of the thought that we detected with the Pre-Socratics: the resistance of the affronted parties and their successful struggle, the "two-in-one," comes to constitute a whole. In extirpating the concrete, the general embraces plurality. But, as Hegel showed via the expressions "the Now is night" and "the Here is a tree,"[9] whose contrariness is equally valid, all that is lived expresses, once uttered, nothing but "generalities." Now, here, I: this is the superposing of all times and all singular "I"s and of their joint *negation*. It is this negation, returned to itself, which constitutes the universal and institutes the superiority of "mediation" over "immediacy." There is seemingly nothing to object to this universal, as it is conceptualized, save that the Nietzschian criticism of language (that it is a double metaphorization of sensation) leaves us with one eye open to the *negative residue* of this overcome negation.

Artists have never been mistaken in this. Their "germinal" eye has never ceased to see Hegel's preliminary condemnation of "sensitive certainty" as a "false start."[10] In reality, this *sinnliche Gewissheit* never abandons them; it is their pedestal, from the first impression ("the *instress*" of the ecclesiastical poet Gerard Manley Hopkins) to its final account ("the *inscape*"). *Sensitive certainty does not need to be educated. It is we who must be taught by it.* If one foregoes the initial fidelity to the formidable impression that sparks the desire for the work, then no concept – be it returned to itself multiple times and mediatized as much as one likes – will assist with creation. In this way, the reality of the universal, which presents a purely negative thickness that seems like a pretense, is coupled with a pretentious projection into the Ideal, a finality "blown away" in spiritual Progress and a "majesty" arrived at just the right moment to make "the machine bend." In reality, one sees how much both the general and the universal are ways of *feigning* the notion of living Totality that Hippias, Hippocrates, and the Stoics aspired to perpetuate, in dismissing and ridiculing it, in making it disappear from human possibilities.

This makes us take an extra step. What constituted the force of ancient thought was concern about granting singularity its entire scope by building a

---

9 Hegel, *The Phenomenology of Mind, Volume 1*, chapter A, "Sense-certainty." Pages 90–103 are essential to the representative discussion of the concepts of singularity and universality.
10 To employ Henri Maldiney's term in "La méconnaissance du sentir et de la première parole, ou le faux-départ de la *Phénoménologie de l'Esprit*" in *Regard, parole, espace*, L'age d'homme Press, Lausanne 1973, 254–321.

Totality *from it*. But this totality was also found in *the intuition of a "singular total-ization*," which Hegel calls "sensitive certainty": the pure sentiment that exists, Rousseau's "pure sentiment of existence" in his musings on the Île Saint–Pierre. *Hen kai pan* refers to the artistic double vision, which considers both the speci-ficity of every phenomenon and the reciprocity of the *impact* of that minuscule entity on the Whole and of the Whole on that minuscule entity. We are dealing with Kafka's *Oriental gaze*,[11] which is staggering for us yet was completely natural for the thinkers who preceded the reign of Reason.

To see the whole *and* the minuscule, to combine the concern for the whole and the presence of each part, to conceive of "total parts" and their energy in tension, this is what the Greeks before Plato were able to do, and it is what Kafka can do so extraordinarily. Put another way, one must change the *direction of the gaze*: to choose the level, kindly gaze, which welcomes multiplicity. Kafka on his "vineyard wall,"[12] Kafka on the watch for intensities (gold tooth, nose),[13] Kafka looking in a different way upon at the child who has fallen in another way.[14] To avoid, above all, both the gaze from on high to below, contemptuous and apprais-ing the advantage that will gain the upper hand over what presents itself, and the gaze from below to above, full of a submission that promises desire for venge-

---

11 Elias Canetti refers to Kafka as the "only Chinese writer" of the Occident, in *Kafka's Other Trial: The Letters to Felice* [*Der andere Prozess: Kafkas Briefe an Felice*], trans. Christopher Mid-dleton, Schocken Books, New York 1988 [1974].

12 "[T]here are things in the woods that one could lie in the moss for years and think about," in Max Brod, *Franz Kafka: A Biography* [*Franz Kafka, eine Biographie*], trans. G. Humphreys Roberts and Richard Winston, Da Capo Press, New York 1995, 117. Kafka imagines lying on the "vineyard wall" in his letter of 24 August 1902 to Oskar Pollack. See Franz Kafka, *Letters to Friends, Family and Editors*, trans. Richard and Clara Winston, Alma Classics, Richmond 2014), 4.

13 On the gold tooth, see: "Travel Diaries," in Franz Kafka, *The Diaries 1910–1923*, ed. Max Brod, trans. Joseph Kresh and Martin Greenberg with cooperation of Hannah Arendt, Schocken Books, New York 1976, 426–487, 441; Gilles Deleuze and Felix Guattari, *Kafka: Toward a Minor Literature* [*Kafka. Pour une littérature mineure*], trans. Terry Cochran, University of Minnesota Press, Minne-apolis 1986, 20. On the nose, see Kafka, *Letters to Friends, Family and Editors*, letter to Max Brod, beginning of May 1920, 236–237; and Kafka, *The Diaries*, 10, 36, 39, 57, 78–79. Kafka sketches "a clean outline that could be drawn in five strokes" (passage from letter after 17 October 1917 to Felix Weltsch, in Kafka, *Letters to Friends, Family and Editors*, 160), as he describes his famous angular shadows. This acuity of the gaze is also painstaking. Like Hopkins's, this gaze searches for the real: "the view from a horse leaping the hurdle, say, certainly shows you the utmost pres-ence, the veritable essence of racing" (letter to Director Eisner, 1907, in Kafka, *Letters to Friends, Family and Editors*, 61).

14 Kathi Diamant, *Kafka's Last Love: The Mystery of Dora Diamant*, Basic Books, New York 2003, 9. Diamant relates that Kafka said to a little boy who had just fallen: "How nimbly you fell and how well you got up again!" thereby silencing those who were about to laugh at the child.

ance. In short, "not to judge," to give every entity its absolute right to presence and its worth as undeniable and irreproducible singularity.

Here we find the stakes of a new thinking. For in the way that a poet can be a philosopher and a philosopher a poet, it is *thought* that changes imperceptibly – and then suddenly topples, in the sense of a "noetic evolutionism," comparable to what happens in the morpho-ecological evolution of a species. Kafka's entire oeuvre summons the opposition between two types of thought, which can be summarized in the terms "abrupt" and "direct." Abrupt thought cannot separate each singular thing from the enveloping and nourishing presence of the Whole. Each thing is signaled and seems surrounded by a halo of the "concern for everything." It is thus much more than itself. From the position of the infinitesimal singular thing, the Whole "is visible." There is thus "an entire world" between one thing and another, which forbids us from any examination in simple and straightforward terms and renders all searching impossible, even if it were to be preceded by an *education*, as a way of bending a "spirit" to a "competence" that makes it suited to an End.

It is the Kafkaesque sense of the "everyday mishap," of the impossible search of *The Castle*, of the painful impossibility of reaching "the last door." Everything has an immense and numbing thickness,[15] that of the non-substantial Whole which gave birth to it and supports it. Consequently, the bridges are capable of sensation and bend in pain when stepped upon. Such an abrupt world, without final conclusion, is numbing, exhausting, grueling – marvelous. In every instant, it demands the energy to confront a "cliff," but derives from it only "stony energy." The world with abrupt borders, with sharp-cut edges, is that of the irremediable fall into chaos, an abolishing hole but also and above all a joyous explosion of infinite differences. Hölderlin, Kierkegaard, Kafka, and Hopkins, among many others, would be the guarantors of this difference "in and for itself," which identity would like to eradicate "at all costs," first forcing it "to atone for its sins."[16]

---

15 "[L]eap up another flight of stairs," from Franz Kafka, "The Advocates" ("Der Neue Advokat"), trans. Tania and James Stern, in *The Complete Short Stories*, ed. Nahum N. Glatzer, Vintage Books, London 2005), 449–451, 451. Also: "For he believed that the understanding of any detail, that of a spinning top, for instance, was sufficient for the understanding of all things," from Kafka's "The Top" ("Der Kreisel"), trans. Tania and James Stern, in *The Complete Short Stories*, 444. It is clear that the "general" of which we speak here is an enlargement to the Whole, a thickness of labyrinthian concreteness. In this sense, Kafka takes up Nietzsche's "pathos of distance."
16 It will have become clear that we are speaking here of Deleuze's thesis in *Difference and Repetition* [*Différence et Répétition*], trans. Paul Patton, Continuum Impacts, London 2004. "Expiating" difference in oneself in order to return it to an Identity is the secret goal of all classical

"Direct" thought first breaks infinite value, the intransitivity (as Baudrillard would say) of each thing as it represents the effigy of the Whole. In this conception, the Whole has nothing to do with singular difference; rather, it is the exemption which, as concept, makes it inaccessible to all-consuming time and to the tumult of differences. It is thus normal that the universal initially embraces the character of the concept, when one extracts it from the "attachments"[17] that still hold it in the singular *situation* and bind it to the singular thing. The *process of secularization*, as Detienne and Vernant discuss it in the Greek context,[18] bears as much upon natural space as on public space; it has purely the same internal structure as the suppression of qualified places, as Aristotle also describes them, in favor of a Newtonian, universal, mathematizable space, where the spirit could go *directly* to its End, doing nothing but repeating its desire for absolute control. The world has become its region, and the mathematization of the real is the other side of an appropriation of every thing, freed from its rough, uneven, abrupt character. That which juts out, which does not offer a space suitable to the progress of theorems and armies, which causes, like the fact of Art, a thick-headed and undefined resistance: this is what Deleuze calls *anhômalos* ("anomalous").

At the same time, how Kafka transforms both conceptual relations and all that allows or favors the domination of one thing over another, beginning with the moment when one thing confiscates another's worth for its own benefit, tends to *manifest a resistance*. One sees this in his abandonment of metaphor, which can easily become the unnoticed accomplice of a discourse of assimilating mastery, as well as its metamorphic conversion. In the same spirit, he transfers conceptual links to physical and topographical relations: *bodies and places*. The Law engraves itself in the bloody furrows of solid flesh; imperceptible domination arises as a Castle; the difficulty of encountering others translates them into a bridge and routes whose going and return do not coincide; ever-present chaos

---

philosophy, according to Deleuze. It is not coincidence that he encounters Kafka, Proust, and Bacon on his philosophical path, *ex abrupto*.

17 See Jean Piaget, *The Origin of Intelligence in the Child: Selected Works, Volume 3*, trans. Margaret Cook, Routledge, London 1997 [1953], where, using the genetic method, he analyzes the constitution of the concept as that which dissociates itself and, more precisely, extracts itself from the context of "singular situations."

18 Jean-Pierre Vernant, *Myth and Thought among the Greeks* [*Mythe et pensée chez les Grecs*], trans. Janet Lloyd with Jeff Fort, Zone Books, New York 2006, Part 3, "The Organization of Space," 157–262, and Part 7, Essay 17, "The Formation of Positivist Thought in Archaic Greece," 371–398. See also Marcel Detienne, *The Masters of Truth in Ancient Greece* [*Les Maîtres de vérité dans la Grèce archaïque*], trans. Janet Lloyd, Urzone Books, New York 1996, chapter 5, "The Process of Secularization," 89–106.

produces holes in the walls of houses; the "universal philosophical problem" of choice becomes the boundless delaying of a "boxer's attitude."[19] As all of this is sufficiently known and the references well documented, we need not dwell on it.

Here, a case for interpretation presents itself, as well as a risk of confusion between *the smooth and the striated* and *the line of flight*, as Deleuze takes up the problem that preoccupies Kafka, in order to push it to its limits. Deleuze's empiricism predisposes him to challenge general ideas, that is to say, the universal breaking the moorings of the real. But when, in transposing Riemann's ideas, he creates the notion of "singularities" and reforms the "qualitative" into "intensive multiplicities," he brings the critique of universal-unique thought to a point of enlightenment never before reached. The *smooth* is that which allows the fluxes to project themselves, without transcendent blockages, into an open space, the "plane of immanence." It is there that the fluxes, encountering other fluxes, enter into syntheses and produce the "plane of composition" from which they derive their full power, while also composing both the virtual to which they have remained close and the current without which they would remain shapeless. Thus, the possibility for the fluxes to run unrestrained, to assume the shape that is closest to the speed of chaos while remaining actualized form, is "smooth." The *line of flight* is the possibility for any system to open itself to "chaotic forms," to run beyond itself, without spoiling in the slowing of a transcendence.[20]

This is not to say that this space, smooth as it may be, is *uniform*, like Newtonian space. *The smooth is ridged*, because it is inhabited by infinite folds. Each of these folds is like Thom's catastrophe, invisible if one does not look at it from the right angle. And yet "all turns" to this point. The singular heterogeneities, the haecceities, follow a path "of broken tones." This plane of immanence and consistency is thus not "even"; it is filled with micro-tears and traps, with "manholes."[21] At every moment, it bends. And the bend, at the points of inversion and of doubling back, at the points where fluxes meet, summons the virtual and produces metamorphosis. The voice of the Kalda stationmaster changing into that of a wolf. A human thorax becomes fluid and knows what the body can do, while the wave becomes a surface carrying adventures and dreams, "heads that sing"

19 See Kafka, *Letters to Friends, Family and Editors*, letter of 19 September 1907 to Hedwig W., 32, and letter of 22 September 1907 to Max Brod, 33.

20 We will attend to the extraordinary sense of speed and continuous movement in Kafka's work.

21 Gilles Deleuze and Felix Guattari, "1914: One or Several Wolves?" in *A Thousand Plateaus: Capitalism and Schizophrenia* [*Mille Plateaux, Capitalisme et Schizophrénie II*], trans. Brian Massumi, Athlone Press, London 2000, 26–38.

(Orpheus), birds of the calm between storms (Alcyon), drunken boats. A flux of a human thorax meets a flux of a wave: this constitutes an "event."

Far from the universal, in full and bent singularity, the event is *what occurs everywhere and always*, the *general* (*allgemein*) yet fragmentary face of singularity. It is entirely constituted of singularities, of intensive multiplicities, which never return to the "same." Therefore, if it can be put this way, it is "granulated," as esteemed scholars Ruyer and Simondon have seen it (independently of Deleuze). These protruding grains explain the feeling that Kafka's writing is shaky, uneven: "Almost every word I write jars against the next, I hear the consonants rub leadenly against each other."[22] In the same way, one understands why Kafka struggles to grasp correctly the "small shapes in a formless clamor."[23] For the goal, Truth, has nothing of the general or the universal. If dignity consists in "rais[ing] the world into the pure, the true, the immutable,"[24] then to believe that these lines might indicate the dream of an ideal world would be pure wandering. The true: this is the paradoxical and heart-rending convergence of the "brilliant" detail and of the whole in which it has its place. Writing is the suffering construction of this convergence.

Death is uniform; life is net-like or granulated, yet continuous, of one piece. Yet these singular grains that so fascinate Deleuze and Hopkins, this Hopkinsian *stain* or *speckling* – constituted by all that is real, small as it may be – do not form any sort of striation. Striated space is charted by concepts and an idea of domination associated with an unfindable and transcendent End. Striated space is made of limits allowing the pinpointing of, the falling back on, a unique norm. Striation is the action of transcendence, which transforms any real place into a machine of war. Thus, the effort to spot the trap is constant for the one who "has an eye" on things or "is an eye, but what an eye!": is it a matter of a grain like a quark or *quanta* of the "real," of an "amorphous shape" giving speed and accelerating the singular fluxes, or of a micro-tower of Control?

We understand why Berkeley, Kafka, Bergson, Proust, Foucault, and Deleuze are *minuti philosophi*, "excavators of detail." For, whether novelist or philosopher, when one engages in this type of thought on singularity, one needs a keen eye to discern in the *stoicheion* the little bit of nothingness, which is nevertheless fundamental: whether it is a matter of a *reply of the universal* and of Universals (which it is advisable, by education and spirit of domination, to repeat so that the real "reaches up" to a Paradise) or of a *grain of the real* (irreducible and unattrib-

---

22 Kafka, *The Diaries*, 29, and the allusion to the "billowing overcoat," 196.
23 Kafka, *The Diaries*, 171.
24 Kafka, *The Diaries*, 387.

utable, which could join a flux and make of it a ball of life). This is what Kafka and Kierkegaard assimilate to a *fall*,[25] and Deleuze to the fulguration of a *lightning bolt*.

These, then, are the *general* ideas and the *universal* laws that these philosophers and artists, these *philosopher-artists*, have decided to eject from thought; they are the angulations, the fragments, which they have decided to return to real thought,[26] thereby restoring an old direction of world thought, despised ever since, constricted, forgotten under platonic *vitrification*. Theoretically, this is possible, albeit on condition of finding again the resistant, "thick" singular, linked to the world as a whole. On condition of replacing a war against unity and against multiplicity – a war to the death, a war that destroys the world – with a secret "understanding" of these two "enemies," each reinforcing the other in an invigorating fight. On condition of being on watch to verify ceaselessly in the singular the promise of life or the certainty of death. On condition of leading a constant battle in order to give back to words their freely inventive worth and their power of affect.[27] Such would be the *charter of singularity*, always to be rewritten.

Works Cited

Brod, Max, *Franz Kafka: A Biography*. Trans. G. Humphreys Roberts and Richard Winston (New York: Da Capo Press, 1995).

Canetti, Elias, *Kafka's Other Trial: The Letters to Felice*. Trans. Christopher Middleton (New York: Schocken Books, 1988 [1974]).

Deleuze, Gilles, *Difference and Repetition*. Trans. Paul Patton (London: Continuum Impacts, 2004).

---

25 On the fall: Kafka, *The Diaries*, 237 and 302; Franz Kafka, *Letters to Milena* [*Briefe an Milena*], trans. Tania and James Stern, Schocken Books, New York 1965, 219; and Kafka, *Letters to Friends, Family and Editors*, letter of 28 August 1904 to Max Brod, 26.

26 This issue necessitates a long discussion to articulate at once how ingenious Hegel's solution with "the concrete universal" is and yet how it distances even further the singularity of the status it deserves. It is likely that this failure results from the collusion that he fabricates between "reality" and "efficiency" in the concept of *Wirklichkeit*. That way, one is sure that all singularity will be submitted (in the inverse sense of the Deleuzian "fold") to the destiny of the Universal, on the way to the *Versöhnung* and the *Vollendung* of the Spirit. One could say that Deleuze chose the way of inefficiency (as witness, his fight for "madness," called "without work") in seeing precisely in *Entfremdung* the real (passive) efficiency of the *Entäußerung*: schizophrenia.

27 And not of affection or of passion, as Deleuze repeats time and again, notably in *What is Philosophy?* [*Qu'est-ce que la philosophie?*] in collaboration with Félix Guattari, Columbia University Press, New York 1994.

Deleuze, Gilles and Felix Guattari, "1914: One or Several Wolves?" in *A Thousand Plateaus: Capitalism and Schizophrenia*, trans. Brian Massumi (London: Athlone Press, 2000), 26–38.

Deleuze, Gilles and Felix Guattari, *Kafka: Toward a Minor Literature*. Trans. Terry Cochran (Minneapolis: University of Minnesota Press, 1986).

Detienne, Marcel, *The Masters of Truth in Ancient Greece*. Trans. Janet Lloyd (New York: Urzone Books, 1996).

Diamant, Kathi, *Kafka's Last Love: The Mystery of Dora Diamant* (New York: Basic Books, 2003).

Hegel, Georg Wilhelm Friedrich, *The Phenomenology of Mind, Volume 1*. Trans. James Black Baillie (New York: Routledge, 2014 [1910]).

Hénaff, Marcel, *The Price of Truth: Gift, Money, and Philosophy*. Trans. Jean-Louis Morhange (Stanford: Stanford University Press, 2010).

Hölderlin, Friedrich, *Essays and Letters on Theory*. Ed. and trans. Thomas Pfau (Albany: SUNY Press, 1988).

Janouch, Gustav, *Conversations with Kafka*. Trans. Goronwy Rees (New York: New Directions, 2012 [1971]).

Janouch, Gustav, *Gespräche mit Kafka* (Berlin: Fischer Verlag, 1968).

Kafka, Franz, *The Diaries 1910–1923*. Trans. Joseph Kresh and Martin Greenberg with cooperation of Hannah Arendt. Ed. Max Brod (New York: Schocken Books, 1976).

Kafka, Franz, *Letters to Friends, Family and Editors*. Trans. Richard and Clara Winston (Richmond: Alma Classics, 2014).

Kafka, Franz, *Letters to Milena*. Trans. Tania and James Stern (New York: Schocken Books, 1965).

Maldiney, Henri, "La méconnaissance du sentir et de la première parole, ou le faux-départ de la *Phénoménologie de l'Esprit*" in *Regard, parole, espace* (Lausanne: L'age d'homme Press, 1973).

Piaget, Jean, *The Origin of Intelligence in the Child: Selected Works, Volume 3*. Trans. Margaret Cook (London: Routledge, 1997 [1953]).

Vernant, Jean-Pierre, *Myth and Thought among the Greeks*. Trans. Janet Lloyd with Jeff Fort (New York: Zone Books, 2006).

Villani, Arnaud, *Lectures du Château de Kafka* (Paris: Belin, 1984).

Section 2: **Before the Law**

Eli Schonfeld
Am-ha'aretz: The Law of the Singular. Kafka's Hidden Knowledge

> It is not so much we who read Kafka's words; it is they who read us. And find us blank.
> – George Steiner, "A Note on Kafka's 'Trial'"[1]

1 Prologue

There is in Franz Kafka's prose a density reminiscent of the literary quality found in the Scripture. In his letter to Gertrud Oppenheim dated 25 May 1927, Franz Rosenzweig writes: "The people who wrote the Bible seem to have thought of God in a way much like Kafka's."[2] Theodor W. Adorno felt it too: paraphrasing the first words of Rashi's[3] commentary on the first verse of *Genesis*, he wrote of Kafka's text: "Each sentence says: interpret me." Adding, immediately after: "and none will permit it."[4]

Adorno's observation applies first and foremost to Kafka's parable "Before the Law" ("Vor dem Gesetz"), a text which, according to George Steiner, contains

---

1 George Steiner, "A Note on Kafka's 'Trial,'" in *No Passion Spent: Essays 1978–1995*, Yale University Press, New Haven and London 1996, 239–252, 251.
2 Quoted by Martin Buber in "The How and Why of Our Bible Translation," in Martin Buber and Franz Rosenzweig, *Scripture and Translation* [*Die Schrift und ihre Verdeutschung*], trans. Lawrence Rosenwald with Everett Fox, Indiana University Press, Bloomington and Indianapolis 1994, 205–219, 219.
3 Rabbi Shlomo Itzhaki, the major eleventh-century French commentator of the Hebrew bible and the Talmud.
4 Theodor W. Adorno, "Notes on Kafka" ("Aufzeichnungen zu Kafka"), in *Prisms* [*Prismen: Kulturkritik Und Gesellschaft*], trans. Samuel Weber and Shierry Weber, MIT Press, Cambridge 1982, 243–271, 246.

This study is the fruit of an ongoing discussion which I have had the good fortune to have with Professor Vivian Liska over the past few years. My reading of Kafka's "Before the Law" would not have been possible without this exchange. Even though our ways are not the same, I believe they meet at more than one crossroad. I am also thankful to Professor Moshe Halbertal and the Berkowitz Fellowship at New York University Law School, during which this work was completed.

"the nucleus of the novel [*The Trial*] and of Kafka's vision."[5] This is one of the most if not the single most commented upon of Kafka's texts. We approach it with fear and trembling, intimidated and vulnerable: "Helplessness seizes one face to face with this page and a half,"[6] notes Steiner. Has everything not already been said, been written, been thought, about this text? Like a detective, the commentator seeks a new clue; he searches for the key that will once and for all resolve the enigma, unveil the mystery that hides so secretively within its depths. A mystery which we know everything depends upon. My reader might skeptically wonder at the discovery of yet another interpretation of "Before the Law": "What more can be added?" he asks himself. And he may be right. Perhaps nothing new can be said here; perhaps nothing original is to be added. Perhaps the gates of interpretation are henceforth sealed. We may have arrived too late.

But before this text, do we not always already come too late? Are we not, by definition, latecomers? Has not the doorkeeper always already shut the door? The moment one realizes there is nothing to add to this text might be the very moment one realizes that, *from the start*, this text, though soliciting interpretation, in fact defies interpretation. We are indeed seized by helplessness. Equally impotent before this text, the first reading equals the last reading, because strictly speaking there is no first and no last here. No one comes better equipped, better prepared. Before this text, as before the law, we find ourselves equally exposed, equally empty, without resources. Before this text, we find ourselves, exactly like the story's protagonist, the countryman, the *Mann vom Lande*: ignorant. And from this position the text inspires us infinitely. Something is revealed. Yet we do not know exactly what, or why. We are ignorant, from the beginning to the end. Ignorance will therefore be my gateway into this story.

---

5 Steiner, "A Note on Kafka's 'Trial,'" 250. "Before the Law" was first published in the 1915 New Year's edition of the Jewish weekly *Selbstwehr*. In 1919 the text was included in *A Country Doctor* ("Ein Landarzt") and Kafka later introduced it in chapter 9 of *The Trial*, published posthumously. A brief synopsis of this parable: a countryman, arriving at the door of the law, requests access to it. The doorkeeper denies entry to the countryman, telling him that he cannot enter now. The countryman waits here for months and years, and eventually spends his life in front of the door, trying to persuade the doorkeeper to allow him entrance. Just before dying, the countryman asks the doorkeeper to answer him one question: I have been sitting here all these years, he says to the doorkeeper, yet how is it that nobody else tried to access the law? To this, the doorkeeper answers: this door was meant only for you; when you die I will shut it and go.
6 Steiner, "A Note on Kafka's 'Trial,'" 250.

2 *Am-ha'aretz*

"Before the Law stands a doorkeeper. A man from the country [*Mann vom Lande*] comes to this doorkeeper and requests admittance to the Law."[7] These are the first two sentences of Kafka's "Before the Law." The protagonist of the story has no proper name: he is simply a *Mann vom Lande*, a countryman, or, more literally, a man from the land, from the soil. For an ear versed in Jewish texts, the term evokes a well-known figure: the Talmudic figure of the *am-ha'aretz*.[8] The term *am-ha'aretz* means, literally, the people (*am*) from the earth (*ha'aretz*). In the book of Ezra, the *am-ha'aretz* is opposed to the *am Yehuda*, the people of Judah.[9] In rabbinic literature the figure came to be associated with the *bur*, the ignorant person, and more precisely the person ignorant of the law. Hillel the Sage states, in the *Sayings of the Fathers*: "A *bur* cannot be sin-fearing, an *am-ha'aretz* cannot be pious."[10] Even though there are contradicting opinions in the Talmud as to the nature of the *am-ha'aretz*,[11] this acceptation eventually became the most current

---

7 Franz Kafka, *The Trial* [*Der Process*], trans. Breon Mitchell, Schocken Books, New York 1998, 215.
8 The first to have drawn attention to the affinities between Kafka's *Mann vom Lande* and the Hebrew *am-ha'aretz* was Heinz Polizer in 1966: "Yet in spite of the fact that the description 'the man from the country' hardly seems appropriate at first, it begins to fit K. as soon as it is translated into its Hebrew equivalent *am-ha'aretz*. Kafka was familiar at least with the Yiddish version of the word, *amhoretz*; since 1911 he had occupied himself intensively with Jewish and Yiddish folklore, and the expression actually occurs in the diaries late in November this year." See Heinz Politzer, *Franz Kafka: Parable and Paradox*, Cornell University Press, Ithaca and New York 1966, 174. This reference has since been quoted routinely in the literature on Kafka's "Before the Law."
9 See the book of Ezra, 4, 4–5.
10 See: *Sayings of the Fathers* (2:6) (my rendering). E. E. Urbach remarks that in this passage *bur* – ignorant – and *am-ha'aretz*, are one and the same thing (cf. Ephraim E. Urbach, *The Sages: Their Concepts and Beliefs*, trans. Israel Abrahams, Magnes Press, The Hebrew University, Jerusalem 1975, 585). For a broad survey of the figure of the *am-ha'aretz* in rabbinic literature, see Urbach, *The Sages*, 630–648. For a sociological account of the role of the *am-ha'aretz*, see Louis Finkelstein, *The Pharisees: The Sociological Background of Their Faith*, The Jewish Publication Society of America, Philadelphia 1966, 24–37.
11 Some of these opinions suggest that the *am-ha'aretz* is not necessarily one who is ignorant. In tractate *Berakoth*, for instance, we learn: "Our Rabbis taught: Who is an *am ha'aretz*? Anyone who does not recite the *Shema'* evening and morning. This is the view of R. Eliezer. R. Joshua says: Anyone who does not put on *tefillin*. Ben Azzai says: Anyone who has not a fringe on his garment. R. Nathan says: Anyone who has not a *mezuzah* on his door. R. Nathan b. Joseph says: Anyone who has sons and does not bring them up to the study of the Torah. Others say: Even if one has learnt Scripture and Mishnah, if he has not ministered to the disciples of the wise, he is an *am ha'arez*. R. Huna said: The *halachah* is as laid down by 'Others'" (*Babylonian Talmud: Tractate Berakoth*, trans. Maurice Simon, Soncino Press, London 1984, 47b). The first definition

one, making its way into Jewish folklore and Yiddish culture (*amhorez* – the Yiddish pronunciation of *am-ha'aretz* – refers in Yiddish to someone ignorant in religious matters). Kafka knew both the Talmudic and the Yiddish usage of the term. In his diary entry of 29 November 1911, he combines the two and writes:

> From the Talmud: when a scholar goes to meet his bride, he should take an *amhorez* along, because, immersed that he is in his study, he will not discern the essential.

> [Aus dem Talmud: Geht ein Gelehrter auf Brautschau, so soll er sich einem amhorez mitnehmen, da er zu sehr in seine Gelehrsamkeit versenkt das Notwendige nicht merken würde.][12]

Kafka does not quote the Talmudic passage accurately: in tractate *Baba Bathra* we learn:

> Abaye said: A scholar [*talmid chacham*] who desires to betroth a woman should take with him a layman [*am-ha'aretz*] [so that another woman] might [not] be substituted for her [who would be taken away] from him.

> [Amar abaye: hai tsurba mi-rabanan de-azil li-kedoushe iteta nidbar am-ha'aretz behedia, dilma michluphu lei minei.][13]

The very passage where Kafka evokes the Talmudic *am-ha'aretz* is one that testifies to his own *am aratzut*, to his own ignorance. Kafka is an *am-ha'aretz*. But, as I will try to demonstrate here, his ignorance is not an ordinary one: it is an ignorance conscious of itself. It is, in a way, a Socratic ignorance. An ignorance that hides knowledge: like Socrates, who *knows* he does not know, Kafka, through his ignorance, possesses a deep, hidden knowledge. This hidden knowledge is the knowledge of this ignorance without which it is impossible to depict the *Mann vom Lande* in front of the door of the Law as Kafka does in his parable. This

---

of the *am-ha'aretz* is thus not ignorance; rather, it refers to disrespect of certain commandments or customs. Nevertheless, there are Talmudic sources that clearly define the *am-ha'aretz* as the non-scholarly individual, as the one who does not study Torah. In Tractate *Pesahim*, for instance, we learn: "It was taught, Rabbi said: An *am ha'aretz* may not eat the flesh of cattle, for it is said: 'This is the law [*Torah*] of the beast, and the fowl.' (Lev. XI, 46) Whoever engages in [the study of] the Torah may eat the flesh of beast and fowl, but he who does not engage in [the study of] the Torah may not eat the flesh of beast and fowl" (*Babylonian Talmud: Tractate Pesahim*, trans. H. Freedman, Soncino Press, London 1983, 49b).

12 Franz Kafka, *The Diaries: 1910–1913*, trans. Joseph.Kresh, Schocken Books, New York 1976, 166 (translation slightly modified).

13 *Babylonian Talmud: Tractate Baba Bathra* (Volume 2), trans. Israel W. Slotki, Soncino Press, London 1976, 168a.

hidden knowledge must be unveiled in order for us to truly hear what "Before the Law" teaches.

Who is the *am-ha'aretz*? In the Talmud, this figure is occasionally character-ized as the one who does not follow the rules of purity. The law applies to him, yet he does not live according to the law. This is not due to heresy, however: the *am-ha'aretz* is not a miscreant, an infidel (a *kofer* or an *apikores*). He is disobedi-ent not because he rejects the divine origin of the law or the truth of prophecy, but rather because, simply, he does not know, because he is ignorant. The one who knows the law and disrespects it, who has studied the law and turned his back to it, has a different name in the Talmud: this is the *shana ve-piresh*, the one who has studied the Torah and abandoned it (and whose hatred of the scholar of the law is said to be greater than the hatred of the *am-ha'aretz* towards the *talmid chacham*[14]). The *am-ha'aretz* is not this kind of person. He, again, is ignorant of the law. Yet the principle is known: *Ignorantia legis neminem excusat*, ignorance of the law excuses no one. Ignorance does not free anyone from the authority of the law. In the Talmud tractate *Baba Mezia* we learn: "the *am-ha'aretz*, his intentional sins (*zedonot*) are accounted to him as unwitting errors (*shegagot*)."[15] In ignorance, there is still a relation to the commandment. Ignorance is not an escape from the law; it is a particular modality of it. In the words of the Talmud: it is a relation characterized by the fact that intentional sins are seen *as if* they are non-intentional. This is the singular position of the *am-ha'aretz*: he is in rela-tion to the law without understanding the nature of this relation. His ignorance is characterized not only by the fact that he does not know the law, but also, and mainly, by the fact that he does not know what it implies to be before the law.[16] He is ignorant of the meaning of being-before-the-law. He is, nevertheless, and perhaps more so than anyone else, *before the law*.

The *Mann vom Lande* is the *am-ha'aretz*, the ignorant. In the Talmud, he is systematically opposed to the *talmid chacham*, the scholar of the law, or, more lit-erally, the wise pupil. In Kafka's text, the *am-ha'aretz* stands before the *Türhüter*,

---

14 Cf. Tractate *Pesahim* 49b: "It was taught: He who has studied and then abandoned [the Torah] [hates the scholar] more than all of them" (*The Babylonian Talmud: Tractate Pesahim*, 49b).

15 *Babylonian Talmud: Tractate Baba Mezia*, trans. H Freedman, Soncino Press, London 1986, 33b

16 This is the only way to understand the end of the passage in tractate *Berakoth* (see supra footnote 11) according to which "even if one has learnt Scripture and Mishnah, if he has not ministered to the wise disciple [*talmid chacham*], he is an *am ha'aretz*." In other words: the *am-ha'aretz* is not necessarily ignorant of the law (he knows Scriptures and Mishnah), but ignorant of what it means to stand before the law: he was never in an existential relation with the master (*Rav*), with the true scholar of the Torah. He never served him.

the doorkeeper. Like the *talmid chacham*, the doorkeeper guards the law – he surrounds the law with a fence.[17] In order to better understand the *am-ha'aretz*, we should look closer at his counterpart, the *talmid chacham*. What is the knowledge that characterizes the *talmid chacham*, the knowledge that the *am-ha'aretz* lacks? What precisely is the knowledge of the wise pupil? Answer: the *talmid chacham* does not possess a specific knowledge; instead, he possesses the art of study, the art of *limoud*. He knows how to study. He is familiar with the particular dialectics involved in Talmudic learning, a dialectics which shape his relation to the law and constitute his relation to the divine. This relation is not one of blind obedience before the authority of the law or even before its divine origin. It is a dialectical relation – or, even better, a dia-logical relation – the ultimate goal of which is to *make sense of our existence in the world*. For the wise pupil, therefore, Torah – the object of his learning, of his *limoud* – never simply amounts to law (as the translation of the *Septuagint* (*nomos*), the *Vulgate* (*lex*), or Luther's (*Gesetz*) suggests). Stated more precisely: the knowledge of the *talmid chacham* is the knowledge of the difference between law and Torah (teaching), between a formal legal system, which creates order by disciplining its subjects through coercion and power, and a teaching through which the world makes sense. The wise pupil knows the difference between *Torah* and *nomos*, between *Torah* and *lex*, between *Torah* and *Gesetz*. And this is precisely the knowledge that the *am-ha'aretz* lacks. Therefore, the *am-ha'aretz* is before the law: "Vor dem Gesetz." In Kafka's parable we are, from the start – indeed, before even having started – placed in the horizon of the ignorant, of the *am-ha'aretz*.

It is here that Walter Benjamin's reading of Kafka becomes extremely precious. In what can be considered among his most surprising insights into Kafka, Benjamin claims – against Gershom Scholem – that following the theme of the law in Kafka does not lead anywhere. In his 11 August 1934 letter to Scholem, Benjamin writes:

---

17 These are the opening lines of the *Sayings of the Jewish Fathers*: "Moses received the Torah from Sinai, and he delivered it to Joshua, and Joshua to the elders, and the elders to the prophets, and the prophets delivered it to the men of the Great Synagogue. They said three things: Be deliberate in judgment; and raise up many disciples; and make a fence to the Torah." See *Sayings of the Jewish Fathers, Comprising Pirqe Aboth in Hebrew and English with Notes and Excursuses*, trans. Charles Taylor, Cambridge University Press, Cambridge 1897, 11.

I consider Kafka's constant insistence on the Law to be the point where his work comes to a standstill, which only means to say that it seems to me that the work cannot be moved in any interpretative direction whatsoever from there.[18]

For Benjamin, focusing on the theme of the law in Kafka leads to an impasse. In his letter of 12 November 1934 to Werner Kraft, Benjamin reiterates this idea, adding a crucial point:

He [Scholem] reproached me with passing over Kafka's notion of the "laws" [*Kafka's Begriff der Gesetze*]. At some later time, I will attempt to demonstrate why the concept of the "laws" in Kafka – as opposed to the concept of *"Lehre"* – has a predominantly illusory character and is actually a decoy [*eine Attrappe*].[19]

The concept of law leads to an impasse, writes Benjamin, and adds: in contrast to the concept of *Lehre* (*im Gegensatz zum Begriff der "Lehre"*). While most commentators have focused on Benjamin's negative claim concerning the law in his letters to Scholem and Kraft, his positive claim is just as important, if not more so: rather than focusing on law, Benjamin states, one should attend to the theme of *Lehre* in Kafka's writing. Law would only be a *simulacrum*, a decoy, whose original is *Lehre*. This is a mostly inspiring statement, whose implications I will try to deploy here. At least one thing is clear: according to Benjamin, in Kafka one should distinguish between law and *Lehre*. Is this distinction similar to the *talmid chacham*'s distinction between law and Torah? That is the question.

---

18 Walter Benjamin, *The Correspondence of Walter Benjamin: 1910–1940*, eds. Gershom Scholem and Theodor W. Adorno, trans. M. R. Jacobson and E. M. Jacobson, The University of Chicago Press, Chicago 1994, 453.
19 Benjamin, *The Correspondence of Walter Benjamin: 1910–1940*, 463. In the quotations from Benjamin I will henceforth intentionally refrain from translating the term *Lehre*, because the question of how to translate this term is at the heart of my study. The existing translations of *Lehre* alternate between "doctrine" and "teaching."

3 What is *Lehre*? Walter Benjamin's Reflections on "Before the Law"[20]

One thing is certain: *Lehre*, for Benjamin, is not *Gesetz*, law. What is it positively? In his notes from "Versuch eines Schemas zu Kafka" ("Tentative Outline on Kafka") Benjamin procures a first answer:

> Haggadah is the name that the Jews give to the stories and anecdotes of the Talmud that serve as explanations and confirmations of the *Lehre* – the *Halachah*.[21]

And in "Franz Kafka: *Beim Bau der Chinesischen Mauer*," Benjamin reiterates this saying: "We may remind ourselves here of the form of the *Haggadah*, the name the Jews have given to the rabbinical stories and anecdotes that serve to explicate and confirm the *Lehre* – the *Halachah*."[22] We have here a firsthand translation of *Lehre*: for Benjamin, it stands for *Halachah*. Before pursuing this clue, I will formulate a first consequence stemming from this translation. If *Lehre* means *Halachah*, and if *Lehre* is to be distinguished from *Gesetz*, then we can at least posit that for Benjamin *Halachah* is not *Gesetz*, that is, *Halachah* is not law. This consequence will reveal itself to be of uttermost importance for the understanding of Benjamin's texts on Kafka.

But we still do not know what *Lehre* actually means. Benjamin offers a description of what *Haggadah* is – those Talmudic stories and anecdotes that explain and confirm *Lehre-Halachah* – yet he does not explain what *Lehre* posi-

---

20 In this part I am not trying to procure a synthesis of Benjamin's reading of Kafka or of Kafka's role in Benjamin's thinking. Instead, I propose to elucidate Benjamin's intuition about the importance of *Lehre* in Kafka through a close reading of selected Benjamin texts that relate – directly or indirectly – to Kafka's "Before the Law." For an extensive analysis of Benjamin's 1934 text on Kafka and the meaning of Law in it, see Rodolphe Gashé's excellent article: "Kafka's Law: In the Field of Forces between Judaism and Hellenism," in *MLN* 117.5 (2002), Comparative Literature Issue, 971–1002. Nevertheless, though Benjamin's intuition about the irrelevance of the law in Kafka (in his letters to Scholem and to Kraft) is central to Gashé's reading (see pages 972 and 997), he does not account for the alternative that Benjamin proposes to law in Kafka in his letter to Kraft (that is, *Lehre*).

21 Walter Benjamin, *Gesammelte Schriften* [*Collected Writings*], Vol. II:3, eds. Rolf Tiedemann and Hermann Schweppenhäuser, Suhrkamp Verlag, Frankfurt/M. 1977, 1204.

22 Walter Benjamin, "Franz Kafka: *Beim Bau der Chinesischen Mauer*," trans. Rodney Livingstone, in *Selected Writings, Volume 2: 1931–1934*, eds. Michael W. Jennings, Howard Eiland, and Gary Smith, Harvard University Press, Cambridge 1999, 494–500, 496.

tively is.[23] We have a clue, at least: *Lehre* is *Halachah*. And as we will see, through-out his Kafka texts, Benjamin is entirely consistent in his use of the term *Lehre*, maintaining systematically the equation *Lehre=Halachah*. He does this especially in the texts where he compares Kafka's relation to *Lehre* to the relation between *Halachah* and *Haggadah*. In order to approach the dimension of *Lehre* in Kafka, let us look closer at these texts.

The most suggestive version of this comparison is in Benjamin's letter of 12 June 1938 to Scholem:

> They [Kafka's parables] don't simply lie down at the feet of *Lehre*, the way *Haggadah* lies down at the feet of *Halachah*. Having crouched down, they unexpectedly cuff *Lehre* with a weighty paw.[24]

In its normal state, the *Haggadah* simply lies before *Halachah*, explains Benjamin: *Haggadah* is at the service of *Halachah*. Just as in his "Versuch eines Schemas zu Kafka," *Haggadah* serves *Halachhah*, by explaining and confirming it. Is this the relation to *Lehre* that is found in Kafka's texts? Benjamin answers: no. The *Haggadah-Halachah* relation is brought up here in order to contrast it with Kafka's texts and their relation to *Lehre*: his texts, *contrarily to Haggadah*, do not submit peacefully to *Halachah*, that is, "They don't simply lie down at the

---

23 I will follow here Benjamin's understanding of the relation between *Haggadah–Halachah* without questioning it, although his presentation is simplistic and fails to account for the nu-anced way *haggadah* and *halachah* interact in the Talmud. Benjamin's sources are unclear. In his correspondence, he repeatedly asks Scholem for a copy of Bialik's essay "Halacha and Agga-dah," but it is difficult to determine whether Benjamin received this text by the time he wrote his Kafka essay (there is no mention in the correspondence of Benjamin thanking Scholem for hav-ing sent Bialik's text). Nevertheless, bearing in mind Bialik's extremely sensible phenomenology of the relation between *Halachah* and *Haggadah* in his essay, it is highly improbable that Benja-min read his text. For instance, from Bialik's text, it is impossible to deduce that *Haggadah* is at the service of *Halachah* (see Haim Nahman Bialik, "Halacha and Aggadah," trans. Leon. Simon, in *Revealment and Concealment: Five Essays*, Ibis Editions, Jerusalem 2000, 45–87). For a schol-arly discussion of the nature of *Haggadah* and its relation to *Halachah*, see Joseph Heinemann, "The Nature of the Aggadah," trans. Marc Bregman, in *Midrash and Literature*, eds. Geoffrey H. Hartman and Sanford Budick, Yale University Press, New Haven 1986, 41–54; Moshe Simon-Sho-shan's introduction to his *Stories of the Law: Narrative Discourse and the Construction of Authority in the Mishnah*, Oxford University Press, Oxford 2012; and Berachyahu Lifshitz, "Aggadah Versus Haggadah: Towards a More Precise Understanding of the Distinction," in *Dine Yisrael* 24 (2007), 11–29 of the English section.
24 Walter Benjamin, "Letter to Gershom Scholem on Franz Kafka," trans. Edmund Jephcott, in *Selected Writings, Volume 3: 1935–1938*, eds. Edmund Jephcott and Howard Eiland, Harvard Uni-versity Press, Cambridge 2002, 322–329, 326.

feet of *Lehre*." Kafka's texts and their relation to *Lehre* are not repetitions of the *Haggadah-Halachah* relationship. Instead, declares Benjamin, Kafka's parables raise a weighty paw against *Lehre*.

In order to understand this comparison – which is in fact an *opposition* – and the metaphor with which it ends we must return to the beginning of Benjamin's reasoning. The theme of Benjamin's text from which the paw metaphor is taken concerns the relation between truth, tradition, and transmissibility. Reflecting on the origins of Kafka's world, Benjamin writes:

> The sole basis for his experience was the tradition to which he wholeheartedly subscribed [...] Kafka listened attentively to tradition – and he who strains to listen does not see.[25]

What is this tradition that constitutes the sole basis of Kafka's experience? Two answers are possible: Judaism and literature. Perhaps both are true, and even interconnected: Judaism as literature or literature as Judaism. For reasons that will become clear, I will suppose that Benjamin is referring here to Judaism. Kafka listened with extreme attention to this tradition, that is, to Judaism. But why this extreme attention, why this great effort, which, according to Benjamin, cost Kafka his eyesight? Benjamin answers:

> This listening requires great effort because only indistinct messages reach the listener [*nur Undeutlichstes zum Lauscher dringt*]. There is no *Lehre* to be learned, no knowledge [*Wissen*] to be preserved. What are caught flitting by are snatches of things not meant for any ear.[26]

Vague, indistinct, shattered messages reach Kafka, as if through a heavy fog: no distinct *Lehre*, no distinct knowledge to which he has access. He is doomed to ignorance. Why did no distinct *Lehre* reach him? Benjamin answers: because this tradition to which Kafka is attentive is a broken tradition, an interrupted tradition, a tradition experiencing *a crisis of transmission*, or, in Benjamin's terms, a sickening of tradition, *eine Erkrankung der Tradition*.[27] This sickness results from the loss of a certain form of truth particular to tradition, that is, wisdom. Or, as Benjamin puts it: the loss of truth in its haggadic consistency:

> Wisdom has sometimes been defined as the epic side of truth. Wisdom is thus characterized as an attribute of tradition; it is truth in its haggadic consistency. This consistency of truth has been lost.[28]

25 Benjamin, "Letter to Gershom Scholem on Franz Kafka," 326.
26 Benjamin, "Letter to Gershom Scholem on Franz Kafka," 326.
27 Benjamin, "Letter to Gershom Scholem on Franz Kafka," 326.
28 Benjamin, "Letter to Gershom Scholem on Franz Kafka," 326.

Let us try to understand this dense text. Two years before his letter to Scholem, it was Benjamin himself, in "The Storyteller" ("Der Erzähler"), who defined wisdom as the epic aspect of truth: "Counsel woven into the fabric of real life is wisdom. The art of storytelling is nearing its end because the epic side of truth – wisdom – is dying out."[29] Truth expressed in an epic form is wisdom, which Benjamin, in "The Storyteller," links to the oral dimension. Transmitted orally, wisdom – the epic form of truth – becomes an "attribute of tradition" (and not, for instance, of pure thinking, of philosophy). And it is here that Benjamin, switching registers, turns to Talmudic categories: wisdom is truth in its haggadic consistency. This is what has been lost. The crisis of tradition is first and foremost a crisis of transmission, that is, a crisis of wisdom. And the proposition can be inverted: the crisis of transmission is the crisis of tradition. And this is what preoccupies Kafka: according to Benjamin, Kafka does not worry about truth as such, but rather about wisdom, this particular modality through which truth can be *transmitted* (and not simply *proven*). The genius of Kafka, according to Benjamin, is that having understood this he made a decision: to save transmissibility, not truth.

> This consistency of truth has been lost. Kafka was by no means the first to be confronted with this realization. Many had come to terms with it in their own way – clinging to truth, or what they believed to be truth, and, heavyhearted or not, renouncing its transmissibility. Kafka's genius lay in the fact that he tried something altogether new: he gave up truth so that he could hold on to its transmissibility, the haggadic element.[30]

Kafka's fundamental decision, according to Benjamin: to sacrifice truth in order to save transmissibility. Yet to separate the consistency of truth from truth itself means to separate form and content, and to choose form over content. Hence the form adopted by Kafka's prose: not simply the parable – which always has a meaning, a content – but the *more-than-the-parable*. As Benjamin notes, "His works are by nature parables. But their poverty and their beauty consist in their need to be *more* than parables."[31] It is in order to formulate this "more than," this surplus of Kafka's parable, that Benjamin addresses the *Haggadah-Halachah* relation and the metaphor of the menacing paw. Kafka's more-than-parables raise a menacing paw to *Lehre*. This very *Lehre* that did not reach Kafka, that tradition failed to transmit. Why does Kafka's prose "unexpectedly cuff *Lehre* with

---

29 Walter Benjamin, "The Storyteller: Observations on the Works of Nikolai Leskov" ("Der Erzähler: Betrachtungen zum Werk Nikolai Lesskows"), trans. Harry Zohn, in *Selected Writings, Volume 3: 1935–1938*, 143–166, 146.
30 Benjamin, "Letter to Gershom Scholem on Franz Kafka," 326.
31 Benjamin, "Letter to Gershom Scholem on Franz Kafka," 326.

a weighty paw"? In order to ensure transmissibility. For this to be possible, the haggadic consistency of truth – and not truth itself – should be able to deploy itself entirely, without any hindrance from *Lehre*. In this way, and only in this way, *Lehre* has a chance – surprisingly – to reemerge.

In order to understand this we should turn to one last text: Benjamin's text on Kafka published on the occasion of the tenth anniversary of the Prague author's death. In this text, and more precisely in the passage contending with "Before the Law," Benjamin addresses the question of the nature of Kafka's parables. And again, he evokes *Haggadah* and *Halachah*.

> The word unfolding has a double meaning. A bud unfolds into a blossom, but the boat which one teaches children to make by folding paper unfolds into a flat sheet of paper. This second kind of 'unfolding' is really appropriate to parable; the reader takes pleasure in smoothing it out so that he has the meaning on the palm of his hand. Kafka's parables, however, unfold in the first sense, the way a bud turns into a blossom. That is why their effect is literary. This does not mean that his prose pieces belong entirely in the tradition of Western prose forms; they have, rather, a relationship to religious teachings similar to the one *Haggadah* has to *Halachah* [...] but do we have the *Lehre* which Kafka's parables accompany and which K.'s posture and the gestures of his animals clarify? It does not exist.[32]

Unlike other parables, Kafka's parables unfold the way a bud turns into a blossom. Each opens up little by little, expanding more and more, revealing its potentialities while never disclosing its mystery. The meaning never discloses itself smoothly in the palm of the reader's hand, it never become transparent. This lack of transparency, the fact that no concealed truth is ever disclosed, is what singularizes the literary effect of Kafka's parables. An effect on the border of literature: Kafka's texts still belong to literature, to the history of literature, to the literary tradition, says Benjamin, but not entirely. A part of them belongs to another tradition: they have "a relation to religious teachings similar to the one *Haggadah* has to *Halachah*." Again, for Benjamin, Kafka's parables are to be understood in light of Talmudic categories: *Haggadah* and *Halachah*. Without concealing the fundamental difference between the two: in Kafka's case, unlike the case of the *Haggadah-Halachah* relation, *Halachah* is absent, *Lehre* is lost. Hence the strange situation of Kafka's parables: they incarnate all the properties of *Haggadah* except one, the most essential: they have lost their message. They are clarifications of a lost, absent, *Lehre*. They are like buds unfolding – *ad infini-*

---

32 Walter Benjamin, "Franz Kafka: On the Tenth Anniversary of His Death" ("Franz Kafka: Zur zehnten Wiederkehr seines Todestages"), trans. Harry Zohn, in *Selected Writings, Volume 2: 1931–1934*, 794–818, 802–803.

tum – into blossoms. The haggadic consistency of truth and not truth: it is only at that cost that Kafka's more-than-parables can assure transmissibility.

And yet, even though *Lehre* does not exist *as such* in Kafka's more-than-parables, it ultimately emerge in an original form, through its absence:

> All that we can say is that here and there we have an allusion to it [*Lehre*]. Kafka might have said that these are relics transmitting the *Lehre*, although we could just as well regard them as precursors preparing the *Lehre*.[33]

Lehre is lost, and yet, in Kafka's parables we find allusions to it: relics from the past, "transmitting the teachings," or precursors, announcing the future, "preparing the teachings." It is as if by choosing transmissibility Kafka unintentionally, as by inadvertence, attains the dimension of *Lehre*. This *Lehre* would be of an extraordinary nature: ironically, it would be accessible through ignorance. Only through ignorance.

Benjamin's lesson is fundamental: in Kafka there is a difference between *Gesetz* and *Lehre*. To distinguish between them allows one to recognize Kafka's choice: transmissibility instead of truth (a choice to be understood in light of the Talmudic categories of *Haggadah* and *Halachah*). Inspired by this insight I wish to return to Kafka's "Before the Law," pushing the analysis further, eventually beyond Benjamin.

4 Before the Law

> For the Jew, in so far as he is not detached from the origin, even the most exposed Jew like Kafka is safe.[34]

The *am-ha'aretz* stands before the law. He stands there because *Lehre* is lost, because tradition is in crisis, because truth was preferred over transmissibility. He stands before the law – and yet he will ultimately hear a meaningful word. *Lehre*, through its absence, in-*forms* Kafka's writing. The task of the reader is to unveil what the *Lehre* of Kafka's text, through its absence, *transmits*.

The *am-ha'aretz*'s starting point is a false knowledge: "The man from the country has not anticipated such difficulties: the Law should be accessible to

---

33 Benjamin, "Franz Kafka: On the Tenth Anniversary of His Death," 803.
34 Martin Buber, *Two Types of Faith* [*Zwei Glaubensweisen*], trans. Norman P. Goldhawk, Routledge and Kegan Paul, London 1951, 168.

anyone at any time, he thinks."[35] The *am-ha'aretz* imagines the law as universal. This is what he was always told. This is what reason, or simple common sense, seems to imply. The man from the country thinks the law is there, once and for all, immobile and indifferent, always open to everyone but addressing nobody specifically. It is a universal and objective law. The man's first surprise: the law is not what he thought it was; it is neither universal nor objective. From the start, the final teaching ("this door was meant solely for you"[36]) is suggested, through the *am-ha'aretz*'s surprised ignorance. He will have to journey a long way before that hidden knowledge will appear in full light. He will have to spend an entire life in front of the doors of the law for this truth to be revealed. And for this to happen, he will need a partner: the doorkeeper.

The doorkeeper, like the *am-ha'aretz*, stands at the threshold of the law. Yet his position is different from the *am-ha'aretz*'s: whereas the *am-ha'aretz* faces the door of the law, the doorkeeper has the law at his back. The *am-ha'aretz* has come to the law, yet the doorkeeper was always already there, as if waiting for the countryman since times immemorial. And mainly: whereas the *am-ha'aretz* is ignorant, the doorkeeper knows. His knowledge is the knowledge of time and the knowledge of the singular. His knowledge of time is the knowledge of the appropriate moment: "jetzt aber nicht" – not yet, not now, says he to the man of the country.[37] Those words contain a promise. It is as if he whispers in the countryman's ear: *be patient*, your waiting is not in vain, do not worry, one day you will eventually reach the law, but now is not that time. The doorkeeper possesses the knowledge of time; he knows the virtue of patience. Moreover, he knows how to maintain the *am-ha'aretz* in this fruitful tension which will, eventually, allow the man of the country to arrive at his destination. Like Socrates's *daimon*, this half-human half-divine creature, Kafka's doorkeeper possesses the wisdom of the appropriate moment (*kairos*, in Greek). The *daimon* restrains Socrates; he does not allow him to follow his inclinations (for instance, to address Alcibiades[38]) until the moment is ripe. His main function is to say: not now. And like Socrates's *daimon*, who cares only for one soul (that of Socrates), the doorkeeper likewise

---

35 Kafka, *The Trial*, 215–216.
36 Kafka, *The Trial*, 216.
37 Kafka, *The Trial*, 215.
38 In the prologue of the *First Alcibiade*, Socrates confesses to Alcibiade: "I have not spoken one word to you for so many years. The cause of this has been nothing human, but a certain spiritual opposition [*daimonion*] of whose power you shall be informed at some later time. However, it now opposes me no longer, so I have come to you, as you see. And I am in good hopes that it will not oppose me again in the future" (Plato, *First Alcibiades*, trans. W. R. M. Lamb, Loeb Classical Library, Harvard University Press, Cambridge 1979, 98–99 [103 a–b]).

cares for only one soul: the soul of the *am-ha'aretz*. Standing between the law and the *am-ha'aretz*, he is there *for* the *am-ha'aretz*. He too spends his life waiting. Watching over the *am-ha'aretz*'s door, he is in fact watching over the *am-ha'aretz*. He cares for the *am-ha'aretz*, warning him that there are other doors to come, with more powerful doorkeepers, so powerful that even he (the first doorkeeper) would not endure the mere sight of the third doorkeeper. And the doorkeeper is unconcerned that nobody save the man from the country has tried to enter the gates of the law during all these years. Exactly as the door itself, he is there for the *am-ha'aretz*. The only difference is that he knows this. And therefore it is he who liberates the *am-ha'aretz*: "this door was meant solely for you."[39]

"Not now" and "this door was meant solely for you." These are the two fundamental sayings of the doorkeeper. These are the two sayings that *make sense*. In chapter nine of *The Trial*, the priest, having just related the parable to Joseph K., engage him in a discussion about the meaning of the parable. The ecclesiastic says:

> The story contains two important statements by the doorkeeper concerning admittance to the Law, one at the beginning and one at the end. The one passage says: "that he can't grant him admission now"; and the other: "this entrance was meant solely for you." If a contradiction existed between these two statements you would be right, and the doorkeeper would have deceived the man. But there is no contradiction. On the contrary, the first statement implies the other.[40]

The first statement echoes the second; it implies the other: the science of the appropriate moment is the science of the singular. And the knowledge of the singular is the knowledge of the appropriate moment.[41] The temporal singularity (*kairos*) and the existential singularity (this door was meant for you, *only for you*)

---

39 Kafka, *The Trial*, 217.

40 Kafka, *The Trial*, 217–218.

41 The prologue of Plato's *First Alcibiades* enacts exactly this link: "In your younger days, to be sure, before you had built such high hopes, the god, as I believe, prevented me from talking with you, in order that I might not waste my words: but now he has set me on; for now you will listen to me" (Plato, *First Alcibiades*, 104–105 [105e–106a]). The *daemon* possesses a very particular knowledge: the knowledge of the right moment (the science of *kairos*). The *daemon* – and only he – knows when *logos* can be effective; when it can affect one's soul, move one's soul. And only an effective speech, one which provokes a *metabolê* of the soul, is a speech worthy of being promulgated. This is why, in the prologue of the *First Alcibiades*, the *daemon* determines at which moment the soul of Socrates can enter into a dialogue with the soul of Alcibiades. Singularity and *kairos* are intimately linked in the inaugural scene of this dialogue.

are intimately bound. Both exceed the regularities, the boundaries, and the universality of the law.

The doorkeeper does not delude the man from the country when he tells him that now is not the time. To Joseph K., who argues that "the doorkeeper conveyed the message of salvation [*erlösende Mitteilung*] only when it could no longer be of use to the man,"[42] and that maybe his task was to let the countryman enter the law, the priest answers in anger: "You don't have sufficient respect for the text and are changing the story."[43] Why is the doorkeeper not deluding the man from the country when he tells him "not yet"? The priest answers: because the two sayings of the doorkeeper are linked. The final words of the doorkeeper are this teaching that the countryman, *without knowing*, waited for all his life. This saying is, as Joseph K. senses, a liberating message, a message of redemption, or a redemptive message: "*erlösende Mitteilung.*"

What is liberating in the doorkeeper's final teaching? What is redemptive in this message?

If the priest's reading is correct, then this can mean only one thing: that the doorkeeper knows that entering the Law, for the *am-ha'aretz*, has no sense. Or better yet: he knows that, even for himself, entering into the law has no sense. The gate does not "lead to the world of meaning," as Buber presents it[44]; the *locus* of meaning does not dwell inside the law, but before the law. Paradoxically, in this Kafkaian world, penetrating the law has no sense. This is precisely the perspective of the *talmid chacham*: the idea of penetrating the law, of *fulfilling* the law, is a false desire. A disastrous desire.

> *En marge*: It is this desire that characterizes Paul's *messianic haste*. According to certain interpretations, Paul's despair of being unable to entirely fulfill the law (*nomos*) is at the origin of his antinomianism. In *Romans* 7, this despair is linked to man's carnality, and Paul, after having depicted the impossible struggle between his inner, spiritual self and his outer, carnal self, proclaims: "O wretched man that I am! who shall deliver me from the body of this death?"[45] Paul, who looks for a *pleromatic* accomplishment of the law, for an absolute fulfillment of the law, cannot find it in the law of works (*nomos ergon*), and therefore abolishes it. He institutes instead a *nomos pisteos*, a law of faith, or a law of love, which is, according to *Romans* (13: 10), the *pleroma* of *nomos*, the fulfillment of the law.[46] The inner (spiritual) law of faith accomplishes and thereby abolishes the outer (carnal) law of

---

42 Kafka, *The Trial*, 217 (translation slightly modified).
43 Kafka, *The Trial*, 217.
44 Buber, *Two Types of Faith*, 165.
45 *Epistle to the Romans*, 7: 24, King James Bible.
46 For a scholarly analysis of the question of the *pleromatic* principle in Paul, see E. P. Sanders, *Paul, the Law, and the Jewish People*, Fortress Press, Philadelphia 1983, 93–100; and Michael

deeds. Nietzsche, in his portrait of Paul in paragraph 68 of *The Dawn of Day* [*Morgenröte*], gives an acute description of the apostle's despair: "This man suffered from a fixed idea, or rather a fixed question, an ever-present and ever burning question: what was the *meaning* of the Jewish Law? And more especially, *the fulfillment of this law?* [...] Now, however, he was aware in his own person of the fact that such a man as himself [...] could not fulfill the Law."[47] Paul could not bear the idea that the Law cannot be fulfilled. Yet not being able to fulfill the law was never a matter of despair for the rabbis, for the *talmid chacham*. Travers Herford, in his remarkable work on the Pharisees, insightfully remarks: "It is safe to say that no Jew before Paul ever thought of the Torah in that way, or ever felt the despair which, according to this theory, he should have felt. Certainly, or let me say probably, no Pharisee ever completely fulfilled all the 'mitzvoth' of the Torah; but I have never come across any Pharisee who was overwhelmed with despair on that account."[48] Contrary to the *talmid chacham*, Paul cannot imagine that there can be a meaningful life before the law that does not consist in the *pleromatic* desire, in the desire to entirely fulfill the law.

If "Before the Law" were to be inscribed in a messianic tradition, it would not be the Paulinian-pleromatic kind, which is a messianism of haste (failing to fulfill the law *now*, it should be superseded *today*: we have to reach the *telos* of the law, the end of the law, which is not law anymore but something different (love, faith)).[49] It would be in the context of a

---

Cranford, "The Possibility of Perfect Obedience: Paul and an Implied Premise in *Galatians* 3:10 and 5:3," in *Novum Testamentum* 36 (July 1994), 242–258.

47 Friedrich Nietzsche, *The Dawn of Days*, trans. J. M. Kennedy, Dover Publications, Inc., Mineola and New York, 2007, 67–68.

48 Travers Herford, *Pharisaism: Its Aims and Its Methods*, G. P. Putnam's Sons, New York 1912, 196.

49 Giorgio Agamben, in his article "The Messiah and the Sovereign: The Problem of Law in Walter Benjamin," goes this way when he reads Kafka's text as a messianic-antinomistic text, which he links to the Paulinian heritage he recognizes at work in Jewish messianism as presented by Scholem (mainly his 1959 essay "Towards an Understanding of the Messianic Idea in Judaism"). Agamben finds the principle of *pleroma* at work both in the relation between *Torah de Briah* and *Tora de Azilut* as depicted in the kabalistic tradition, and in Paul: "What is decisive here is the concept of fulfillment, which implies that the Torah in some way still holds and has not simply been abrogated by a second Torah commanding the opposite of the first. We find the same notion in the Christian tradition of the *pleroma* of the law, for example in *Matthew* 5:17–18 [...] and in the theory of the law proposed by Paul in the *Epistle to the Romans* (8:4). What is at issue here are not simply antinomical tendencies but an attempt to confront the pleromatic state in which the Torah, restored to its original form, contains neither commandments nor prohibitions but only a medley of unordered letters." See Giorgio Agamben, "The Messiah and the Sovereign: The Problem of Law in Walter Benjamin," in *Potentialities: Collected Essays in Philosophy*, trans. Daniel Heller-Roazen, Stanford University Press, Stanford 1999, 160–176, 167. Further in the text, Agamben links those unordered letters to Scholem's definition of the law in Kafka as a law being in force without significance. For Scholem, writes Agamben, "this is the correct definition of the state of law in Kafka's novel. A world in which the law finds itself in this condition and where 'every gesture becomes unrealizable' is a rejected, not an idyllic, world" (page 169). Every gesture becomes unrealizable: this is the messianic situation which characterizes Kafka's text according

messianism of patience, which is the only messianic attitude that does not lead to a (messianic) *aufhebung* of Judaism (Paulinism, Sabbatheanism, Hegelianism, etc.), and thus to an abolishment of Judaism.[50] The countrymen, as well as the doorkeeper, are waiting. Their

---

to Agamben: "The thesis that I intend to advance is that this parable [Kafka's "Before the Law"] is an allegory of the state of law in the messianic age, that is, in the age of its being in force without significance" (page 172). Agamben's analysis is possible only if one maintains the dichotomy of the inside and the outside (the idea of the ban supposes an inside and an outside, a logic of exclusion), or of *nomos* and *anti-nomos* (the idea of fulfillment supposes an unfulfilled law versus an ideal of fulfillment without law), whereas what is singular in "Before the Law" is precisely that this parable deactivates those classical dichotomies. Everything happens in the outside, and therefore the outside becomes the *locus* of meaning. And the Law is there only in order to be placed before it. Not in order to enter it, or to accomplish it. This is true if we follow the priest's lesson, and if we are attentive to Benjamin's remark about the centrality of *Lehre* in Kafka. For a critique of Agamben's Paulinian reading of Kafka's parable see Vivian Liska, "'Before the Law stands a doorkeeper. To this doorkeeper comes a man...': Kafka, Narrative, and the Law," in *Naharaim* 6/2 (June 2013): 175–194, 179–183.

50 This messianism of patience, nevertheless, should not be confounded with Derrida's logic of "indefinite adjournment" and "interminable *différance*." Derrida, in his "Before the Law" writes: "After the first guardian there are an undefined number of others, perhaps they are innumerable, and progressively more powerful and therefore more prohibitive, endowed with greater power of delay. Their potency is *différance*, an interminable *différance*, since it lasts for days and 'years', indeed, up to the end of (the) man. *Différance* till death, and for death, without end because ended. As the doorkeeper represents it, the discourse of the law does not say 'no,' but 'not yet,' indefinitely." See Jacques Derrida, "Before the Law" ("Devant la loi"), trans. Avital Ronell and Christine Roulston, in *Acts of Literature*, ed. Derek Attridge, Routledge, New York 1992, 181–220, 204. Derrida's reading of Kafka's parable – like Agamben's – is possible only if one dissociate the two doorkeepers' respective sayings ("not yet" and "this door was meant only for you"). His reading is possible only if the doorman's last saying is not the accomplishment of a promise ("not yet"), as the coming true of the man from the country's hope (which is not a fulfillment or an accomplishment of the Law, but the redemptive apparition of *Lehre*). If, contrary to Derrida and according to the priest's exegesis in *The Trial*, the two sayings are connected, then the waiting of the "*Man vom Lande*" acquires a completely different meaning. This waiting is not in vain anymore; it now leads somewhere (to *Lehre*, precisely). It is a messianic patience, not messianicity without messiah. The best way to illustrate the difference between my reading and Derrida's is by evoking a symptomatic passage in his text where he refers explicitly to the "Jewish Law": "There is an analogy with Judaic law here. Hegel narrates a story about Pompey, interpreting it in his own way. Curious to know what was behind the doors of the tabernacle that housed the holy of holies, the triumvir approached the innermost part of the Temple, the center of worship. There, says Hegel, he sought 'a being, an essence offered to his mediation, something meaningful (*sinnvolles*) to command his respect; and when he thought he was entering into the secret, before the ultimate spectacle, he felt mystified, disappointed, deceived. He found what he sought in 'an empty space' and concluded from this that the genuine secret was itself entirely extraneous to them, the Jews; it was unseen and unfelt" (Derrida, "Before the Law," 208). Pompey, as related by Hegel in *The Spirit of Christianity and Its Fate*, tells us, according to Derrida, the truth of "Jewish law": entering

main trait is patience, a patient hope which eventually will be realized not as the abolishment of the law but as the apparition of a *Lehre*. "Before the Law" is not a text enacting the messianic accomplishment-abolishement of the law, but a text about the conditions of possibility of *Lehre* in an epoch of crisis of tradition.[51]

From the perspective of the *talmid chacham*, as noted previously, the issue is not the *fulfilling* of the law. The doorkeeper never enters the law. Perhaps he has never entered the law. Indeed, he does not even see it: in facing the man from the country, he has the door at his back. He already knows that the door is there not to be entered but to remain open, until the one for whom this open door is destined – the *am-ha'aretz* – dies. This the *talmid chacham* knows: no one penetrates the law, not because it is impossible but because penetrating the law is, in fact, to violate it. Incarnating it means abolishing it. Standing in front of the open gates of the law is not a sign of failure; rather, it is the only disposition that will eventually render it possible to hear a *Lehre*. There is no accomplishing of the law, no entering the law. Instead, there is a lifelong existential study of one's place

---

into the saint of saint, one would encounter... nothing, "an empty space." Instead of listening to what the sages of Israel have to say about the divine commandment and the saint of saint (*kodesh ha-kodashim*), Derrida reposes on Hegel's authority, himself telling a story about Pompey. This surely serves Derrida's reading ("The law is silent, and of it nothing is said to us. [...] Is it a thing, a person, a discourse, a voice, a document, or simply a nothing that incessantly defers access to itself [...]" (page 208)), though it is unclear if it clarifies anything about Jewish law.

51 Moreover, this text is not a Paulinian text but a Pharisaic text. In bringing up the categories of *haggadah* and *hallachah*, which are genuine rabbinic categories, Benjamin anticipates this perspective. In fact, in *The Trial*, it is Kafka himself who very clearly alludes to the Talmudic-Pharisaic context. The parable is referred to as Scripture ("I've told you the story word for word according to the Scripture [*der Schrift*]," says the priest to Joseph K, and further: "You don't have sufficient respect for the Scripture [*der Schrift*]"). Scripture, the text insists time and again, has commentators, but most importantly, the discussion itself between the priest and Joseph K., as is obvious from the text and as was noted by numerous commentators, has all the traits of a Talmudic debate. Derrida for instance qualifies this sequence as "a prodigious scene of Talmudic exegesis" (Derrida, "Before the Law," 217). For a more detailed analysis of Kafka's Talmudic exegesis in *The Trial* see Iris Bruce, *Kafka and Cultural Zionism: Dates in Palestine*, The University of Wisconsin Press, Madison 2007, 102. Nevertheless, if this passage says something essential about Kafka's parables in general, then Benjamin's analysis should be revisited. Indeed, if the debate between the priest and Joseph K. echoes the Talmudic way of debating, then, strictly speaking, the parable occupies the place of Scripture, which the Talmud (more precisely its later layer, the *Guemara*) refers to so as to construct its argumentations and convey its teachings. The relation of Kafka's parable to *Lehre* should then be compared not to *Haggadah* and *Halachah*, but to *Tora she bi'chtav* (written Torah, or the Hebrew Bible) and *Tora she beal pe* (oral Torah, or the Talmudic reading of the Written Torah), between the biblical verse and its dialectization. But I will not engage in this direction, as it leads us too far.

in relation to the law. The doorkeeper and the countryman in this text are first and foremost students, subjects questioning their existences, their place in the world, in front of an open door. In this study there are degrees. Degree zero: the *am-ha'aretz*, the ignorant. What does the *am-ha'aretz* know? What is his hidden knowledge? Answer: he knows – without knowing – that in being before the law he is at his place. He does not accomplish the law, and nevertheless he is – body and soul – before the law. *The am-ha'aretz does not accomplish the law without being for this reason an outlaw.*[52] He is, on the contrary, in a living relation with the facticity of the law, with the very fact of standing before a commandment. His life is, from beginning to end, an existence before-the-law.

Inspired by Benjamin's reading, let us push the analysis a step further: what is the hidden knowledge of the ignorant person? In his existence, he in fact knows that law is not the issue here. He knows without actually knowing – he has a deep, implicit, knowledge – that what is at stake here is *Lehre*, and not some kind of cold, meaningless and oppressive law. If he did not have this (hidden) knowledge, he would not stay at the gate of the law. Indeed, no one obliges the man from the country to stay there: "Now the man is in fact free: he can go wherever he wishes [...]. If he sits on the stool at the side of the door and spends the rest of his life there, he does so of his own free will; the story mentions no element of force,"[53] explains the priest to Joseph K. But the man from the country does not leave. He is there and there he stays. Does he not have a life of his own? Affairs he must attend to? A wife? Children? The man from the country stands where he is supposed to be. This is his place. He knows that what is at stake here is his existence, the meaning of his existence. And this will be the final teaching of the doorkeeper: this place was destined for you. You were where you were supposed to be. You were, until the end, where you were supposed to be, attentive to the call. Before the Law: an *am-ha'aretz*.

The first trait of ignorance is the confusion between *Gesetz* and *Lehre*, the impossibility to see, beyond the law, a teaching. In Kafka's parable, the death of the *am-ha'aretz* is also the death of ignorance, of his ignorance. Not because the *am-ha'aretz* dies, but because his death is simultaneous with the unveiling of

---

52 As in opposition to Derrida, for whom "since he is before it because he cannot enter it, he is also *outside the law* (an outlaw)" (Derrida, "Before the Law," 204). The equivalence outside the law=outlaw is possible only in a Paulinian world, where the pleromatic realization of the law is the ideal. And indeed, Derrida, even though very far from Agamben, situates his reading in the Paulinian horizon (see Derrida, "Before the Law," pages 203, 217, and 219).

53 Kafka, *The Trial*, 221. At the end of the chapter, the Priest concludes on a similar note: "The court wants nothing from you. It receives you when you come and dismisses you when you go" (page 224).

what was always already there, beyond the visible, beyond the superficial, beyond the law: *Lehre*. The doorkeeper, who has withheld his teaching until the ultimate moment, which is the appropriate moment, is now able to say: "No one else could gain admittance here, because this entrance was meant solely for you. I'm going to go and shut it now."[54] The law, says the doorkeeper to the *am-ha'aretz*, is meaningful only so far as it is addressed to the singular. This you always already knew. In saying this, the doorkeeper is revealing to the man from the country the hidden law of the man's existence, the very sense of his awaiting, of his patience.[55] True law is not universal. True law is such only so far as it is the law of the singular. And therefore, only so far as it is not law anymore, but teaching: *Lehre*.

In "Before the Law" Kafka brings us to the point where law becomes teaching, where *Gesetz* becomes *Lehre*. He brings us to the point where the forgotten and absent *Lehre*, this *Lehre* that is ignored and to which Kafka's parables are *Haggadah*, unexpectedly – as by a miracle – appears; as a revelation *full of sense*.[56] "Here and there we have an allusion to *Lehre* in Kafka," writes Benjamin in his Kafka text.[57] This is what happens at the end of Kafka's parable. Not a suspension, not a *différance* or a *déférance* of the law, not a deferral or a procrastination of the time under the law, but the appearance, against all odds, of this law which is not a law, of this law which defies the concept itself of law along with all the dichotomies that accompany this concept (inside/outside, oppressive/anarchic,

---

54 Kafka, *The Trial*, 217.

55 In this sense, what Benjamin says about Kafka's "The Truth about Sancho Panza" ("Die Wahrheit über Sancho Pansa") can be said of "Before the Law": Kafka, on at least one occasion, "has found the law of his journey" (Benjamin, "Franz Kafka: On the Tenth Anniversary of His Death," 815).

56 Here is where my interpretation strongly differs from Scholem's, which defines the law in Kafka's texts as "the Nothing of Revelation" (*Nichts der Offenbarung*): "You ask what I understand by the 'nothingness of revelation'? I understand by it a state in which revelation appears to be without meaning, in which it still asserts itself, in which it has validity but no significance [*Geltung ohne Bedeutung*]. A state in which the wealth of meaning is lost and what is in the process of appearing (for revelation is such a process) still does not disappear, even though it is reduced to the zero point of its own content" (see Walter Benjamin and Gershom Scholem, *The Correspondence of Walter Benjamin and Gershom Scholem: 1932–1940*, ed. Gershom Scholem, trans. Gary Smith and Andre Lefevre, Harvard University Press, Cambridge 1992, 142). Even though Scholem's idea of validity without significance is a very powerful idea, "Before the Law" defies this idea: there is a moment of positive revelation at the end of the parable. As readers, meaning overflows us: there is an excess of sense in the doorkeeper's final words, a sense that retroactively colors all the parable with a redemptive tint. An excess that makes us, readers, shiver. Agamben, who takes Scholem's intuition and reads "Before the Law" according to it (see *supra* footnote 49), can do this only by silencing the redemptive character of the doorkeeper's final words.

57 Benjamin, "Franz Kafka: On the Tenth Anniversary of His Death," 803.

nomistic/antinomistic, liberal/state-of-exception, etc.): the appearance of *Lehre*. The genius of Kafka is that he understood that this appearance could be rendered possible only through pushing the logic of ignorance to its last consequences. In this time, which is the time of the crisis of tradition, only the ignorant can recognize, beyond the law, a teaching. Only he is capable of recognizing – if he is prepared to spend his entire life before the law – a Torah.

And maybe Kafka, this Socratic ignorant, transmits truth – and not only the haggadic consistency of it – through his ignorance. Maybe the *amhorez* indeed saves the essential.

Works Cited

Adorno, Theodor W., *Prisms*. Trans. Samuel Weber and Shierry Weber (Cambridge: MIT Press, 1982).

Agamben, Giorgio, *Potentialities: Collected Essays in Philosophy*. Trans. Daniel Heller-Roazen (Stanford: Stanford University Press, 1999).

Babylonian Talmud: Tractate Baba Bathra (Volume 2). Trans. Israel W. Slotki (London: Soncino Press, 1976).

Babylonian Talmud: Tractate Baba Mezia. Trans. H Freedman (London: Soncino Press, 1986).

Babylonian Talmud: Tractate Berakoth. Trans. Maurice Simon (London: Soncino Press, 1984).

Babylonian Talmud: Tractate Pesahim. Trans. H. Freedman (London: Soncino Press, 1983).

Benjamin, Walter, *The Correspondence of Walter Benjamin: 1910–1940*. Eds. Gershom Scholem and Theodor W. Adorno. Trans. M. R. Jacobson and E. M. Jacobson (Chicago: The University of Chicago Press, 1994).

Benjamin, Walter, *Gesammelte Schriften*, Vol. II:3. Eds. Rolf Tiedemann and Hermann Schweppenhäuser (Frankfurt/M.: Suhrkamp Verlag, 1977).

Benjamin, Walter, *Selected Writings, Volume 2: 1931–1934*. Eds. Michael W. Jennings, Howard Eiland, and Gary Smith (Cambridge: Harvard University Press, 1999).

Benjamin, Walter, *Selected Writings, Volume 3: 1935–1938*. Eds. Edmund Jephcott and Howard Eiland (Cambridge: Harvard University Press, 2002).

Benjamin, Walter and Gershom Scholem, *The Correspondence of Walter Benjamin and Gershom Scholem: 1932–1940*. Ed. Gershom Scholem. Trans. Gary Smith and Andre Lefevre (Cambridge: Harvard University Press, 1992).

Bialik, Haim Nahman, *Revealment and Concealment: Five Essays* (Jerusalem: Ibis Editions, 2000).

Bruce, Iris, *Kafka and Cultural Zionism: Dates in Palestine* (Madison: The University of Wisconsin Press, 2007).

Buber, Martin, *Two Types of Faith*. Trans. Norman P. Goldhawk (London: Routledge and Kegan Paul, 1951).

Buber, Martin and Franz Rosenzweig, *Scripture and Translation*. Trans. Lawrence Rosenwald with Everett Fox (Bloomington and Indianapolis: Indiana University Press, 1994).

Cranford, Michael, "The Possibility of Perfect Obedience: Paul and an Implied Premise in *Galatians* 3:10 and 5:3," in *Novum Testamentum* 36 (1994): 242–258.

Derrida, Jacques, *Acts of Literature*. Ed. Derek Attridge (New York: Routledge, 1992).

Finkelstein, Louis, *The Pharisees: The Sociological Background of Their Faith* (Philadelphia: The Jewish Publication Society of America, 1966).

Gashé, Rodolphe, "Kafka's Law: In the Field of Forces between Judaism and Hellenism," in *MLN* 117. 5 (2002) Comparative Literature Issue: 971–1002

Heinemann, Joseph, "The Nature of the Aggadah," trans. Marc Bregman, in *Midrash and Literature*. Eds. Geoffrey H. Hartman and Sanford Budick (New Haven: Yale University Press, 1986), 41–54

Herford, Travers, *Pharisaism: Its Aims and Its Methods* (New York: G. P. Putnam's Sons, 1912).

Kafka, Franz, *The Diaries: 1910–1913*. Trans. Joseph Kresh (New York: Schocken Books, 1976).

Kafka, Franz, *The Trial*. Trans. Breon Mitchell (New York: Schocken Books, 1998).

Lifshitz, Berachyahu, "Aggadah Versus Haggadah: Towards a More Precise Understanding of the Distinction," in *Dine Yisrael* 24 (2007): 11–29 (English Section).

Liska, Vivian, "'Before the Law stands a doorkeeper. To this doorkeeper comes a man...': Kafka, Narrative, and the Law," in *Naharaim* 6/2 (2013): 179–183.

Nietzsche, Friedrich, *The Dawn of Days*. Trans. J. M. Kennedy (Mineola and New York: Dover Publications, Inc., 2007).

Plato, *First Alcibiades*. Trans. W. R. M. Lamb (Cambridge: Loeb Classical Library, Harvard University Press, 1979).

Politzer, Heinz, *Franz Kafka: Parable and Paradox* (Ithaca and New York: Cornell University Press, 1966).

Sanders, E. P., *Paul, the Law, and the Jewish People* (Philadelphia: Fortress Press, 1983).

Sayings of the Jewish Fathers, Comprising Pirqe Aboth in Hebrew and English with Notes and Excursuses. Trans. Charles Taylor (Cambridge: Cambridge University Press, 1897).

Simon-Shoshan, Moshe, *Stories of the Law: Narrative Discourse and the Construction of Authority in the Mishnah* (Oxford: Oxford University Press, 2012).

Steiner, George, *No Passion Spent: Essays 1978–1995* (New Haven and London: Yale University Press, 1996).

Urbach, Ephraim E., *The Sages: Their Concepts and Beliefs*. Trans. Israel Abrahams (Jerusalem: Magnes Press, The Hebrew University, 1975).

Arthur Cools
Desire and Responsibility: The Case of K.

The category of the universal does not seem to fit well in relation to literary texts. There are many reasons not to relate this notion to literature. It is obvious that the meaning of literary expressions can never have the same transparency or necessity as a mathematical formula, not least because of the metaphoric operations characteristic of literary language. Moreover, it is generally accepted that literary works are dependent of the context in which they originate and that their meaning is relative to this context.[1] Nevertheless, literary texts have often been considered as bearers of universal meaning, especially in religious traditions. Since modern times, however, various claims have been made concerning the epistemological status of literary texts. Realism is based upon an empirical claim, namely, that literary narratives describe the experience of life as it is. German idealism claims that literary texts are able to express universal ideas. It considered the tragic genre to be the expression of the idea of freedom as embodied by the acceptance of responsibility with regard to a situation that did not result from a choice. Marxist theories claim that literary works contribute to an emancipated society by unraveling ideological mechanisms and power relations in society. Whatever the differences between these theories, the basic argument underlying all of them is ethical, the universality of which is taken as something absolute: for realism, this is the idea of faithfulness; for German idealism, the idea of freedom; and for Marxism, the idea of a true emancipation.

Attributing a universal meaning to Kafka's work – which is among the most commented-upon literary works of the twentieth century – seems to be an entirely justified and self-evident adjudication. However, it is difficult to assess this universality within the limits of the respective frameworks of the literary theories of realism, German idealism, and Marxism. It seems that Kafka's modernist writings escape such categories and resist elucidation in terms of faithfulness, freedom, and emancipation. Moreover, it seems similarly problematic to state that Kafka's work has a universal meaning because of its belonging to the Jewish tradition. As is known, Kafka's relations to Judaism are far more complex than Max Brod was willing to say. And even when these relations to Judaism do play a role in Kafka's writings, it does not imply that his texts can be considered to express the univer-

---

1 This view is called "contextualism" and generally accepted as the main theory about the ontological status of literary artworks. Cf. Peter Lamarque, *The Philosophy of Literature*, Blackwell, Oxford 2009, 78–81.

sal meaning of the religious Jewish tradition as such.[2] On the contrary, it is generally accepted that Kafka's narratives contribute to the modernist transformation of the novel.[3] Are there other candidates by which to ensure the foundation of the universal meaning of Kafka's work?

In this article, I will focus on Zygmunt Bauman's proposal, from *Postmodern Ethics*, to understand Kafka's story "Before the Law" ("Vor dem Gesetz") in terms of Emmanuel Levinas's concept of responsibility.[4] I confront this interpretation with a reflection upon the kind of narrative in Kafka's novel *The Trial* [*Der Process*], in which "Before the Law" is told. I will consider the question whether, in what way, and to what extent it is possible to interpret this narration in continuation with the tragic model of narration as articulated by German idealism. Indeed, this tragic model still retained important influence in the development of the modern novel during the nineteenth century. I will show that the narration in *The Trial* is, in certain respects but not in others, a continuation with this model, and I will examine the implications of these narrative transformations as concerns the question of the universal meaning of Kafka in terms of responsibility.

1 Universality as a Singular Rule? Zygmunt Bauman on "Before the Law"

In his book *Postmodern Ethics*, Zygmunt Bauman establishes a remarkable connection between Emmanuel Levinas's philosophy of responsibility and Kafka's story "Before the Law." After discussing the modern concept of universality and its discontents, he presents the condition of morality in a new way, via introducing Levinas's concept of selfhood in which Bauman welcomes the idea of a non-generalizable uniqueness and the idea of the non-reversibility of personal responsibility. For Bauman, "[b]eing a moral person means that I *am* my brother's keeper. But this also means that *I* am my brother's keeper whether or not my brother sees his own brotherly duties the same way I do; and that I am my brother's keeper whatever other brothers, real or putative, do or may do." Bauman quotes the well-

---

2 For an interesting reflection on this issue, see Eli Schonfeld's contribution, "*Am-ha'aretz*: The Law of the Singular. Kafka's Hidden Knowledge," in this volume.

3 Cf. Vivian Liska, "Kafka, Modernism, and Literary Theory," in *A Handbook of Modernist Studies*, ed. Jean-Michel Rabaté, Wiley-Blackwell, Oxford 2013, 75–86.

4 Zygmunt Bauman, *Postmodern Ethics*, Blackwell, Oxford 1993, 52.

known sentence which Levinas takes from a novel of Dostoyevsky: "The I always has one responsibility *more* than all the others." He continues:

> only on this assumption is a *"moral* party," as distinct from contractual partnership, thinkable and realizable. My responsibility is always a step ahead, always greater than that of the Other. I am denied the comfort of the already-existing norms and already-followed rules to guide me, to reassure me that I have reached the limit of my duty and so spare me that anxiety which I would account for as "guilty conscience." If my responsibility can be at all expressed as a rule, it will be (like in the famous Kafka parable of the door to the Palace of Justice through which no one ever entered, as it had been kept open but for a single penitent and was bound to be closed the moment he died) just a *singular* rule, a rule which for all I know and care has been spelled out for me only and which I heard even if the ears of others remained blocked. "Appel de la sainteté précédant le souci d'exister. [...] Le moi de celui qui est élu à répondre du prochain ... Unicité de l'élection."[5]

Because of this explicit connection with Levinas's philosophy, Bauman seems able to add a new reading of Kafka's "Before the Law," one of Kafka's most commented-upon texts.[6] However, his comparison between Levinas's concept of responsibility and Kafka's story of the man before the law is mistaken. It is not difficult to say why. First, the law to which the door is open, in Kafka's story, is not the law of the Palace of Justice, in which case it would be possible to generalize the law and to guarantee reciprocity between the subjects of the law; it is also different from the ethical commandment "you should not kill," as is revealed in the face of the other in Levinas's account of responsibility: the normativity of this injunction is universal, but does not guarantee justice. Second, Kafka's story relates the uniqueness of one's selfhood not to the response given to one's neighbor but rather to the impersonal presence of the law which binds the man of the country and the doorkeeper to its own authority; in Levinas's philosophy, however, the uniqueness of one's selfhood appears in relation to the encounter of the other person before any reference to a third party. And finally, Kafka's story is ethically indifferent, without consideration of what is good and what is evil – the man of the country is simply waiting and dying hopelessly, and the guardian undertakes nothing to interrupt this dying: it is never even suggested that he gives food, clothes, and shelter; it is mentioned only that he looks powerful and that he regularly interrogates (in an apathetic way) the unfortunate man of the

---

5 Bauman, *Postmodern Ethics*, 51–52.
6 For an overview see Vivian Liska, "'Before the law stands a doorkeeper: to this doorkeeper comes a man...': Kafka, Narrative, and the Law," in *Naharaim* 6/2 (June 2013), 175–194. See as well Rodolphe Gasché, "Kafka's Law: In the Field of Forces between Judaism and Hellenism," in *MLN* 117.5 (2002): 971–1002.

country. Yet Levinas still wishes to say something about goodness: a common world and the possibility of justice in the world are dependent on one's response to the other person.

Consequently, it seems right to conclude that the respective universes of the works of Kafka and Levinas are incompatible. Nevertheless, in his examination of Levinas's philosophy, Bauman points to a condition which he has good reason to refer to Kafka. Bauman, rejecting the universality of modern rationality (because of its internal contradictions which neutralize moral autonomy and depersonalize the effects of this rationality), welcomes in the works of Kafka and Levinas the attempt to account for the sense of a singular commitment before any reference to a pre-given logos (as in ancient Greek philosophy), to a shared belief (as in a pre-modern Christian society), to a faculty of reason (as in Kant), to a universal idea of freedom (as in German idealism), or to an hermeneutic understanding of one's being together with others (as in Heidegger's ontology). In this respect, Bauman's reference to Kafka's story "Before the Law" in his considerations of postmodern ethics is not accidental. For Bauman, the story reveals at once the commitment of the individual (the man from the country seeking access to the law), and the singularity of the commitment: the door where he requests access was open only to him and "was bound to be closed the moment he died." In other words, uniqueness is not so much a question of giving answer to an appeal (let it be a universal one), as it is a question of being chosen or accused by an appeal that is addressed only to oneself and to which one does not have access.

There is no doubt that Kafka's work reaches without restraint into these depths of uniqueness and singularity, even more than the philosophy of Levinas, who still wishes to say something about both the sender of the address (the face of the other) and the ethical sense of justice in one's relation to the other. *The Trial* opens with the arrest of Josef K. and the accusation of a court that commits him individually; this arrest is one from which he will never be able to be delivered and it is based upon reasons that will never become clear. It is in this novel that the story "Before the Law" appears: a priest relates it to Josef K. Given the differences already noted, it is clear that the problem of the universal is not the same for Kafka as it is for Levinas, who considers his philosophy of responsibility compatible with an intellectualism of reason. Yet Bauman, in referring to Kafka while explaining Levinas, opens, without realizing it, the possibility of a reading which undermines this compatibility and in which Kafka's expression of uniqueness functions as an uncontrollable disorder of Levinas's argument that articulates the singular position of responsibility in relation to the possibility of a just world. Is it possible to recover the sense of the universal, which is required in order to do justice, starting from the unique position of the elected and the accused? Levinas's answer to this question is a complex articulation of different steps which implies a diachronic temporality: the independence of an enjoying and egocentric self, the trace of the other's face, the responsibility for the non-desirable other, the presence of the third, and the eschatology of the time of generations.[7] Yet what about Kafka? How does the narrative of a singular commitment, the position of being accused in *The Trial*, express meaning that can be considered as universal? Does the law reveal at the end its power of justice, as Bauman seems to suggest in his interpretation of "Before the Law"? Or does the law fail to assess its universality? Does Kafka's narrative reveal an impediment to joining any sense of the universal?

2 Kafka's Narrative and the Legacy of the Tragic Model

The difficulty in answering these questions is related to particular features of Kafka's fictional work, especially its enigmatic, fragmentary, and disorientating character, which invites an infinite hermeneutics. But it may be that the difficulty concerns a preliminary question as well: the difference between philosophical discourse and fictional writing. Since Plato, i.e., since the existence of a philosophical discourse, distinct from mythos, this distinction has been established on the basis of the notion of representation (mimesis). Philosophical discourse defines itself as a criticism of representation and formulates new access to truth by means of conceptual clarification. This remains the case in Levinas's philosophy, which intends to delimitate, as did Plato, the role of representation in the general understanding of existence. Thus, Plato and Levinas agree upon the universal meaning of the idea of goodness being distinct from representation of this idea. Levinas, moreover, articulates this meaning in terms of an ethical injunction. Yet Aristotle, in his *Poetica*, shows that philosophy does not need to dismiss representation; moreover, he argues that poetics, as the art of representation, not only contributes towards understanding of the human condition but is able to present the essentials while contending with the possible instead of being addicted to the factual. It seems therefore that the Aristotelian notion of representation (and its legacy) sets the stakes for an approach that can answer the question of the universal in Kafka's narrative of Josef K.

---

7 Cf. Arthur Cools, "Levinas' Defense of Intellectualism: an Undecidable Ambiguity?" in *Debating Levinas' Legacy*, eds. Andris Breitling, Chris Bremmers, and Arthur Cools, Brill, Leiden and Boston 2015, 3–15.

At first sight, it may seem problematic to refer to a Greek notion in order to approach the question of the universal in Kafka's fictional work, which, according to so many commentaries, has its origin in a Jewish tradition. In fact, there is a striking parallel between the Aristotelian approach to representation and Kafka's narrative in *The Trial*. The main issue of tragedy – tragedy, according to Aristotle, being the model of representation *par excellence* – is the problem of being chosen or accused by a demand that is addressed only to the individual, a demand that he or she is unable to undo and to which he or she does not have access. This is the case for Oedipus and Antigone alike. The problem we face here seems to be similar to the case of K. in *The Trial* or the man from the country in "Before the Law." Moreover, since German idealism, and especially since the reflections of Schelling and Hegel on tragedy and Hölderlin's translations of ancient tragedies, the reference to the Greek model and the attempts to actualize it in a modern condition have played a major role in aesthetic theory, in the development of the German mourning play (*Trauerspiel*), and in the transformation of the modern novel. I am inspired here by Philippe Lacoue-Labarthe's analyses of the destiny of mimesis in modern times.[8] It is quite unlikely that Kafka, reading and writing novels and stories in German in the early decades of the twentieth century, was unfamiliar with this context and not involved in this transformation. It may be that the representation of the accused who is victim of a destiny he or she could not choose is not at all specific to Kafka's narratives. It may be moreover that this representation entails a question by which modern times confront the art of narrative, for it is in modern times that the question of the meaning and relevance of the tragic model is raised as such and thereby invites exploration of new approaches.[9]

For these reasons, in order to answer the question of the universal in the case of Kafka's *The Trial*, it is interesting to examine to what extent it is possible to say that the Greek legacy of representation is transformed in this novel and to what extent the novel still repeats features of the tragic model. For this kind of examination, Marthe Robert's interpretation of Kafka merits particular attention,

---

8 Philippe Lacoue-Labarthe, *L'imitation des modernes. Typographies II* [*Typography: Mimesis, Philosophy, Politics*], Galilée, Paris 1986. Philippe Lacoue-Labarthe, *La fiction du politique. Heidegger, l'art et la politique* [*Heidegger, Art, and Politics: the Fiction of the Political*], Christian Bourgeois, Paris 1998. Philippe Lacoue-Labarthe, *Heidegger. La politique du poème* [*Heidegger and the Politics of Poetry*], Galilée Paris, 2002.
9 About the transformation of the Greek legacy of tragedy in the context of German idealism, especially in the case of Hölderlin, see for instance Frans van Peperstraten, "Modernity in Hölderlin's Remarks on Oedipus and Antigone," in *The Locus of Tragedy*, eds. Arthur Cools, Thomas Crombez, Rosa Slegers, and Johan Taels, Brill, Leiden and Boston 2008, 105–120.

owing to the explicit connection she establishes with the Greek epopee. She considers Kafka's *The Castle* [*Das Schloss*] a modern imitation of Homer's *Odyssey*, and articulates the search of K. in this novel in terms of tragic conflict. Although she does not consider the tragic model and does not examine its relevance for Kafka's fictional work, she rightly observes "the dramatic organization" and "the striking theatrical expositions" of various scenes in his novels.[10] Indeed, in *The Trial* the majority of the scenes are located strictly within single rooms, each of which functions as the décor of the narrated interaction: these rooms include the bedroom, the living room, the office, the storage room, the atelier of the artist, the office of the lawyer, the church. Moreover, many scenes have immediate theatrical effect, owing to detailed descriptions of bodily presence and movements: the two men arresting K. at the beginning and end of the novel, the old couple looking indifferently through the window into the living room as K. is arrested, the scene of punishment in the storage room, the dispute and competition with the vice-director, K.'s suffocation each time he begins to know something about the trial.

Commenting on the protagonist's search, Robert implicitly points to a main feature of the tragic model: the excessiveness and opacity of desire which is the driving force behind the protagonist's choices until the tragic ending – for Oedipus, this is the desire to know the truth of his own destiny; for Antigone, it is the desire to properly bury her deceased brother, even at the cost of her own life.[11] In *The Trial*, K.'s desire to know the object of the charge, the instance of the accusation, and the rules of the trial, and his desire to free himself from the accusation constitute the main dynamic of the sequence of chapters; these desires determine the regulations and permissions which upend K.'s daily life, and they disturb continuously all his various interactions with others. Faced with his accusation, K. is no longer in a position where he can avoid being obsessed by it. As with the tragic hero, the exorbitance of K.'s desire to make the court withdraw its

---

10 Marthe Robert, *L'Ancien et le nouveau: de Don Quichotte à Kafka* [*The Old and the New: From Don Quixote to Kafka*], Payot, Paris 1967, 27: "l'allure étonnamment théâtrale de ses romans laisse supposer une passion dont on trouve effectivement mainte preuve dans son *Journal* –, l'organisation dramatique de leur œuvre est tellement frappante qu'elle tente continuellement les adaptateurs, en les persuadant qu'ici au moins, ils peuvent adapter sans trahir, ayant somme toute peu de choses à faire pour transformer le roman en pièce."
11 Jean-Pierre Vernant recalls that this desire, being intrinsically determined by a blindness, cannot yet be interpreted in the modern term of (free) will. Cf. Jean-Pierre Vernant, "Ébauches de la volonté dans la tragédie grecque" ("Intimations of the Will in Greek Tragedy"), in J.-P. Vernant and Pierre Vidal-Naquet, *Mythe & tragédie en Grèce ancienne* [*Myth and Tragedy in Ancient Greece*], Maspero, Paris 1972, 41–74.

accusation is misleading for him and continuously compels him towards interpretations and examinations beyond the limits of the ordinary. It is most striking to observe that K. becomes interested in his trial despite there being no reason to afford credence to the charge against him.

The exorbitance of this desire is partially comprehensible because of its relation to another important feature of the tragic model: the ambiguity of guilt and innocence, the contingency of the accusation, what Aristotle calls the "hamartia." The accusation testifies that K. is guilty, but K., convinced of his innocence, considers the accusation a mistake. Therefore, his desire to speak before the court is motivated by the purpose to prove his innocence. However, as in the tragic model, not only do the origins of the accusation remain inaccessible to the protagonist, but his attempts to prove his innocence inevitably fail. Finally, another key characteristic of the tragic model is the sacrificial logic which, at the end, punishes the culprit. It would seem that the final scene of *The Trial*, where K. is slaughtered like a dog, repeats this logic.

It appears that we can go a long way with the model of tragedy in order to understand the case of K. in *The Trial* – long enough, at least, to become aware of a certain presence of the former in the narration of the latter. Even so, other essential features of the model of tragedy are absent from Kafka's novel. First, the novel does not refer to a given destiny previously announced by an oracle or a name or a past: the initial K., for example, entails no information about the character's origin or destiny. Furthermore, one cannot discern a plot in the narration: the different scenes and acts do not lead to a moment of insight in the sequence of scenes or in the reasons of the trial. Indeed, the plot is neutralized by the arrest of K., in the first chapter. In a realistic story, this scene would inaugurate the story of the events which had led to the arrest, or to the story of the events which lead to the judgment of the trial. In the case of K., however, there is no such ordered concatenation of events. Moreover, Kafka's narration affords no catharsis: the distanced, almost indifferent descriptions of K.'s experiences in no way appeal for either approval or sympathy from the reader/spectator. This may be the most disturbing aspect of the narration: the estrangement of the reader before the images of the story and his or her incapacity to join the world of K. Finally, there is no chorus: the narration does not incorporate or accommodate commentary, save for K.'s comments. A potential exception is the priest's comment about the parable "Before the Law": his observations seem to figure in the text the experience of the reader challenged by the multi-interpretability of the descriptions, though they shed no light upon the figure Josef K. or on the meaning of his actions. Unlike the words of the priest Tiresias in respect to Oedipus, the priest's comments in Kafka's parable offer nothing as to the truth of Josef K. or his lack of insight about his own destiny.

It is thus also possible to conclude that Kafka's novel is something quite different than mere imitation of the tragic model, different enough at least to undermine the intended effects of the tragic operations. The transformation of the narration in *The Trial* is such that the reader or spectator is no longer in a position where he or she can arrive at insight into the protagonist's desires or even sympathize with him. Yet how does one then address the question of the universal in Kafka's novel?

According to German idealism's interpretation of the Greek tragedy, the universal meaning of the tragedy is the paradox of the recognition of human freedom in the protagonist's defeat and punishment. This interpretation is based upon the conflict between the power of destiny and the finitude of the protagonist's capacities to contest this fatality. The moment of insight reveals the tragic meaning of his freedom: accepting his destiny, the protagonist resigns himself to punishment for a crime which was inevitable but for which he takes responsibility. Recognition of freedom through the protagonist's acceptance of being responsible for his actions in being punished: this recognition is a spiritual defeat of the power of destiny, for it creates the condition for a self-esteem which is appropriate for man and elevates him beyond the vicissitudes of his destiny. Nothing of all this is applicable to Kafka's novel, because there is no given destiny of the protagonist and there is no insight into the accusation of the trial. Although K. resigns at the end to the punishment to which he is subjected, this resignation does not reveal any particular meaning of his freedom and/or of his responsibility. After all: what is the crime for which K. is put to death? What kind of responsibility does K. assume when he consents to his own death? The end of the novel reveals certainly the power of the court, but it does not reveal the possibility of the sense of justice. On the contrary, in defeating K.'s indignation and struggle against a trial without cause and whose rules never become transparent, this end takes away the possibility of self-esteem.

From this, it might become clear why "Before the Law" can be understood as a kind of abstract symbol of the narrative of *The Trial*. Despite K.'s various attempts to establish contact with the court's authorities, there is no progression in the events. At the end of the novel there is no more than in the beginning: the protagonist, accused of a charge that remains unclear, seeks to address himself to the relevant authority, so as to be admitted to its rules and to be able to prove his innocence; but he never receives access to the actual circumstances of the charge against him and his death follows from his tenacious efforts to retain his demand. Nevertheless, the narrative of the novel differs from the story "Before the Law" in that the former is able to reveal something about the opening scene of the demand and about the protagonist's perseverance not to give up. Indeed, from the first chapter the protagonist's freedom and responsibility appear as the effect of the unique position of his being chosen or accused by an appeal that is addressed only to him and to which he has no access. K.'s choices and claims – in fact, his whole existence – are presented and described as the effects of this accusation, as if there had never been a life of K. without his being accused. Consequently, his case shows the impossibility of clear distinction between, on one hand, his desire to know the origins of the accusation and the rules and authority of the court and, on the other, his self-affirmed responsibility to contest the groundless charge.

3 Uniqueness of Desire or Uniqueness of Responsibility?

This impossibility may well be at the core of the difference between Kafka's novel and the tragic model. In K.'s case, the desire to know is an effect of the law that accuses him in a singular way. In Greek tragedy, the desire to know is excessive because the law is in default. K.'s attempts to justify himself before the court do not infringe the rules of the law; instead, they manifest its power. In contrast, the protagonists of the tragic model by their very actions transgress the law, thereby revealing its weakness and finitude. This strange reversal of the tragic model may have its origin in another difference. The subject of Greek tragedy is the law of the city, and what this law is about is clear: enemies of the city are punished; beneficiaries and what is good for the city are approved. In the tragic representation, this law is in default: it is confronted with a conflict that it cannot manage or resolve and where the distinction between enemies and benefactors becomes unclear and instable. In Kafka's story, however, it is never certain whether the law is the law of the city. Obviously, the law concerns a community, for there are court administrators and lawyers who conduct the trial, other people know about the trial, and it is said that "the law should be accessible for everyone at any time." Some commentators have thought that it is possible to recognize the presence of the Torah in Kafka's description of the law,[12] but this identification does not allow for revealing fundamental ambiguities in Kafka's description. The authority of the law is unaffected and indisputable, but the terms and the rules of the law are not clear: it is never entirely discernible whether they prescribe moral duties, religious prohibitions or political agreements, and the content of the charge against K. is never articulated. As a consequence, in Kafka's narrative the law remains an

---

12 Cf. the contribution of Eli Schonfeld in this volume.

abstract entity, whose anonymous omnipresence K. immediately feels yet also rejects as inacceptable, inescapable, unjust, and merciless.

In other words, there is no outside the law in the case of K. "Before the Law" is the law. The law does not accept a beyond where its power is neutralized or suspended. All ambiguities stem from this "not beyond." The law is as much external as it is internal; it is as much the instance of an accusation whose authority K. is unable to undo as it is the object of his desire. K.'s strivings to claim his freedom and to prove his innocence before the court, and his laziness or distractedness are equal effects of the omnipresence of the law. The indistinctness of K.'s desire and responsibility becomes especially evident in the scenes of his attempts to take responsibility for his trial, attempts which are time and again disturbed by erotic escapes with women he meets (apparently by accident) in the immediate proximity of the instances of authority: these include the woman of the examining magistrate in the session of the empty courtroom; the nurse Leni tending to the ill lawyer whom K.'s uncle has requested to defend K. before the court; the hunchbacked girl who is close to the painter who is asked to paint the judges of the court. In these scenes, K.'s approach to the court's authority is each time mediated by the presence of a woman who seems, to K., to be familiar with the instances of the court, yet who also attracts and seduces him, precisely because of his being accused. It is the same position of the accused that both leads him to look for support in regard to the inaccessible court's authority and renders him the chosen object of an erotic desire; hence, the distinction between K.'s interest in the court and his erotic attraction becomes unclear. In his conversation with the woman of the magistrate, K.'s intention to plead his innocence before the court is easily substituted by another aim:

> And probably there could be no more fitting revenge on the Examining Magistrate and his henchmen, than to wrest this woman from them and take her himself. Then some night the Examining Magistrate, after long and arduous labor on his lying reports about K., might come to the woman's bed and find it empty. Empty because she had gone off with K., because the woman now standing in the window, that supple, voluptuous warm body under the coarse heavy, dark dress, belonged to K. and to K. alone.[13]

The indistinctiveness between the intention to prove his innocence and the intention of his erotic desire can also be shown in a reverse way, as when K. contem-

---

13 Franz Kafka, *The Trial*, translated by Willa and Edwin Muir, revised and with additional materials translated by E.M. Butler, Vintage Books, New York 1969, 70–71.

plates profiting from his arrest by exploiting it as a means to seduce his flatmate, Fräulein Bürstner.[14]

However, the ambiguity is not restricted to K.'s unfortunate position with regard to the authority of the court. *The Trial* is not just a narrative about the double bind of the protagonist's behavior in a world ruled by an abstract, omnipresent law. The law's authority is itself represented as the origin of that ambiguity, in that it is both (and each through the other) the instance that accuses and the object of erotic desire. The painter shows K. the portrait of a judge that he is painting. He explains that it is a picture of justice, "actually it is Justice and the goddess of Victory in one" and that he has to paint it according to the instructions given by the court: "my instructions were to paint it like that."[15] The picture attests the relations between the painter and the judges of the court, and these relations guarantee the authenticity of the representation as required by the court. Yet the painting is not the representation of a general idea of justice; rather, it is the portrait of a single man: "their superiors give them permission to paint them like that. Each one of them gets precise instructions how he may have his portrait painted."[16] However, upon looking closer, K. realizes that the figure resembles "a goddess of the Hunt in full cry": "But the figure of Justice was left bright except for an almost imperceptible touch of shadow; that brightness brought the figure sweeping right into the foreground and it no longer suggested the goddess of Justice, or even the goddess of Victory, but looked exactly like a goddess of the Hunt in full cry."[17] The ambiguity is not only that the authority of the judge is represented by a goddess and that the representation of the goddess of Justice is so easily transformed into the representation of the goddess of Hunt; what is more important is that the court's authority authorizes these ambiguities. This authority installs simultaneously a law of justice that accuses and a law of desire that attracts, a law of justice as a law of erotic desire. Being accused is being in search of an erotic substitution.

From this, it follows that the court and all its representatives are in the ban of a radical, unresolvable ambiguity. The girls and women whom K. encounters in his attempts to make contact with the court are time and again considered to be trustworthy guides to the representatives of the court: "Thanks to her [the hunchback], he was able to make straight for the right door."[18] Yet, in their bodily

---

14 Cf. Kafka, *The Trial*, 29–38.
15 Kafka, *The Trial*, 182.
16 Kafka, *The Trial*, 183.
17 Kafka, *The Trial*, 184.
18 Kafka, *The Trial*, 178.

appearances in their encounters with K., they are immediately described as being "depraved" (*verdorben*), and their intimate relations to men (or at least their ever present intentions for such relations) leave no doubt for imagined ascriptions: "The girl, who was slightly hunchbacked and seemed scarcely thirteen years old, nudged him with her elbow and peered up at him knowingly. Neither her youth nor her deformity had saved her from being prematurely debauched. She did not even smile, but stared unwinkingly at K. with shrewd, bold eyes. K. pretended not to have noticed her behavior."[19] The warders, who have the power to announce the arrest, are as much the "trustworthy services" of the court's authority as they are submitted to the court's authority and punished by its executors. In the scene of the lumber-room, one of the two men who arrested K. and who are now submitted to the punishment of being flogged, remarks: "Both of us, and especially myself, have a long record of trustworthy service as warders – you must yourself admit that, officially speaking, we guarded you quite well – we had every prospect of advancement and would certainly have been promoted to be Whippers pretty soon, like this man here."[20] The humiliations inflicted to the various representatives of the court (women, warders, lawyers) manifest not only the power of the court, but moreover the state of being a representative of the court's authority. Even K., in the final scene, "submitted himself to the guidance of his escort," assuming even the initiative, "pull[ing] his companions forward" before the policeman who seemed to stop their journey going outside the city (a figure whose appearance indicates that the court's authority does not coincide with the law of the city) and convinces himself to be "grateful for the fact that these half-dumb, senseless creatures have been sent to accompany me on this journey, and that I have been left to say to myself all that is needed."[21]

It may be clear now what is lost if one interprets the story "Before the Law" without embedding it in the context of the narrative of *The Trial*. In fact, the ambiguity of the law, the double bind of its manifestation, remains unseen. Only "the fleas in his [the doorkeeper's] fur collar" in the story "Before the Law" remind us of the image of the goddess of hunt, and the "radiance that streams inextinguishably from the door of the Law" reminds us of the law's irresistible attraction – albeit in an abstract (not gender-based) way. What one loses here is nothing less than the question of the singular effectivity of the law, its double bind of accusing and attracting, which cannot be approached without revealing the intrinsic connection between the omnipresence of the law and the imagined relations to the

---

19 Kafka, *The Trial*, 177.
20 Kafka, *The Trial*, 105.
21 Kafka, *The Trial*, 283–284.

law's authority as articulated in and through the singular chain of images in *The Trial*. This chain of images is but the unique door to the law which reveals what it means that "[n]o one but you could gain admittance through this door, since the door was intended for you."[22]

4 Concluding Remarks

Where has our consideration of the Greek legacy in Kafka's novel *The Trial* led us? First, it has taken us to the conviction that, though, it is possible to insert the narrative of *The Trial* into the legacy of the tragic model, Kafka's narrative actually reverses the meaning of the tragic as understood in German idealism, for it shows the progressive loss of both self-esteem and recognition of human freedom. This reversal has its origin in a new presence and a new approach of the law: it is not the law of the city which has defaulted, leaving space for human initiative. The law, in the case of K., is abstract, anonymous; it has no outside; it is omnipresent and the protagonists are all in the ban of this "not beyond" which constitutes a law that accuses as much as it attracts, a law that meanwhile is inescapable as well as inaccessible. With regard to this law, the protagonist can only be a victim and an executor, an accused and an accuser… an executor because of being a victim, an accuser because of being accused. Second, and moreover, it has brought us to the point where Bauman mentions the story "Before the Law" in order to establish a new moral condition as a singular commitment in Levinasian terms of the uniqueness of responsibility; nonetheless, it enables us to state that it is in fact doing exactly the opposite from what Bauman claims: in short, rather than revealing the non-ambiguous meaning of a unique responsibility for the non-desirable other person, it erases the moral sense of this uniqueness, by undermining the clear distinction between desire and responsibility without which it is not possible to conceive of a just world. Third, it has helped us to approach the question of the universal in Kafka's literary work. For, as the confrontation with Aristotle's concept of representation has made clear, there is no possibility and no guarantee to define the universal in the narrative of *The Trial*: there is no insight into the meaning of the protagonist's action, no insight into the meaning of the accusation against the protagonist, no insight into the court's authority – the law itself is, despite its omnipresence, not transparent and therefore not universal. In other words, the narrative of *The Trial* denies the very

---

22 Kafka, *The Trial*, 268–269.

possibility of grasping the universal in terms of an (ethical) idea (be it the idea of justice, of faithfulness, of freedom, or of emancipation). Is Kafka therefore not the writer who shows why the question of the universal is misguided in relation to literary fiction, claiming the autonomy of the literary text and withdrawing it from any discourse about truth? Unless literary fiction reveals, in the concreteness of the image and in the singular chain of images, the true condition of any approach to the universal. In this respect, it may be possible to say that the narrative in *The Trial* reveals the paradox of the universal that situates each of us into a singular position before the law.

Works Cited

Bauman, Zygmunt, *Postmodern Ethics* (Oxford: Blackwell, 1993).

Cools, Arthur, "Levinas' Defense of Intellectualism: An Undecideable Ambiguity?" in *Debating Levinas' Legacy*. Eds. Andris Breitling, Chris Bremmers, and Arthur Cools (Leiden and Boston: Brill, 2015), 3–16.

Gasché, Rodolphe, "Kafka's Law: In the Field of Forces between Judaism and Hellenism," in *MLN* 117:5 (2002): 971–1002.

Kafka, Franz, *The Trial*. Trans. Willa and Edwin Muir, revised and with additional materials trans. E.M. Butler (New York: Vintage Books, 1969).

Lacoue-Labarthe, Philippe, *Heidegger. La politique du poème* (Paris: Galilée, 2002).

Lacoue-Labarthe, Philippe, *L'imitation des modernes. Typographies II* (Paris: Galilée, 1986).

Lacoue-Labarthe, Philippe, *La fiction du politique. Heidegger, l'art et la politique* (Paris: Christian Bourgeois, 1998).

Lamarque, Peter, *The Philosophy of Literature* (Oxford: Blackwell, 2009).

Levinas, Emmanuel, *Otherwise than Being, or Beyond Essence*. Trans. Alphonso Lingis (Pittsburgh: Duquesne University Press 2006).

Levinas, Emmanuel, *Totality and Infinity. An Essay on Exteriority*. Trans. Alphonso Lingis (Pittsburgh: Duquesne University Press, 1969).

Liska, Vivian, "'Before the law stands a doorkeeper: to this doorkeeper comes a man…': Kafka, Narrative, and the Law," in *Naharaim* 6/2 (2013): 175–194.

Liska, Vivian, "Kafka, Modernism, and Literary Theory" in *A Handbook of Modernist Studies*. Ed. Jean-Michel Rabaté (Oxford: Wiley-Blackwell, 2013), 75–86.

Robert, Marthe, *L'Ancien et le nouveau: de Don Quichotte à Kafka* (Paris: Payot, 1967).

van Peperstraten, Frans, "Modernity in Hölderlin's Remarks on Oedipus and Antigone," in *The Locus of Tragedy*. Eds. Arthur Cools, Thomas Crombez, Rosa Slegers, and Johan Taels (Leiden and Boston: Brill, 2008), 105–120.

Vernant, Jean-Pierre and Pierre Vidal-Naquet, *Mythe & tragédie en Grèce ancienne* (Paris: Maspero, 1972).

Michal Ben-Naftali
Derrida-Reads-Kafka

"He took all conceivable precautions against the interpretations of his writings," wrote Benjamin about Kafka. "One has to find one's way in them circumspectly, cautiously, and warily."[1] Cautious, circumspect, wary, and anti-hermeneutic is also Derrida-reads-Kafka: thus, in one breath, the way one says Derrida-reads-Celan or Derrida-reads-Shakespeare or Derrida-reads-Blanchot, each time producing a deconstructive exemplar, enacting differently the role of the philosopher-reading-literature that Derrida performed, a role that served him as a quasi-starting-point in an attempt to contend with all elements which constitute the philosophical architechtonics throughout Western tradition; a role whose fulfilment brings us closer to Derrida's own conception of writing.

Though Derrida is not a Kafkologist, in two of his three essays on Kafka he makes the question of literature itself a central question, as if he gave this highly specific encounter between himself and Kafka a meta-literary status. Derrida's "Before the Law" ("Devant la loi"), which discusses Kafka's ascetic parable, juxtaposes the literary thing to a legal and a moral discussion in order to address alternately the law of literature and the narrativity of law as communicating vessels; the chapter "Literature in Secret: An Impossible Filiation" ("La Littérature en secret: une filiation impossible"), which concludes *The Gift of Death* [*Donner la mort*] and reads Kafka's hyperbolic "Letter to His Father" ("Brief an den Vater") in relation to the Sacrifice of Isaac, links the literary and the religious, searching after the fundamental plot of literature. In each discussion literature is embodied in secret and as a secret which is more radical than any intentional concealment of content; in each discussion literature is half described and half performed in the very philosophical text by a philosopher who declares himself, in his turn, as someone who does not want to say or, better, is unable to say. Despite the differences between these two texts and their respective protagonists, one can read them together, namely, read the one through motifs that are raised by the other. The issues of marriage, the desire for women, parasitism, and de-socialization thus pervade "Before the Law" ("Vor dem Gesetz"), while the question of the fiction of the law and the validity of the Oedipal Law gnaw at the "Letter to His Father."

1 Walter Benjamin, "Franz Kafka: On the Tenth Anniversary of His Death" ("Franz Kafka: Zur zehnten Wiederkehr seines Todestages"), trans. Harry Zohn, in *Selected Writings*, Volume 2: Part 2: 1931–1934, The Belknap Press of Harvard University Press, Cambridge 1999, 794–818, 804.

Let us first tarry with each discussion separately. Derrida chose Kafka's German – as well as French, English, and Hebrew – idiomatic title, "Before the Law," as his own essay's title, a gesture seemingly unique in his writing. This choice of course joins the idiom's repetition both in the title and at the beginning of Kafka's text, thereby creating a non-synonymic homonymic chain, for each appearance of the same words does not carry the same semantic content. As a title that mediates between the text and the world of law, the expression "Before the Law" gives the text its proper name, attaching to it a unity and an identity which makes it classifiable. A title, Derrida argues, belongs to literature but is heterogeneous to it, while the reiteration of "Before the Law" in the parable is homogeneously assimilated to the text: it opens it and situates the characters both in the scene's interior space – that is, before the Law, namely, at a certain distance from it (the doorkeeper turns his back, as if he were ignoring, deserting, or perhaps even transgressing the Law, while the man from the country faces both the doorkeeper and the law) – and in time, for the characters precede the law and perhaps condition it. But, as is his way, the incorporation that Derrida enacts does not relate only to the title that will occur again and be cited and mentioned throughout his text. The impressive incorporation, more effective than absorption of a sheer motif or notion of the other (such as *pharmakon*, trace, *Shibboleth*, etc.), that transpires here swallows the temporality of Kafka's text, namely, the time of the story's deferral: expectation, regression, aging, the différance of days and years until the man's death. Derrida defers, at the beginning, his discussion of the parable itself – indeed, we must undertake a considerable detour until he reaches Kafka's text – in order to postpone the discussion once again, and then to promise, time and again, that he is about to end and will continue, until the moment comes when he finally closes the text. Never has Derrida's incorporation been so comprehensive. It seems that Kafka is totally absorbed in this melancholic friendship between two sons-brothers, a friendship that transforms, as we shall see, the Oedipal rules of the game.

Neither Kafka's "Before the Law" nor Derrida's discloses to what Law it refers. This silent Law might be the moral, natural, legal, or political, or, more precisely, the Law of the Law, the very notion of the Law, namely, the transcendent Law that is beyond space and time, and not the contingent phenomenal law. Derrida avoids interpreting the Law in the Jewish terms of the Tora or the Halakha. As his discussion advances, he quotes what he calls the most religious moment of Kafka's parable: "At length his eyesight begins to fail, and he does not know whether the world is really darker or whether his eyes are only deceiving him. Yet in his darkness he is aware of a radiance that streams inextinguishably from the gateway of the Law."[2] This is the only moment where an analogy to the Jewish Law is mentioned; this analogy is insistently raised by Kafka's door- or archive-keepers, yet here, as we shall learn, it offers no help in unveiling something that may have escaped other discourses. The analogy is presented precisely in order to expose the Holy of Holies as an empty space, which is profaned or secularized within literature's secret. The rigorous conceptual examination of the notion of the Law conducts Derrida towards Kant's idea of pure morality; the latter is an iron Law that allegedly exists from time immemorial and gains authority from its categorical neutralization of any empirical genesis which might refer, at the most, to the exterior circumstances of its revelation. The Law of "Before the Law" has never taken place. In his essay "Force of Law" Derrida will write:

> The being "before the law" that Kafka talks about resembles this situation, both ordinary and terrible, of the man who cannot manage to see or above all to touch, to catch up with the law: it is transcendent [...] The law is transcendent, violent and nonviolent, because it depends only on who is before it (and so prior to it), on who produces it, founds it, authorizes it in an absolute performative whose presence always escapes him. The law is transcendent and theological, and so always to come, always promised, because it is immanent, finite, and thus already past. Every subject is caught up in this aporetic structure in advance.[3]

The man from the country is thus caught in this structure like everyone else, that is, in an aporia that leads him towards a voyage, both impossible and inevitable, to the origin of the Law. He fails to recognize that what he perceives as general and available to everyone is in fact singular and transcends any historical sequence. The origin is always a moment of foundation without foundation, a moment which in other contexts Derrida terms "constitutive violence": "These are difficulties the man from the country has not expected; the Law, he thinks, should surely be accessible at all times and to everyone."[4] When sobriety comes, before a gate that was until then not closed but by the force of the doorkeeper's words, the man's consciousness can no longer contain the doorkeeper's statement: "No one else could ever be admitted here, since this gate was made only for you. I am now going to shut it."

---

2 Franz Kafka, "Before the Law," trans. Willa and Edwin Muir, in *The Complete Stories*, ed. Nahum N. Glatzer, Schocken Books, New York 1971, 3–4, 4.
3 Jacques Derrida, "Force of Law: The 'Mystical Foundation of Authority'" ("Force de loi: Le 'Fondement mystique de l'autorité'"), trans. Mary Quaintance, in *Acts of Religion*, ed. Gil Anidjar, Routledge, New York 2002, 228–298, 270.
4 Kafka, "Before the Law," 3.

For Kafka's abstract and solitary figures, Derrida finds quasi-replicas in some of the major protagonists of modern thought, including Marx, Nietzsche, and Freud. The historicist or hermeneutical efforts to tell the history of the Law, that is, to describe an entity that pushes, in principle, any genealogical gesture, share something of the vain journey made by the man from the country. Derrida's long detour to Freud does not ask to interpret the literary text through semantic, psychoanalytic, or philosophical contents. On the contrary, though Freud, in *Totem and Taboo* [*Totem und Tabu*] attempts to historically and narratively reconstruct the origin of moral Law, he wanders just like the man from the country. Apparently free to enter the Law, he is also forbidden to do so, by the Law. Freud invents a story that nobody experienced, the story of the murder of the primitive father, in order to explain in a phylogenetic manner the origin of the Oedipal Law's persistence, namely, the feelings of guilt and regret which overwhelm the neurotic sons and which in their turn augment the power of the dead father. Yet for these feelings to be evoked in the first place, the Law should have already existed. In other words, morality does not generate from this hopeless crime that keeps the murdered father alive. Morality should have been possible before the crime. The sons thus transgress an already existing Law rather than giving birth to it. This quasi-event does not generate anything, since one should assume the originary guilt of the sons, a guilt not connected with any specific crime. In the end the Freudian Law is history-free as well. In inscribing the Kantian Law into history, without reducing it to history, Freud repeats the Law's impenetrability and the unrecoverable nature of its origin. Here, as in Kafka's story, respect for the Law or the very relation to Law means forfeiting the relation to Law, ignoring who or what or where it is. Here also the subject stands before the Law outside the Law. What seems to be a re-appropriation of the Law is revealed as a futile effort before something that in principle excludes any cognitive relation to it. The Law is neither a subject nor an object before which one stands, and this includes Freud. Scholarly discussions are both necessary and superfluous, since they enact the same incapacity. Kafka and Freud's respective texts relate an impossible story, one that neither describes nor tells anything but itself. This is the case without, on one hand, Freud "influencing" Kafka, or, on the other, Kafka entering ipso facto an Oedipal pattern.

In fact, we experience the same paralysis before the Law and before the story, as if the Law shared with the literary object the same conditions of possibility. In this deconstruction, the Law is summoned before literature and literature is summoned before the Law, where both are simultaneously legible and illegible. Whatever the craft, erudition, or pretention of a certain nobility of interpretation, the text remains closed to reading, though illegibility, for Derrida, does not contradict legibility. The rule makers of literature, that is, the doorkeepers of the text – interpreters, critics, editors, scholars, translators, and teachers – receive and lose their privileged authority. For no apparent hierarchy can bypass the essence without essence of the singular Law of the text, a Law which is inaccessible to all, including the author him- or herself. Literature legislates its own Law. Like the reader, it is before the Law it legislates, as a singular performance that embraces the categorical and the idiomatic. No literary text belongs to literature as a phenomenon contained within a tradition whose borders are indivisible. The work should overcome its genre in order to be itself. The man from the country, writes Derrida, does not understand that the singular crosses the universal, and thus has difficulties not only with the Law but with literature. In "Literature in Secret" Derrida will formulate this differently: "every text given over to the public space, relatively legible or intelligible, but of which the content, the meaning, the reference, the signatory and the addressee are not fully determinable *realities*, realities at the same time *non-fictive* or *pure of all fiction*, realities handed over, as such, by an intuition, to some determinative judgment, can become a *literary* thing."[5] The description that follows is more specific, since it engages with the literary plot: "Literature would begin there where one no longer knows who writes and who signs the account of the call, and of the 'Here I am!' between the absolute Father and Son." The writer and the one who signs are undefinable, but their contours are absolute. The story, Derrida claims, is one of a call and a responsiveness between the absolute figures of father and son, which are replaceable in their very absoluteness. But to whom do the categories of writer and signatory relate? Are they characters inside the text, or do they refer to the addressor and addressee outside the text? Could the latter stay altogether undefinable? The passage from, on one hand, the abstract figures of the man from the country and the doorkeeper to, on the other, Kafka and his father complicates the picture. Moreover, it problematizes any attempt to distinguish, at least in the modern literary space beginning with the seventeenth century, between the author as an identified citizen, who signs and has legal rights, and the Orphean or Blanchotian writer; the latter is condemned by writing to de-subjectivization and expropriated from every possession, yet is afforded an infinite hyperbolic responsibility, neither ethical nor civil, in relation to the content of writing and its referent.[6]

---

5 See: Jacques Derrida, "Literature in Secret: An Impossible Filiation" in *The Gift of Death* [Second Edition] *and Literature in Secret,* trans. David Wills, The University of Chicago Press, Chicago 2007, 117–158.
6 "We say Proust, but we sense that it is the entirely other who writes, not only someone else but the very demand of writing, a demand that uses the name Proust but does not express Proust, that expresses him only by disappropriating him, by making him Other." See: Maurice Blan-

This is a story with no woman, Derrida emphasizes in *The Gift of Death*, in the chapter on the Sacrifice of Isaac. He refers also to Melville's Bartleby, wondering whether a woman's presence would have softened the law. One can say in the same vein that Kafka's "Before the Law" is a story of two alienated and solitary men, with no family, a story devoid of combat for possession of the woman or the mother. It is a scene of naked life and of years of expectation which inscribe themselves on the body with no mediation, no medicine, no work, no distraction. The man from the country stops working, in a kind of Blanchotian "worklessness" [*désoeuvrement*]. In a certain sense, by approaching the Law, he ceases being a man from the country; he leaves everything behind. He stays there, even after being forbidden to enter, and does not return to his homeland. Before the Law also means outside family and genealogy. Derrida, who dedicates himself to Kafka's abstraction, raises these motifs only indirectly, noting the increasing difference in height between the two protagonists: they create a kind of intimate encounter that blurs the borderline between the private and the public, or the infantile and the adult – the man dies as a little boy, on all fours, while the doorkeeper stands, looking down at him. De-territorialization and infantilization reveal the lining which links, for both men – who seem to share the same language and perhaps even a specular identification – between law and abjection, between the sacred and the profane.

Turning now to "Letter to His Father" means deepening what stands at the basis of Derrida's reading of Kafka, namely, the matrix of the plot deployed between the literary and the non-literary, de-socialization, literature as a language of withdrawal – the common language of the man from the country and the doorkeeper, which links literature to secret and involves religious space and non-ethical, absolute responsibility. There is, however, something delicate and complex in this trajectory. Of course, this is not done from a psychoanalytic stance that discerns in "Letter to His Father" a key to the work of someone who apparently did not escape a hyperbolic Oedipal complex. Moreover, Derrida expropriates the letter from its context, perceiving it as a foundation to literary creation in general, albeit precisely not by way of a hermeneutic key but instead as a secret that forms its heart. He does not present a key to Kafka's oeuvre. Interestingly, Kafka's most autobiographical work becomes a meta-literary work. In a direction somewhat opposite to the Oedipal, which, in *Archive Fever* [*Mal d'Archive*], he elaborates for example in relation to Yerushalmi and Freud, namely, to the monologue with the Father that reproduces the Father's score, here Derrida imagines another scenario. What was altogether omitted from his description of "Before the Law" – the motifs of the Law's brightness, or the Gate of Law which keeps the Law's Halls – receives apparent compensation through the affinity Derrida establishes between "Letter to His Father" and the Sacrifice of Isaac. Yet the Sacrifice is presented in turn as a narrative elaboration of the paradox of responsibility. The link with the Bible does not make Kafka Jewish. This is an affinity of literature whose Biblical origin, which indeed differs from that of the Greek epos, transcends the sacred ipso facto. Moreover, in Derrida's reading, the Sacrifice itself, namely, the willingness to sacrifice the most dear and unique, de-sacralizes the world, constituting a moment that profanes or secularizes the Sacred Writings, a moment which is by definition emptied of sacred signification or content. In "Literature in Secret" we learn that the crucial interest posed by the Sacrifice is neither in Isaac nor in the gift of death to the son. Instead, it lies in the secret that excludes any others and any generality, in Abraham's obligation to keep a secret no matter what. Through this affinity Derrida presents literature as a unique alliance, outside society: a locked unity betrayed by transmission, translation, interpretation and tradition. Literature generates from revelation yet necessarily both profanes and betrays it.

The connection to the Sacrifice is thus crucial. It concerns the de-socialization of Abraham the father. The son seemingly inhabits ethical generality, whereas the father, via Derrida's curious juxtaposition of him and Bartleby, transcends ethical normalcy towards non-ethical religiosity; thus the father inhabits the heart of the aporia of Law or responsibility, a singular law destined for him alone. Abraham, unlike the man from the country, knows what literature is; he dwells within the literary element, between the general and the singular, the communicative and the silent and secretive. The father is expelled from society, addressing himself against the future, against his son, against the promise, and keeping a secret unknown to himself. In order to draw the plot of the Sacrifice closer to the "Letter to His Father," which, given Kafka's stance regarding the father, seems far from the Sacrifice, Derrida uses Kierkegaard's parables from the beginning of *Fear and Trembling*. Kierkegaard here invents Isaac's response to facing a secret, undecipherable father. Because Abraham is neither epic nor tragic, a genre-less Knight of Faith, Kierkegaard can imagine Isaac and redeem him from generality, in a way that can, in a sense, link him to Kafka the son. Isaac witnesses his father without his father's knowledge, yet he is ordered to keep his father's secret. Derrida associates between Isaac, Hamlet, Kierkegaard, and Kafka: in each of these cases, the son gives the father the right to speech, but also dictates to him what he should say in response to his (the son's) letter. In each case, the son actually speaks to himself. It is as if Derrida were saying, following Kierkegaard – a pertinent possibility even if not explicit, given the son's writing which releases him from ethical generality – that Isaac invents Abraham as someone who is about to sacrifice him.

Abraham never considered it, being too preoccupied with earning a living, and thus Isaac himself hallucinates the whole affair from beginning to end through his parasitic tool, namely, writing. The son is afraid of the social burden and task imposed on him, from being the son of the promise; yet what he really wants is to write – he does not want to marry, he does not wish to further his familial lineage, he does not want a commitment that does not fit his own measures. He wishes that his father would sacrifice him in order to put an end to all this, once and for all, because he experiences the very pattern of his life and its telos as a sacrifice. Isaac does not want to live; he is Abraham's "mute," "dry," "doomed" son. This is the plot that Kafka seemingly formulates, a plot which is opposed to *Totem and Taboo* and which is written by the son, a plot whose interest is not a fight over power, women, or desire. Following this, Derrida formulates what he calls an absolute axiom: "there is in each case a sort of Letter to His Father before the event [*avant la lettre*] – before that by Kafka – signed by a son who publishes pseudonymously."[7]

To grant such a text –which was not meant to be published, and surely not as a literary work – the status of a foundational plot of literature, is a gesture that calls for explanation. If indeed this letter constitutes an autobiography – the most comprehensive one Kafka ever writes – then still, as Derrida insists, Kafka invents in it the letter his father should or could have written his son in response to it. We are facing the figure of a son who is not unlike the figure of the man from the country, a figure of someone who has failed, to use Benjamin's expression. Benjamin describes the fathers' corrupt world, which resembles the bureaucratic world in its degeneration and filth, but while Benjamin emphasizes the parasitism of the father who eats away at his son's existence, Derrida speaks of the parasitism of the son who cannot marry, who is neither respectable nor strong, and who fails to compete with his father for his place: "Parasitism is the whole cause to which the son has devoted his life, everything to which he admits having unforgivably devoted his life. He has committed the error of writing instead of working; he has been content to write instead of marrying normally."[8] Sacrifice is here conceived as part of the father's socialization and not as an anti-social act. Society sacrifices the parasitical sons who threaten its continuity, who stand outside ethical normalcy while unveiling it. Concerning Noah's son Ham, who witnesses his father's nakedness and tells his brothers, Derrida writes later in this chapter: "The fable

---

7 Derrida, "Literature in Secret," 128.
8 Derrida, "Literature in Secret," 138.

that we never stop recounting, the ellipse of time of every (hi)story, is also the nudity of the father."[9]

I noted that Derrida-reads-Kafka is a unique exemplar of deconstructive melancholia. Yet at the end of our short journey, we find Kafka distilling Derrida's Blanchotian voice, a voice crucial for understanding Derrida's writing gesture in general, also where he supposedly addresses worldly issues. Blanchot's words thus shed light on its most vital characteristics: "The work demands that [...] the man who writes it sacrifice himself for the work, become other – not other than the living man he was, the writer with his duties, his satisfactions, and his interests, but he must become no one, the empty and animated space where the call of the work resounds."[10]

Works Cited

Benjamin, Walter, "Franz Kafka: On the Tenth Anniversary of His Death," trans. Harry Zohn, in *Selected Writings*, Volume 2: Part 2: 1931–1934. Eds. Michael W. Jennings, Howard Eiland, and Gary Smith (Cambridge: The Belknap Press of Harvard University Press, 1999), 794–818.

Blanchot, Maurice, "The Search for Point Zero," in *The Book to Come*. Trans. Charlotte Mandell (Stanford: Stanford University Press, 2003), 202–210.

Blanchot, Maurice, "'Where now? Who now?'" in *The Book to Come*. Trans. Charlotte Mandell (Stanford: Stanford University Press, 2003), 210–217.

Derrida, Jacques, "Force of Law: The 'Mystical Foundation of Authority,'" trans. Mary Quaintance, in *Acts of Religion*. Ed. Gil Anidjar (New York: Routledge, 2002), 228–298.

Derrida, Jacques, "Literature in Secret," in *The Gift of Death* [Second Edition] *and Literature in Secret*. Trans. David Wills (Chicago: The University of Chicago Press, 2007), 117–158.

Kafka, Franz, "Before the Law," trans. Willa and Edwin Muir, in *The Complete Stories*. Ed. Nahum N. Glatzer (New York: Schocken Books, 1971), 3–4.

---

9 Derrida, "Literature in Secret," 138.
10 Maurice Blanchot, "'Where now? Who now?'" ("Où maintenant? Qui maintenant?"), in *The Book to Come*, 210–217, 215–216.

Section 3: **Animals**

Rodolphe Gasché
Of Mammoth Smallness:
Franz Kafka's "The Village Schoolmaster"

What is it, precisely, that the village schoolmaster has discovered in Kafka's short story "The Village Schoolmaster [The Giant Mole]" ("Der Dorfschullehrer [Der Riesenmaulwurf]") and over which he and the narrator, a businessman from the city, are engaged in a struggle that opposes them and ties them to each other? Obviously, it is the discovery of a giant mole in the neighborhood of the schoolmaster's remote, small village. Yet this is also no ordinary mole, but a truly *giant* mole, the size of "two yards," as the schoolmaster, "somewhat exaggerating the length of the mole in exasperation,"[1] exclaims while reporting his discovery to a hostile and mocking scholar whose help he has sought. In other words, it is a mole which, as the title of the pamphlet that he wrote about the case suggests, is "'larger in size than ever seen before.'"[2] Since, indeed, the size of the animal is of the order of the incredible and improbable, the fact that the schoolmaster has made the matter – which is, he avers, "infinitely [*himmelhoch*] [above the narrator's] intellectual capacity"[3] – "his lifework"[4] – a life-task as huge as the giant mole itself – raises the question of what precisely this gigantic mole actually is and what is at stake in its gianthood or giantism. Could it be that the prodigious size of this mole – a size which is indicative of a significance so huge that, in the schoolmaster's words, it infinitely transgresses the narrator's understanding – which, from the start, sets it apart from that of all other individual moles, who, as a rule, are small, has something to do with the abstract problematic of generalization, or universality? Is the tremendous size of this unique mole an instance of singularity which standard universal categories are unable to classify, or do this mole's dimensions, on the contrary, point toward a universality so heaven-wide that it becomes overbearing? In any case, with this small animal of gigantic proportions, Kafka not only seems to complicate the philosophical distinction between the universal and the singular, but, perhaps, also to suggest that, par-

1 Franz Kafka, "The Village Schoolmaster [The Giant Mole]," trans. Willa and Edwin Muir, in *The Complete Stories*, ed. Nahum Glatzer, Schocken Books, New York 1971, 168–182, 169–170. All references in the text are to this edition.
2 Kafka, "The Village Schoolmaster [The Giant Mole]," 171.
3 Kafka, "The Village Schoolmaster [The Giant Mole]," 173.
4 Kafka, "The Village Schoolmaster [The Giant Mole]," 169.

adoxically, the towering significance of the animal in question is, perhaps, also infinitely insignificant, but, as such, also all the more oppressive.

Throughout literature and philosophy, the imagery associated with the mole has, since the biblical book of Leviticus, related to an impure (because chtonic) animal. Yet the mole has also been commonly depicted, in Shakespeare and Karl Marx, for example, as a diligently toiling animal tunneling through the earth. Moreover, in what has been termed "l'univers talpologique de Franz Kafka," the figure of the mole is shown to be involved in the construction of an elaborate labyrinthine underworld of tunnels, i.e., burrows.[5] In Gilles Deleuze and Félix Guattari's *Kafka: Toward a Minor Literature* [*Pour une littérature mineure*], such burrowing is established as a guiding thread in their reading of Kafka's work, if not of this work's line of flight itself.[6] According to Karlheinz Stierle, this emphasis on burrowing, which Stierle interprets as a metaphor for "the objectification of a subjective complex of experience," is a major aspect of what he characterizes as Kafka's "development of a new meaning of the image of the mole which, at the same time, keeps alive a whole field of metaphorical relations through forms of complex metaphorical polysemy."[7] Yet although this feature of the mole's underground labor is not altogether absent from the "The Village Schoolmaster," which Kafka wrote between 1914 and 1915 but, supposedly, left uncompleted, it is, in comparison to this mole's prominent size, of secondary importance.[8] This is one reason why the story of "The Burrow" ("Der Bau"), from 1923, cannot, in my view, provide directives for how to read "The Village Schoolmaster." As several critics have noted, it is quite improbable that the animal of "The Burrow" is even a mole. The story features a much bigger animal, more likely a badger, and some have held (though I have not yet been able to discern any basis for doing so) that Kafka had initially wished to entitle the story "The Badger."[9] Be it as it may, the

5 Maurice Fleurent, *Célébration de la taupe* [*Celebration of the Mole*], ed. Robert Maurel, Editions R. Morel, Les hautes plaines de Mane 1970–1971.
6 Gilles Deleuze and Felix Guattari, *Kafka: Toward a Minor Literature*, trans. D. Polan, University of Minnesota Press, Minneapolis 1986.
7 Karlheinz Stierle, "Der Maulwurf im Bildfeld: Versuch zu einer Metapherngeschichte" ("The Mole in the Image Frame: An Attempt At Metaphoric History"), in *Archiv für Begriffsgeschichte* [*Archives of Conceptual History*] XXVI, no. 1 (1982): 101–143, 133.
8 In his diary entry of 19 December 1914, Kafka notes that on the previous night he had written "The Village Schoolmaster" "almost without knowing," but did not finish it; on 6 January 1915 he notes that "for the time being he has abandoned it." See Franz Kafka, *Diaries 1914–1923*, trans. M. Greenberg, Schocken Books, New York 1974, 103, 107.
9 Hartmut Binder, *Kafka Kommentar zu sämtlichen Erzählungen* [*Kafka Commentary on Selected Stories*], Winkler Verlag, Munich 1975, 304. See also Fleurent, *Célébration de la taupe*.

critics' embarrassment in making sense of the giant mole in "The Village School-master" is, perhaps, best illustrated by Karl-Heinz Fingerhut's study of animal figures in Kafka's work. On the basis of the enormous dimensions of the burrow in the homonymous story from 1923, Fingerhut concludes that the animal in "The Village Schoolmaster" is no other than "The Giant Mole" of the earlier story, thereby relieving himself from having to address what this mole's gigantic size is actually all about.[10] Giantness has not figured among the mole's distinguishing features in its characterizations in literature and philosophy. However, as we will see, this does not mean that Kafka invented the giant mole.

Chronologically, "The Village Schoolmaster" follows by one month the com-position of the parable "Before the Law" ("Vor dem Gesetz"). If the story presents few of the many traditional aspects of the mole metaphor as found in literature and philosophy; and if, furthermore, the rather frequent references to moles in Kafka's diaries and letters leading up to the period of the story's composition in 1914/1915 are not particularly helpful in addressing the issue of the giantism of the mole in question[11]; and if, finally, most of the sources that are considered as potential stimuli for this story, such as Ernst Hardt's "Morgengrauen" ("Dawn"),[12] shed no light on the mole's size – except, perhaps, Micha Josef Bin Gorion's *Die Sagen der Juden* [*The Legends of the Jews*](1913), a work Kafka possessed – I suggest that, when turning to the text of the story, we keep in mind Kafka's other short stories from the same period – in particular the parable "Before the Law" (written in 1914) and "The Judgment" ("Das Urteil") (from 1912).

At this juncture it is appropriate to offer some consideration of the qualify-ing adjective "giant." According to Elias Canetti, Kafka is the only Western poet who "practices, with a sovereign skill matched only by the Chinese," the art of "transformation into something small."[13] Canetti, over the course of several won-derful pages, documents Kafka's interest in "very small animals," and his trans-formation into them, precisely by way of Kafka's early accounts of his encounters with moles.[14] Yet Kafka also has a genius for the opposite talent, the skill of cre-

10 Karl-Heinz Fingerhut, *Die Funktion der Tierfiguren im Werke Franz Kafkas* [*The Function of Animal Characters in the Works of Franz Kafka*], Bouvier, Bonn 1969, 190, 225.
11 Klaus Wagenbach, to my knowledge, is the first to have recorded the presence of the figure of the mole (especially in Kafka's early writings). See Klaus Wagenbach, *Franz Kafka: Eine Bi-ographie seiner Jugend 1883–1912* [*Franz Kafka: A Biography of His Youth*], Francke Verlag, Bern 1958, 111.
12 Ernst Hardt, *Gesammelte Erzählungen* [*Collected Stories*], Insel Verlag, Leipzig 1922, 78–82.
13 Elias Canetti, *Kafka's Other Trial: The Letters to Felice* [*Der andere Prozeß. Kafkas Briefe an Felice*], trans. C. Middleton, Calder and Boyars, London 1974, 89.
14 Canetti, *Kafka's Other Trial*, 92.

ating giants. His concern with giants, and giant things, is easily documented: for example, "the dove [...] as big as a cock," from "The Hunter Gracchus" ("Der Jäger Gracchus")[15]; the "curious animal[s], half kitten, half lamb," "huge [*riesenhafte*] whiskers," from "A Crossbreed" ("Eine Kreuzung")[16]; the "overlarge egg" noted in the sixth blue octavo notebook[17]; and the "huge city" mentioned in the second notebook.[18] There are also giant persons, beginning with the "gigantic form" of the narrator in the first notebook who, in a low-ceilinged room, receives a Chinese visitor whose eyes are half-closed.[19] There is also "the huge [*riesige*] man, my father," from the "Letter to His Father" ("Brief an den Vater") whose "mere physical presence" weighed Kafka down.[20] To him Kafka says: "You were such a giant in every respect."[21] Another such figure is the "political careerist" evoked in "Fragments from Note-Books and Loose Pages" ("a man with a gigantic jaw that was gigantically moved, too, by strong muscles") as well as "the accused [who] grated his huge teeth in suspense" during the trial alluded to in these "Fragments."[22] And what about the doorkeeper of "Before the Law" (not to mention the Law itself) whose size, toward the end of the story, has, to the extent that the man from the country has shrunk, "altered much to the [country] man's disadvantage."[23] However, as is already the case in "Before the Law," and even more so in "The Village Schoolmaster," Kafka does not simply depict giants. Rather, his art consists in describing processes that inexorably cause something, or some being, to become gigantic, overbearing, and even oppressive. Yet, if it is not simply a question of things, or creatures – a mole, for example – having grown excessively large, then what is it precisely that has become gigantic?

A useful preamble to commentary on "The Village Schoolmaster" is a passage from the *Anthropology from a Pragmatic Point of View* [*Anthropologie in pragmatischer Hinsicht*] in which Kant, while distinguishing sincerity from simplicity (in

---

15 Franz Kafka, "The Hunter Gracchus: A Fragment," trans. Willa and Edwin Muir, in *The Complete Stories*, 226–230, 228.
16 Franz Kafka, "A Crossbreed [A Sport]," trans. Willa and Edwin Muir, in *The Complete Stories*, 426–427, 426, 427.
17 Franz Kafka, *The Blue Octavo Notebooks*, ed. Max Brod, trans. Ernst Kaiser and Eithne Wilkins, Exact Change, Cambridge 1991, 70.
18 Kafka, *The Blue Octavo Notebooks*, 9.
19 Kafka, *The Blue Octavo Notebooks*, 2.
20 Franz Kafka, *Letter to His Father / Brief an den Vater*, trans. Ernst Kaiser and Eithne Wilkins, Schocken Books, New York 1973, 17, 19.
21 Kafka, *Letter to His Father*, 41.
22 Franz Kafka, *Wedding Preparations in the Country and Other Posthumous Prose Writings*, trans. Ernst Kaiser and Eithne Wilkins, Secker and Warburg, London 1954, 366, 369.
23 Franz Kafka, "Before the Law," trans. Willa and Edwin Muir, in *The Complete Stories*, 4–5, 4.

short, from naïveté) and from the forced appearance of one's own personality, writes:

> The plain manner of expressing oneself, as a result of innocence and simple-mindedness (ignorance in the art of pretence), as evidenced in [...] a peasant [*Landmann*] unfamiliar with urban manners, arouses a cheerful laugh among those who are already practiced and wise in this art [...] It is a momentary cheerfulness, as if from a cloudy sky that opens up just once in a single spot to let a sunbeam through, but then immediately closes up again in order to spare the weak mole's eyes of selfishness [*um der blöden Maulwurfsaugen der Selbstsucht zu schonen*].[24]

Undoubtedly, these lines merit lengthier commentary on the metaphor of the proverbial blindness of moles. For the moment, however, it is important to note that here it is the city dweller whose short-sighted self-interest reveals him as an idiotic and nearsighted mole, when the man from the country's unsophisticated simplicity elicits in him a momentous, cheerful laughter. This passage is further notable because, in analyzing the countryman-and-city-dweller "dialectic" that structures Kafka's short story, one may encounter something like a significant variation of this theme. It should also be noted that among the antagonists in the story's struggle, not only is one from the country and the other from the city, but the man from the country is an older man, whereas the man from the city is a young man – a child, in fact, in the words of a schoolmaster.[25] Furthermore, it is a struggle between differing forms of deception. "Most old people," the young businessman submits, "have something deceitful, something mendacious, in their dealings with people younger than themselves"; however, it turns out that he himself is, admittedly, not "entirely sincere" in his dealings with the man from the country, precisely to the extent that the latter is an old man.[26]

The literature on Kafka offers few references to this short story, thereby raising the question of why this particular narrative, which possesses a remarkable formal structure, has scarcely interested scholars.[27] Most critics hold that,

---

24 Immanuel Kant, *Anthropology from a Pragmatic Point of View*, trans. R. B. Louden, Cambridge University Press, Cambridge 2006, 21. For further references to moles in Kant, see David Farell Krell, "Der Maulwurf: Die philosophische Wühlarbeit bei Kant, Hegel und Nietzsche," in *Boundary II* 9/10 (1981), 155–167.
25 Kafka, "The Village Schoolmaster [The Giant Mole]," 176.
26 Kafka, "The Village Schoolmaster [The Giant Mole]," 176.
27 A notable exception is Bernard Dieterle, "Der Dorfschullehrer (<Der Riesenmaulwurf>)" ("The Village Schoolmaster [The Giant Mole]") in *Kafka-Handbuch* [*Kafka Handbook*], eds. M. Engel and B. Averochs, Metzler Verlag, Stuttgart 2010, 266–268. This volume also contains the short bibliography of scholars who have addressed the story in question (page 280).

compared to the conflict between the two protagonists, the mole's role in the narrative is negligible.[28] Undoubtedly, it is true that by being qualified from the outset as an apparition, or even mirage (*Erscheinung*), and, furthermore, not just a rumor (*Gerücht*) but a rather "sluggish"[29] one that was never investigated in any precise fashion, the mole remains rather elusive. All we learn is that this mole is atypical and has been seen only once – all of which, not unlike the curious animal in "A Crossbreed," invites "the strangest questions," such as "why is there only one such animal?" and why "rather than anybody else" should a school-teacher have discovered it and, in this very capacity of being its discoverer, thus "own it"?[30] But even though the village teacher stylizes himself the discoverer (*Entdecker*) of the apparition, it is far from certain that he has actually seen it. As the narrator notes, the schoolmaster was not even the discoverer of the mole[31]; all he seems to have done is been the first to interrogate "those who had seen or heard of the mole"[32] and to have written "the sole account in black and white of the incident."[33] Apart from the schoolmaster's angry and exaggerated response to the scholar that the mole is two yards in size, one learns nothing else about "the mole itself."[34] Thus it might seem justified to brush aside the topic of the mole in favor of the conflict between the two protagonists. As will be shown, however, this conflict between the antagonists concerns the mole and cannot be addressed by abstracting from the topic they quarrel about.

Before turning to their fight, one should recall Kafka's statement, in "Fragments," that fighting "is the only thing to do" and that if one stops fighting, one is already definitively lost.[35] In "The Village Schoolmaster," struggle is the very condition of the protagonists. Indeed, both the village schoolmaster and the narrator from the city are, like the wrestlers from "Description of a Struggle," involved in a fight[36] or, what amounts to the same, in "working against" each

28 As one critic even remarks, "'Der Riesenmaulwurf,' another example of the motif of the mole, again serves [Kafka] only as a pretext for a lengthy discussion on our most vital, yet 'camouflaged' subject: religion." See Joachim H. Seyppel, "The Animal Theme and Totemism in Franz Kafka," in *The American Imago* 13 (1956): 69–93, 75.

29 Kafka, "The Village Schoolmaster [The Giant Mole]," 168.

30 Kafka, "A Crossbreed," 426.

31 Kafka, "The Village Schoolmaster [The Giant Mole]," 172.

32 Kafka, "The Village Schoolmaster [The Giant Mole]," 171.

33 Kafka, "The Village Schoolmaster [The Giant Mole]," 168.

34 Kafka, "The Village Schoolmaster [The Giant Mole]," 174, translation modified.

35 Kafka, *Wedding Preparations in the Country*, 334, 343–344.

36 Franz Kafka, "Description of a Struggle," trans. Tania and James Stern, in *The Complete Stories*, 9–51, 33–34.

other (*entgegenarbeiten*, that is, working against and toward each other) in a way not unlike how, in the story "My Neighbor," the businessman recounts his neighbor's actions.[37] Now, although Kafka notes of the two schoolmates from "The First Long Train Ride" ("Die erste lange Eisenbahnfahrt") that they experience in variable ways attraction and repulsion,[38] a remark from "A Little Woman" clarifies the kind of struggle that opponents in Kafka undergo. Of his relation to this little woman, who, despite her sickness, is "a fighter by nature,"[39] the narrator observes that, though he is a complete stranger to her, she "is very ill-pleased with [him]" and that "any connection between [them] is her own invention and entirely one-sided [*die Beziehung, die zwischen uns besteht, nur von ihr hergestellt ist und nur von ihrer Seite aus besteht*]."[40] In other words, the struggle between Kafka's characters is grounded in relations to others; these relations originate in one character without reciprocity from the other, and thus they will never meet midway, as it were. Speaking of his relation to his own father, Kafka evokes their mutual "helplessness" as the reason for the "impossibility of getting on calmly together."[41] Indeed, what is significant is that while Kafka's siblings and father "were always in a fighting position," and thus involved in a "terrible process [...] pending between" him and them (Kafka himself had lost the fight from early on), this struggle is not in any way "chivalrous combat, in which independent opponents pit their strength against each other."[42] It is always a non-symmetrical struggle, where each opponent's relation to the other is always created by only one of them, independently of the other, and thus it is a struggle that is mutually entirely one-sided. It is the very helplessness of each protagonist that makes him or her invent the relation to the other; moreover, this helplessness embroils them in endless struggle, not only because help is never available, but also because each opponent refuses help even while calling for it. As explained in "The Hunter Gracchus,"

> no one will come to help me; even if all the people were commanded to help me, every door and window would remain shut [...] And there is sense in that, for nobody knows of me, and if anyone knew he would not know where I could be found, and if he knew where I could

---

37 Franz Kafka, "My Neighbor," trans. Willa and Edwin Muir, in *The Complete Stories*, 424–425, 425.

38 Franz Kafka, *Erzählungen* [Stories], Fischer Verlag, Berlin 1946, 295.

39 Franz Kafka, "A Little Woman," trans. Willa and Edwin Muir, in *The Complete Stories*, 317–234, 320.

40 Kafka, "A Little Woman," 319.

41 Kafka, *Letter to His Father*, 33.

42 Kafka, *Letter to His Father*, 65, 69, 123.

be found, he would not know how to deal with me, he would not know how to help me. The thought of helping me is a sickness that has to be cured by taking to one's bed. I know that, and so I do not shout to summon help. Even though at moments [...] I think seriously of it."[43]

The struggle (over the mole) between the village schoolmaster and the businessman from the city is one waged by helpless men who invent their relation to others in search for help that they can, at best, only think of. And yet, though the participants are equal in their helplessness, the asymmetry of their mutual struggle holds as far as its outcome is concerned. One antagonist will lose the battle; the other will score a victory, however ambiguous it may be.

Concerning *The Trial* [*Der Process*] it has been remarked, for example by Hannah Arendt, that this work has from the start been recognized as "critique of the bureaucratic form of government of the old Austria in which the numerous nationalities which mutually fought each other were governed by a uniform hierarchy of civil servants."[44] Not surprisingly, one of the earliest prevailing assumptions in Kafka scholarship, one that Arendt fully shares, is that Kafka's heroes are caught in an oppressive and malicious bureaucratic machine whose machinations they seek to destroy but against which they rebel in vain. The assumption holds that Kafka's heroes always, from the start, face overpowering force against which they can only react before eventually being crushed by it. But if Kafka in the third notebook can advance that "one of the most effective means of seduction that Evil has is the challenge to struggle [*Aufforderung zum Kampf*]," is it not precisely because the struggle itself engenders, through the very machinations of the combatants, the oppressive force that destroys them?[45] What follows from this is that Kafka's heroes are anything but innocent cogs in the machine that ultimately crushes them. Rather than being entangled in a preexistent machine, it is they themselves who, through their combative machinations rooted in their very helplessness, create, with ineluctable necessity, something bigger than themselves that, inevitably, gets the better of them. As will be seen, in the struggle between the village schoolmaster and the businessman from the city, something terrible emerges from the antagonists' merciless struggle, something for which they themselves fully bear responsibility rather than simply being its innocent victims. Much Kafka scholarship is undergirded by still another assumption, or rather temptation, one which, though only implicitly, I must take issue so as to

43 Kafka, "The Hunter Gracchus," 230.
44 Hannah Arendt, "Franz Kafka," in *Die verborgene Tradition. Acht Essays* [*The Hidden Tradition. Eight Essays*], Suhrkamp, Frankfurt/M. 1976, 88–107, 92, see also 90–91.
45 Kafka, *The Blue Octavo Notebooks*, 16.

account for what happens in the story in question. I certainly do not claim anything new in noting that Kafka's main protagonists do not even have names. In the case of "The Village Schoolmaster" all that determines the two main characters are their professions and thus, at best, the social roles assigned to them in society. They lack the depth of real people; as merely a businessman and a schoolteacher they cannot be approached in any psychological or psychoanalytical manner, however seductive this temptation might be. They are exclusively a function of their actions and relations with each other, that is, of what follows from one being a man of the city and the other of the country, one being younger and the other older, one being steeped in the art of deception and the other naïve, and so forth. They will have constructed their identities as a result of their words and deeds.

The previous claim about the combative relation of Kafka's protagonists might, at first sight, be contradicted by the narrator's decision to aid the village schoolmaster. Indeed, the businessman, notwithstanding his thorough disgust for even small, ordinary moles, and his comment that the view of a giant mole would certainly have killed him, decides to come to the schoolmaster's defense.[46] From the start, of course, it is clear that his decision is hardly unselfish. On the contrary, it immediately takes the form of competition. Indeed, since in his response to the businessman's help the schoolmaster claims that he is "the first man publicly to vindicate the mole [*der erste* öffentliche *Fürsprecher des Maulwurfs zu sein*],"[47] it is unmistakably clear that the businessman has stylized himself as a *Fürsprecher* (an intercessor or advocate). But a *Fürsprecher* is also, especially in Swiss German, an attorney, that is, someone who pleads the cause of someone else in a court of law. Moreover, as we know from *The Trial*, writing reports always takes place in view of a pending examination, or trial. Hence, by writing pamphlets and engaging in a battle of documents, the advocates and attorneys in "The Village Schoolmaster" are, from the beginning, set for some sort of trial. One attorney, or *Fürsprecher*, usurps the priority of the other and earns, therefore, from the discoverer of the mole (*Maulwurf*) the constant reproach (*Vorwurf*) of seeking to disown him of his finding and rob him of his fame. Furthermore, as the schoolmaster argues, the city dweller's help is essentially no help at all and has in fact "damaged [the schoolmaster's] credit"[48] in a case (*Sache*) that is all but credible. The question, therefore, arises as to the motives and sincerity of the

---

46 Throughout the popular literature about the mole, disgust is not only regularly associated with the animal but also inspires incredible violence against it.
47 Kafka, "The Village Schoolmaster [The Giant Mole]," 172.
48 Kafka, "The Village Schoolmaster [The Giant Mole]," 171.

businessman in seeking to assist the schoolmaster in this incredible case. Even he admits that although he came to help the schoolmaster, "instead of helping him I myself would probably require support [*statt zu helfen, für mich einen neuen Helfer brauchen würde*], which was most unlikely to appear."[49] The struggle between the antagonists is about help, which the schoolmaster rejects yet continues to expect, and which the businessman seemingly wishes to provide but not, as will be seen, in full honesty, and this in turn renders him in need of help that cannot be offered. Everyone needs help, everything necessitates a supplement, and every *Wurf* requires a *Gegenwurf*, as it were. If, in this war that opposes one advocate, or attorney, against another, there is a trial, it can result only from the asymmetry of the positions and actions of both antagonists, even though at first sight this war appears to be a struggle in which one agent seeks to help the other (while at the same time usurping the other's elusive fame) and the other rejects the help he so acutely needs (yet also continues to request such support).

As noted earlier, giantism is not one of the features that commonly characterize the figure of the mole in literature and philosophy. Rather, with respect to size, it is the smallness of the extremely laborious animal that is generally highlighted, especially in contrast to its vast underground constructions and to the devastations that it creates. So far, my diggings to unearth a giant mole in the corpus of Western literature and philosophy preceding Kafka have been in vain, save for one exception, that of Jonathan Swift. In *Gulliver's Travels*, Swift notes that Gulliver, during his visit to the Brobdingnagians, after "walking to the Top of a fresh Molehill [...] fell to [his neck], in the hole through which that Animal had cast up the Earth."[50] Kafka knew this passage extremely well, as evidenced in a letter he wrote to Max Brod in 1922. But the inventor of the giant mole in Kafka's story, that is, Swift, may also have stood as a model for the battle of the pamphlets, rather than of books, that characterizes the antagonists' actions in the short story. "The Village Schoolmaster" is a story, narrated by a businessman from the city, about an exchange of pamphlets (*kleine Schiften*) variously supplementing, replacing, and disowning one another. Everything starts with a small pamphlet that the village schoolmaster writes in order to testify to the veracity

---

49 Kafka, "The Village Schoolmaster [The Giant Mole]," 170.
50 Jonathan Swift, *The Writings of Jonathan Swift*, eds. R. A. Greenberg and W. B. Piper, W.W. Norton, New York 1973, 94. It is, of course, difficult to assess whether Kafka, who in a letter to Max Brod refers to Gulliver's encounter with the Maids of Honor, whose naked bodies instill in Gulliver horror and disgust, was aware that the giant hairy blemishes on their skin – "as broad as a Trencher, and Hairs hanging from it thicker than Pack-threads" (see Swift, *The Writings of Jonathan Swift*, 95) – are, in English, moles. The letter to Max Brod is from August 1922. See Franz Kafka, *Briefe 1902–1924* [*Letters 1902–1924*], Fischer Verlag, Frankfurt/M. 1958, 405.

of the giant mole's appearance in the vicinity of his village. This small piece of writing soon gives rise to a battle of pamphlets of somewhat giant proportions, a *gigantomachia*, of sorts, concerning the existence of the giant mole. Indeed, several years after its publication, the schoolteacher follows up his pamphlet with another "brief brochure [*kleiner Nachtrag*],"[51] as the first one had passed unnoticed, not least by those who should have been especially concerned, namely, the scholarly establishment. Of course, this should hardly have been surprising, the narrator observes, since neither the abilities nor the equipment of this "excellent man in his own profession [...] made it possible for him to produce an exhaustive description that could be used as the foundation by others, far less, therefore, an actual explanation of the occurrence [*Erscheinung*]."[52] The only response to the schoolmaster's writings comes from the businessman, who is also the narrator. He is an unlikely advocate of the schoolmaster's cause, not least as he is equally unqualified to explain exhaustively the witnessed phenomenon. As soon as he reads (it is not stated where) about the schoolmaster's mistreatment by scholars, he decides to come to the defense of this "honest but uninfluential man"; before even familiarizing himself with the teacher's pamphlet, he resolves "to collect and correlate all the information [he] could discover regarding the case."[53] He muses: "If I wanted to convince people I could not invoke the teacher, since he himself had not been able to convince them. To read his pamphlet could only have led me astray, and so I refrained from reading it until I should have finished my own labors. More, I did not even get in touch with the teacher."[54] As a result, the businessman from the city shoulders a "great burden of work" in that he is "compelled to undertake anew all the inquiries [the village schoolteacher] had already made."[55] In fact, he inadvertently reduplicates everything the teacher had accomplished in the original pamphlet, such that "from my words one might have thought nobody had ever inquired into the case before, and I was the first to interrogate those who had seen or heard of the mole, the first to correlate the evidence, the first to draw conclusions."[56] The businessman's reduplication of the schoolmaster's efforts, which characterizes their conflict, is itself already a usurpation not only of the schoolmaster's initial efforts to reduplicate witnesses' accounts of the phenomenon, as well as efforts of those who had heard about it,

---

51 Kafka, "The Village Schoolmaster [The Giant Mole]," 169.
52 Kafka, "The Village Schoolmaster [The Giant Mole]," 168–169.
53 Kafka, "The Village Schoolmaster [The Giant Mole]," 170.
54 Kafka, "The Village Schoolmaster [The Giant Mole]," 170.
55 Kafka, "The Village Schoolmaster [The Giant Mole]," 170.
56 Kafka, "The Village Schoolmaster [The Giant Mole]," 171.

but also of something that belongs properly to the schoolmaster. Indeed, commenting on how the schoolmaster responds to the businessman's statements, the latter notes "the old teacher's habit of repeating the other person's answers."[57] As a teacher, the schoolmaster is, in a way, a champion of reduplication.

Of course, in the introduction to his pamphlet, the narrator states that his intention is only to give "the schoolmaster's book the wide publicity it deserves"[58] and that, once this goal has been reached, that his name should be effaced from the affair. However, by completely ignoring the schoolmaster's pamphlet, the businessman not only forces himself (*drängte ich mich*), in the schoolmaster's words, into the discovery itself, but also substitutes his pamphlet for the schoolmaster's and thus potentially robs the latter of the fame of being the mole's first public advocate. Admittedly, there are differences between the two pamphlets; yet this lack of agreement on certain important points partially invalidates the schoolmaster's conclusions. Furthermore, the businessman, although he declares in the introduction of his pamphlet that he has no wish to achieve anything for himself through these efforts but seeks only to help the first discoverer of the mole become publicly recognized, by "disclaim[ing] expressly any major participation in the affair [*Sache*]" and by suggesting that he is merely interested in defending the teacher's honesty, in fact belittles (*entwerten*) the significance of the teacher's so-called discovery. As the schoolmaster observes, this new pamphlet, under the pretext of helping him, instead draws attention to the discovery "merely for the purpose of depreciating it."[59]

As the businessman undertakes anew all of the schoolteacher's investigations in order to write his own first pamphlet in the aftermath of the schoolteacher's two publications, the latter places myriad obstacles in his way. When the businessman finally contacts the schoolteacher, the difference of opinions not only prevents establishment of friendly relations; it also triggers a battery of reproaches from the latter. It is important to note that although the narrator considers the reproaches that he receives for his efforts as an intercessor in the schoolmaster's case to be "unbelievable reproaches [*Vorwürfe*]," he also claims to have "in some manner foreseen" them.[60] He even observes that "there was a faint show of justice in what [the schoolteacher] said or rather hinted"[61] and that the latter's perspicacity (*Scharfsinn*) regarding his intentions was to the point.

---

57 Kafka, "The Village Schoolmaster [The Giant Mole]," 175.
58 Kafka, "The Village Schoolmaster [The Giant Mole]," 172.
59 Kafka, "The Village Schoolmaster [The Giant Mole]," 173.
60 Kafka, "The Village Schoolmaster [The Giant Mole]," 172.
61 Kafka, "The Village Schoolmaster [The Giant Mole]," 172.

Furthermore, following the schoolmaster's claim that the businessman does not understand the significance of his discovery, that he does "not prize it at its true value," and that he has "no real feeling for it" because "it was infinitely above [his] intellectual capacity [*himmelhoch* über *meinen Verstand hinaus*]," the narrator admits not only that he lacks the necessary scientific qualifications for the affair, but also that his interest in the matter was perhaps "really too trivial" and that even if he "had been the discoverer [of the mole, he] would probably never have come forward so gladly and voluntarily in defense of the mole as [he] had in that of the schoolmaster."[62]

Writing a pamphlet in support of the fate of the schoolmaster usurps from the start his originality, and thus supplants it. However much the schoolmaster may have depended on help from a man of the city, he cannot but respond to the latter's work by way of a series of reproaches. In the schoolmaster's words, the businessman's pamphlet is double-faced (*doppelzüngig*). It is divided in itself, as are the reproaches of the schoolmaster himself, insofar as he, without hesitation, accepts the businessman's financial generosity. There is also the fact that, just as the schoolmaster's two pamphlets were unsuccessful, that of the businessman also fails to achieve success; the two pamphlets even become confused with each other. This happens when a comment on the businessman's piece appears (albeit in "small print") in "a leading agricultural journal." This article not only derides the whole affair; it mistakes the pamphlet of the businessman for one of those of the teacher, thereby demonstrating that neither man's research has been read by the article's author.[63] This review of the case complicates, and even exasperates, the battle of the pamphlets, particularly when the schoolmaster learns about the article. He even suggests, in a letter sent ahead of his visit to the businessman, that the latter not only is responsible for the confusion in question, but also had smoothed the path for it to occur. Furthermore, the businessman, in his verbal reply to the schoolmaster's accusation – a reply of which he "made a note [...] shortly after [their] interview": hence, in another piece of writing – declares that their "ways part from this moment."[64] One should not overlook the businessman's offer to eventually publish in the agricultural journal an admission of his failure to help the schoolteacher, so that the confusion concerning their pamphlets could be undone and the schoolmaster's original authorship be restored; as the businessman confesses, these words "were not entirely sincere, but what

62 Kafka, "The Village Schoolmaster [The Giant Mole]," 173–174.
63 Kafka, "The Village Schoolmaster [The Giant Mole]," 174.
64 Kafka, "The Village Schoolmaster [The Giant Mole]," 175.

was sincere in them was obvious enough."[65] Resultantly, the old man's response is, in the young businessman's words, unsurpassably mendacious (*unübertrefflich Lügnerische*). Indeed, despite denying any need of help throughout all their exchanges, the schoolteacher now professes, not without some ambiguity and only after his advocate admits his failure, to have looked forward to the businessman's help. What makes this "new decree" a "final deceit," as the translator renders "*unübertrefflich Lügnerische*," is that it is, paradoxically, more self-evident (as if there could be an intensification [*Steigerung*] of the self-evident, as Kafka muses) than what the schoolmaster had always said, which itself was thus always also already mendacious.

Before turning to the narrator's final response to this decree from the visiting schoolmaster, it should be kept in mind that he has "sent out a circular [*Rundschreiben*] demanding the return of all the copies" of his own pamphlet.[66] Most of these copies have been returned to him and lie piled upon the table. The schoolmaster has not yet seen the circular, which, according to its own wording, is intended to annul the businessman's intervention in the affair and to restore all credit for the mole's discovery to the schoolteacher. Yet, there is no evidence in the story that the businessman will eventually show it to the schoolmaster. For the moment, at least, the narrator keeps his hand over the circular, in which he declares that he is withdrawing his pamphlet but not because the expressed opinions about the case were erroneous. However, without the schoolmaster having seen the circular, the retroactive annulation of the advocate's intervention will not have taken effect. It will not have ended their struggle, nor will it lead to the separation that the businessman seeks. That there is seemingly no end to the case becomes evident in the businessman's lengthy response to the schoolmaster's decree.

The businessman, still hiding the circular from the schoolteacher, reminds him that his discovery is not necessarily more important than any other discovery, and that his expectations that his findings would be embraced by the learned societies were entirely unrealistic. He then submits:

> While I myself still hoped that something might come of my pamphlet, the most I expected was that perhaps the attention of a professor might be drawn to our case, that he might commission some young student to inquire into it, that this student might visit you and check in his own fashion your and my inquiries once more on the spot, and that finally, if the result seemed to him worth consideration – we must not forget that all young students are full of

---

65 Kafka, "The Village Schoolmaster [The Giant Mole]," 176.
66 Kafka, "The Village Schoolmaster [The Giant Mole]," 178.

skepticism – he might bring out a pamphlet of his own in which your discoveries would be put on a scientific basis.[67]

The businessman conjectures that, in the best of scenarios, an even younger man than himself would, after independently verifying the evidence for the existence of the giant mole, have written another – this time, properly scientific – pamphlet. At this point the businessman wonders about the implications of the unlikely scenario in which this hypothetical pamphlet would have met not ridicule but acceptance. Some people, perhaps, may then have paid attention to the schoolmaster, and the agricultural journal might possibly have had to publicly apologize for its dismissal of his discovery; in all likelihood, however, the scientific establishment would have soon sent him back to his village. Even worse, by being recognized by scientific societies the village schoolmaster would have been disowned of his discovery. Furthermore, as the businessman argues, the schoolmaster would no longer "hear much more about it," and what he would hear would be scarcely understandable to him: the discovery, as "related to fundamental axioms" so abstract as to be impossible for people like themselves to understand, would have been "raised on these axioms into the very clouds."[68] The schoolmaster, who had claimed that his discovery infinitely (*himmelhoch*) surpassed the businessman's intelligence, would no longer be in a position to recognize his own discovery. In short, his discovery, though he "clung to his mole, so to speak, with both hands,"[69] "would [have been] taken out of [his] hands,"[70] without possibility of reproach or protest.

It merits noting again the businessman's claim that, in wanting to help the schoolmaster, it was bound to happen that he himself would be misunderstood "and that instead of helping him I myself would probably require support [*einen neuen Helfer brauchen würde*], which was most unlikely to appear."[71] In speculating about a young student who could have offered such help, it becomes evident that this assistance would have been effectively the exact opposite of help and in fact would have cemented the schoolmaster's total disownment from his discovery. And thus the businessman's last speech, in which he acknowledges his

---

67 Kafka, "The Village Schoolmaster [The Giant Mole]," 179.

68 Kafka, "The Village Schoolmaster [The Giant Mole]," 180. The qualification of the discovery as one of skyward importance that infinitely surpasses the understanding of the city dweller is a rare occasions in the story in which Kafka resorts to, and transforms, a classical connotation of the figure of the mole in literature and philosophy, namely, the mole's binary opposition to the figure of the imperial eagle.

69 Kafka, "The Village Schoolmaster [The Giant Mole]," 173.

70 Kafka, "The Village Schoolmaster [The Giant Mole]," 180.

71 Kafka, "The Village Schoolmaster [The Giant Mole]," 170.

failure, is the final effort to "withdraw now and undo what I've done [*es ungesche-hen zu machen*] as far as I'm able."[72] It is, indeed, an attempt to withdraw from the struggle by conceding defeat. However, before examining how the schoolmaster frustrates the advocate's attempt to withdraw on his own terms (that is, in a way that would prevent him from having entirely lost the struggle) and undo what he has done, namely, to extirpate himself from the battle of pamphlets (and the accompanying speeches) and the trial of sorts that he has engendered, it is necessary to return to the question of the mole, and its giantness.

As has been seen, the village schoolmaster has made the appearance of a giant mole in the neighborhood of his village into his lifework. In devoting himself to investigating (*untersuchen*) this phenomenon, the schoolmaster, who, on one of his visits to the businessman, wears "an old-fashioned padded overcoat [*eigentümlich wattierten Rockes*],"[73] has dug through all the witnesses' reports and quarried an immense amount of work, not unlike the proverbial mole. And yet the discovery of the mole "failed to penetrate [*durchdringen*]."[74] By making the discovery (*Entdeckung*) of this giant mole his lifework – unearthing it, so to speak (*entdecken* originally means *aufdecken*) – and always claiming, in his struggle against any attempts to reduplicate his discovery, to be the original discoverer, the schoolmaster clearly asserts his privilege, or prerogative, over the mole. It is, indeed, a gigantic mole, and thus much is at stake in it. It is so sizable, in fact, as to affect the schoolmaster's life; as his efforts and appearance reveal, he has even assumed some of the animal's features.

At the beginning of this article I raised the question about what is at stake in the giantness of the mole. Any ordinary mole is a small animal. So what is at stake in rendering as oversized this animal that is so small and, therefore, so insignificant? In the context of the story, is smallness and insignificance not also the fate of all country people? Do the city people not far surpass them? Are they not infinitely insignificant, even tiny in, every regard? And, finally, are the country people, and in particular the peasants, not themselves all moles, clinging to the soil, digging through the earth, nearsighted, if not even blind, in short, disgusting? In contacting the scientific societies in the city did the village schoolmaster not endeavor to attain their recognition and, in order to do this, thus need a mole significantly larger than any previously witnessed? Yet what, indeed, is a giant mole? Since ordinary moles are small animals, the giant mole is, perhaps, not just a mole that measures some two yards, as the schoolteacher holds when

---

72 Kafka, "The Village Schoolmaster [The Giant Mole]," 181.
73 Kafka, "The Village Schoolmaster [The Giant Mole]," 175.
74 Kafka, "The Village Schoolmaster [The Giant Mole]," 174.

defending himself against an incredulous scholar. In my view, the question of proportion concerns not so much the animal itself as its characteristic smallness. Is the giant mole, then, not rather a *mammoth small* animal whose distinguishing trait is its oversized smallness? That is, is not this gigantically tiny creature in fact a small animal whose very smallness has been magnified to such an extent that its tininess appears monstrously huge? But how is one to *think* such mammoth smallness? Rather than just a single, magnified mole, might not the giant mole be the incarnation of the species "mole," that is, the entire species in the shape of one oversized mole? If so, what the village schoolmaster discovered would in fact be the universal mole, the hyperbolic blow-up of all particular moles. Perhaps! But it should be kept in mind that in the story only one particular mole has been sighted, one that is oversized, even gigantic. From the start, what is in question is a singular mole, which is unique in that it is a mammoth animal. The very size of this small animal makes it universally significant. Yet, Kafka's story is in no way a literary illustration of the philosophical distinction between the universal and the singular; rather it is a radical reconception of it. Indeed, if something small is perceived and conceived as huge, without being defined by species-related criteria, then such mammoth smallness would thereby hint at a novel conception of the universal. Furthermore, if the mole's gigantic size is an "analogon" of universality, this universality is also necessarily singular in a sense. The singularity of the mole's importance, paradoxically, is its unique insignificance.

As noted earlier, the schoolmaster qualified his discovery of the giant mole as being sky-high (*himmelhoch*), infinitely surpassing the businessman's understanding. In inflating the mole's smallness, does his discovery not rather consist of a disproportioned smallness that rises above the earth and soars, eagle-like, into the heavens – a mammoth smallness of imperial dimensions? Moreover, in defending his discovery and forging it into his lifework, he takes responsibility not only for its smallness, even made gigantic, but also for the overwhelming significance of whimsical, or droll, insignificance. However, as suggested previously, the mole is the schoolmaster's privilege; thus he, and not the businessman from the city, has a prerogative in the affair. Yet what, essentially, is a privilege? In answering this question, it is important to note, especially as here the schoolteacher's quarrel is with a city dweller, that, traditionally, the law is always the law of the city. So, again, what does a privilege consist of? Is it not, as its derivation from the Latin *privus* ("single," "each every individual," "one's own," "peculiar," and "particular") and *lex* ("law"), suggests, a law for one, a law that is peculiar to only one singular case or to one individual? A privilege, then, rather than being an abstract generality or universality, is a singular law. As suggested, not only has this giant mole been sighted only once: like the animal in "A Crossbreed," there is only one exemplar of it – and it is the schoolmaster who, in a way, is its only owner, in that he has made it his life's task to render the giant mole's existence public. In the same way as the law in "Before the Law" reveals itself as one accessible (and thus defined) by a gate made exclusively for the countryman, the giant mole, I contend, is the law of the schoolteacher. In this context, it is important that the businessman suggests that the schoolmaster "had hit upon [his] discovery more by chance than by design" and that it remained "one case [*Einzelfall*]"[75] – just as, in "Before the Law," the gate before which the man from the country waits was made solely for him. With Keats in mind, who, in "Isabella," evokes "a demon-mole,"[76] I submit that the appearance of the giant mole, rather than being just a specter or ghostly apparition, is the schoolmaster's individual *daimon*, "the divine something" within him alone, of which Socrates speaks. If the giantism of the mole is repeatedly qualified in the narrative as improbable and laughable, is it not also because this giantism is construed as a law for only one? Therefore the project of proving this giantism requires all the help it can get, even though such help, because of its intrinsic ambiguity, is counterproductive.

But the schoolmaster, by writing a pamphlet about the discovery of an over-sized mole, has also thrown down the gauntlet to the city dwellers. He is not only the one who discovered the giant mole but, driven by this *daimon*, also the one who initiated the struggle, the war of pamphlets. In seeking the attention of the scientific establishments of the city, he initiated the "dialectic" between the country person and city dweller, between mole-like blindness and enlightenment, between naïveté and the art of appearance. This "dialectic" leads the schoolmaster's advocate from the city to have, as he boasts, "probed deeply [*eingebohrt*]"[77] into the former like only a mole can and thus to have been countrified in turn. But the conflict is not symmetrical. It initially seems that the businessman has manipulated, and thus dominated, the struggle; however, the shift that occurs after it has "turned out [*gewendet*]"[78] that all his efforts have been a failure, causing him to disengage from the conflict and wash his hands of it, suggests that in fact the schoolmaster has gained the upper hand in the struggle. It is he who will pronounce the final verdict. Furthermore, as a result of their struggle, the sky-high important discovery of the schoolmaster's giant mole has become transformed: it no longer represents a law, or universal, applicable to only one singular person; it has become a most oppressive reality. Indeed, although the businessman has bidden him a last farewell, thereby seeking to permanently disengage himself

---

75 Kafka, "The Village Schoolmaster [The Giant Mole]," 180.
76 John Keats, *Poetical Works*, ed. H. W. Garrod, Oxford University Press, London 1966, 190.
77 Kafka, "The Village Schoolmaster [The Giant Mole]," 176.
78 Kafka, "The Village Schoolmaster [The Giant Mole]," 179.

from the conflict, the schoolmaster does not budge and continues to burden his host with his "silent presence."[79] The narrator observes: "As I contemplated the stubborn little fellow from behind, while he sat at the table, it seemed an impossible idea ever to show him the door." On previous visits, the schoolmaster had often disturbed (*befremdet*) him, but this time "his silent presence as he sat there was an actual torture."[80] By characterizing the village schoolmaster as a "little fellow" (*kleinen zähen Alten*), the struggling young businessman is seen as rising beyond the old man and all his self-deluded importance. But when the schoolmaster recounts to the businessman the conversation he had with his wife after he had learned that a man of the city had felt compelled to enter into his affair, he "pushed his chair back from the table, got up, spread out his arms, and stared at the floor, as if his tiny little wife were standing there and he were speaking to her."[81] Rising before his wife while explaining to her how the businessman could help him in bringing his discovery of a giant mole to the attention of the city, the little fellow, indeed, becomes a giant who is no match for the businessman. Furthermore, in the final scene, the little fellow, who, with all his bitter reproaches (*Vorwürfe*) against the businessman, has proven to be somewhat mole-like, is not only regarded by the narrator as a giant, but also, seen from behind – clad, it can be assumed, in his old-fashioned padded overcoat – he actually looks like a giant mole. Not unlike, in *The Trial*, the judge in the painting, about whom Leni informs Josef K. that "he's a small man, almost a dwarf" and "yet in spite of that he had himself drawn out to that length in the portrait," the schoolmaster has enhanced his size.[82] It is as if the insignificant village schoolteacher, who has, the narrator asserts "in a certain sense [...] become [his] teacher,"[83] has also, for his part, learned from the man of the city the art of deceptive appearance of which Kant spoke. The narrator, as described at the beginning of the story, finds even a small, ordinary-sized mole utterly disgusting. But the stink of the schoolmaster's tobacco is so penetrating as to be unbearable. Thus, it can easily be assumed that the presence in his room of this giant mole, who shows no desire or inclination to stir forth, is oppressive enough to conclude the conflict, and the trial, with a death sentence for the narrator – a sentence resulting from a law that he himself has labored to bring about, but whose sight is so disgusting as to kill him on the spot. The little fellow, whom the businessmen cannot show the door, will have

---

79 Kafka, "The Village Schoolmaster [The Giant Mole]," 182.
80 Kafka, "The Village Schoolmaster [The Giant Mole]," 181.
81 Kafka, "The Village Schoolmaster [The Giant Mole]," 177.
82 Franz Kafka, *The Trial*, trans. Willa and Edwin Muir, Schocken Books, New York 1974, 108.
83 Kafka, "The Village Schoolmaster [The Giant Mole]," 176.

won the struggle that he initiated. Indeed, now that the verdict has been rendered, it is he, though not budging from his seat in the businessman's apartment, who will replace the man from the city. His singular law will have substituted itself for the law of the city. Yet the death of the businessman is the death of the story's narrator. His execution leaves no one to help by testifying or speaking for someone denied a hearing. No one remains to advocate his case, that is, to publicly vindicate the giant mole and its mammoth smallness. The schoolmaster's victory is thus, to say the least, ambiguous: In the narrator's place only "the silent presence" of the man of the country can be "heard," or, rather, is no longer heard. With the destruction of the law of the city, i.e., the law for the many, the law for one will also have been reduced to silence.

Kafka owned a copy of Micha Josef Bin Gorion's *Die Sagen der Juden*, and thus would likely have been familiar with the Jewish legend about the three strange or monstrous creatures that God created in distinction from all other creatures: these three are the mole, the snake, and the frog. It is true that only the snake and the frog are described as giant creatures. But of the mole it is expressly stated that "if it sees the light of day, no being is capable of continuing to exist anymore [*wenn er das Tageslicht erblickt, so kann kein Wesen vor ihm bestehen*]."[84] In other words, no other creature can possibly subsist the presence and the sight of this monstrous mole. But, in light of the logic of Kafka's short story, it follows that the very day the mole sees the light of day and succeeds in imposing his own law, his own presence is also reduced to inexistence. Before himself even he cannot subsist.

Works Cited

Arendt, Hannah, "Franz Kafka," in *Die verborgene Tradition. Acht Essays* (Frankfurt/M.: Suhrkamp, 1976): 88–107.
Bin Gorion, Micha Josef, *Die Sagen der Juden* (Frankfurt/M.: Rutten and Loening, 1913).
Binder, Hartmut, *Kafka Kommentar zu sämtlichen Erzählungen* (Munich: Winkler Verlag, 1975).
Canetti, Elias, *Kafka's Other Trial: The Letters to Felice*. Trans. C. Middleton (London: Calder and Boyars, 1974).
Deleuze, Gilles and Felix Guattari, *Kafka: Toward a Minor Literature*. Trans. D. Polan (Minneapolis: University of Minnesota Press, 1986).
Dieterle, Bernard, "Der Dorfschullehrer (<Der Riesenmaulwurf>)," in *Kafka-Handbuch*. Eds. M. Engel and B. Averochs (Stuttgart: Metzler Verlag, 2010), 266–268.

---

84 Bin Gorion, Micha Josef, *Die Sagen der Juden*, Rutten and Loening, Frankfurt/M. 1913, 70. I thank David Suchoff for this reference.

Fingerhut, Karl-Heinz, *Die Funktion der Tierfiguren im Werke Franz Kafkas* (Bonn: Bouvier, 1969).

Fleurent, Maurice, *Célébration de la taupe*. Ed. Robert Maurel (Les hautes plaines de Mane: Editions R. Morel, 1970–1971).

Kafka, Franz, *The Blue Octavo Notebooks*. Ed. Max Brod. Trans. Ernst Kaiser and Eithne Wilkins (Cambridge: Exact Change, 1991).

Kafka, Franz, *Briefe 1902–1924* (Frankfurt/M.: Fischer Verlag, 1958).

Kafka, Franz, *Diaries 1914–1923*. Trans. M. Greenberg (New York: Schocken Books, 1974).

Kafka, Franz, *Gesammelte Erzählungen* (Leipzig: Insel Verlag, 1922).

Kafka, Franz, *Letter to His Father / Brief an den Vater*. Trans. Ernst Kaiser and Eithne Wilkins (New York: Schocken Books, 1973).

Kafka, Franz, "The Village Schoolmaster [The Giant Mole]," trans. Willa and Edwin Muir, in *The Complete Stories*. Ed. Nahum Glatzer (New York: Schocken Books 1971), 168–182.

Kafka, Franz, *Wedding Preparations in the Country and Other Posthumous Prose Writings*. Trans. Ernst Kaiser and Eithne Wilkins (London: Secker and Warburg, 1954).

Keats, John, *Poetical Works*. Ed. H. W. Garrod (London: Oxford University Press, 1966).

Krell, David Farell, "Der Maulwurf: Die philosophische Wühlarbeit bei Kant, Hegel und Nietzsche," in *Boundary II* 9/10 (1981): 155–167.

Seyppel, Joachim H., "The Animal Theme and Totemism in Franz Kafka," in *The American Imago* 13 (1956): 69–93.

Stierle, Karlheinz, "Der Maulwurf im Bildfeld: Versuch zu einer Metapherngeschichte," in *Archiv für Begriffsgeschichte* XXVI, no. 1 (1982): 101–143.

Swift, Jonathan, *The Writings of Jonathan Swift*. Eds. R. A. Greenberg and W. B. Piper (New York: W.W. Norton, 1973).

Wagenbach, Klaus, *Franz Kafka: Eine Biographie seiner Jugend 1883–1912* (Bern: Francke Verlag, 1958).

David Suchoff
Irreducible Pluralities: The Jewish Legacy of Franz Kafka

In revisiting the Jewish reception of Kafka, I would like to begin with a story that Franz Kafka told Milena Jesenská, his Czech translator and lover. In this story, Kafka tells Milena of his own interest in the problem of "universal" definitions – those ways we categorize other people. The topic of Kafka's story is the commonplace definitions that are used to distinguish Germans from Jews. The tale concerns Mathilde, the wife of Heinrich Heine, the greatest – we could say the most universally loved – German-Jewish writer before Kafka. "Next we come to Judaism," Kafka tells Milena, after a sardonic discussion of Franz Werfel, "but then again, you should hear a pretty story from me once in a while." The promise here is of pleasure, expressed in Kafka's awareness that he is both defining and crossing a linguistic line: he is telling this tale about Heine's family, after all, in response to Milena's request to define his Jewish identity: and to do so, as one would say in the Jewish tradition, while standing on one foot.

"You ask me if I am a Jew," Kafka reminds his correspondent, with his next line posing the question of his own singularity with a difference: as the "particular" that transforms its universal box into a liberating variety of terms. "Perhaps you were joking around," is how he makes his opening, as he introduces his preferred and in a strict sense most essential approach to such questions of definition: "or perhaps you are asking whether I am one of those anxious Jews." From the outset it is evident that Kafka's answer proceeds in his characteristic fashion: he sets two popular, and limiting, notions of Jewish difference – laughter, and anxiety – in contact with one another. In terms of Kafka's own bestiary, he moves forward like his "giant mole," that creature difficult to discover: as an animal who works to establish covert passageways, and pleasurable, underground tunnels that connect two. Whereas the "anxious Jew" acts out uncertainty over his lack of fit with the "universal" and plays a predictable vaudeville role, the prospect that Milena was "just joking around" uncovers a different formulation: that Kafka took pleasure in his own Jewish difference, and viewed the "universal" less as a source of "paradox" or contradiction than as a repository of irreducibly plural perspectives and differences to be excavated and enjoyed.

Kafka first apologizes before telling the story of his Jewish identity: one reason for this might be that Milena is not herself Jewish and the story he is about to retell includes various stereotypes, some of which she may not know how to apply. But since, as Kafka writes elsewhere in an aphorism, "what is intended to be actively destroyed must first of all have been firmly grasped,"[1] he recounts the tale in the following form:

> Mathilde was constantly irritating [Meissner] with her outbursts against the Germans: they were spiteful, opinionated, overly clever, quibbling, and pushy – in short, an unbearable people. "You don't know the Germans at all," Meissner finally answered back. "Henry's social circle here in Paris consists entirely of German journalists," he told her, "and they are all Jews." "Come on," she responded, "you're exaggerating, of course there might be a Jew here or there in the bunch. Take Seiffert, for instance." "No," said Meissner, "he is the only non-Jew." "Really?" said Mathilde. "What about Jeitteles?" she asked, who was a strong, blond specimen of a man: "could he be a Jew?" "Of course," said Meissner. But "Bamberger?" "Him too." "Arnstein?" "Just the same." And so it followed as she went down the list of all his acquaintances. Finally, Mathilde became angry and said: "You're just trying to make fun of me! Now you'll try to top it off by telling me that 'Kohn' is a Jewish name, but Kohn is a cousin of Henry's and Henry is a Lutheran!" (to this Meissner had no response).[2]

Kafka concludes by entertaining his future readers with this moral: "in any case, you don't seem frightened of Judaism at all": Mathilde is thereby redeemed from her role as the idiot of the Jewish family by her failure to master the terms that would place every individual in a universal box. In this failure to reduce Germans and Jews to their dominant paradigms, Mathilde becomes quite beautifully singular, as she makes a mockery of universally valid categories. Her wisdom therefore refers us neither to the philo-Semite, sometimes defined as an anti-Semite who likes Jews, nor to the Talmudic adage that all praise carries within it the seeds of its opposite by holding us to a pattern we can only fail to match. In her own inimitable fashion, Heine's wife points us toward those multiple differences that fit no priestly definition – national, religious, or otherwise: she is, in other words, the potential *mensch* of the story, or the Jewish definition of the human being.

Why would Kafka – like Wittgenstein – highlight these multiple pleasures of the universal? The reason, as his own story about Heine suggests, was that such categories for identity had already reduced Jews, and other others, into a stage comedy of types that were much less enjoyable in his period. And by discussing "whether I am a Jew" with his translator, Kafka was raising the question of his reception as a Jewish writer with this negative – that is, reductive – form of

---

1 Franz Kafka, *The Blue Octavo Notebooks*, ed. Max Brod, trans. Ernst Kaiser and Eithne Wilkins, Exact Change, Cambridge 1991, 95; Franz Kafka, *Nachgelassene Schriften und Fragmente II* [*Posthumous Writings and Fragments II*], ed. Jost Schillemeit, S. Fischer, Frankfurt/M. 1992, 133: "Was tätig zerstört warden soll, muß vorher ganz fest gehalten worden sein."
2 Franz Kafka, letter to Milena Jensenská, 30 May 1920, in *Briefe an Milena* [*Letters to Milena*], Fischer, Frankfurt/M. 1983, 93, my translation.

comedy in mind. Such acts of self-definition, for Kafka, were thus a special kind of pain: something less than a pursuit of philosophical meaning, yet also more profound, in that his writing cleverly internalizes and explodes the narrowness of national clichés. "You as a woman of Prague," Kafka therefore tells Milena, "will not be so innocent." For "innocent," Kafka uses the German word *harmlos*: for while universal definitions can indeed inflict much *harm*, we are not so easily *los*, or rid of them, especially, as he means to relate to her, where the Jews are concerned. Joking, according to some definitions of humor, indeed sought to singularize this gift as a "Jewish" capacity (one often heralded in the Yiddish writers Kafka studied) to produce a literature of "laughter through tears." However, Jewish literature, the baby in this quotation, should not be thrown out with the bathwater. For Kafka defined his own reception as a writer in these German Jewish terms. "Thoughts of Freud," Kafka wrote in 1912, when reflecting on his story "The Judgment" ("Das Urteil") but also on Max Brod and his *Arnold Beer: das Schicksal eines Judens* [*Arnold Beer: The Fate of a Jew*] (1912) and on Jakob Wasserman, who in 1918 would produce the classic *Mein Weg als Deutscher und Jude* [*My Life as German and Jew*] (1921).[3] For just as Kafka was famously opposed to psychoanalysis, he regarded his peers as those German Jewish writers able to take deadening – and ostensibly universal – national definitions and make them come alive.

It would be the "universalist" Freud who, in 1927, defined "humor" as the ability of the ego to obtain pleasure from a painful situation.[4] Kafka found this position through a Jewish doorway to the plural, and took it far from home. Scholars generally agree that Kafka would never have experienced his "breakthrough" to stature as a universal modernist writer without his having fallen in love, in 1911–1912, with the Yiddish theater he brought to Prague. In this same period, Kafka carefully read Meyer Pines's *Histoire de la littérature Judeo-Allemande* [*History of Judeo-German Literature*], noting the following – one wants to say Freudian – description of Jewish writing and its unique European voice: in defining the style of Mendele, Pines states, "c'était un rire à travers des larmes," that is, "it was a laughter through tears, more painful and full of sorrow than tears themselves."[5] This intensified feeling of sorrow, according to Pines, became the trigger

---

3 Franz Kafka, diary entry of 23 September 1912, in *The Diaries 1910–1923*, ed. Max Brod, trans. Joseph Kresh and Martin Greenberg with the cooperation of Hannah Arendt, Schocken Books, New York 1976 [1948], 213.
4 Sigmund Freud, "Humour," in *The Standard Edition of the Complete Psychological Works of Sigmund Freud*, ed. James Strachey, Hogarth Press, London 1961, XXI: 163.
5 Meyer Pines, *Histoire de la littérature Judeo-Allemande*, Jouve et Cis, Éditeurs, Paris 1911, 410.

that unleashed "this spirit of gaiety and good-natured openness" that Yiddish literature makes the reader feel. This quiet openness to multiple influences finds its surprising "father" figure, as he was called, in Sholem Aleichem, who borrowed the motto "laughter through tears" from the famous Chapter VII of Gogol's *Dead Souls*. Yiddish, Kafka learned, was less than averse to lifting its pleasures from more "universal" European languages – that is, "great" literatures that had cornered the market on prestige. And so Kafka understood that, as follows from this version of Jewish tradition, "tears" could be cried with a hidden smile as Russian and other literary influences entered through the door.

Kafka expressed his joy at this discovery in his famous diary entry of 25 December 1911. There, Kafka outlines his concept of "small" or "minor" literatures, as French post-structuralist theory calls them, though his use of Jewish tradition deserves a more enjoyable description than that. A better name for the Jewish and universal Kafka would be post-pleasure-less: for in Yiddish and the new writing of modern Hebrew, he noted, the "antithesis between sons and fathers, and the possibility of discussing this," appears in a new way: as the "presentation of national faults in a manner that is painful, to be sure, but also liberating and deserving of forgiveness."[6] "Pain," in Kafka's formulation, thus signals a process of liberation already underway. The "faults" of the nation – the signs of its struggles – were to be regarded as different forms of "universal" patterns as they emerged – and forgiveness as the art of an unbinding that set these multiple forms of energy free. Were Freud to be summoned from the dead to join a discussion, we might discover him sitting in the back of the room, in the same spot where a Talmudic parable places Moses: the position in Talmudic academies awarded to the worst readers of the Torah.[7] If, in the tradition of Jewish commentary, the author of the Law itself – Moses, our Teacher – gets the cheap seats, then Freud should be similarly honored, albeit in Kafka's perspective. Where Freud imagined a father killed by his sons – envious, no doubt, of the father's Egyptian as well as Hebrew origins – Kafka saw a house with many mansions: "Abraham," after all, means *Av Hamon* [אב המון], or "father of a multitude," in the Hebrew text.[8] In the Jewish tradition, the author of the Law sits at the back of the Talmudic Academy because

---

6 Kafka, diary entry of 25 December 1911, in *The Diaries*, 148.

7 *Babylonian Talmud*, Tractate Menahot 29B. For the text and discussion, see Jeffrey L. Rubenstein, *Talmudic Stories: Narrative Art, Composition, and Culture*, The Johns Hopkins University Press, Baltimore and London 1999, 271–272.

8 See Genesis 17:5: "but your name shall be Abraham, for I make you the father a multitude of nations," footnote b: [Abraham]: "understood as 'father of a multitude.'" *Tanakh: A New Translation of the Holy Scriptures According to the Traditional Hebrew Text*, The Jewish Publication Society, Philadelphia 1985, 23.

he is the "worst" student of his own text: because, as this Mosaic figure suggested to Kafka, the "universal" meaning of the father is more varied – and ultimately more marked by the traces of many nations – than the author himself could see.

In Kafka's view, the "people" or "nation" suffers from uniformity because of the narrow roles accorded to "others": like the odd woman or gay male, whose pleasures are judged a failure rather than as the new forms of reading and expression they actually are. In this respect, Kafka's innovation re-discovered "forgiveness" as a Jewish pleasure: in his re-reading of Abraham and the binding of Isaac, for instance, it is the patriarch, who would impose his deadly form of universality on the son, who receives the honored position of Moses and is thus placed at the back of the class. "I can imagine," Kafka wrote, "a different Abraham for myself."[9] Instead, Kafka's original patriarch is re-imagined as an "old clothes dealer," whose assemblage of a nation from different, cast-off sources was his grandest human quality of all. In this same spirit, Kafka identified what he called "the old story" – "universal" roles of father and son that he thought were deserving of "Verwandlung," or transformation: that is, of being situated on a new stage for the German Jewish voice.

1 Paradox as Comedy: Kafka and Beckett

As Kafka recorded in a notebook, "universal" and "particular" were, as terms for the father-son struggle, already stale formulations: they constituted a staging that made one forget that a bad – because limiting – script was not the real thing. The problem, for Kafka, was therefore not that Freudian interpretation was Jewish; rather, it was that such interpretation was not Jewish enough in its ability to take pleasure from these vaudeville scenes. In this way, Adorno's quip – that in psychoanalysis only the exaggerations are true – can be understood as his own version of Kafka's reading of Freud.[10] For "while psychoanalysis lays stress on the father-complex and finds the concept intellectually fruitful," as Kafka wrote to Max Brod in 1921, "in this case I prefer another version, where the issue revolves not around the innocent father but the father's Jewishness," that is, a version where exaggerations are already implicit and waiting to have their truth values

---

9 Franz Kafka, "Abraham," trans. Clement Greenberg, in *Parables and Paradoxes in German and English*, Schocken Books, New York 1946, 36–41, 41.

10 Theodor Adorno, *Minima Moralia: Reflections from Damaged Life* [*Minima Moralia: Reflexionen aus dem beschädigten Leben*], trans. E.F.N. Jephcott, Verso, London 1978, section 29, "Dwarf Fruit," 49.

uncovered in the canonical text.[11] Kafka's reflections on Abraham, the original Jewish father figure, already envision, in 1918, this notion of "general" paternal authority as a displacement of actual life, its lively borrowings and trades – as a theater to be renewed. "It is as if," Kafka writes, "the back and forth between the general and the particular were taking place on the real stage, and, as if, on the other hand, life in general were only sketched in on the background scenery."[12]

Samuel Beckett's relation to English was similar in this respect to Kafka's feeling for German: both encountered languages that needed to be re-created, and each found his own way out. With English having reduced Irish culture to stereotype, Beckett's desire to break the hold of that language through humor is particularly evident in the Shakespearean sonnet presented in *Watt*, his final English novel. In this miniature poem that critics have discovered hiding amidst his prose, Beckett uses an English form to find his Irish voice. Repunctuating the prose sentence (and adding a rhyme scheme) yields the following poetic form:

> The wacks, (A)
> the moans, (B)
> the cracks, (A)
> the groans. (B)
>
> The welts, (C)
> the squeaks, (D)
> the belts, (C)
> the shrieks. (D)
>
> The pricks, (E)
> the prayers, (F)
> the kicks, (E)
> the tears. (F)
>
> The skelps, (G)
> and the yelps. (G)

With this sentence Beckett has in fact produced the most classic form of English poetry: the fourteen points follow the rhyme scheme of the Shakespearean sonnet, even as they scream against the English brutality that wears gentleman's clothes. The hatred of English becomes the pleasure of rejecting its most "British," and

---

11 Franz Kafka, letter to Max Brod, June 1921, in *Letters to Friends, Family, and Editors*, trans. Richard and Clara Winston, Schocken Books, New York 1977, 286–289, 289.
12 Kafka, *The Blue Octavo Notebooks*, 55.

thus most sickening, assumptions about his people: learning the language, in other words, begins when "life begins to ram her fish and chips down your gullet and you puke."[13]

Beckett did eventually expel the English language, subsequently writing his greatest works in French. As Mark Nixon has noted, Beckett was, as early as 1931, when he published his "A Casket of Pralinen for a Daughter of a Dissipated Mandarin," already conceiving of "waste" as a model for his literary products.[14] This process intensified in the 1930s, when his final English works appeared; these were published in the journal *transition*, alongside early translations of Kafka and the first sections of Joyce's *Finnegans Wake*. Beckett's "Casket" was quite alive: much in the spirit of Kafka's story that begins "I Was A Visitor Among the Dead" [*Ich War Unter den Toten zu Gast*], where the underworld contains a "Jewish maiden" [*ein Judenmädchen*] who refuses to wear a shroud.[15] Beckett likewise thought of national literary categories as deathly for the living force of literary creation: he sought, as he states in a German-language letter to Axel Kaun, "to bore one hole after another" [*ein Loch nach dem anderen in ihr zu bohren*] in what he called "official" language and literature.[16] The only writing truly alive for Beckett – as Kafka's Jewish figure already suggests – had re-opened the connections between different languages, to escape the living death of literature as separate and sealed-off national spheres. Beckett's "Casket of Pralinen" therefore recognized the sweets of national literatures as productive of "memory's involuntary vomit"[17]: the creation of canons that could not be swallowed, and whose tastes for the voices of other nations needed to be read anew. And it would be the remnants – those multiple differences – of this mother tongue that would speak with the greatest eloquence in Beckett's French-language novel *Molloy*, an Irish name that combines "mother" with a recapture of his linguist "alloy."

Kafka's attitude toward German was quite similar, if his "Letter to the Father" ("Brief an den Vater," translated as "Letter to His Father"), from 1921, is any guide. "Six months of German Studies," Kafka recalls, followed by law studies

---

13 Samuel Beckett, *Watt*, Grove Press, New York 1953, 55, 44
14 Mark Nixon, *Samuel Beckett's German Diaries 1936–1937*, Continuum, New York 2011, 58.
15 Franz Kafka, "Bei den Toten zu Gast" ("A Guest Among the Dead"), in *Die Erzählungen und andere ausgewählte Prosa* [*The Stories and Other Selected Prose*], ed. Roger Hermes, Fischer Taschenbuch Verlag, Frankfurt/M. 2002, 354–356, 356.
16 Samuel Beckett, "German Letter of 1937," in *Disjecta: Miscellaneous Writings and a Dramatic Fragment*, ed. Ruby Cohn, Grove Press, New York 1984, 51–55, 52.
17 See Samuel Beckett, "A Casket of Pralinen for a Daughter of a Dissipated Mandarin," in Lawrence Harvey, *Samuel Beckett: Poet and Critic*, Princeton University Press, Princeton 1970, 278–283, 281.

at Prague's German university, had each given him the pre-Beckett experience of digesting a literary and legal language that was pablum, especially from a German national point of view: "I was positively living, in an intellectual sense," Kafka notes, "on sawdust, which had, moreover, already been chewed for me in other people's mouths."[18] In his discussion of the Jewish vernacular in Prague, Kafka notes that in Yiddish he found what he called the "youngest European language," that is, a memory of the translation roots which languages like German and Yiddish shared.[19] He had thus discovered a multiple perspective on a German language whose myth of origin, like that of Beckett's English, he felt had been ruthlessly forced upon him. Whereas English claimed cultural priority in Ireland – and branded the Irish as comic imitators – French, for Beckett, exposed many of the pieces from which English was composed. And whereas German forced the "Jewish mother" into a cold, staged role as a would-be Christian – "the Jewish 'Mutter' is no mother," Kafka wrote – Yiddish exposed those holes, in Beckett's sense, between "official" and unofficial forms of the national voice.[20] The original German form of "we are," Kafka observed, had in fact become secondary: the earlier form was actually preserved in the Yiddish "mir seien," thus rendering the Yiddish, itself closer to middle high German, more "original" than standard German itself. Kafka therefore urges his audience in Prague to be wary not of Yiddish, their own deliciously varied language, but rather "of yourselves" for running from its multiple national embrace: "for we did not come to punish you," Kafka concludes.[21]

Beckett's English was much like Kafka's German in this respect, especially given Beckett's dislike for universals and the humor he attained by switching to French. Thus in *Molloy*, when the hero declares – first in French, and then in Beckett's English translation – that he was "born out of my mother's arse, if I am correct,"[22] no Irish self-hatred or misogyny is involved. Beckett's object is English, his mother tongue: Molloy reminds us that he was, as the original French so aptly puts it, born "par le trou," – that is, "by the truth"; in other words, the "whole"

---

18 Franz Kafka, "Letter to His Father," trans. Ernst Kaiser and Eithne Wilkins, in *The Basic Kafka*, ed. Erich Heller, Pocket Books, New York 1979, 186–236, 223.

19 Franz Kafka, "Einleitungsvortrag über Jargon" ["Talk on the Yiddish Language"], in Franz Kafka, *Nachgelassene Schriften und Fragmente I* [*Posthumous Writings and Fragments I*], ed. Malcolm Pasley, S. Fischer, Frankfurt/M. 1992, 188–193, 189.

20 Kafka, diary entry of 24 October 1911, in *The Diaries*, 88.

21 Kafka, "Einleitungsvortrag über Jargon," 190, 193, my translation.

22 Samuel Beckett, *Molloy*, trans. Patrick Bowles in collaboration with Samuel Beckett, in *Three Novels: Molloy, Malone Dies, The Unnamable*, Grove Press, New York 1955, 12; Samuel Beckett, *Molloy*, Les Éditions de Minuit, Paris 1951, 20.

of English generalizations about the Irish should be expelled and treated as utter waste. The true "hole" – or "Loch," as Beckett writes in his "German Letter of 1937" – is where original identity arrives already defaced by prejudiced attitudes: precisely that point where a multiple, trans-national channel of influence receives its sign. As in Kafka, however – who referred to "The Judgment" as a story that emerged "covered in filth and slime"[23] – birth imagery is used as the opportunity to re-imagine one's native ground. And in a doubly original sense: Beckett reclaims the Irish tradition of scatological humor in this passage, using Kafka to explain that German and English notions of identity are indeed a pain in the behind, so to speak, and establishing a breakthrough from closed national attitudes to multiple-linguistic style. Hence Beckett's allusion to the French version of Kafka's diary entry, as provided by Max Brod in 1945.[24] One would, of course, very much like to say that *ceteris paribus*, or all other things being equal, Kafka's Jewish attitude toward German works the same way as Beckett's self-delivery from English, that is, via the courtesy of French. The point of humor, for both Beckett and Kafka, is precisely to discover the positive and multiple meanings of the different, in those many linguistic passageways that already inhabit the universal judgments of a more prestigious tongue.

Such is the "way out" described in Kafka's "A Report to an Academy" ("Ein Bericht für eine Akademie"), a story published in Martin Buber's monthly journal *Der Jude* [*The Jew*] in 1917. This tale – of an African ape who is captured, boxed, and shipped to Berlin by the German circus – is Kafka's most Jewish story in this humorous sense, as it encourages the reader to de-identify with the German language the narrator has so carefully acquired. Little wonder, then, that Beckett's "Premier Amour," or first love – one of his first French compositions after the Second World War – would visit the grave of the "wild animal collector Hagen-

---

23 Kafka, diary entry of 11 February 1913, in *The Diaries*, 214. The passage reads: "the story came out of me like a real birth, covered with filth and slime, and only I have the hand that can reach to the body itself, and the strength of desire to do so."

24 The quotation, from Kafka's diary in French translation, reads: "car ce récit est sorti de moi comme par un veritable accouchement, couvert de souillures et de mucus." See Max Brod, *Franz Kafka: souvenirs et documents* [*Franz Kafka, Memories and Documents*], trans. Hélène Zylberberg, Gallimard, Paris 1945, 149. Beckett's final library contained the version cited here: a French translation of Brod's *Franz Kafka: Eine Biographie: Errinerungen und Dokumente* [*Franz Kafka: A Biography: Reminiscences and Documents*], Heinrich Mercy Sohn, Prague 1937. See Dirk Van Hulle and Mark Nixon, *Samuel Beckett's Library*, Cambridge University Press, Cambridge 2013, 239.

beck," the "Führer," or "leader," of Kafka's earlier tale.[25] The obvious Jewish, as well as African, paradox of Kafka's story has always been that Peter, though he is the "animal" of the tale, is far more human than his German captors. Less obvious is how the similarity between Jews and Africans opens the vulgar stereotypes in which both were confined. Indeed, Arthur Holitscher's *Amerika Heute und Morgen* [*America Today and Tomorrow*] – Kafka's source for his novel *Amerika* – reports a conversation between the author and an African American he met on the streets of New York's Tin Pan Alley: the young man informs him that "our fates share much in common: we negroes and the Jews!"[26] In this, the source for Kafka's "ape" – who has been enslaved by his German captors and then carried over sea to Berlin – the African American from the vaudeville world effectively tells his Jewish friend: "We're in the same boat!"

The African ape of "A Report to an Academy" is therefore deeply Jewish, though for exactly the opposite reason that Kafka scholars have traditionally suggested. The standard reception of the story regards Peter as "Jewish" because he is "assimilated" and "aping" German customs: the comedy of the story reveals more than one hole in the vaudeville reductions that the philosophic tradition has substituted for thought. Germans are of course the ostensible "apes" in this story, having assimilated stereotypes in unthinking fashion, thus constituting what Beckett termed the "risus purus," or the laugh at that which is "unhappy."[27] This purest laughter – in Beckett as in Kafka – occurs when one escapes from the highest – and also stupidest – concepts that give so much pain, and approaches the multiple forms of our common human ground. As Kafka's narrator relates, with a broad range of cultural reference present in his voice, "The whole construction was too low for me to stand up in, and too narrow for me to sit down in."[28] These Germans, he informs the reader, have also imitated a Jewish sage:

---

25 Samuel Beckett, "First Love," in *Samuel Beckett: The Complete Short Prose 1929–1989*, ed. S.E. Gontarski, Grove Press, New York 1995, 25–45, 27. Kafka's Red Peter recalls the "hunting expedition sent out by the firm of Hagenbeck – by the way, I have drunk many a bottle of good red wine since then with the leader of that expedition." See Franz Kafka, "A Report to an Academy," trans. Willa and Edwin Muir, in *The Complete Stories*, ed. Nahum N. Glatzer, Schocken Books, New York 1972, 250–259, 251; Franz Kafka, "Ein Bericht für eine Akademie," in *Die Erzählungen und andere ausgewählte Prosa*, 322–333, 323: "Jagdexpedition der Firma Hagenbeck – mit dem Führer habe ich übrigens seither manche gute Flasche Rotwein geleert."
26 My translation. The original German reads: "Unsere Schicksale haben ja viel Ähnlichkeit miteinander. Und dann kommen wir beiden aus Afrika, wir Neger und die Juden." See Arthur Holitscher, *Amerika Heute und Morgen*, S Fischer Verlag, Berlin 1912, 365.
27 Beckett, *Watt*, 48.
28 Kafka, "A Report to an Academy," 252.

their arrangement recalls a passage from Moses Maimonides, who himself had taken his definition of the African from the Aristotelian-Arabic philosophers of the middle ages. In this respect, one could say that in Kafka's fiction Jews have the potential to become the best kind of human animals: creatures so full of "varieté" – a job that Peter is offered – that they break out of any German or Jewish cage.[29]

2 Bite Your Tongue: Kafka's Jewish Multi-lingualism

In Kafka's "The Judgment," Georg Bendemann offers this tasty and ultimately open response to his father: "'You Comedian!' Georg could not resist the retort, realized at once the harm he had done and, his eyes starting in his head, bit his tongue back, only too late, till the pain made his knees give."[30] Georg's attempt at self-stifling is only the surface meaning of this phrase: when he "bit his tongue back" [*biß in seine Zunge*] the bite triggers a trembling gesture – "a *Beltschmerz*,"[31] according to Beckett – that one feels when multiple meanings begin their transition to expressive form. A transfer and indeed a translation are acted out in this scene. First, the son indicates the staged quality of the father's angry performance – "You Comedian!" is reminiscent of the "transitional generation of Jews" as described in Kafka's "Letter to His Father": the vaudeville terms suggest how Jewish fathers of his generation would resort to Yiddish curses in their anger and rage.[32] "Biting the Tongue" indicates a taste for the multiple in this respect – Kafka's translation of what in Yiddish has been called "Pronouncing the Magic Word *Kholile* and its Relatives."[33] Loosely translatable into English as "Horrors!" or "Perish the Thought," these "Kholile" expressions can be termed an opening to multiple pleasures: in Kafka's translation, "Kholile" appears in German where

---

29 On Maimonides in Kafka's text, and "varieté" as an allusion to connections between disparate national traditions, see David Suchoff, *Kafka's Jewish Languages: the Hidden Openness of Tradition*, University of Pennsylvania Press, Philadelphia 2012, 4.
30 Franz Kafka, "The Judgment," trans. Willa and Edwin Muir, in *The Complete Stories*, 77–88, 86.
31 Samuel Beckett, "What A Misfortune," in *More Pricks Than Kicks*, Grove Press, New York 1972, 114–151, 118.
32 Kafka, "Letter to His Father," in *The Basic Kafka*, 186–236, 217.
33 James A. Matisoff, *Blessings, Curses, Hopes and Fears: Psycho-Ostensive Expressions in Yiddish*, Stanford University Press, Stanford 2000, 48–49.

the bite, or *biß*, in other words, opens our tastes to a series of trans-linguistic meanings, alive on the tip of the filial – that is, a complex and ramified tongue. For "it was not so long ago," as Kafka informs his audience in Prague in 1912, that "the familiar colloquial language [*Verkehrsprache*] of German Jews [...] seemed to be a remoter or closer approximation to *Jargon*, and many nuances remain to this day."[34]

"Bite Your Tongue," in this signal gesture, holds back: in a way that fully tastes the variety of the pleasure withheld: a good description of the richness that comes across in Kafka's German style. In much the same fashion, the *Kholile* principle of Yiddish, as James Matisoff notes, is most often used sarcastically: telling us something is terrible – God forbid – as a way of admitting a fuller viewpoint and its pleasures. The saying about comedy that Kafka cites bites its own tongue in just this sense: – "a joke can, *kholile*," lay waste to an entire world, when abhorrence, that is, is at the same time enjoying a more expressive voice: already tasting, as it were, the plural meanings of both the German and Jewish tongue.[35] As a model for reading Kafka, this "bite" in the "tongue" also offers a morsel of Kafka's sense of humor, whose joys have been savored far too little in the reception he has received. Of this crime, however, Freud can certainly be forgiven, even in Kafka's own Jewish terms, since Kafka exemplifies this version of recapturing the past by taking the father's place in a more pleasurable way: in this case, in the small connections that Kafka draws between German and Jewish speech. In this minute instance, abhorrence already enjoys an expanded form of linguistic pleasure: namely, the "biß" that is already tasting, as it were, "a bisl" – *a little bit*, or *bite*, in English – of the meanings common to both the German and Jewish mouth.[36]

Kafka's Jewish reception could therefore be said to be lacking because – *Kholile!* – readers have taken such "Comedian!" moments in a singular way. Georg's gesture also enacts a completion of Goethe's "loosening one's tongue" [*die Zunge los*].[37] *Kholile*, essentially a form of biting one's tongue – that is, of

---

34 Franz Kafka, "An Introductory Talk on the Yiddish Language," trans. Ernst Kaiser and Eithne Wilkins, in Mark Anderson, ed., *Reading Kafka: Prague, Politics and the Fin de Siècle*, Schocken Books, New York 1989, 263–266, 266; Kafka, "Einleitungsvortrag," in *Nachgelassene Schriften I*, 192.
35 Matishoff, *Blessings, Curses, Hopes and Fears*, 49
36 Kafka thus preferred books, as he wrote in 1904, "die einen beißen und stechen" – "that bite and stick." See Franz Kafka, letter to Oskar Pollak, 27 January 1904, in *Briefe* [*Letters*] *1902–1924*, Schocken Books, New York 1958, 27.
37 See Kafka, diary entry of 16 November 1910, in *The Diaries*, 28: "I'm reading *Iphigenie auf Tauris* [*Iphigenia in Tauris*]. Here, aside from some isolated, plainly faulty passages, the dried up

magically neutralizing a painful state of affairs, and thus enjoying the broadest secular tastes – enjoys a rich tradition in the Hebrew language. In the Hebrew Bible the root of the word for "horrors" in this Yiddish sense was deeply antithetical from the start and appears in boundary-crossing forms that suggest the universal pleasure involved. Thus the same Hebrew root that means "desecrate, ruin, make unfit" – but also "to begin anew" – first appears in the Hebrew text when Abraham pleads with God to spare Sodom and Gomorrah; he tells God that destroying the cities would be an act of desecration: "Far be it from You" – literally *Kholila* – "to bring death upon the innocent as well as the guilty" (Genesis 18:25).[38] A related form of the word appears in Jeremiah 31:5, a source that Kafka alludes to in *The Castle* via the name of the character Jeremias, one of the two playful "assistants." In the biblical book of Jeremiah, Hebrew accordingly gives a form of *khalel* and its "horrors" as a form of reaping joy: "men shall plant, and live to enjoy common things," as the verse is translated in a version that highlights "Khol" – literally, "sand." In modern Hebrew this everyday word now means "secular," as opposed to a religiously narrow point of view. In this particulate and grammatical sense, "Khol" in the Hebrew of Jeremiah can be said to speak of the common and multiple soil from which all life grows and thus to offer a hint of the many differences in our language and of the lives that bear the most enjoyable human fruit.

Kafka's humor performs a secular version of these Jewish linguistic pleasures. In his diary entry of 26 January 1912, he notes the "eastern Jewish habit of biting one's lips" [*Ostjudische Gewohnheit des an den Lippen Beißens*] as being another model of such expansive linguistic control – such as when we taste meanings that are ready to explode.[39] This expressive potential well describes a figure like Kafka's Odradek, in his aptly named "The Cares of a Housefather" ("Die Sorge eines Hausvaters") (translated into English as "The Cares of a Family Man"), who gives forth "only the kind of laughter that has no lungs behind it."[40]

German language in the mouth of a pure boy is really to be regarded with absolute amazement. The verse, at the moment of its reading, lifts every word up to heights where it stands in perhaps a thin but penetrating light." "Vom alten Bande löset ungern sich/Die Zunge los," as Goethe's Iphigenia says, "ein lang verschwiegenes / Geheimniß endlich zu entdecken" [Its ancient bands reluctantly my tongue Doth loose, a long-hid secret to divulge].

38 See Francis Brown, Samuel Rolles Driver, and Charles Augustus Briggs, "חלילה, חלל," in *A Hebrew and English Lexicon of the Old Testament*, Clarendon Press, Oxford 1968, 370.

39 Kafka, diary entry of 26 January 1912, in *The Diaries*, 174; Franz Kafka, *Tagebücher II: 1912– 1914*, Fischer Taschenbuch Verlag, Frankfurt/M. 1994, 25.

40 Franz Kafka, "The Cares of a Family Man," trans. Willa and Edwin Muir, in *The Complete Stories*, 427–429, 428

In biblical Hebrew, "lip" designates what other languages call "tongue" – that is, a bit, as it were, of the language that helps the reader to discover the many senses of what Odradek's breathless laughter might mean. "Safa" – "lip," in English – in biblical and modern Hebrew also means "language": and breath, forced through lips, teeth and tongue, shapes one's voice, in what is known as pronunciation [*Aussprache*], or how a particular accent is given to the words brought to speech. In this spirit, it would be correct to say that what worries the "Housefather" of Kafka's story is the peculiar accent of the son – Odradek – whose voice – like the meanings of his name – can be pronounced so many ways. That Odradek is also a figure from Jewish tradition is clear in the story: for while this creature looks like a "spool" for collecting many threads, he is also "star-shaped" and promises to be there "at the feet of my children, and my children's children,"[41] recalling the wording of many Hebrew prayers. Not surprisingly, this figure for the open future of the tradition provokes a *kholile* reaction – Žižek calls him an emblem of "castration"[42] – that fearful reaction of the master toward the "lachen" or "laughter" of the son. That Odradek lacks "lungs" suggests a Hebrew vernacular that had long remained unspoken – except for the "Blätter" or dead "leaves" of tradition – while this same figure who remains "Od" – Hebrew, meaning "more," "another," or "differently" – names the potential of a language whose best days are still to come.

This "horror" at transformed future was not to be taken that seriously – at least in the sources Kafka knew. "The idea that he is likely to survive me I find almost painful" [*ist mir eine fast schmerzliche*], the Haus-Vater, or House-Father, declares – worrying his way to pleasure, like balabustas of every national taste.[43] A Talmudic story Kafka possessed – the debate over ritual purity known as "The Oven of Akhnai" – suggests the sources from which this humor drew.[44] Like much Jewish commentary, this parable was less concerned with purity than with how the Hebrew tradition could flourish in the actual world. And like Kafka's father figures, Rabbinic authority initially turns the world upside down in its quest for interpretive judgment and control. A stream of water flows in reverse, a carob tree uproots itself one hundred yards from its place: all without convincing the academy of any single answer. And when "the very walls of the schoolroom

41 Kafka, "Cares of a Housefather," 428, 429.
42 Slavoj Žižek, *The Parallax View*, MIT Press, Cambridge 2006, 121.
43 Franz Kafka, "Die Sorge eines Hausvaters," in *Die Erzählungen und andere ausgewählte Prosa*, 343–344, 344.
44 Baba Metzia 59b here is quoted from Jakob Fromer, *Der Organismus des Judentums* [*The Organism of Judaism*], Selbstverlag des Verfassers, Charlottenburg 1909, 118, my translation. The book was in Kafka's library and is discussed in his diary.

began to topple" in support of Rabbi Eliezer, the decree that the answer "is not in heaven" settles the case. And what did the Holy one, blessed be he, do in that hour?" the prophet Elijah is asked at the end. "God smiled," according to the text, then spoke the following words – "my children have defeated Me, my children have defeated Me" – For the superiority of our children – as all good parents know – is the most lasting Jewish pleasure of all.[45] For just as Latin lives on in English and German – "Vater"("Father") might be the best example – Odradek's "laughter," like the "rustling" of apparently dead linguistic "leaves," suggests what Hebrew calls *kedusha* – the blessing of a life that thrives in new and unexpected forms "unto all generations" (Psalms 146:10).

Kafka's Judaism was thus quite universal, in its own secular and different form. "The Messiah will come," as Kafka wrote, "as soon as the most unbridled individualism of faith becomes possible – when there is no one to destroy this possibility and no one to suffer its destruction."[46] This kind of Jewish expectancy is the reverse of a self-fulfilling prophecy that holds us back: for once we have discovered the many differences in ourselves, Kafka tells us, the idea of waiting for someone to liberate us can truly be left behind. As in a Jewish joke, Kafka's messiah comes only when he's no longer necessary: and so will he will appear in the figure of the nudnik when he finally arrives: the messiah is a pest who has been superseded – "no longer needed" – once we have become the multiple creatures that we are.[47] The way Kafka waited for this possibility was quite singular – a posture dramatized in my concluding passage, from Kafka's "Investigations of a Dog" ("Forschungen eines Hundes"):

---

45 Kafka's story is likewise less concerned with the name of the father than with the meanings to be discovered in the name of the son. "Some say the word 'Odradek' is of Slavonic origin, and try to account for it on that basis," Kafka begins his story of filiation: "others believe it to be of German origin, only influenced by the Slavonic," indulging in a form of self-citation. For such was precisely the linguistic history of Yiddish, which, as Kafka told his Prague audience when lecturing on that language, was spoken in different versions – more influenced by German or Slavic sources – depending on whether the Jews lived in East or West. See Kafka, "An Introductory Talk on the Yiddish Language," 266.

46 Kafka, *Parables and Paradoxes*, 81.

47 In terms of a distinction between two kinds of messianism, in which a global – one would say, universal – form requires the destruction of existing arrangements, while a smaller form of the messianic spirit consists of the work of mending the world. The latter is known as *tikkun olam*: mending by discovering and accepting its openness to others, and establishing a universalism worth its name. Kafka's messianic spirit would find its voice in his comic use of the former, as a screen for ultimately the more open form of the latter.

Our forefathers appeared threateningly before me. True, I held them to be responsible for everything, even if I dared not say so openly; it was they who involved our dog life in guilt, and so I could easily have responded to their menaces with counter-menaces: but I bow before their knowledge, it came from sources of which we know no longer, and for that reason, much as I may feel compelled to oppose them, I shall never actually overstep their laws, but content myself with wriggling out through these gaps, for which I have a fine sense of smell.[48]

For the Kafka who called the "revolutionary" process a "continuous" one, such potential was ready to break out at any time.[49] "Certainly such freedom as is possible today is a wretched business," Kafka assures us, "but nonetheless freedom, nonetheless a possession"[50] to discover the hidden openness of closed traditions to one another with the devotion of a research dog. As Kafka's canine wisdom suggests, it is only these gaps in our legacies from the past that connect us and make us fully human – while allowing us to experience laughter, that animal in us all.

Works Cited

Adorno, Theodor W., *Minima Moralia: Reflections from Damaged Life*. Trans. E.F.N. Jephcott (London: Verso, 1978).

Anderson, Mark, *Reading Kafka: Prague, Politics and the Fin de Siècle* (New York: Schocken Books, 1989).

Beckett, Samuel, "A Casket of Pralinen for a Daughter of a Dissipated Mandarin," in *Samuel Beckett: Poet and Critic*. Lawrence Harvey (Princeton: Princeton University Press, 1970). 278–283.

Beckett, Samuel, *The Complete Short Prose of Samuel Beckett 1929–1989*. Ed. S.E. Gontarski (New York: Grove Press, 1995).

Beckett, Samuel, *Disjecta: Miscellaneous Writings and a Dramatic Fragment*. Ed. Ruby Cohn (New York: Grove Press, 1984).

Beckett, Samuel, "First Love," in *The Complete Short Prose of Samuel Beckett 1929–1989*. Ed. S.E. Gontarski (New York: Grove Press, 1995), 25–45.

Beckett, Samuel, "German Letter of 1937," in *Disjecta: Miscellaneous Writings and a Dramatic Fragment*. Ed. Ruby Cohn (New York: Grove Press, 1984), 51–55.

---

48 Franz Kafka, "Investigations of a Dog," trans. Willa and Edwin Muir, in *The Complete Stories*, 278–316, 309–310; Franz Kafka, "Forschungen eines Hundes," in *Die Erzählungen und andere ausgewählte Prosa*, 411–455, 447–448.

49 Kafka, Aphorism 6, in *The Basic Kafka*, 237; Kafka, *Nachgelassene Schriften und Fragmente II*, 114.

50 Kafka, "The Cares of a Family Man," 316.

Beckett, Samuel, *Molloy* (Paris: Les Éditions de Minuit, 1951).

Beckett, Samuel, *Molloy*, trans. Patrick Bowles in collaboration with Samuel Beckett, in *Three Novels: Molloy, Malone Dies, The Unnamable* (New York: Grove Press, 1955).

Beckett, Samuel, *Watt* (New York: Grove Press, 1953).

Beckett, Samuel, "What A Misfortune," in *More Pricks than Kicks* (New York: Grove Press, 1972), 114–151.

Briggs, Charles Augustus et al., *A Hebrew and English Lexicon of the Old Testament* (Oxford: Clarendon Press, 1968).

Brod, Max, *Franz Kafka, souvenirs et documents*. Trans. Hélène Zylberberg (Paris: Gallimard, 1945).

Freud, Sigmund, "Humour," in *The Standard Edition of the Complete Psychological Works of Sigmund Freud*. Ed. James Strachey (London: Hogarth Press, 1961), XXI 161–166.

Fromer, Jakob, *Der Organismus des Judentums* (Charlottenburg: Selbstverlag des Verfassers, 1909).

Harvey, Lawrence, *Samuel Beckett: Poet and Critic* (Princeton: Princeton University Press, 1970).

Holitscher, Arthur, *Amerika Heute und Morgen* (Berlin: S Fischer Verlag, 1912).

Kafka, Franz, "Abraham," trans. Clement Greenberg, in *Parables and Paradoxes in German and English* (New York: Schocken Books, 1946), 36–41.

Kafka, Franz, *The Basic Kafka*. Ed. Erich Heller (New York: Pocket Books, 1979).

Kafka, Franz, "Bei den Toten zu Gast," in *Die Erzählungen und andere ausgewählte Prosa*. Ed. Roger Hermes (Frankfurt/M.: Fischer Taschenbuch Verlag, 2002), 354–356.

Kafka, Franz, "Ein Bericht für eine Akademie," in *Die Erzählungen und andere ausgewählte Prosa*. Ed. Roger Hermes (Frankfurt/M.: Fischer Taschenbuch Verlag, 2002), 322–333.

Kafka, Franz, *The Blue Octavo Notebooks*. Ed. Max Brod. Trans. Ernst Kaiser and Eithne Wilkins (Cambridge: Exact Change, 1991).

Kafka, Franz, *Briefe 1902–1924* (New York: Schocken Books, 1958).

Kafka, Franz, *Briefe an Milena* (Frankfurt/M.: Fischer, 1983).

Kafka, Franz, "The Cares of a Family Man," trans. Willa and Edwin Muir, in *The Complete Stories*. Ed. Nahum N. Glatzer (New York: Schocken Books, 1972), 427–429.

Kafka, Franz, *The Complete Stories*. Ed. Nahum N. Glatzer (New York: Schocken Books, 1972.

Kafka, Franz, *The Diaries 1910–1923*. Ed. Max Brod. Trans. Joseph Kresh and Martin Greenberg with the cooperation of Hannah Arendt (New York: Schocken Books, 1976 [1948]).

Kafka, Franz, "Einleitungsvortrag über Jargon," in *Nachgelassene Schriften und Fragmente I*. Ed. Malcolm Pasley (Frankfurt/M.: S. Fischer, 1992), 188–193.

Kafka, Franz, *Die Erzählungen und andere ausgewählte Prosa*. Ed. Roger Hermes (Frankfurt/M.: Fischer Taschenbuch Verlag, 2002).

Kafka, Franz, "Forschungen eines Hundes," in *Die Erzählungen und andere ausgewählte Prosa*. Ed. Roger Hermes (Frankfurt/M.: Fischer Taschenbuch Verlag, 2002), 411–455.

Kafka, Franz, "An Introductory Talk on the Yiddish Language," trans. Ernst Kaiser and Eithne Wilkins, in *Reading Kafka: Prague, Politics and the Fin de Siècle*. Ed. Mark Anderson (New York: Schocken Books, 1989), 263–266.

Kafka, Franz, "Investigation of a Dog," trans. Willa and Edwin Muir, in *The Complete Stories*. Ed. Nahum N. Glatzer (New York: Schocken Books, 1972), 278–316.

Kafka, Franz, "The Judgment," trans. Willa and Edwin Muir, in *The Complete Stories*. Ed. Nahum N. Glatzer (New York: Schocken Books, 1972), 77–88.

Kafka, Franz, "Letter to His Father," trans. Ernst Kaiser and Eithne Wilkins, in *The Basic Kafka*. Ed. Erich Heller (New York: Pocket Books, 1979), 186–236.

Kafka, Franz, *Letters to Friends, Family, and Editors*. Trans. Richard and Clara Winston (New York: Schocken Books, 1977).
Kafka, Franz, *Nachgelassene Schriften und Fragmente I*. Ed. Malcolm Pasley (Frankfurt/M.: S. Fischer, 1992).
Kafka, Franz, *Nachgelassene Schriften und Fragmente II*. Ed. Jost Schillemeit (Frankfurt/M.: S. Fischer, 1992).
Kafka, Franz, *Parables and Paradoxes in German and English* (New York: Schocken Books, 1946).
Kafka, Franz, "A Report to an Academy," trans. Willa and Edwin Muir, in *The Complete Stories*. Ed. Nahum N. Glatzer (New York: Schocken Books, 1972), 250–259.
Kafka, Franz, "Die Sorge eines Hausvaters," in *Die Erzählungen und andere ausgewählte Prosa*. Ed. Roger Hermes (Frankfurt/M.: Fischer Taschenbuch Verlag, 2002), 343–344.
Kafka, Franz, *Tagebücher II: 1912–1914* (Frankfurt/M.: Fischer Taschenbuch Verlag, 1994).
Matishoff, James, A., *Blessings, Curses, Hopes and Fears: Psycho-Ostensive Expressions in Yiddish* (Stanford: Stanford University Press, 2000).
Nixon, Mark, *Samuel Beckett's German Diaries 1936–1937* (New York: Continuum, 2011).
Pines, Meyer, *Histoire de la littérature Judeo-Allemande* (Paris: Jouve et Cis, Éditeurs, 1911).
Rubenstein, Jeffrey L., *Talmudic Stories: Narrative Art, Composition, and Culture* (Baltimore and London: The Johns Hopkins University Press, 1999).
Suchoff, David, *Kafka's Jewish Languages: the Hidden Openness of Tradition* (Philadelphia: University of Pennsylvania Press, 2012).
Van Hulle, Dirk, and Mark Nixon, *Samuel Beckett's Library* (Cambridge: Cambridge University Press, 2013).
Tanakh: A New Translation of the Holy Scriptures According to the Traditional Hebrew Text (Philadelphia: The Jewish Publication Society, 1985).
Žižek, Slavoj, *The Parallax View* (Cambridge: MIT Press, 2006).

Anna Glazova
Kafka's Cat-Lamb: Hybridization of Genesis and Taxonomy

A passage in Kafka's diaries contains a highly peculiar representation of the universal natural and cultural history. It combines the notion of technical progress with a vision of origin as described in the Book of Genesis:

> Inventions hasten on ahead of us as the coast always hastens on ahead of the steamer, which is ceaselessly shaken by its engine. Inventions achieve all that can be achieved. It is unfair to say, for instance: The airplane does not fly like the bird, or: We shall never be capable of creating a living bird. Of course not, but the error lies in the objection, just as if the steamer were expected ever and again to arrive at its port of departure in spite of keeping on a straight course. – A bird cannot be created by means of an original act, for it is already created, is continually coming into existence as a result of the first act of Creation, and it is impossible to break into this series, created on the ground of an original, unceasing will, a living series continually showering forth; it is just as is recounted in a legend: although the first woman was created out of the man's rib, this was never repeated, but from then on men always took to wife the daughters of others. – The method and tendency of the creation of the bird – this is the point – and the airplane need not, however, be different; and the savage's way of interpreting things, confusing a shot from a gun with a roll of thunder, may have a limited truth.[1]

Technical progress is described here from the modern scientific perspective, whereas the story of the human origin refers to the creation of Adam and Eve as it appears in the Book Bereshit.[2] Kafka invents here a hybrid of a specific Jewish metaphysical narrative and a modern, universal scientific belief. Progress, in Kafka's understanding, is the unfolding of the original will – which is synonymous with the will to unfold – and thus history as a whole can be understood as a progression of individual creatures and creations (in the sense of *Erfindungen*, "inventions") related to each other, even if their individual geneses become forgotten and unreconstructable. As an example, Kafka traces the genesis of birds and airplanes to a common origin. Airplanes are not born of birds, and yet, from a certain point of view, they are descendants of birds – not in blood and not so

---

1 Franz Kafka, *Nachgelassene Schriften und Fragmente II* [*Posthumous Writings and Fragments II*], ed. Jost Schillemeit, Fischer, Frankfurt/M. 1992, 67; Franz Kafka, *The Blue Octavo Notebooks*, ed. Max Brod, trans. Ernst Kaiser and Eithne Wilkins, Exact Change, Cambridge 2004: 51–52. Translation modified.
2 Genesis 1:24–28.

much in shape as in the same will that is responsible for flying forms. The phylogeny Kafka has in mind is essentially different from Darwin's model of evolution. For Kafka, birds and airplanes are close relatives sharing the same branch on the tree of life. Darwin, in contrast, would find the very idea of a relation between a living organism and a man-made construct puzzling at best. Creatures and inventions, for Kafka, are bound by the principle of semblance, and this semblance leads back to the hidden origin of all life, which Kafka calls, in the previously noted diary entry, "the original, unceasing will." Creatures as well as creations represent stages in the genesis of this will, and these stages give rise to a taxonomy that is based on existential facts rather than blood relations or similarities in genetic codes. In this taxonomy, airplanes stem from birds, guns from thunder, and literary creations can be traced to the same root of the universal tree of life. As Kafka notes in his diary, "Tree of life – lord of life."[3] Everything that exists, be it an animal, a vehicle, or a literary invention, springs forth from this same tree.

This model of genesis is particularly recognizable in Kafka's stories about animals and inanimate creatures, all of whom occupy a place directly next to humans in Kafka's taxonomy – creatures like the ape-human Red Peter, the childlike wooden spool Odradek, and the crossbreed of cat and lamb who sheds human tears of compassion. This genus of creatures has a common predecessor, a hybrid of hound and donkey from a dream that Kafka records in his diary in 1911:

> I dreamed today of a donkey that looked like a greyhound, it was very cautious in its movements. I looked at it closely because I was aware how unusual a phenomenon it was, but remember only that its narrow human feet could not please me because of their length and uniformity. I offered it a bunch of fresh, dark-green cypress leaves which I had just received from an old Zürich lady (it all took place in Zürich), it did not want it, just sniffed a little at it; but then, when I left the cypress on a table, it devoured it so completely that only a scarcely recognizable kernel resembling a chestnut was left. Later there was talk that this donkey had never yet gone on all fours but always held itself erect like a human being and showed its silvery shining breast and its little belly. But actually that was not correct.[4]

Kafka sees this creature in a dream on the night following an evening spent in the Jewish theater together with his friend Yitzhak Löwy, whose last name is essentially identical to that of Kafka's maternal uncle Joseph Loewy. Kafka felt close to both men, and their common surname was important for him, not only because it was shared by two people whom he esteemed but also because of its semantic content (just as his own surname is a homophone of "kavka," the Czech term for a jackdaw). We know from Kafka's notorious "Letter to the Father" ("Brief an den Vater") that he felt torn between his paternal and maternal bloodlines, the Kafkas and the Loewys, respectively. He depicts the mild and non-offensive Loewys as the precise opposite of the assertive and easily irritable Kafkas.

But being born into the Kafka-Loewy household was also to be born into a linguistic reality co-defined by these two conflicting names. Werner Hamacher shows in his imaginative analysis of names and the naming power in Kafka's texts[5] that the discrepancy between the two names, Kafka and Loewy, serves as a model for the creature in the short story "A Crossbreed" ("Eine Kreuzung").[6] Since the word "Kafka" means "jackdaw" in Czech and the name Loewy derives from "Löwe," or "lion," being a child of Kafka and Loewy entails, if the names are taken literally, being both a bird and a cat, that is, prey and predator simultaneously. This is the existential condition of the cat-lamb in Kafka's story: it "flees cats" and "wants to assault lambs." Its conflicted double-nature tears it apart; yet this conflict, as Hamacher shows, originates in Kafka's language and in the logic of his literary production, where the figurative pairs with the non-figurative, making it impossible to interpret metaphors, as each undermines its own metaphoric content. Following this observation, Hamacher shifts the focus of his analysis away from the figure of the hybrid and towards the underlying problem of the hybridization of language, in which proper names transform into general terms and general terms mixed with names lose their signifying function. This hybridization allows Kafka to work towards the disintegration of linguistic means of representation, but also to work in anticipation that this disintegration may give rise to some new, unprecedented form of language. Taking this analysis as my starting point, I would like to linger on the logic of hybridization of names and figures in Kafka's stories.

It is true that the Czech word "kavka" happens to mean "jackdaw" and that Franz's father, Hermann Kafka, was well aware of this when he chose a figure of a jackdaw for an emblem of his store's sign-plate. It is also true, however, that the surname Kafka derives from the biblical name Jacob and its Yiddish diminutive form, Kovka. This proper name mantels itself in a familiar general term in

---

5 Werner Hamacher, "The Gesture in the Name: On Benjamin and Kafka" ("Die Geste im Namen. Benjamin und Kafka"), in *Premises: Essays on Philosophy and Literature from Kant to Celan*, trans. Peter Fenves, Stanford University Press, Stanford 1999, 294–336.
6 Here and in the following: Franz Kafka, *Nachgelassene Schriften und Fragmente I* [*Posthumous Writings and Fragments I*], ed. Malcolm Pasley, Fischer, Frankfurt/M. 1993, 372–374; Franz Kafka, "A Crossbreed [A Sport]," trans. Willa and Edwin Muir, in *The Complete Stories*, ed. Nahum N. Glatzer, Schocken Books, New York 1976, 426–427. Translation modified.

order to enter the sphere of a language – Czech, in this instance – by means of homophony. In this transformation the name becomes a nomad between languages, homeless among proper names as much as among ordinary nouns. Precisely this is the fate of the homeless name and figure called Odradek in Kafka's story "The Cares of the Family Man" ("Die Sorge des Hausvaters"). "A Crossbreed" also tells a story of a nomad, except this nomad is not a traveler but rather a host for a nomadic origin within its own body. This creature has no place in the taxonomy of living things, because its creation is still *en route*: "it only developed in my time; formerly it was far more lamb than kitten." The narration captures the moment in the history of its development when the two fighting natures within its body are in a balance: "Now it is both in about equal parts." The genesis of the creature is exactly half-completed but it remains unclear what further development would bring and whether the animal would become only a cat, only a lamb, or something else entirely. This literary invention, Kafka's cat-lamb, is a figure of thought that pairs a notion of natural history with a notion of an ahistorical origin within it. Creation, from the perspective of this story, is not only an ongoing process; it is also a process that is intrinsically bound to history yet that does not share history's linear progression. Widely diverging branches on the phylogenetic tree reveal themselves as potential origins of another degree. Kafka formulates this thought laconically, noting in his diary that "Adam's first domestic pet after the expulsion from paradise was the serpent."[7] This thought establishes an alternative genetic succession, in which all pets and livestock are offspring of the snake – a succession as wildly divergent from Darwin's view as from the biblical Genesis. In Kafka's succession, cats and lambs appear to be as easily crossbred as horses and donkeys.

The specificity of the hybrid in Kafka's story is that its phylogenesis is unfinished and, as long as it remains unfinished, secures a succession of generations: the creature, though it does not (and probably cannot) have progeny, is a "piece of heirloom" (*Erbstück*) that ensures a continuation of heritage in the narrator's family, even if this continuation comes as a personal sacrifice for the creature. If all pets and livestock are offspring of the original sin – itself mediated by one particular animal, the snake – then, as Kafka's aphorism suggests, the cat-lamb must likewise have a specific place in this natural history of human and animal co-existence. From the little that Kafka tells us, we know that at least a partial destiny of this crossbreed is to become a sacrificial animal. He writes, "Perhaps the knife of the butcher would be a redemption (*Erlösung*) for this animal." As long as the animal remains unscathed, no redemption can seal its destiny, and nothing in the

---

7 Kafka, *Nachgelassene Schriften und Fragmente II*, 65; Kafka, *The Blue Octavo Notebooks*, 33.

common destiny of humans and sacrificial animals can be changed; the animal will remain sinful. If we take for granted that the family history of the cat-lamb and its owner is a Jewish history, we can situate Kafka's cat-lamb on the ladder of Jewish living things; however, this requires that we first consider both the role that lambs play in Judaism and in related monotheisms, as well as the Halakhic status of crossbreeds.

Sheep are sacrificial animals in many traditions. All Abrahamic monotheisms respect this exclusive status of sheep, and one such sacrifice lies at the very foundation of Judaism, namely, in the narrative of the Aqedah. After Abraham is tested and called to sacrifice his only son, Isaac, a ram appears miraculously in the bushes on the Mount Moriah; Abraham is ordered to sacrifice the animal instead of Isaac. After this test, Abraham becomes the arch-patriarch of the Jewish tradition, as his son later becomes a father and there follows a sequence of generations. In this story, a ram enters between the father and his child and has to give its life, so that the child can live. There is a similar constellation in Kafka's story, except that the sacrifice seems to have gone entirely awry. The narrator inherits an animal that wants to be sacrificed but cannot be, precisely because it is a piece of inheritance. What if Abraham had not killed that ram found in the bushes of Mount Moriah? Would he have walked it back home and given it as a pet to his son? Would this animal, whose miraculous appearance was caused by divine intervention, have been mortal or would it have continued living until the entirety of human (or Jewish) history had run its course? Kafka's story reads like a narrative of one of the possible futures of this ram. The fatal change in the procedure of the sacrifice has caught up with the lamb and imprinted itself on the animal's body, just as the original sin became imprinted in the body of the snake, who is cursed to crawl on its stomach. The sacrificial lamb who has failed to be sacrificed becomes haunted by original sin. After the expulsion from paradise, lambs and lions no longer live in peace with each other, at least not until the world of creation is redeemed, as the prophet Isiah envisioned. In the current – sinful – world, lions hunt lambs; the unsacrificed lamb, however, is torn from within by its natural predator, and seems to retain some memory that it was supposed to have been sacrificed. Its desire to be butchered does not remain secret to the man, to whose household the lamb belongs; but it is precisely because the fatal mistake of the unfinished sacrifice has become a part of the family history that this solution is no longer possible, at least not until the family line ends. The animal cannot stop wanting to be sacrificed, yet its owner cannot kill it, because both stand in a relation of guilt toward each other that remains the same, no matter how much the animal and the human may change. This is why the cat-lamb's owner considers questions about the existence of this piece of his inheritance inadequate: its existence is inseparable from the existence of the owner himself. "[T]he strangest questions are asked, which no human being could answer: Why there is only one such animal, why I rather than anybody else should own it, whether there was ever an animal like it before and what would happen if it died, whether it feels lonely, why it has no children, what it is called, etc." These questions are, like the question of human origin, impossible to answer.

The relation of guilt between the owner and the cat-lamb replaces the sacrifice. When the intended offering is not presented, it manifests itself in what the owner calls "heiliger Schutz" ("sacred protection"): "It remains faithful to the family that brought it up. In that there is certainly no extraordinary mark of fidelity, but merely the true instinct of an animal which, though it has countless step-relations in the world, has perhaps not a single blood relation, and to which consequently the protection it has found with us is sacred." The animal has no blood relatives, because its blood remains reserved for a blood offering that never transpired. It can have no other blood relation to anyone or anything on the tree of life except for the relation to the family who *owes* its blood and *owns* it. From the perspective of the Halakhic rules, the blood of one such crossbreed would not be kosher; thus no ritual slaughter of this animal could occur within the legal bounds prescribed by the Jewish law.

There are good reasons to believe that as Kafka wrote this story he had in mind the rules of kosher slaughter. He and Yitzhak Löwy may have recently discussed *shechita* (ritualistic slaughter), and it is beyond doubt that together they had seen a play that alludes to the ritualistic slaughter. In a diary note from 24 November 1911, Kafka mentions Jacob Gordin's play *Di shkhite* [*The Slaughter*] and records quotations from the Talmud that appear in this play. A member of Kafka's family, his paternal grandfather, Jakob Kafka, had been a ritual slaughterer. Kafka, who was a vegetarian, once noted in a letter: "my grandfather on the paternal side was a butcher in a village near Strakonitz; I have to not eat as much meat as he has slaughtered."[8] A similarly strange food economy is the fate of the cat-lamb: the creature can survive only on milk, because its lamb-half cannot eat meat and its cat-half cannot eat grass. It is remarkable, too, that in this same letter Kafka labels his lack of musical talent "a piece of heirloom" ("ein Erbstück der

---

8 The original German reads: "mein väterlicher Großvater war Fleischhauer in einem Dorf bei Strakonitz, ich muß soviel Fleisch nicht essen, als er geschlachtet hat." Franz Kafka, letter to Milena Jesenská from 25 June 1920, in *Briefe an Milena. Erweiterte Ausgabe* [*Letters to Milena. Extended Edition*], eds. Jürgen Born and Michael Müller, Fischer Verlag, Frankfurt/M. 1995, 79; Franz Kafka, *Letters to Milena*, trans. Philip Boehm, Schocken Books, New York 1990, 33. Translation modified.

Vorfahren"), repeating an expression from "A Crossbreed," in which the cat-lamb is identified as "a piece of heirloom" ("ein Erbstück").

The cat-lamb, being a hybrid of a feline and a ruminant, could not be eaten by people. The Mosaic law prescribes that certain animals may be eaten, some may not, and some may not even be touched. The list of clean and unclean animals in Deuteronomy 14:5 contains a *hapax legomenon*, which has led to various diverging speculations about the species in question. The name of the animal as it appears in the Tanakh is זָמֶר (*zamer*); this animal is, according to the Mosaic law, kosher, like other cloven-hoofed ruminants. The current consensus is to identify the *zamer* as a wild sheep (*Ammotragus tragelaphus*). Because the exact species has never been identified with certainty, translators of the Bible have faced considerable difficulty in finding an adequate translation. Both the Septuagint and the Vulgate translate *zamer* as "camelopard," likely deriving this word from Pliny's *Naturalis Historia*, where the word stands for "giraffe." The giraffe, however, could hardly be the *zamer* of the Tanakh, as it is most unlikely that this animal, native to Central and South Africa, would have presented much of a concern to the Rabbinic authorities of the time.[9] Despite the eventual clarification and the resulting general agreement to identify the *zamer* as a wild sheep, the history of its shape-shifting has left a trace in the Halakhic tradition. The Greek and Latin translations mentioning the giraffe provoked discussion among rabbis as to the animal's Halakhic status. The giraffe does fulfill the criteria for being kosher, though this hardly means that it will ever become a staple product. Interestingly, the question of whether giraffe meat is kosher has become a bit of a new lore in contemporary Israel. The profane curiosity most commonly associated with giraffe slaughter concerns where to cut the neck. The rabbinic authority response to this is simple: "anywhere."

Giraffe's meat is kosher meat yet that of the "camelopard," the name given to the giraffe by Pliny and later adopted by Linnaeus, is not. The giraffe's name in modern binomial nomenclature is *Giraffa camelopardalis*, a designation that reflects Pliny's belief that the animal was a crossbreed of camel and leopard, with the hooves of an ungulate and the spotted fur of a feline. As such, should a half-camel half-cat animal ever exist, it would be unquestionably non-kosher, according to the Halakhic rules. It is curious that the kosher *zamer*'s non-kosher modern name "camelopard" has become part of the Biblical tradition, passing through translation into Greek and Latin with a detour through Pliny. It is even more

---

9 *The Jewish Encyclopedia*, Funk and Wagnalls, New York 1906. The complete articles are now available online. See also the page on "chamois" (the translation of *zamer* in the King James Bible): http://www.jewishencyclopedia.com/articles/4227-chamois

curious, though, that this same tradition has the need to classify this animal – born, as it were, in translation – in accordance with the Halakhic order of things.

The Talmud mentions a creature that, like the cat-lamb, is a transitory life form, whose Halakhic status changes when it reaches maturity. This is a dirt-mouse: a mouse whose hind legs, until fully formed, are dirt, indivisible from the earth. There are at least two instances when the dirt-mouse is invoked, one in Chullin 9:10: "A mouse [*achbar*] which is half flesh and half earth; if someone touches the flesh part, he becomes *tamei* [unclean]; if he touches the earth part, he remains *tahor* [clean]"; and in Sanhedrin 91a: "A certain sectarian said to Rabbi Ami: You say that the dead will live again – but they become dust, and can dust come alive? He replied... Go out to the field and see the rodent that one day is half flesh and half earth, and on the next day it has transformed into a creeping creature and has become entirely flesh."[10] As long as one can differentiate between the mouse's two parts, the question of its Halakhic status is easily answered. One cannot say this about Kafka's cat-lamb, because its two halves cannot be differentiated with certainty. Furthermore, cat and lamb do not seem to be the only two natures fighting for the creature's body. There is something dog-like about it, even human-like: it has "the ambitions of a human being." When the narrator notes that it "simply cannot be parted from me" and that its place of choice is "lying on my loins," the animal indeed appears to be of one flesh with him. The hybridization of the animal affects even its human owner. Divided as it is within its own body, the creature has no place within the taxonomy of the Judaic animals.

Like the camelopard of Deuteronomy, the dirt-mouse of the Talmud does not have a corresponding life form in Linnaean taxonomy. It has been suggested, however, that the dirt-mouse ended up being mentioned in the Talmudic tractate through Greek and Roman sources (Diodorus Siculus and Pliny the Elder, among others).[11] These sources, of course, had no rabbinic authority as such. Yet Diodorus's authority as a natural historian was revered even by the rabbis, so much so that they became concerned with a creature not mentioned in the Tanakh. If a dirt-mouse indeed existed, it would be imperative to define its Halakhic status. This much stands to reason. Less comprehensible is that this

---

10 Natan Slifkin, *Sacred Monsters. Mysterious and Mythical Creatures of Scripture, Talmud and Midrash*. Zoo Torah / Yashar Books, New York 2007, 329–330.

11 Sid Z. Leimann, "R. Israel Lipshutz and the Mouse that is Half Flesh and Half Earth: A Note on Torah U-Madda in the Nineteenth Century," in *Hazon Nahum*, eds. Norman Lamm and Jeffrey S. Gurock, New York, Yeshiva University Press, 1998, 449–458. He cites Johann Link, a German biologist, who discusses the passage about the "springmaus" in Diodorus (see page 453).

creature, whose existence was supported only by anecdotal evidence from a Greek source, somehow burrowed its way into the Talmud. If the law prescribes a particular Halakhic status to the dirt-mouse, it must also, by necessity, assume that a dirt-mouse actually exists; otherwise, the animal would be of no interest to scholars of Jewish law. The law prescribes that the flesh part of the dirt-mouse is unclean, thereby establishing that the dirt-mouse does indeed exist. Diodorus's description may well have referred to an animal identifiable within the Linnaean system (modern scholars suggest a jerboa); however, the dirt-mouse of Mishnah, having been defined as "legal," can no longer be assimilated into any scientific taxonomy. Like its "cousin" the camelopard of the Septuagint, the dirt-mouse entered into Halakhah through a door in Greek natural history, via cross-cultural inclusion. Kafka's cat-lamb, "an animal which, though it has countless step-relations in the world, has perhaps not a single blood relation," entered into the order of creatures that are "step-relations" of those belonging to Linnaean taxonomy (such as lambs or cats), but only by means of language. The cat-lamb – a mix of predator and ruminant, and thus, in the Halakhic perspective, an abomination – is a crossbreed whose flesh is essentially and entirely language.[12]

The etymological histories of words that signify things in nature do not always correspond to natural history. The history of the transition of *zamer* to camelopard to giraffe captures a development not found in any systematic

---

12 Jorge Luis Borges, a dedicated reader of Kafka, explored fantastic creatures as well as fantastic classifications of real animals. In his *Book of Imaginary Beings* [*El libro de los seres imaginarios*], Borges collected concise descriptions of mystical creatures from antiquity to modern times. The book contains, among others, the *barometz*, a hybrid of lamb and plant, described by Pliny the Elder, and Kafka's "Crossbreed," which is cited in its entirety. Furthermore, Borges, in his short story "The Analytical Language of John Wilkins" ["El idioma analítico de John Wilkins"], invented a Chinese encyclopedia entitled "Celestial Emporium of Benevolent Knowledge," which offers a fantastic taxonomy of animals arranged according to no principle save the author's imagination. All animals in this "encyclopedia" are divided into the following categories: "Those that belong to the emperor; Embalmed ones; Those that are trained; Suckling pigs; Mermaids (or Sirens); Fabulous ones; Stray dogs; Those that are included in this classification; Those that tremble as if they were mad; Innumerable ones; Those drawn with a very fine camel hair brush; Et cetera; Those that have just broken the flower vase; Those that, at a distance, resemble flies" (see Jorge Luis Borges, "John Wilkins' Analytical Language," in *Selected Nonfictions*, trans. Eliot Weinberger, Penguin Books, New York 1999, 229–232, 231). Besides thematizing hybridization in its narrative, this text, as are many by Borges, is an example of a hybridization of common genres: the essay genre, which is supported by facts, quotations, and references, undergoes a crossing with the genre of the fantastic short story. Some interpreters take Borges's fantastic figures to be references to actual sources and have sought to locate them among existing books. Thus, these interpretations have a similar fate as that of the word *zamer* in its translations: pieces of scientific knowledge become mixed with a generous portion of free imagination.

account of natural history. Most of this development occurs in the transitory zone between languages, and it is precisely this transitory zone that is the place of abode of Kafka's Odradek, who is homeless in at least two languages, German and Czech. Kafka's writings present at least one other invented creature whose place on the tree of living things remains unknown. Unlike with Odradek, this animal's place of abode is entirely definite; in contrast to the cat-lamb, however, its relation to people is veiled and unclear. This creature, as described by Kafka in an unpublished fragment (likely written in 1922), belongs to a place rather than to an owner:

> In our synagogue there lives an animal about the size of a marten. One can often see it very well; it allows people to approach to a distance of about two meters. It is pale blue-green in color. Nobody has ever yet touched its fur, and so nothing can be said about it, and one might almost go as far as to assert that the real color of its fur is unknown, perhaps the color one sees stems only from the dust and mortar with which its fur is matted, and indeed the color does resemble that of the paint inside the synagogue, only it is a little brighter.

It is asserted that the animal would stay here even if the building were no longer being used as a synagogue. It is also related that generations ago someone had attempted to banish the animal; the proposed action, however, had introduced problems pertaining to Halakhic regulations:

> There is evidence that at that time the question whether the presence of such an animal might be tolerated in the house of God was investigated from the point of view of the religious laws. Opinions were sought from various celebrated rabbis, views were divided, the majority were for the expulsion of the animal and a reconsecration of the house of God. But it was easy to issue decrees from afar, in reality it was simply impossible to banish the animal.[13]

If the cat-lamb in the earlier story is the token both of the family's continued history and of its inheritance, the blue-green creature of the synagogue[14] has a history preceding the community of people who, in relation to this creature,

---

13 Kafka, *Nachgelassene Schriften und Fragmente II*, 405–411; Kafka, *Parables and Paradoxes*, 49–59.

14 It is unlikely that Kafka ever read the Talmudic tractate Berakhot in Seder Zeraim, but it is entirely plausible that he heard about the regulation concerning when the morning prayer should be recited. The earliest time for the morning *Shema*, as Rabbi Eliezer ben Hurcanus proposed, is when the natural light is bright enough for the human eye to recognize the difference between blue and green (m.Ber.1.2; I thank Yulia Shtutina for this reference). The color of Kafka's blue-green creature would thus create a noticeable obstacle for someone intending to say a morning prayer in the synagogue.

appear to be its guests rather than its owners. Precisely for the reason that the animal's genesis precedes the foundation of the synagogue, the Halakhic regulations prove inadequate for defining its status and proper place. Walter Benjamin, though he would not have seen this fragment at the time, recognized that animals in Kafka's stories were representatives of an order preceding the systematized view of creation in Judaism. As Benjamin observed, in 1931, in his notes for an unwritten essay on Kafka:

> [G]anz verschollen ist [die prähistorische Stufe der Menschheit] in der Torah nicht. Die Reinigungs- und Speisegesetze beziehen sich auf eine Vorwelt, von der nichts mehr erhalten ist als diese Abwehrmaßnahmen gegen sie.
> [The prehistoric stage of humanity has not gone completely missing in the Torah. The laws of purification and food preparation refer to a pre-world, from which there remains nothing besides these mechanisms of defense against it.][15]

The cat-lamb is not only an abomination from the point of view of the Halakha because it is an unclean animal; the problem also lies in the heterogeneity of its nature. The animal's two taxonomic identifications are mixed to the extent that no part of its body can be discerned as clean or unclean. The transitory nature of its existence sets it beyond the taxonomy of creatures; taxonomy is powerless in the face of mixed origins. Kafka's furry creature, because of its birthright, renders this same taxonomy powerless: its existence in the synagogue is primogenital in relation to the Jewish community with its set of beliefs and laws. In this text it is the community, rather than the animal, that exists in a transitory state. The community must adopt their fellow tenant, even if its nature does not fit within the taxonomy defined by the community's laws. Either way, the transition as such appears to be problematic for laws and regulations.[16] Kafka investigates pre-

---

15 Walter Benjamin, *Benjamin über Kafka* [*Benjamin on Kafka*], ed. Hermann Schweppenhäuser, Suhrkamp, Frankfurt/M. 1981, 116. English translation my own. Mary Douglas, who researched rules and rituals of purity and purification extensively, saw the reason of the distinction between clean and unclean animals in Judaism in the need to expand the special status of Jews: they were God's chosen people, and the kosher animals were God's chosen creatures. See Mary Douglas, *Leviticus as Literature*, Oxford University Press, New York 2000. Benjamin's statement is more radical. For him, the distinction between kosher and non-kosher animals is a sign of the prehistoric dividing line between humans and animals.

16 Mary Douglas suggests that unclassified animals cause danger to taxonomy and thus are banned from the order of Jewish animals as impure: "I proposed a theory of anomaly, a universal feeling of disquiet (even of disgust) on confrontation with unclassifiables. Taking the Levitical classification system as it revealed itself, the said abominable species failed to show the taxonomic requirements of inhabitants of the three environmental classes, land, air, water, and the abominability of species that 'go upon the belly' in all environments went by the same rule: the

cisely this transitory zone in order to reach the critical point, at which the law, as the tool of systematization, loses its ability to separate and define. Benjamin terms this transitory zone *die Vorwelt* [pre-world]. Yet there is no going back to the prehistoric stage, when the powers of the pre-world were not yet contained by and within laws; thus, there is no access to the origin of these laws. In order to describe the world together with its origin hidden in the depths of the pre-world, Kafka collapses in his texts the law with what it seeks to regulate. The blue-green creature of the synagogue does not, as such, give birth to the generations of Jews inhabiting the building; it does, however, reference a time when the future of this Jewish community was only germinating. The animal is not the community's progenitor and yet it signifies the prehistoric stage in its world. As in Benjamin's note about the laws and regulations of the Torah, the animal in Kafka's story survives as a sign of the Jewish community's prenatal stage without disclosing anything about its own origin. The animal and the community have a common history without sharing a common genesis and yet they are related – not by blood but by history – through something hidden in their pre-history. This logic can be extended to Kafka's literary practice as a whole. His literary inventions resemble a crossbreed of a bird and an airplane: the history, natural and cultural, that separates them on the chronological scale abbreviates their genesis without answering as to where the origin of the inherent will for such hybridization is to be sought. Kafka's prose gives shape to this abbreviation.

Origin and continuation, as Kafka shows in the passage (on technical progress) cited at the beginning of this article, stand in a paradoxical relation to each other. On one hand, origin defines the sequence of what originates from it; on the other, origin is unlike any other element in this sequence and thus is excluded from it. In mathematics, for example, zero is unlike any other number and thus a special set of rules applies exclusively to it. Kafka explains this mechanism through the example of Eve, the first woman. She, unlike any other woman in history, was born from Adam's rib; being the first woman, she gives birth to the generations to come but her own birth remains unrepeatable and exclusive to her alone. In order to generate a sequence, one must be or become excluded from it.

This logic is reflected in the story of Abraham and Isaac as re-told repeatedly by Maurice Blanchot. Blanchot, too, like Kafka in his story "A Crossbreed," speaks about an animal's sacrifice for a human family's sake and alludes to Abraham's sacrifice. This allusion appears in Blanchot's works at least three times: in two

---

forbidden animals were species that escaped being classified." See Douglas, *Leviticus as Literature*, vii. I thank Mikhail Iampolskii for this reference.

essays on Kafka and in a short story.[17] In the latter, entitled *At the Desired Moment* [*Au moment voulu*], Blanchot writes:

> When Abraham came back from the country of Moriah, he was not accompanied by his child but by the image of a ram, and it was with a ram that he had to live from then on. Others saw the son in Isaac, because they didn't know what had happened on the mountain, but he saw the ram in his son, because he made a ram for himself out of his child. A devastating story [histoire accablante].[18]

"Accablante," from "accabler," traces to "katabole," the Greek word meaning "laying down," in the sense of both "laying a foundation" but also, metaphorically, the physiological act of conception.[19] In view of this etymology, Blanchot's words "histoire accablante" characterize the Aqedah as a story (or a history) of Abraham sacrificing his right to found a family and tradition rather than proving this right. In order to start the sequence of generations and become the arch-patriarch of the Jewish people, Abraham must be excluded from this very succession. Just as Eve, the mother of all women, can have no mother herself, so too Abraham, in Blanchot's version, can be the father of all Jewish sons only if he gives up his own son. We know the story of the Biblical Abraham's life prior to his journey to Moriah and thus we know that he does not stand outside human history; Blanchot's point in his description of the Aqedah is that God's demand to sacrifice Isaac tears Abraham from the generations' succession. If Abraham sacrifices his only son, he will cede all hope of becoming the forefather for generations

---

17 My focus in this article is specific to the problem of mixed origin, human and animal, in Kafka's prose, and my reading thus limits itself to the discussion of the constellation involving Isaac and the ram. Chris Danta's excellent book-length study of the Aqedah in Kafka, Blanchot, and Kierkegaard offers a much more detailed analysis of Kafka's and Blanchot's respective versions of the Biblical story. See Chris Danta, *Literature Suspends Death: Sacrifice and Storytelling in Kierkegaard, Kafka and Blanchot*, Continuum, New York 2011.
18 Maurice Blanchot, *When the Time Comes*, trans. Lydia Davis, Station Hill Press, New York 1985, 65; Maurice Blanchot, *Au moment voulu*, Gallimard, Paris 1951, 147.
19 The word occurs several times in the New Testament and always, with only one exception, in the expression "από καταβολῆς κόσμου," "from the foundation of the world" (Matthew 13:35; Matthew 25:34; Luke 11:50; John 17:24; Ephesians 1:4; Hebrews 4:3; Hebrews 9:26; 1 Peter 1:20; Revelation 13:8; Revelation 17:8). The only exception is Hebrews 11:11, where the word occurs in connection with Isaac's conception: "Through faith also Sara herself received strength to conceive seed, and was delivered of a child when she was past age, because she judged him faithful who had promised [Πίστει καὶ αὐτὴ Σάρρα δύναμιν εἰς καταβολὴν σπέρματος ἔλαβεν καὶ παρὰ καιρὸν ἡλικίας ἔτεκεν, ἐπεὶ πιστὸν ἡγήσατο τὸν ἐπαγγειλάμενον]." It is not clear, however, whether Blanchot explicitly intended this use of the word "accablante" to be an allusion to its Biblical precursors and the Aqedah or whether the link is incidental.

of Jews, and yet it is precisely his willingness to sacrifice this future that renders him, in God's eyes, worthy of becoming the Jewish arch-patriarch.

This paradox of sacrificing the future for the future's sake recurs in a later text by Blanchot, "Kafka and the Work's Demand" (from 1958), where he explains to a fuller extent that Abraham's sacrifice concerns waiving his belief in the future, for the sake of his son's future and for the future sons:

> What is demanded of Abraham is not only that he sacrifice his son, but God himself. The son is God's future on earth, for it is time which is the Promised Land – the true, the only dwelling place of the chosen people and of God in his people. Yet Abraham, by sacrificing his only son, must sacrifice time, and time sacrificed will certainly not be given back in the eternal beyond. The beyond is nothing other than the future, the future of God in time. The beyond is Isaac.[20]

Kafka, as Blanchot explains here, faces a paradox similar to Abraham's. In order to be able to write, he must sacrifice his belief in being a writer. This comparison also appears in Blanchot's "Kafka and Literature" (from 1949):

> As soon as [the writer] starts writing, he is within literature and he is there completely: he has to be a good artisan, but he also has to be a word seeker, an image seeker. He is compromised. That is his fate. Even the famous instances of total sacrifice change nothing in this situation. To master literature with the sole aim of sacrificing it? But that assumes that what one sacrifices exists. So one must first believe in literature, believe in one's literary calling, make it exist – to be a writer of literature and to be it to the end. Abraham was willing to sacrifice his son, but what if he was not sure that he had a son, and what he took for his son was really just a ram?[21]

Blanchot knew Kafka's own variations of the Aqedah from a letter Kafka had written to Robert Klopstock[22]; however, Blanchot's comparison of Kafka and Abraham has little to do with these variations, or at least not directly. The parallel he draws emphasizes one sole aspect: both Abraham and Kafka are not sure whether they exist in the only respective quality that, for each, has the utmost existential meaning: Abraham as father, Kafka as writer. In Blanchot's baffling description, Kafka's existence as a writer is firmly rooted in the very uncertainty as to whether he is able to enter the realm of literary tradition, whereas Abra-

---

20 Maurice Blanchot, *The Space of Literature*, trans. Ann Smock, Nebraska University Press, Lincoln 1982, 61.
21 Maurice Blanchot, *The Work of Fire*, trans. Charlotte Mandell, Stanford University Press, Stanford 1995, 15.
22 See Franz Kafka, *Briefe 1902–1924. Gesammelte Werke* [*Letters 1902–1924. Collected Works*], Fischer Verlag, Frankfurt/M. 1998, 332–334.

ham's existence as a father is rooted in his uncertainty about whether he does indeed have a son. This uncertainty, for Blanchot, contains the true essence of sacrifice. Isaac must become a ram in Abraham's doubting eyes so that he (Isaac) can remain human in the eyes of others; Abraham himself must reduce his son to an animal so as to exclude him from the progression of sons born of sons and thus establish himself as the original arch-patriarch. With this procedure Abraham becomes dissolved in the origin of this progression. "The desired moment" – "un moment voulu," in Blanchot's formulation – is the zero point in this sequence, the moment of founding a history of the Jewish people. The will to originate embodied by Abraham lies at the foundation of this sequence and projects itself into the future.

Blanchot, like Kafka, seeks to capture in his narration the border between the animal and the human. To become human, the human must step beyond being just animal, that is, the human must make a conscious choice to sacrifice willingly in response to God's calling. This ethical dimension in the relation of man to God forms the core of Judaism. Abraham incorporates the ethical principle of choosing God and being chosen by God, in that he chooses to sacrifice his own flesh and blood, Isaac. Blanchot claims that this is possible only if Abraham reduces Isaac to *mere* flesh and blood, that is, if he sees him as just a living organism, an animal rather than an individual capable of his own choices. Blanchot's version of the Aqedah is a narration in which the human is separated from the animal at the precise moment when the separating line is drawn by Abraham's sacrificial knife.

Kafka's story about the cat-lamb-dog-human is an invention of a hybrid whose body as a whole encloses the demarcation between the human and the animal. Within its body the common origin of the human and of the animal lies hidden. The border between the animal and the human natures cannot be located and described, as it is not possible to identify the exact evolutionary moment when humans became a separate species. Humanity does not remember its origin, just as no person remembers his or her own birth. It is possible, however, to include this critical moment in a narration about human origin and humans' separation from animals. The same can be said, too, about being Jewish. It is not possible to draw a separating line in one's nature between what is Jewish and what is universally human. It is possible, though, to live a life doubting the existence of this very division, as did Kafka. His doubt became the foundation of his existence and the source of his literary inspiration. Moreover, his doubt about whether there was anything Jewish about his literary creation[23] made him into a writer whose works embody the impossibility and necessity of choosing to be Jewish as much as that of choosing to be human.

Works Cited

Benjamin, Walter, *Benjamin über Kafka*. Ed. Hermann Schweppenhäuser (Frankfurt/M.: Suhrkamp, 1981).

Blanchot, Maurice, *Au moment voulu* (Paris: Gallimard, 1951).

Blanchot, Maurice, *The Space of Literature*. Trans. Ann Smock (Lincoln: Nebraska University Press, 1982).

Blanchot, Maurice, *When the Time Comes*. Trans. Lydia Davis (New York: Station Hill Press, 1985).

Blanchot, Maurice, *The Work of Fire*. Trans. Charlotte Mandell (Stanford: Stanford University Press, 1995).

Borges, Jorge Luis, *The Book of Imaginary Beings*. Trans. Andrew Hurley (New York: Penguin Classics, 2006).

Borges, Jorge Luis, "John Wilkins' Analytical Language," in *Selected Nonfictions*. Trans. Eliot Weinberger (New York: Penguin Books, 1999), 229–232.

Danta, Chris, *Literature Suspends Death: Sacrifice and Storytelling in Kierkegaard, Kafka and Blanchot* (New York: Continuum, 2011).

Douglas, Mary, *Leviticus as Literature* (New York: Oxford University Press, 2000).

Hamacher, Werner, "The Gesture in the Name: On Benjamin and Kafka," in *Premises: Essays on Philosophy and Literature from Kant to Celan*. Trans. Peter Fenves (Stanford: Stanford University Press, 1999), 294–336.

The Jewish Encyclopedia (New York: Funk and Wagnalls, 1906).

Kafka, Franz, *The Blue Octavo Notebooks*. Ed. Max Brod. Trans. Ernst Kaiser and Eithne Wilkins (Cambridge: Exact Change, 2004).

Kafka, Franz, *Briefe 1902–1924. Gesammelte Werke* (Frankfurt/M.: Fischer Verlag, 1998).

Kafka, Franz, *Briefe an Milena. Erweiterte Ausgabe*. Eds. Jürgen Born and Michael Müller (Frankfurt/M.: Fischer Verlag, 1995).

Kafka, Franz, *The Complete Stories*. Ed Nahum N. Glatzer (New York: Schocken Books, 1976).

Kafka, Franz, *Diaries 1910–1913*. Ed. Max Brod. Trans. Joseph Kresh (New York: Schocken Books, 1965).

Kafka, Franz, *Letters to Milena*. Trans. Philip Boehm (New York: Schocken Books, 1990).

Kafka, Franz, *Nachgelassene Schriften und Fragmente I*. Ed. Malcolm Pasley (Frankfurt/M.: Fischer, 1993).

Kafka, Franz, *Nachgelassene Schriften und Fragmente II*. Ed. Jost Schillemeit (Frankfurt/M.: Fischer, 1992).

Kafka, Franz, *Parables and Paradoxes*. Ed. Nahum N. Glatzer (New York: Schocken Books, 1987).

---

23 Kafka wrote about the impossibility and necessity of being a German-Jewish writer in a letter to Max Brod. See Kafka, *Briefe 1902–1924. Gesammelte Werke*, 334–338.

Leimann, Sid Z., "R. Israel Lipshutz and the Mouse that is Half Flesh and Half Earth: A Note on Torah U-Madda in the Nineteenth Century," in *Hazon Nahum*. Eds. Norman Lamm and Jeffrey S. Gurock (New York: Yeshiva University Press, 1998), 449–458.

Slifkin, Natan, *Sacred Monsters. Mysterious and Mythical Creatures of Scripture, Talmud and Midrash* (New York: Zoo Torah / Yashar Books, 2007).

Section 4: **Modernism**

Jean-Michel Rabaté
Kafka's Anti-Epiphanies

My approach to the "paradox of the universal" reopens a critical debate concerning Kafka. This debate, now almost forgotten yet still full of meaning, opposed the American art critic Clement Greenberg, the main exponent of modernism as Abstract Expressionism, and the British critic and Cambridge professor F. R. Leavis. Their discussion commenced in the spring of 1955. Greenberg had previously translated several of Kafka's short stories, including "Josephine the Singer, or The Mouse Folk" ("Josefine, die Sängerin oder Das Volk der Mäuse") for a co-edition of *Parables*, published in 1947. In 1955, he published "The Jewishness of Franz Kafka: Some Sources of His Particular Vision," in which he explained that Kafka's vision could not be dissociated from his being Jewish. According to Greenberg, Kafka's tradition was the Halachah, even if he, an emancipated and enlightened Jew, did not believe in the promise of a Messiah. If the meaning of his texts was not exhausted by Jewish mysticism, the form itself was Jewish. As in the Halachah, Kafka's tales and parables revolve around the interpretation of the law "with a patient, if selective, circumstantiality that belongs more to description and logical exposition than to narrative."[1] Thus, according to Greenberg,

[Kafka's] shorter efforts are generally more successful than his novels or extended short stories like "The Metamorphosis." [...] Beyond a certain point the peculiarly stealthy, gradual movement in time and perception that Kafka is able to achieve tends to bore the reader – whose patience is further taxed by the insufficient promise of a resolution. [...] States of being are what are conclusive here, and these for Kafka can have no beginnings or endings, only middles. What is more, these exclude moral issues, and hence no moral choices are made in Kafka's fiction. To the extent that this fiction succeeds, it refutes the assumption of many of the most serious critics of our day – F. R. Leavis is notably one of them – that the value of a work of literary art depends ultimately on the depth to which it explores moral difficulties."[2]

---

1 Clement Greenberg, "The Jewishness of Franz Kafka: Some Sources of His Particular Vision," in *The Collected Essays, Volume 3: Affirmations and Refusals, 1950–1956*, ed. John O'Brian, University of Chicago Press, Chicago 1993, 202–209, 208.
2 Greenberg, "The Jewishness of Franz Kafka," 208.

Parts of this essay overlap with sections from a chapter of *Crimes of the Future*, Bloomsbury, New York 2014, 171–184.

Beyond the revealing admission that he found Kafka's novels boring, Greenberg was challenging Leavis's ethical type of criticism. This elicited a counter-attack from the British critic, who reiterated his idea that good literature engages with ethical issues and that Kafka, in this respect, was no exception. Leavis objected to Greenberg's emphasis on Kafka's limitations as a creative writer[3] – indeed, did Greenberg's argument not in fact merely underscore that the meaning of Kafka's works was opaque for readers not familiar with Jewish culture? Leavis was clearly on the side of the universal, explaining that he himself, though neither Jewish nor Catholic, could sense Kafka's greatness just as he could recognize the point of one of Graham Greene's Catholic novels. For Leavis, Kafka transcended both his local neurosis – but Greenberg doubted this point – and the Jewish tradition, a tradition that had the disadvantage of remaining "particularist" or even "non-Western," the latter phrase coming from Greenberg.

Greenberg responded by highlighting Kafka's humor, which he saw as a means by which Kafka transcended his fragmentariness and "imprisonment" in a tradition. Kafka's greatness, for Greenberg, appeared more in his mannerisms than in grand projects, which often were no more than abortive schemes. Thus, stories like "Josephine the Singer," "Investigations of a Dog" ("Forschungen eines Hundes") and "The Hunter Gracchus" ("Der Jäger Gracchus") would offer the full measure of Kafka's genius. There should be, Greenberg argued, a dialectical relationship between universal appeal and the specific conditions of production:

> What I cannot see at all is why the resemblances I find between the method of Kafka's imagination and Halachic logic should have any more *special* – that is, exclusive – an interest for "those familiar with Jewish culture and tradition" than Shakespeare's echoes of Montaigne have for experts in 16th-century French literature, or the cosmological scheme of the *Divine Comedy* has for Catholic medievalists. I hoped I was explaining the cause of an effect in Kafka's writings that those unacquainted with Jewish tradition feel as much as I do – who am not, in my ignorance of Hebrew and many other things, *that* familiar with Jewish tradition anyhow. The explanation of the cause was not intended to enhance one's opinion of the effect, nor was the Jewishness of Kafka's art expected to recommend it in any way that it could not recommend itself at first hand to any reader, Gentile or Jew.[4]

Greenberg touched a nerve here. A longer reply followed, in which Leavis insisted on a discrepancy between Greenberg's evaluation of Kafka and his account of Kafka's work.[5] Kafka's humor, according to Leavis, could not suffice to offset the

3 Greenberg, "The Jewishness of Franz Kafka," 208.
4 Greenberg, "The Jewishness of Franz Kafka," 212–213.
5 Greenberg, "The Jewishness of Franz Kafka," 213.

absence of moral issues. He argued that Greenberg, having fallen into the trap of aestheticism, was in fact denying that our discriminations about art and literature have no bearing on "our future personal living." This triggered a reply from Greenberg that marked the end of the exchange. Greenberg agreed that Leavis was right. Greenberg did indeed reject any form of moralism and preferred aestheticism to moralism: "I do hold with art for art's sake. [...] If I agreed with Dr. Leavis, I would have to conclude that art was a substitute for life and experience."[6] Greenberg flaunted a Kantian aestheticism. His letter's conclusion has much to say about the "paradox of the universal":

> In his *Critique of Aesthetic Judgment* Kant demonstrated that one cannot prove an aesthetic judgment in discourse. Let Dr. Leavis see whether he can, in practice or theory, refute Kant's arguments. For what he [Kant] is claiming in effect is that one can so adequately exhibit in *words* one's grounds for an aesthetic judgment that agreement with it is compelled by the rules of evidence and logic. Kant holds that one can appeal only to the other person's *taste* as exercised through experience of the work of art under discussion.
> [...] Morality is built into the mind, and works of art have to respect the limitations that morality imposes on fancied action; otherwise the reader's or observer's interest cannot be held, whether in high- or lowbrow literature. But this does not mean that we have to learn from literature in order to enjoy it properly or that those who do not learn from it are in no position to judge it. Art, in my view, explains to us what we already feel, but it does not do so discursively or rationally; rather it acts out an explanation in the sense of working on our feelings at a remove sufficient to protect us from the consequences of the decisions made by our feelings in response to the work of art.[7]

The reference to Kant functioned as an absolute weapon. Greenberg would later use it to define modernism as such; at that time, it was heavy enough to silence Leavis. Greenberg's catharsis left him no wiser than before, but he had made his point. The chain of reasons leads from a stylistic preference for Kafka's shorter texts to a general theory that not only establishes the laws of art but also finds, in Kant's third Critique, a means of connecting modernism and theory. This is a clear opposition to a universalist concept of literature, which corresponds to Leavis's position, a universalism that must be reinforced by the ethical function attributed to literature. According to such a concept, Kafka's appeal is universal; he helps us make sense of the "human condition" and this understanding will in its turn make us better people. Literature, in other words, contains "universals of fantasy," as Giambattista Vico would have it, thanks to which we imaginatively merge with other points of view. In the name of a postulated empathy with such

---

6 Greenberg, "The Jewishness of Franz Kafka," 216.
7 Greenberg, "The Jewishness of Franz Kafka," 216.

views (those of people whose religion the reader does not share, for instance) the experience of reading literature offers tools for living better. Ethics –an Ethics of the Other, to be sure – remains the *telos* and horizon of literary criticism, a position taken more recently by deconstructive critics like Derek Attridge.

However, Greenberg also insists on a Jewish particularism; it is a welcome limitation, and such a limitation will later echo the idea that modernism is fundamentally defined by its limitations; indeed, these limitations, once accepted and understood, can then be successfully transformed into aesthetic programs. Here, the limitations of Kafka's thought and origins return us to a question about the judgments needed by literature. These should not be confused with aesthetic judgments, for there is something specific to the latter, as Kant shows in his third Critique. We have accordingly moved from a Jewish reading of Kafka to a Kantian appreciation of the function of judgments (not a priori but reflexive in this case) about art. In experiencing the beauty and depth of Kafka's writings, one learns about both oneself and the judgments one inevitably makes when appreciating works of art.

Greenberg does not believe in the ethical power of Kafka's works; rather, he insists upon the works' beauty and aesthetic value. In short, Kafka's works are powerful precisely because they bypass the ethical mode; they do so by hesitating between the aesthetic and the religious, to use Kierkegaard's useful categories. The story aptly called "The Judgment" ("Das Urteil") offers a case in point. Here, a son is condemned to death, by his father, for no other reason than perhaps having wished to supplant his father in his roles as a businessman. Despite the son's profession that he loves his father dearly, he finds himself torn on an evening when he writes to his best friend, who now lives in Russia, about his recent engagement and other news. In deploying the convoluted dynamics of "judging" as a verdict invariably leading to a "death sentence," Kafka spurs any personal awareness of how the reader reacts to authority as "sons." Since we are always already caught up in Oedipal patterns of subversive and punishable desires, love for our parents is ambivalent, and love must make room for hate; the apparently unexpected condemnation can then be re-interpreted as the only logical resolution. Yet this logical resolution – so effective when it allowed Kafka to dramatize his own inability to marry – is also, of course, a logical absurdity.

For *Parables and Paradoxes* Greenberg had translated "The Building of the Temple" ("Der Tempelbau"), "The Watchman" ("Der Wächter"), "The Sirens" ("Die Schweigen der Sirenen"), "The New Attorney" ("Der Neue Advokat), "Couriers" ("Kurier") and "Josephine the Singer"; one of his earlier essays served as the volume's introduction. Greenberg specialized in Kafka's shorter forms, or what can be termed the "aphoristic" in Kafka. I will try to understand, via using Richard T. Gray's systematic analysis of aphorisms in Kafka, how the shorter forms aim at mediating between the universal and the particular.[8] This does not mean that aphorisms should be considered as more "universal" because of their closeness to philosophy or traditional morality. As a genre, the aphoristic fragment is often classified as "classical" or "romantic" yet it also has serious claims to a modernist status. Aphorisms (not to be confused with "sentences"), in fact, resemble what I would call "philosophemes," that is, philosophical maxims of a certain type. "Philosophemes" are pithy phrases replete with meaning: they include tags, mottos, and apophthegms that can be mentioned independently of their original context. They are cryptic, dense, and often paradoxical or truly oxymoronic.[9] Such arresting sentences sustain their tension and usually avoid mere sententiousness. Their brevity and notable structural parallels transform them into maxims that are easily memorized. A highly subjective list, to exemplify what I mean: *"Die Sprache spricht"* (Heidegger), *"Tout autre est tout autre"* (Derrida), *"Le coeur a des raisons que la raison ne connaît pas"* (Pascal), *"Die Welt ist alles, was der Fall ist"* (Wittgenstein), *"Je est un autre"* (Rimbaud), *"Les non-dupes errent"* (Lacan), *"Verum Ipsum Factum"* (Vico), *"Das Wirkliche is das Reale"* (Hegel), *"Rien n'aura eu lieu que le lieu"* (Mallarmé), *"O my friends, there are no friends"* (Aristotle, translated by Derrida), *"D'ailleurs c'est toujours les autres qui meurent"* (Duchamp), *"Ubi nihil vales, ibi nihil velis"* (Geulincx), *"I wouldn't want to belong to any club that would accept me"* (Groucho Marx). One could easily add myriad other examples or adduce Oscar Wilde's famous paradoxes. However, the number of such sentences, great as it is, is not infinite. These sentences, moreover, share characteristics, including a notable syntactic compression[10] and a high dependence on the given language's amphibologies, which often render literal translation almost impossible; often, the sentences can be used only in their original languages.

This is highlighted by Kafka's aphorism 46 from *Contemplation* [*Betrachtungen*]: "The word *sein* means two things in German: 'being' and 'belonging-to-him.'"[11] It is unclear where exactly Kafka sought to go with this. I would argue that the obviousness in his semantic remark (*sein* as the possessive pronoun

---

8 Richard T. Gray, *Constructive Destruction: Kafka's Aphorisms: Literary Tradition and Literary Transformation*, Niemeyer, Tübingen 1987, 264.

9 See the wonderful collection gathered by Mardy Grothe, *Oxymoronica: Paradoxical Wit and Wisdom from History's Greatest Wordsmiths*, Harper, New York 2004. Kafka is quoted only once: "Don't despair, not even over the fact that you don't despair" (page 164).

10 See Virginia Tufte, *Artful Sentences, Syntax as Style*, Graphics Press, Cheshire 2006.

11 Franz Kafka, "The Collected Aphorisms," in *The Great Wall of China and Other Short Works*, ed. and trans. Malcolm Pasley, Penguin, London 1991, 79–98, 86. In the original: "Das Wort 'sein' bedeutet im Deutschen beides: Dasein und Ihm-gehören." See Franz Kafka, *Nachgelassene*

"his" doubling as the noun or verb for "to be" and "being") hides a deeper destabilization of ontology, and that this has as foundational an impact, as when Heidegger differentiates between *Sein* (as capitalized "Being") and *Seiendes* (as the lowercase-b "being being" of a *Dasein* understood as existence). The tantalizing semantic ambiguity of these aphorisms has triggered proliferating commentaries that lead in various directions and which evince the inexhaustible richness of the expression.

Is this comparable to certain similarly dense and cryptic writings of James Joyce, which he termed epiphanies? In Joyce's Epiphany 36 (a dream epiphany) we see him similarly and subtly questioning ontology via a comparable accident of language:

> Yes, they are the two sisters. She who is churning with stout arms (their butter is famous) looks dark and unhappy: the other is happy because she had her way.
> Her name is R . . . . Rina. I know the verb "to be" in their language.
> – Are you Rina?
> – I knew she was.[12]

The dream is triggered by Ibsen: Rina is a character in *Hedda Gabler*; she is the old aunt who is terminally ill and dies at the end of the play. We see that Joyce remembers the verb *å vaere* – meaning "to be," in Norwegian – and also linking its signifier, *Være*, with the Latin *Vera*, or "Truth," a truth apparently disclosed in dreams. For Joyce and Kafka, are ontology and language pitted against each other, placed at the extreme poles of a long conceptual arc, or are they instead like two sides of a coin? Does it help if, in one's native French, one can hallucinate the *vrai* as a "true" *sein*, a breast that will owe to Melanie Klein's split object, that one can divide between a good and a bad breast? Such seemingly irrelevant questions can be answered more rigorously by examining the parallel corpuses referred to previously, namely, Kafka's aphorisms and Joyce's epiphanies.

The Joycean epiphany and the Kafkan *Betrachtung* share a degree of commonality. However, attempts to set Kafka and Joyce into straightforward or unmediated dialogue seem glib or forced. Many have felt that these two authors come from worlds so fundamentally different that any attempt to align them appears problematic. Yet there are points of entry into a comparative study of their respective aphoristic works. Such points include the aphorisms' connections to Nietzsche, their common reverence for Flaubert's style, their similar awareness

---

Schriften und Fragmente II [*Posthumous Writings and Fragments II*], ed. Jost Schillemeit, Fischer, Frankfurt/M. 1992, 123.
12 James Joyce, *Poems and Shorter Writings*, Faber, London 1991, 196.

that clichés or "received ideas" constitute the basis for popular wisdom, their reduction of myth to catchphrases, and their wish to condense culture to a synthetic idiom.

If one tries to compare the Kafkan aphorism to the Joycean epiphany, an important difference becomes apparent almost immediately. Joyce began his career with these short texts, which date from 1902 to 1904; they are disseminated throughout *Stephen Hero*, *A Portrait of the Artist as a Young Man*, and *Ulysses* and even reappear in *Finnegans Wake*. Kafka, in contrast, was near the end of his literary career when he composed his two collections of aphorisms: those in the first collection, known as "He," date from the fall and winter of 1917 and 1918; the others, known as the Zürau aphorisms, were copied from notebooks and compiled in 1920, at a moment when he had renounced writing novels. This fundamental difference between the two sets of aphorisms must be kept in mind when noting their formal similarities. These short fragments, ranging in length from a single sentence to a paragraph, often have a content that is essentially cryptic or so condensed that the meaning is not immediately apparent. The main point of convergence between the aphorisms and the epiphanies is that they share a dialectical relationship between the particular and the universal. This is achieved via the link between fragment and totality: "Only fragments of a totality," Kafka notes, in his third octavo notebook.[13] Above all, their tensions generate "dialectical images" (to quote Walter Benjamin), in that they deploy, in a startling figurative language, a broader consideration of the whole, be it named "Truth" or "Life."

Any study of the aphorism should begin by considering its literary tradition, as does Richard Gray, as noted previously, in his *Constructive Destruction: Kafka's Aphorisms: Literary Tradition and Literary Transformation*. Gray reminds us that the word aphorism derives from the Greek *aphorismos*, a term coined by Hippocrates to designate a set of symptoms; indeed, the medical sense adheres to Joyce's epiphanies. Over time, the genre of the aphorism addressed a wider range of discourses. Aphoristic writing as practiced by Pascal, Vauvenargues, de La Rochefoucault, Novalis, Lichtenberg, Kierkegaard, Nietzsche, and Wittgenstein moves easily between philosophy and autobiography, religion and cultural critique. The aphorism's innate tendency to straddle genres contributes to its complexity. A working definition of an aphorism is that it is a short, condensed, apodictic statement that aims at giving a striking shape to an abstract truth. Gray

---

13 Franz Kafka, *The Blue Octavo Notebooks*, ed. Max Brod, trans. Ernst Kaiser and Eithne Wilkins, Exact Change, Cambridge 1991, 14.

concludes that the aphorism is "the ultimate expressive form of modernism."[14] His main thesis is that aphorism is the embodiment of modern skepticism facing the arrogance of the Universal when the latter becomes identical with Reason. Fittingly, the aphorism's resistance to any single definition parallels the form itself, since the tension between the universal and the particular generates series of dense, cryptic, tantalizing hermeneutical puzzles to be savored and solved one at a time.

Yet what it is that renders such short forms distinctly "Kafkan" or "Joycean"? These fragments compress the struggle of a subject who balances language and reality; indeed, they point to the discrepancy between linguistic capabilities and the shock of a real perceived as foreign, opaque, threatening. A Kafkan or Joycean aphorism thus presents the shortest narrative form capable of capturing the interaction – at times quite aggressive, disturbing or enigmatic – of Self and Other. I will study Joyce's practice first, not only because it took place earlier, around 1903–1904, but also because, despite being invoked by many critics, it retains an enigmatic air. We do not understand everything in the Joycean epiphany, and one of my contentions is that a detour via Kafka can bring new elements. Conversely, a detour through Joyce yields new insights into Kafka's literary practice.

I will survey two main features: the first is that these short texts are numbered in a manner that is either continuous (for Kafka) or discontinuous (for Joyce); the ongoing struggle to understand the logic behind these numberings is often reminiscent of the long-raging critical debate about Pascal's ordering of his *Pensées*. The second feature is the necessary fragmentation of the texts. In Joyce's case, the short texts exhibit countless ellipses; the many periods dot the texts, opening them up. In Kafka's fragments, the ellipses are more conceptual: we find myriad breaks, reversals in syntax, and countless evasions and self-referential loops. In each case, the vignettes enact a certain dynamism, often by evoking physical movement. For Joyce this may be a person who reads a book and identifies with characters who are moving, as in Epiphany 2. Epiphany 21 depicts two female mourners hurrying through a crowd, while Epiphany 23 presents a male dancer who moves noiselessly in an amphitheater: "He begins to dance far below in the amphitheatre with a slow and supple movement of the limbs, passing from movement to movement, in all the grace of youth and distance, until he seems to be a whirling body, a spider wheeling amid space, a star."[15] Dancers, dream animals, passers-by: all move with an oneiric precision. Epiphany 16 depicts "an

---

14 Gray, *Constructive Destruction*, 135.
15 Joyce, *Poems and Shorter Writings*, 183.

artic beast": "Something is moving in the pool."[16] The dreamer pushes it with a stick: "He moves his paws heavily and mutters words of some language which I do not understand."[17] Epiphany 6 presents bearded satyrs – each half-man and half-goat – who threateningly "move about me, enclosing me."[18] Epiphany 31 has a more urgent tone: "What moves upon me from the darkness subtle and murmurous as a flood [...]?"[19] Epiphany 32 begins with a crowd moving in a dream: "The human crowd swarms in the enclosure, moving through the slush."[20] Epiphany 33 evokes society ladies who "pass in twos and threes amid the life of the boulevard."[21] Many of these vignettes have an inchoative and exhortatory function: they shake the speaker and push him to an action or a decision. Typical in this respect is Epiphany 30 (reused at the end of *A Portrait of the Artist as a Young Man*), in which the plural voices of adventure beckon: "they call to me their kinsman, making ready to go, shaking the wings of their exultant and terrible youth."[22] Even Epiphany 7, a vignette that evokes a moment of pious devotion and presents the young man after communion in a church, begins "It is time to go away now."[23]

To grasp what Joyce does with his epiphanies, we must return to *Stephen Hero*, to the introduction of the term. Near the end of the remaining fragments of this long autobiographical novel, the eponymous hero, Stephen, overhears a discussion between a man and a woman; this takes place in Eccles Street one misty evening and resembles a scene written for the stage:

The Young Lady – (drawling discreetly) . . . O, yes . . . I was . . . at the . . . cha . . . pel . . .

The Young Gentleman – (inaudibly) . . . I . . . (again inaudibly) . . . I . . .

The Young Lady – (softly) . . . O . . . but you're . . . ve . . . ry . . . wick . . . ed . . . [24]

This is, admittedly, disappointing; dots and ellipses count more than what is said. This may leave the impression that an epiphany leads to a quintessentially Pinterian mode of dialogue, in that silences are more significant than what is spoken.

---

16 Joyce, *Poems and Shorter Writings*, 176.
17 Joyce, *Poems and Shorter Writings*, 176.
18 Joyce, *Poems and Shorter Writings*, 166.
19 Joyce, *Poems and Shorter Writings*, 191.
20 Joyce, *Poems and Shorter Writings*, 192.
21 Joyce, *Poems and Shorter Writings*, 193.
22 Joyce, *Poems and Shorter Writings*, 190.
23 Joyce, *Poems and Shorter Writings*, 167.
24 James Joyce, *Stephen Hero*, Jonathan Cape, London 1956, 216.

These three lines of – broken – dialogue nevertheless manage to touch the young poet's sensitivity, spurring his decision to collect similar vignettes, in a "book of epiphanies." His definition of epiphany follows: "The triviality made him think of collecting many such moments together in a book of epiphanies. By an epiphany he meant a sudden spiritual manifestation, whether in the vulgarity of speech or of gesture or in a memorable phase of the mind itself. He believed that it was for the man of letters to record these epiphanies with extreme care, seeing that they themselves are the most delicate and evanescent of moments."[25]

For Joyce, the lack of content in the actual words of the exchange is constitutive; it is the equivalent of a maximum of content, and such a dialectical reversal is something that we find in Kafka's *Contemplation* as well. Here, ellipses condense Irish paralysis, adding curious sexual innuendoes: for example, what was the young lady doing at the chapel that is so unspeakable? This almost forces the reader to be "wicked," though the actual exchange may well have been banal and harmless. Was there a priest in the dark, to whom she was muttering her soft "O... yes..."? Was she doing something to him? What does she suggest with her sensual drawling of "O"s? Excited, seduced, baffled, the reader becomes an involuntary voyeur. Joyce is trying to capture less a moment of plenitude or revelation than gaps in speech, pauses or loopholes in dialogues. In this, he testifies to the always surprising emergence of truth as a hole in discourse, to use a formulation shared by Jacques Lacan and Alain Badiou. Hence this systematic attempt at voiding language of its meaning. Such an attempt is apparent elsewhere in *Stephen Hero*, such as in the following passage, which, in describing the experience, calls up an identical hollowing out of meaning:

> As he walked thus through the ways of the city he had his ears and eyes ever prompt to receive impressions. It was not only in Skeat that he found words for his treasure-house, he found them also at haphazard in the shops, on advertisements, in the mouths of the plodding public. He kept repeating them to himself till they lost all instantaneous meaning for him and became wonderful vocables. [...] In class, in the hushed library, in the company of other students he would suddenly hear a command to begone, to be alone, a voice agitating the very tympanum of his ear, a flame leaping into divine cerebral life. He would obey the command and wander up and down the streets alone, the fervour of his hope sustained by ejaculations until felt sure that it was useless to wander any more: and then he would return home with a deliberate, unflagging step piecing together meaningless words and phrases with deliberate unflagging seriousness."[26]

---

25 Joyce, *Stephen Hero*, 210–211.
26 Joyce, *Stephen Hero*, 30–31.

This passage is rarely linked to the account of the epiphany, yet it is obvious that both are describing the same process. This affords a rationale for the striking lack of content in the initial dialogue in Eccles Street. The words lose all content, and, once they have become almost meaningless, they can be reshuffled at will, reworked in patient combinations as required by the creative process. Moreover, the literary task is triggered by an order from outside; it is initiated by a commandment from the Other. The idea of obeying this voice from above may strike one as irrational and unhinged, yet the literary task would be impossible otherwise, since it aims at opening the whole world to artistic recreation. Thus Joyce first empties the Real of meaning; he then leaves the mark of the hole open for a while, until he manages to knot it with other holes. Epiphany 19 offers an illustration of this process:

(Dublin: in the house in Glengariff Parade: evening)

Mrs Joyce – (*crimson, trembling, appears at the parlour door*) . . . Jim!

Joyce – (*at the piano*) . . . Yes?

Mrs Joyce – Do you know anything about the body? . . . What ought I do? . . . There's some matter coming away from the hole in Georgie's stomach . . . . Did you ever hear of that happening?

Joyce – (*surprised*) . . . I don't know . . .

Mrs Joyce – Ought I send for the doctor, do you think?

Joyce – I don't know . . . . . . What hole?

Mrs Joyce – (*impatient*) . . . The hole we all have . . . . . . here (*points*)

Joyce – (*stands up*)[27]

The vignette found its way into *Stephen Hero* as the conclusion of chapter XXII, where it becomes more dramatic: the blank page that follows the last spoken word (" – The hole ... the hole we all have ... here") leaves the reader in intolerable suspense. The next chapter jumps ahead and the reader learns that Isobel (in the novel, she has replaced real-life George) has indeed died. The setting is also more theatrical. Stephen had been playing the piano, and he stops to hear something. Dusk is coming when death is announced to him. The characters are steeped in

---

27 Joyce, *Poems and Shorter Writings*, 179.

dramatic shadows: "A form which he knew for his mother's appeared far down in the room, standing in the doorway. In the gloom her excited face was crimson. A voice which he remembered as his mother's, a voice of terrified human being, called his name. The form at the piano answered."[28]

The fragment then refers to a nameless hole, perhaps the navel or anus. The text leaves the readers as startled as the protagonists. In naming the impossible site of death, the fragment allegorizes the presence of a void at the core of the epiphany. The epiphany allegorizes the function of letters, which, in Lacanian terms, function as the rim of the hole of *jouissance*. The foundational role of such a hole derives from the emergence of Truth in the Real. The truth can then be disseminated in the social fabric, as seen in Epiphany 22:

[Dublin: in the National Library]

Skefflington – I was sorry to hear of the death of your brother . . . . sorry we didn't know in time . . . . . to have been at the funeral . . . . .

Joyce – O, he was very young . . . . a boy . . . .

Skefflington – Still . . . . . it hurts . . . .[29]

From the outset, Joyce recognized that his epiphanies would become discrete parts of a greater whole – either a series of short texts, or integrated into a novel. He used many of the epiphanies as fragmentary sketches for scenes and conversations. From the opening scene of *A Portrait of the Artist as a Young Man* to Stephen's recurrent dreams of his mother in *Ulysses*, the epiphany plays a central role throughout Joyce's oeuvre. The form reinforces and anchors the rest of the text. I argue for the central porosity of the Joycean epiphany. In using "porous," I mean to convey the Greek meaning of *"poros,"* the way. In short, wherever there is a linguistic hole, there is a way, or, rather, there is a way of tying this hole to another hole.

Kafka's experience, though starting from a similar "triviality," that is, identical urban crossroads, leads instead to an *aporia*. The aporia, as with Plato's aporetic dialogues, requires a different passage, and often this dead-end can be overcome only by an ascent, a groping for a revelation. This is allegorized in Kafka's "Unmasking a Confidence Trickster" ("Entlarvung eines Bauernfängers"), one of the shorter texts that echo with Joyce's urban epiphanies. This short story, dating

---

28 Joyce, *Stephen Hero*, 162–163.
29 Joyce, *Stephen Hero*, 162–163.

from 1913, features a narrator who explains that he has come to a fine house because he has been invited for a party. On his way, he has been followed for two hours by a stranger who has thrust himself upon him. Finally, having decided to shake off this stranger, the narrator confronts him. The unwanted companion then makes a mistake: in trying to be seductive and pleasant, he stretches his arm along the wall, leans his cheek upon it, and, closing his eyes, smiles. This smile reveals to the narrator that the man is a confidence trickster (*Bauernfänger*). "Caught in the act!" the narrator exclaims. He is then able to climb the stairs, alone, and give his coat to a servant. What is revealing in this tale is the suggestion, at the moment of the unmasking, of shame ("shame suddenly caught hold of me") and the idea of doubling: the man of the city and the peasant are successive versions of the same person.[30] But where are they planning to visit?

Indeed, if we examine the text closely, the signs become even more opaque. The story was triggered by a visit that Kafka and Max Brod made to a Parisian brothel during their 1911 trip. During these excursions into the red-light district, the two friends had to fend off seedy barkers, aggressive touts, and conniving middlemen trying to lure customers into their establishments. The final sense of ease at the story's close contrasts with the embarrassment felt by Kafka, who once fled, in shame and disgust, from a Parisian brothel. Here, the confidence trickster appears more like Alfred Prufrock's confidant, a reminder of sordid street-corners seductions, someone ready to use his urban cunning to ensnare gullible "peasants" – in this case, clearly, non-Parisian visitors. Here we meet triviality with a vengeance. However, this is the rare Kafka text in which the narrator actually reaches his aim, that is, he moves on, unimpeded, to a company and enjoys a successful social life. The text ends thusly: "With a deep breath of relief and straightening myself to my full height, I then entered the drawing room." Yet, as we know from most of his other texts, above all *The Trial* [*Der Prozess*], in Kafka's world one cannot shake a confidence trickster so easily...

What matters, then, both for Joyce and Kafka, is to capture such evanescent signs when the flash of the Real is perceptible. Even though the truncated signs are displayed in corners so as send one on the path to writing, they appear on the spot of a missing corner; thus, they are literally blind spots, not unlike that darkened parallelogram in Euclid's "gnomon," itself the geometrical figure evoked at the beginning of the first story in Joyce's *Dubliners*.

Kafka's Zürau aphorisms outnumber Joyce's epiphanies, as only forty vignettes survived of the seventy-one numbered by Joyce. The epiphanies include

---

30 See Franz Kafka, "Unmasking a Confidence Trickster," trans. Willa and Edwin Muir, in *The Complete Stories*, ed. Nahum N. Glatzer, Schocken Books, New York 1971, 396–397.

dream transcriptions, fragments of dialogues, first drafts of objective narratives and lyrical, autobiographical confessions. Curiously, the term becomes derogatory in *Ulysses*: Stephen muses ironically on his juvenile fantasy of sending copies of his "epiphanies on green oval leaves" to "all the great libraries of the world, including Alexandria."[31] Did Joyce, by the late 1910s, no longer believe in his theory of the epiphany? Has the term been swallowed by the movement of mimesis seen as the work of writing itself?

In rewriting *Stephen Hero*, Joyce erased the Romantic echoes lurking in the first version of his theory. In *A Portrait of the Artist as a Young Man*, the same phraseology recurs, without being founded on the term "epiphany." The "manifestation" showing the divine nature of Jesus belongs to a discourse of disclosure and revelation, but in the negative sense rather than in the positive. In "The Dead," set on the night of the Epiphany, Gabriel Conroy has no "good news" to bring to anyone at the party. At the story's end, he comes to terms with his own blindness, selfishness, and emotional limitations. He discovers these limits in facing a wife who emerges as a more opaque "Other," and this leads to revision of all his values. This process of divesting himself of his last illusions parallels the process of the Joycean epiphany. Again, the epiphany is relayed by a narrative process, its deadly work accompanying the radiance of the Thing. While pointing to the radiance of pure manifestation, the "shine" of epiphanies does not conceal their blindness. This is why the term retains the suggestion of "betraying," which finds an equivalent in how most of Kafka's *Contemplation* seems obsessed with issues of lies, deception, and self-deception. By revealing something that had been concealed, the fragment condenses a process of *aletheia* – that is, it gives birth to truth as unconcealment. Joyce's epiphany is never far from a Freudian symptom, albeit with a political twist – in the context of an Ireland endlessly abused and betrayed. According to Joyce's brother Stanislaus, the "manifestations or revelations" in which the epiphanies consist undo the very process of ideological concealment while exhibiting ironically the type of repression at work: "these notes were in the beginning ironical observations of slips, and little errors and gestures – mere straws in the wind – by which people betrayed the very things they were most careful to conceal."[32] In Epiphany 12, Hanna Sheehy, asked who her favorite German poet is, replies sententiously, after a pause and a hush: "I think ... Goethe ..."[33] A Proustian irony is created by the multiplication of

---

31 James Joyce, *Ulysses*, ed. H. W. Gabler, Garland Press, New York 1986, 143.
32 Stanislaus Joyce, *My Brother's Keeper: James Joyce's Early Years*, Viking Press, New York 1958, 134–135.
33 Joyce, *Poems and Shorter Writings*, 172.

dots. The pretensions of provincial culture – here, a young woman taking herself too seriously – are exposed by a conflation of personal, social, and cultural symptoms.

A similar complexity is observable in Kafka's aphorisms, parables, and paradoxes. These short texts range from single sentences – such as "A cage went in search of a bird"[34] and "Never again psychology!"[35] – to longer paragraphs that condense a short tale. These aphorisms tend to be serious, enigmatic, at times even grotesque; often they evince a weird sense of humor. Most of these aphorisms are bound together by a deconstructive dialectic that Richard Gray labels "constructive destruction" and Stanley Corngold calls "chiastic recursion." In this structure, each new term, consisting of elements syntactically and conceptually parallel to those of a previous term, arises by means of an inversion of similar elements. Patterns of "chiastic recursion" construct parallel lines of inverted meaning and fold the text back upon itself.

Thanks to such an inbuilt logic of paradox, each aphorism contains its own undoing. For instance, the first aphorism – "The true way is along a tightrope, which is stretched aloft but just above the ground. It seems designed more to trip one than to be walked along."[36] – exemplifies the deconstructive energy of the Kafkan aphorism. Kafka sets forth the idea of a pure truth and then deconstructs it in three stages: the first stage describes the image of an ideal, lofty truth suspended in the air; the second inverts the image of a rope suspended above: the rope is now just on the ground; and in the third stage, the transformation of the tightrope to a tripwire juxtaposes the image of a true path with its inverted parallel, a tripwire. The ascendance of truth that the aphorism initially invokes is deconstructed through negation, inversion, and chiastic recursion.

Where does this trope come from? As Peter Sloterdijk has argued, the aphorism makes better sense if we understand it as Kafka's ironical response to Nietzsche's axiom, from *Thus Spake Zarathustra* [*Also Sprach Zarathustra*], that "man is a rope over the abyss." The latter axiom is from the Prologue, when Zarathustra gives his first discourses. He asserts: "Man is a rope, fastened between animal and Superman – a rope over an abyss [*Der Mensch ist ein Seil, geknüpft zwischen Tier und Uebermensch, – ein Seil über einem Abgrunde*]."[37] Even before Zarathustra had expressed this idea, the crowd had called him a "tight-rope

---

34 Kafka, *The Blue Octavo Notebooks*, 88.
35 Kafka, *The Blue Octavo Notebooks*, 42.
36 Kafka, "The Collected Aphorisms," 79.
37 Friedrich Nietzsche, *Thus Spake Zarathustra*, trans. R.J. Hollingdale, Penguin, London 1969, 43.

walker"[38] (*Seiltaenzer*) and an actual tightrope walker appears in section 6 of the Prologue. This tightrope walker walks between two towers in the village; however, when he is midway the devil appears on the rope and quickly overtakes the man, jumping over him and causing the tightrope walker to fall to his death. As the dying man sees Zarathustra kneeling next to him, he says that he knew the devil would trip him. Zarathustra refuses to pity him and mocks his belief in god and the devil.[39]

For Peter Sloterdijk, this marks a general shift from asceticism to acrobatics in European thought.[40] Nietzsche's dying tightrope walker prefigures the dying artist in Kafka's story "A Hunger Artist" ("Ein Hungerkünstler"). Kafka manages to condense a tension already present in Nietzsche. After all, Zarathustra could take the fallen acrobat as a disciple, even if a clumsy follower; instead, he berates the dying man, without sympathy. This gives a more ominous overtone to a sentence he had uttered previously: "What is great in man is that he is a bridge and not a goal; what can be loved in man is that he is a *going-across* and a *down-going* [*ein* Übergang *und ein* Untergang *ist*]."[41]

Thus we see that if the aphorisms stage a tension between the particular and the universal, this tension should generate "dialectical images" (to quote Walter Benjamin). Their implied dialogism (here, between Nietzsche and Kafka, between Zarathustra and the acrobat, between rise and fall, etc.) prevents them from deploying a single thesis. Thus the apodictic structure of statements that sound as necessarily true, their authoritative aspect disguise more malleable and proliferating meanings. Fittingly, the aphorism's resistance to a single definition parallels the form itself, in that the aphorism presents a set of cryptic, fragmented hermeneutical puzzles to be unwound. Yet this does not explain what makes a particular aphorism distinctly "Kafkan." These fragments can be read as compressed fictions presenting a subject who struggles to balance language and reality. They point to a discrepancy between linguistic capabilities and the shock of a real perceived as foreign, opaque, threatening. A Kafkan aphorism would be the shortest narrative form capable of capturing the sometimes quite aggressive interaction of Self and Other, while noting that the point of view is more often than not that of the Other.

---

38 Nietzsche, *Thus Spake Zarathustra*, 43.
39 Nietzsche, *Thus Spake Zarathustra*, 48.
40 Peter Sloterdijk, "Last Hunger Art: Kafka's Artistes" ("Letzte Hungerkunst: Kafkas Artistik"), in *You Must Change Your Life* [*Du mußt dein Leben ändern*], trans. Wieland Hoban, Polity, Cambridge 2013, 61–72, 64.
41 Nietzsche, *Thus Spake Zarathustra*, 44 (emphasis in original).

Although it is impossible to identify a common structure among the various epiphanic forms, some trends are worth noting. Richard Gray, countering Max Brod's thesis of a religious Kafka, suggests that Kafka's aphorisms move away from revelation. They pose complex hermeneutical puzzles and seem shrouded in a "willed obscurity," since truth remains a blinding truth. For example: "In a certain sense you deny the existence of this world. You explain life as a state of rest, a state of rest in motion."[42] This paradox leads us to the Way – yet there are several ways at once, and the fragment always battles with Freudian over-determination. One of the "ways" I would choose to negotiate the paradoxes of Kafka's "Reflections on Sin, Pain, Hope, and the True Way" ("Betrachtungen über Sünde, Leid, Hoffnung und den wahren Weg") would be by focusing on the paradigm of movement.

> Aphorism 14: "If you were walking across a plain, had every intention of advancing and still went backwards, then it would be a desperate matter; but since you are clambering up a steep slope, about as steep as you yourself are when seen from below, your backward movement can only be caused by the nature of the ground, and you need not despair."[43]

> Aphorism 15: "Like a path in autumn: scarcely has it been swept clear when it is once more covered with leaves."[44]

> Aphorism 21: "As firmly as the hand grips the stone. But it grips it firmly only to fling it away the further. But the way leads into those distances too."[45]

> Aphorism 26: (second half) "There is a goal, but now way; what we call a way is hesitation."[46]

> Aphorism 38: "There was one who was astonished how easily he moved along the road of eternity; the fact is that he was racing along it downhill."[47]

> Aphorism 76: "This feeling: 'Here I will not anchor,' and instantly to feel the billowing uplifting swell around one."[48]

---

42 Kafka, *The Blue Octavo Notebooks*, 47.
43 Kafka, "The Collected Aphorisms," 81.
44 Kafka, "The Collected Aphorisms," 81.
45 Kafka, "The Collected Aphorisms," 81.
46 Kafka, "The Collected Aphorisms," 83.
47 Kafka, "The Collected Aphorisms," 85.
48 Kafka, "The Collected Aphorisms," 91.

This movement is indeed "moving" yet outside any psychology. Aphorism 93 famously states: "Never again psychology!"[49] Why then should we dismiss all psychology? The answer, as Maurice Blanchot well understood in his own fragments and short novels, is that psychology moves one too easily and generates an excess of fictional comprehension or empathy. As Kafka explains, "Nausea after too much psychology. If someone has good legs and is admitted to psychology, he can, in a short time and in any zigzag he likes, cover distances such as he cannot cover in any other field. One's eyes overbrim at the sight."[50] Is this nausea or ecstasy? No matter what causes it, the moving excess brought about by psychology must be reduced by a writing of the outside. Truth will be opposed to the field of psychological masks and disguises, fictions, and lies about oneself and others. The result is a certain stillness, as delineated in Aphorism 109: "It is not necessary that you leave the house. Remain at your table and listen. Do not even listen, only wait. Do not even wait, be wholly still and alone. The world will present itself to you for its unmasking, it can do no other, in ecstasy it will writhe at your feet."[51]

Of course, the trajectory returns us to the writing desk... For Kafka, writing must go deep enough; the subjectless subject can remain still, and he may end up cutting his body and writing on it, as in the famous parable of "In the Penal Colony" ("In der Strafkolonie"). Meanwhile, the world will also have unmasked itself, an unmasking that would offer the promise of an absolute *jouissance*. Stanley Corngold has rightly mentioned a Gnostic streak in Kafka. One might be tempted to add, as Lacan, does in Seminar XX, a mystical *jouissance* of the Real as pure Otherness. It is the lack of narrative placement that makes the aphorisms difficult to decipher. The technique evokes the abysmal aura of a Truth that will be withheld. If the aphorisms aim at truth, truth is always blinded by an excess of aura – as if the epiphany had become a little sun, its light a blinding glare. All that remains is an afterimage of the blinding process, a flicker of lost revelation.

Kafka's main novels are marked by the absence of expected revelation. In *The Castle* [*Das Schloss*] and *The Trial* he constructs intricate labyrinths of relationships and possibilities in tracing the respective protagonists' futile and seemingly endless journeys. *The Castle* concludes mid-sentence, lost amidst a tangle of narrative possibilities. *The Trial* ends with Josef K.'s humiliating death. This death can be read as an anti-revelation, for it removes any possibility of illumination or final understanding. It serves to obfuscate the plot further. Against this tendency, Kafka's aphorisms correspond to a desire to reach the truth quickly

49 Kafka, "The Collected Aphorisms," 95.
50 Kafka, *The Blue Octavo Notebooks*, 79.
51 Kafka, "The Collected Aphorisms," 98.

and immediately; in other words, they echo what Hermann Broch has called the "impatience of knowledge." Yet, even when the aphorisms manifest this impatience, they also debunk it, as in Aphorism 3: "There are two cardinal human sins from which all others derive: impatience and indolence. Because of impatience they were expelled from Paradise, because of indolence they do not return. But perhaps there is only one cardinal sin: impatience. Because of impatience they were expelled, because of impatience they do not return."[52]

Driven by "impatience," Kafka's aphorisms explore the metaphorical division between the material world and a higher state of being even as they challenge this barrier in its impossibility. It does not matter that the ground is limited to where the subject can stand, as per Aphorism 24: "What it means to grasp the good fortune that the ground on which you stand cannot be greater than what is covered by your two feet."[53] A tension between the local and the eternal, the trivial and the universal, provides the dynamism to the verbal engine. Kafka's negative dialectics imply contrapuntal relationships in the flow from universal to trivial. The effect is one of deconstruction or demystification rather than revelation, yet the concept of Truth is not destroyed. On the contrary, Truth plays a role similar to that I have analyzed in Joyce's epiphanies: namely, that of a decentering tool, a hole in discourse. Kafka goes further, since this Truth risks devouring all others and thereby destroying both the world and the subject.

We have seen that the porosity of Joyce's epiphanies led to a practice of writing that was buttressed by the letter. For Joyce the letter provides a key because it contains and rims a hole. In a similar manner, the logical impossibilities in Kafka's aphorisms evoke a principle of verticality. Any hope that a vision of the vertical truth will bypass the obscure labyrinths of *The Trial* and *The Castle* is frustrated. The aphoristic style achieves a shortcut, yet, when it literally puts an end to the narrative, it undercuts itself. Kafka generates perpetual movement by using a very small textual surface. Thus, what moves him is the possibility of jumping from an ethics of language to a perception of the Law as such. This means not that singularity is abolished but rather that the writer tends to see himself from the outside. The writing becomes once more the writing of the Real, at least insofar as the divided subject is told to side with the world and not with subjectivity. Three aphorisms are relevant here, namely, Aphorism 52: "In the struggle between yourself and the world, second the world"[54]; Aphorism 53:

---

52 Kafka, "The Collected Aphorisms," 79.
53 Kafka, "The Collected Aphorisms," 82.
54 Kafka, "The Collected Aphorisms," 87.

"One must not cheat anyone, not even the world of its triumph"[55]; and the aphorism "He": "He has discovered the Archimedean principle, but he has turned it to account against himself; evidently it was only on this condition that he was permitted to discover it."[56]

We can distinguish three modernist attitudes facing what I have called the "Style of the Real." First, there is Proust's position: a writer must come to terms with the signs written in him by reality and time – involuntary memory tells him that Time can be abolished. The operation of involuntary memory supposes that, in the end, all particular places, names, or sensations can be brought together by the text. Time will be abolished once two sensations are superimposed. One could read this as a certain Platonism.

Kafka would not allow such a way out. He is haunted by an ethics in which God, the, Real, or an Unconscious to which we have no access, wholly dominate. With Proust, the writer can, in the end, learn to trust this Unconscious and find reassurance in the thought that the work of art continues being written, as it will in each of us. Thus, each of us should not only enjoy but also make use of this process of writing. What Proust calls a "metaphor" depends upon a utopia in which time is abolished in exchange for the promise of a work of art to come. Moreover, Proust's promise of writerly bliss is granted without any personal God being present or relevant; Kafka, however, needs the framework of messianic promise, or, as a second-best theory, Kierkegaard's or Pascal's overcoming of the ethical by the religious. The Jewish Messiah embodies the principle of the "to come" – it will come, as we know, not on the last day but on day after the last day, or, as Kafka puts it, "The Messiah will come only when he is no longer necessary; he will come only on the day after his arrival; he will come, not on the last day, but on the very last day."[57]

Joyce contents himself with the promise of a law of seriality: he believes in the text to come. There will always be other privileged moments to jot down; the task may be infinite but it remains possible. Yet, there is another version of the Unconscious at work here, the aptly named "agenbite of inwit" that Stephen feels gnawing at his soul. That one can trust history does not liberate it from the taint of original sin; and thus *Finnegans Wake* becomes a universal history of the original sin. Finally, whereas Joyce seems to always gain (loss is his gain, as Beckett would argue), Kafka prefers to always lose: gain is his loss. In this sense, he paves

---

55 Kafka, "The Collected Aphorisms," 87.
56 Kafka, "The Collected Aphorisms," 105.
57 Franz Kafka, "The Coming of the Messiah," in *The Basic Kafka*, ed. Erich Heller, Washington Square Press, New York 1979, 182.

the way for Beckett's poetics of impotence and deprivation. Yet, these three positions still imply a hermeneutic circle, one that must be run through over and over again. This mechanism is best illustrated by Kafka's famous text "On Parables" ("Von den Gleichnissen"), which, in the version proposed by Willa and Edwin Muir, perhaps with help from Clement Greenberg, ends thusly:

> Concerning this a man once said: Why such reluctance? If you only followed the parables you yourselves would become parables and with that rid of all your daily cares.
> Another said: I bet that is also a parable.
> The first said: You have won.
> The second said: But unfortunately only in parable.
> The first said: No, in reality: in parable you have lost.[58]

The first speaker addresses the utopia of pure aestheticism: if one agrees that the only life worth living is that of literature, as Proust suggests, then, indeed, one should be able to live happily ever after, for life will always be inferior to fiction. Yet, if the parables' true meaning simply yields a tautology, such as the idea "that the inconceivable is inconceivable," then this fictional world would seem too remote, too far from the need to battle every day with life's intractable concerns and dramas. Thus the second speaker is right to tell the first that he has not progressed toward the truth and has merely added a level of fiction to the problem. The first speaker is obliged to concede that he has been beaten. Yet when the second speaker believes that he has won, the first qualifies the victory: he has won in reality and lost in parable, that is, he may have won a space for reality as distinct from fiction, but in doing so has relegated the world of fiction to an "other" world, one marked by lies and alienation. He will be safer in his everyday life but will have lost the possibility of consolation in the name of literature – hence his life, deprived of the imagination, will be all the poorer. Commenting on this exchange, Stanley Corngold wittily remarked that one can always add to the last comment: "I bet that is also a parable."[59] The movement of what Sartre would call a "whirligig" (*tourniquet*) in his book on Jean Genet or of what Barthes had called "bathmology" (the "science of degrees") is virtually unstoppable. We can only quote from Kafka's final diary entry: "Every word, twisted in the hands of the spirits – this twist of the hand is their characteristic gesture – becomes a spear turned against the speaker. Most especially a remark

---

58 Franz Kafka, "On Parables," trans. Willa and Edwin Muir, in *Parables and Paradoxes*, ed. Nahum N. Glatzer, Schocken Books, New York 1961, 11.
59 Stanley Corngold, "Kafka's Later Stories and Aphorisms," in *The Cambridge Companion to Kafka*, ed. Julian Preece, Cambridge University Press, Cambridge 2002, 95–110, 105.

236 — Jean-Michel Rabaté

like this. And so ad infinitum."[60] Or Aphorism 29: "The beast wrests the whip from the master and whips itself in order to become master, not knowing that this is only a fantasy produced by a new knot in the master's whip-lash."[61] A similarly constitutive division is at work in Joyce and Kafka alike. It can be summed by a portmanteau word that Joyce coins in *Finnegans Wake*, where an "individual" is called an "individuone."[62] Division and wholeness are combined when the body turns into writing, as is the case of Shem the Penman. Shem unfolds all history as a universal but dividual chaosmos: "his own individual personal life unlivable, transaccidentated through the slow fires of consciousness into a dividual chaos, perilous, potent, common to allflesh, human only, mortal."[63] What, then, in this universalizing context, of Kafka's own epiphanies? I thought I had found one, in a recent translation of his *Abandoned Fragments*: "The first epiphany I've had since the move to"[64] Alas, no sooner had I checked the original than I had to admit that this was a translator's invention; the German text is simply *"Die einzige Erkenntnis, die ich der Uebersiedlung in"*[65] – "The only insight [realization] I had since the move to" (my translation). Well: did Kafka have his epiphany in the end? Probably not, at least not insofar as his *Uebersiedlung* remained infinite or indefinite. We will have to re-read once more these fragments, maxims, and aphorisms, and then, perhaps, we will decide.

Works Cited

Corngold, Stanley, "Kafka's Later Stories and Aphorisms," in *The Cambridge Companion to Kafka*. Ed. Julian Preece (Cambridge: Cambridge University Press, 2002), 95–110.
Gray, Richard T., *Constructive Destruction: Kafka's Aphorisms: Literary Tradition and Literary Transformation* (Tübingen: Niemeyer 1987).
Greenberg, Clement, "The Jewishness of Franz Kafka: Some Sources of His Particular Vision," in *The Collected Essays, Volume 3: Affirmations and Refusals, 1950–1956*. Ed. John O'Brian (Chicago: University of Chicago Press, 1993), 202–209.
Grothe, Mardy, *Wit and Wisdom from History's Greatest Wordsmiths* (New York: Harper, 2004).
Joyce, James, *Finnegans Wake* (Oxford: Oxford University Press, 2012).

---

60 Quoted by Corngold, "Kafka's Later Stories and Aphorisms," 106.
61 Kafka, "The Collected Aphorisms," 83.
62 James Joyce, *Finnegans Wake*, Oxford University Press, Oxford 2012, 51.
63 Joyce, *Finnegans Wake*, 186.
64 Franz Kafka, *Abandoned Fragments: The Unedited Works of Franz Kafka 1897–1917*, trans. Ina Pfitzner, Sun Vision Press, 2012, 177.
65 Franz Kafka, *Nachgelassene Schriften und Fragmente I*, ed. Malcom Pasley, Fischer, Frankfurt/M. 1993, 331.

Joyce, James, *Poems and Shorter Writings* (London: Faber, 1991).

Joyce, James, *Stephen Hero* (London: Jonathan Cape, 1956).

Joyce, James, *Ulysses*. Ed. H. W. Gabler (New York: Garland Press, 1986).

Joyce, Stanislaus, *My Brother's Keeper: James Joyce's Early Years* (New York: Viking Press, 1958).

Kafka, Franz, *Abandoned Fragments: The Unedited Works of Franz Kafka 1897–1917*. Trans. Ina Pfitzner (Sun Vision Press, 2012).

Kafka, Franz, *The Basic Kafka*. Ed. Erich Heller (New York: Washington Square Press, 1979).

Kafka, Franz, *The Blue Octavo Notebooks*. Ed. Max Brod. Trans. Ernst Kaiser and Eithne Wilkins (Cambridge: Exact Change, 1991).

Kafka, Franz, "The Collected Aphorisms," in *The Great Wall of China and Other Short Works*. Ed. and trans. Malcolm Pasley (London: Penguin, 1991), 79–98.

Kafka, Franz, *The Complete Stories*. Ed. Nahum N. Glatzer (New York: Schocken Books, 1971).

Kafka, Franz, *Nachgelassene Schriften und Fragmente I*. Ed. Malcom Pasley (Frankfurt/M.: Fischer, 1993).

Kafka, Franz, *Nachgelassene Schriften und Fragmente II*. Ed. Jost Schillemeit (Frankfurt/M.: Fischer, 1992).

Kafka, Franz, *Parables and Paradoxes*. Ed. Nahum N. Glatzer (New York: Schocken Books), 1961.

Nietzsche, Friedrich, *Thus Spake Zarathustra*. Trans. R.J. Hollingdale (London: Penguin, 1969).

Sloterdijk, Peter, "Last Hunger Art: Kafka's Artistes," in *You Must Change Your Life*. Trans. Wieland Hoban (Cambridge: Polity, 2013), 61–72.

Tufte, Virginia, *Artful Sentences, Syntax as Style* (Cheshire: Graphics Press, 2006).

Lorraine Markotic

Modernism's Particulars, Oscillating Universals, and Josefine's Singular Singing

1 The Universal in Modernity: Lost and Found

> And it really was kind of the moon to shine on me, too, and out of modesty I was about to place myself under the arch of the tower bridge when it occurred to me that the moon, of course, shone on everything.
> – Franz Kafka, "Description of a Struggle"[1]

Without a doubt, Kafka's works have a universal feel about them. The very short stories include rewritings of ancient Greek myths; others are set in distant lands (distant from a German-speaking, European audience, at least) or in past times. References to concrete places are few: Laurenziberg, the hill in Prague, Riva in Italy, and the United States (although this is an imaginary country, where the Statue of Liberty carries a sword and Oklahoma is spelt "Oklahama"[2]). Neither are Kafka's narratives temporally located; they never begin, for example, "In 1903" or "At the end of the previous century" or even "Many centuries ago." In several stories, characters go unnamed and are referred to otherwise, such as by physical characteristics ("a small woman"), role ("doorkeeper," "father of the family"), or profession ("village schoolmaster," "starvation artist," "trapeze artist"). In *The Trial* [*Der Process*] and *The Castle* [*Das Schloss*], each protagonist is designated only by the initial "K." Animals speak in some stories, which gives them the quality of fables.

In certain ways, then, Kafka's texts seem to eschew particulars, despite the detailed and meticulous quality of the writing. Adorno, following Benjamin, considers Kafka's works to have the attribute of parables.[3] But as Adorno also percep-

---

1 Franz Kafka, "Description of a Struggle" ("Beschreibung eines Kampfes"), trans. Tania and James Stern, in *The Complete Stories*, ed. Nahum N. Glatzer, Schocken Books, New York 1976, 9–51, 19.
2 As noted in *A Franz Kafka Encyclopedia*, following Max Brod and Alfred Wirkner, Kafka was likely influenced by Arthur Holitscher's critical book *Amerika heute und morgen: Reiseerlebnisse* [*America Today and Tomorrow: Travel Experiences*] (1912), which contains such a spelling. See *A Franz Kafka Encyclopedia*, ed. Richard T. Gray, Greenwood Press, Westport 2005, 128.
3 Theodor W. Adorno, "Notes on Kafka," in *Prisms*, trans. Samuel and Shierry Weber, The MIT Press, Cambridge 1997, 243–271.

tively notes in his *Aesthetic Theory*: "Artworks have no power over whether they endure; it is least of all guaranteed when the putatively time-bound is eliminated in favor of the timeless." Kafka's abjuring of the time-bound is not, therefore, what affords his works their enduring power; neither, I would argue, is it what gives them their universal quality. Adorno continues: "It was out of Cervantes' ephemeral intention to parody the medieval romances that *Don Quixote* originated."[4] Analogously, I would postulate, it was out of Kafka's (often parodic) rejoinder to modernity and modernism, and precisely to its concern with universals and particulars, that *his* enduring works originated.

Kafka's texts respond to prevalent aspects of modernity: increased urbanization, isolation, and enlarged state bureaucracies. Both the novels and short stories are concerned with hierarchical institutions and with oppressive relations within institutions, including the family. Of course, Austro-Hungarian society had always been hierarchical, and the bourgeoisie family patriarchal, but, in early-twentieth-century Europe, entrenched authoritarian structures and apparently natural spheres of control were fundamentally questioned. What had previously been regarded as universal forms of knowledge, social structures, and power relations came under scrutiny. The ways in which these apparently universal – yet actually quite contingent and particular – structures and relations nevertheless permeate our being and our bodies is something Kafka spiritedly attests to and explores. Many of his texts portray what Bourdieu will come to depict as the "habitus," the system of non-conscious social dispositions we inculcate, including at the bodily level. Others demonstrate what Foucault will refer to as "capillary" power,[5] the decentralized, defining, and intricate power that invisibly extends its tentacles into the thinking, discourses, and minutest practises of our lives.

In "The Metamorphosis" ("Die Verwandlung"), even after awaking to find himself transformed into an insect, Gregor's main concern is to go to work. An elderly father's condemnatory words in "The Judgment" ("Das Urteil") impel his son to commit suicide. The story "In the Penal Colony" ("In der Strafkolonie") literalizes the idea that language is inscribed upon the body (subsequently psychoanalytically elaborated by Lacan) through an apparatus invented precisely for the purpose. The very short story "Fellowship" ("Gemeinschaft") recounts five friends who live together simply because they had exited a house in succes-

---

4 Theodor W. Adorno, *Aesthetic Theory* [*Ästhetische Theorie*], ed. and trans. Robert Hullot-Kentor, Bloomsbury Academic, London 2013, 38.
5 Michel Foucault, "Prison Talk," in *Power/Knowledge: Selected Interviews and Other Writings, 1972–1977*, ed. Colin Gordon, Harvester Press, Brighton, 1980, 37–54, 39.

sion and stood before it, and people noticed them having done so. Based on this simple, arbitrary event, they become a community and are displeased that a sixth person wishes to join them and intrude on their fellowship – even though this fellowship has no intrinsic basis.

Many of Kafka's works delineate forces of convoluted and labyrinthine origins and directions. In "The Refusal" ("Die Abweisung"), the narrator tells of a town so far from the frontier that to reach it one must cross desolate highlands and wide fertile plains. It is unlikely anyone from the town has ever been to the frontier, for "to imagine even part of the road makes one tired, and more than one part one just cannot imagine."[6] Even further than the frontier is the capital, but the town humbly submits to it. The town's highest official is from the capital. He consistently refuses petitions; these assured refusals are something the town seems to need, however, though they allegedly are not a formality. The narrator explains: "Time after time one goes there [to the official from the capital] full of expectation and in all seriousness and then one returns, if not exactly strengthened or happy, nevertheless not disappointed or tired"[7] – despite one's petition having been refused. Like many of Kafka's texts, "The Refusal" depicts the tangled formations and the remote and obscure origins of power – power that shapes bizarre practices and even more bizarre understandings.

Kafka's figures and narrators generally seem less like individuals than like illustrations and embodiments of forces with which all humans must contend, and which, insofar as we contend with them, become constitutive. Kafka's characters hardly exhibit the defiant and critical hyper-consciousness of Dostoyevsky's singular underground man. They are more likely to manifest the clichéd (and prejudicial) thinking of Schnitzler's Lieutenant Gustl, of the eponymous novella that appeared at the opening of the twentieth century. *Lieutenant Gustl* was the first German-language literary work to present a character's "stream of consciousness."[8] Schnitzler's restriction of his text to inner monologue nonetheless paints an expansive social scenery, each brushstroke adding detail to a recognizable landscape: the Austrian world of the "k. und k." ("kaiserlich und königlich," or "imperial and royal"), the defining ethos of the Austrian-Hungarian empire.

---

6 Franz Kafka, "The Refusal," trans. Tania and James Stern, in *The Complete Stories* ed. Nahum N. Glatzer, Schocken Books, New York 1976, 263–267, 263.
7 Kafka, "The Refusal," 267.
8 Approximately two decades later, the interior consciousness of individuals became key to the works of high modernism: Joyce's *Ulysses*, Woolf's *Mrs. Dalloway*, Proust's *Remembrance of Things Past*, and (later on) Faulkner's *The Sound and the Fury*. Individual subjectivities were portrayed as containing and revealing something universal – including the loss of universal truths or universally accepted social understandings.

Gustl's particular, innermost thoughts disclose a broader, more universal (albeit hollow and crumbling) social world. Literary modernism seemed to respond to the erosion of traditional beliefs systems, the loss of putative social cohesion, and experiences of individual isolation by focussing on the perspective of one or more characters.

The idea that the universal can be gleaned through the particular is something Kafka mocks in his brief story "The Top" ("Der Kreisel"), in which a philosopher believes that he can grasp the universal by grasping the particular: "For he believed that the understanding of any detail, that of a spinning top, for instance, was sufficient for the understanding of all things."[9] Part of the story's humour, of course, is that when the philosopher grasps the top, it stops spinning, that is, it ceases to function as a top and becomes a "silly piece of wood."[10] More generally, the tale questions whether one can ever grasp a particular, or whether by "grasping" it one simultaneously isolates it and hence loses it.

Literary modernism tries not to isolate the individuals upon whom it focuses but rather to keep them moving, and in this way simultaneously to illustrate the social vista that emerges in and through such individuals. In response to a modern world that seems increasingly fragmented and fragmentary, a point of view that presents a particular perspective is considered a more illuminating and ultimately more truthful form of representation. Pirandello illustrates this in *Six Characters in Search of an Author*. The play's clichéd characters are more universal, because they are eternal and unchanging, whereas the actors, who are individual and sometimes inconsistent, are more true. Literary modernism suggests that particular perspectives and individual subjectivities provide both an apt sense of experience in modernity and a propitious way to access the modern world. In general terms, literary modernism can be said to approach or investigate the universal through the particular.

Kafka's works, I would argue, go further. They not only seek to access the broader, more universal social world through individual thinking and experiences; they also depict the ubiquitous nature of social and institutional power, its reach and its vagaries. Moreover, Kafka's works suggest that we can never know how far and how deeply power and convention permeate us, or the ways and the extent to which they constitute and affect us. In "Unhappiness" ("Unglücklichsein"), a child-ghost blows into the protagonist's room and converses with him. Soon, however, the protagonist has had enough of the fractious ghost and leaves the room. He then encounters a neighbor who does not believe in ghosts. The

---

9 Franz Kafka, "The Top," trans. Tania and James Stern, in *The Complete Stories*, 444.
10 Kafka, "The Top," 444.

protagonist says that he does not believe in ghosts either, but that he cannot see how his not believing will help him. The neighbor explains that if one does not believe in ghosts then one need not "be afraid any more if a ghost really turns up."[11] The protagonist responds that such a fear is only a secondary fear: "The real fear is fear of the cause of the apparition. And that fear sticks."[12] Kafka's humorous, imaginative, and expressively rich story concludes with the protagonist becoming suddenly panicked that the neighbor will steal his ghost. The ghost could represent the protagonist's loneliness or fear of loneliness – a fear that could be experienced by anyone. For if the ghost can be stolen by the neighbor, the protagonist's "fear of the cause of the apparition" may not be a particular fear, but one potentially shared by others. To the contrary, the ghost could represent the protagonist's intimate personal anxieties (including sexual ones); thus, his becoming incensed at the possibility that his ghost might be taken from him could be understood (psychoanalytically) insofar as some neurotics cling to their neuroses. What is important, in my view, is that the conclusion remains ambiguous: universal fears may have induced the presence of the conversing apparition; or, the protagonist may have highly particular, idiosyncratic fears that lead to his being visited by a talking ghost.

Kafka's works go further than modernist works that approach the universal through the particular, further than works that focus on the particular to disclose the disintegration of the universal, and even further than works that contrast the two. Many of Kafka's texts question whether and to what extent one can even distinguish universal from particular. This is an explicit theme in the story "Conversation with a Supplicant" ("Gespräch mit dem Beter"), which also appears as part of "Description of a Struggle" ("Beschreibung eines Kampfes"). At one point in the story, the supplicant relates to the narrator his overhearing a conversation between his mother and another woman:

> "When as a child I opened my eyes after a brief afternoon nap, still not quite sure I was alive, I heard my mother on the balcony asking in a natural tone of voice: 'What are you doing my dear? Isn't it hot?' From the garden a woman answered: 'Me, I'm having my tea on the lawn.' They spoke casually and not very distinctly, as though this woman had expected the question and my mother the answer."[13]

---

11 Franz Kafka, "Unhappiness," in *The Metamorphosis and Other Stories*, trans. Joyce Crick, Oxford University Press, Oxford 2009, 15–18, 18.
12 Kafka, "Unhappiness," 18.
13 Franz Kafka, "Description of a Struggle," trans. Tania and James Stern, in *The Complete Stories*, 9–51, 34.

This particular yet completely ordinary conversation baffles the supplicant.[14] At this point, fairly late in the story, the supplicant's response may not seem especially surprising, for he has already indicated that he experiences many ordinary things as insubstantial. But the narrator, too, seems to consider the conversation "a most remarkable incident," stating that he cannot "make head or tale of it"[15] yet also noting that he does not believe the incident is true. By the end of the story, however, the narrator seems to have grown weary of the garrulous supplicant, and seeks to disengage himself from their conversation by retracting his earlier comments. He tells the supplicant that he does not, in fact, find the story of the conversation so remarkable, that he has heard many such stories and has even participated in some, and that it was "quite an ordinary occurrence."[16] The supplicant appears unconvinced by the retraction, however, referring to the narrator's earlier statement as a "confession." Kafka's "Conversation with a Supplicant" implies that what seems universal and ordinary may actually be particular and peculiar – or at least that one should not easily presume to differentiate them. Kafka's works go beyond the quest to illuminate the universal (including its disintegration) through the particular, suggesting that they may, in fact, be indistinguishable.

2 Hegel, Kafka, Derrida

> And so long as you say "one" instead of "I," there's nothing in it and one can easily tell the story.
> – Kafka, "Wedding Preparations in the Country"[17]

> I put on my gloves, sighed for no good reason, as one is inclined to do at night beside a river.
> – Kafka, "Description of a Struggle"[18]

---

14 Vivian Liska analyzes the importance of this passage, including its staggering significance for Ilse Aichinger and probable influence on Aichinger's story "Doubt about Balconies." See Vivian Liska, *When Kafka Says We: Uncommon Communities in German-Jewish Literature*, Indiana University Press, Bloomington and Indianapolis 2009, 193–199.
15 Kafka, "Description of a Struggle," 34.
16 Kafka, "Description of a Struggle," 36.
17 Franz Kafka, "Wedding Preparations in the Country" ("Hochzeitsvorbereitungen auf dem Lande"), trans. Ernst Kaiser and Eithne Wilkins, in *The Complete Stories*, 52–76, 53.
18 Kafka, "Description of a Struggle," 14.

Do you think you're the only one who can shut doors? [spoken by the ghost]
– Kafka, "Unhappiness"[19]

The longer one hesitates before the door, the more estranged one becomes.
– Kafka, "Home-Coming"[20]

Hegel's *Phenomenology of Spirit* explores the conceptual and historical oscillation between the universal and the particular. The opposition of subject and object, of universal and particular, is introduced into the broader socio-historical context in the chapter on "Spirit." Unsurprisingly, Hegel opens his discussion of societal Spirit by turning to ancient Greece. Somewhat surprisingly, Hegel draws not upon the many and influential ancient Greek philosophical works, but upon a work of literature: Sophocles's *Antigone*. Therein Hegel sees a concern not unfamiliar to modernism: the fragmentation of an apparently harmonious whole – although in this case, the schism involves only two parts: state and family, or man and woman, or human and divine. In the tragedy, Antigone comes into conflict with Creon, king of Thebes, by burying her brother Polynices. This brother had been a traitor to the polis, and consequently Creon decreed that his body not be buried; Antigone buries him nevertheless and is condemned by Creon.

For Hegel, what is significant in the tragedy is that Antigone and Creon each believe her- or himself to be acting ethically and, more important, to be acting on the basis of a higher, universal law. Antigone states that, as a woman, her duty is to the family and hence to her brother; in short, according to immemorial custom, it is the duty of women to perform funeral rites and bury the dead. Creon believes it his duty as ruler to punish anyone who betrays the polis, even if this entails proscribing burial rites; also, he believes it is his further duty to condemn anyone who disobeys his prohibition. On the face of it, Antigone represents something smaller and more particular (the family, the sphere of individual, biological relationships and attachments), whereas Creon represents something larger and more universal (the state, the realm of wider social commitment and political action). But the family, by performing religious rites for the dead, insists upon both the value of the deceased to the community and the meaning of the deceased's existence and memory. In this way, the family ethically enacts a law – namely, divine law – that is higher than the law of the state. The family is particular in relation to the more universal law of the state; divine law, however, is ultimately higher and more uni-

---

19 Kafka, "Unhappiness," 16.
20 Franz Kafka, "Home-Coming" ("Heimkehr"), trans. Tania and James Stern, in *The Complete Stories*, 445–446, 446.

versal than state law. Moreover, there are many states, as Hegel notes; Thebes is only one, which renders Creon's decree a particularity. To summarize: Antigone represents the particularity of the family and familial relations, but she also represents the universality of divine law; Creon represents the more universal state law, which is nevertheless the law of only a single state and therefore particular. In Hegel's reading of *Antigone*, universal and particular can be said to oscillate.

The possibility that what seems universal may actually be particular and vice versa is wittily presented in Kafka's short work "Poseidon." Kafka depicts Poseidon, God of the Sea, as a discontented administrator who spends his days in his palace at the bottom of the ocean, sitting at his desk and reviewing accounts. What most annoys Poseidon is the wholly inaccurate image people have of him supposedly "dashing over the waves with his trident."[21] In fact, Poseidon has barely seen the oceans; he is counting on a quiet moment just before the end of the world to "make a quick little tour."[22] Kafka amusingly portrays Poseidon as a universal administrator chained to his desk; whenever Poseidon is able to take leave and go somewhere, he visits his brother Jupiter (usually returning in a rage). On the one hand, Kafka's Poseidon seems little different from a high-level bureaucrat of today who has never travelled to the places where his international institution does business, or from a colonial administrator of Kafka's time who has never seen the territories he controls. Poseidon also differs little from a sibling who continues to frequent a more powerful, more respected sibling even though the visits are enraging. Thus, Poseidon loses his singularity as God of the Sea and becomes the universal bureaucrat and family member. On the other hand, however, Kafka's Poseidon also becomes more particular, more like an actual individual, insofar as he is overwhelmed with paperwork, occasionally visits his family (where there are constant tensions), and intends to travel at some future, unspecified date. The universal image of Poseidon riding the waves, trident in hand – the classical image familiar from sculpture, painting, and literature – is shown to be general and idealized. In the end, Kafka's Poseidon, the busy administrator, is both more universal and more particular than the Greek God of the Sea.

Kafka's "A Starvation Artist" ("Ein Hungerkünstler") and "Eleven Sons" ("Elf Söhne") can also each be interpreted in terms of ambiguity and oscillation between universal and particular. "A Starvation Artist" is a story of self-deprivation, which is itself a universal phenomenon found in countless cultures and

---

21 Franz Kafka, "Poseidon," in *Kafka's Selected Stories: New Translations, Backgrounds and Contexts, Criticism*, ed. and trans. Stanley Corngold, Norton Critical Edition, Norton, New York and London 2007, 131.
22 Kafka, "Poseidon," 131.

throughout various historical periods; yet the starvation artist seems singular in his ability to fast for lethal lengths of time. He is so dedicated to his art that he objects when his manager forces him, after forty days, to cease fasting. At the story's conclusion, when the starvation artist has finally managed to fast for well over forty days, he reveals the real reason he ceased eating: it was simply because "I could not find the food I liked."[23] The artist seems to be confessing that he is far less talented than he had suggested, that he is hardly the artist he had seemed, and that his unique fasting ability does not render him so singular. He is simply like everyone else who eats the food they like. But surely almost any food would taste good to someone starving; thus, the starvation artist's inability to find a food he liked is truly singular. Preferring to eat what one likes is universal; not being able, even when starving, to settle for any other food is quite singular.

Similarly, Kafka's "Eleven Sons" depicts either a completely universal tendency or a very particular, singular disposition. In this story, a parent, apparently the father, describes his sons, one by one. Even when this father begins by lauding a particular son, he ends up finding fault with him. Each son is rendered as a particular, an individual (the descriptions are not repetitive), but each is ultimately portrayed as flawed. This tendency to find fault in others, regardless of their positive qualities, may be universal, and the tendency of fathers to be critical of their sons may be fairly common. The story's title, however, evokes the biblical Jacob and his remaining eleven sons after his favourite, Joseph, has (as his other sons allege) been killed by a wild animal. Jacob may be inclined to find fault with his surviving sons, because he (consciously or unconsciously) faults them for not having protected Joseph, or possibly because he (consciously or unconsciously) wonders if something about their story is amiss. "Eleven Sons" could be illustrating a universal phenomenon or evoking an exceedingly particular event.

This returns us to *Antigone*. As noted, both Antigone and Creon believe they are acting on the basis of higher universal laws. Each believes that her or his own personal inclination plays no role in decisions and subsequent actions. Yet Creon's punishment of Antigone is excessively harsh. Although rulers are supposed to condemn traitors and to expect that their decrees will be obeyed, Creon's behaviour is despotic. And although Antigone claims to be acting only based on her familial obligation and duty as a woman, her sister, Ismene, acts differently (initially, at least), a juxtaposition that makes Antigone's behaviour seem peremptory. Creon's disproportionate retribution and Antigone's intractable self-will each disclose particularities. They both claim to be acting according to higher, universal laws; nonetheless, each is more singular than either would admit.

---

23 Franz Kafka, "A Starvation Artist," in *Kafka's Selected Stories* 86–94, 94.

A Kafkan figure who similarly does not want to contend with his singularity in the face of universal laws is the "man from the country" in the parable "Before the Law" ("Vor dem Gesetz"). Therein, a man from the country comes seeking admittance to the law. The door to the law stands open, but the doorkeeper refuses to grant the man permission to enter, although he concedes that permission may be granted at some future time. The doorkeeper further informs the man that if he passes through the open door, he will encounter another doorkeeper, and then another, each more powerful than the last. The man from the country spends years waiting; he pleads with the doorkeeper and even tries to bribe him, to no avail. Near the end of the parable, as the man is dying, he seems to see a radiance streaming from the doorway. He forms a final question for the doorkeeper, inquiring how it is that, although everyone strives for the law, in all these years no one except him has ever asked for admittance. The doorkeeper responds that no one else could gain admittance, since this door was intended only for him (the man from the country), and that he (the doorkeeper) will now go and shut it.

Derrida interprets Kafka's parable as suggesting that although the law may be universal, everyone encounters it in her or his own particular way. Derrida succinctly states that the law is "always an idiom."[24] Because the man from the country is a particular individual, he has his own particular entrance into the law (although the law in itself is not something he can ever reach, as Derrida makes clear). In other words, when the singular collides with the universal, it does so only in a particular way.

In "Before the Law," as in *Antigone*, universal and particular can be said to fluctuate. The man from the country is patently singular, having his own door to the law and indeed his own doorkeeper. At the same time, this man is universal. He is all of us. We have all been "from the country" insofar as we have felt "inurbane" in the face of intimidating laws into which we sought entrance. Moreover, we have all, at some time (as children or as "from the country," for example) felt that we did not understand the law, could not grasp it – as if the law could be grasped. But the law, like the philosopher's top, is not something that can be grasped. It must be interpreted. Derrida states: "Perhaps man is the man from the country as long as he cannot read" or assumes that the law is to be read rather than "deciphered."[25] Derrida later notes that "the 'man' is both Man and anybody, the anonymous subject of the law"[26]: that is, insofar as the man chooses to wait

---

24 Jacques Derrida, "Before the Law," trans. Avital Ronell and Christine Roulston, in *Acts of Literature*, ed. Derek Attridge, Routledge, New York 1992, 181–220, 210.
25 Derrida, "Before the Law," 197.
26 Derrida, "Before the Law," 202.

before the law, before the open door as if it was not his own particular entrance, he is this anonymous subject, anybody, a universal. At the same time, however, the door is for him only, a particular individual.

The doorkeeper may hardly seem particular. We do not know where he is from (is he also a man from the country, or is he from this or some other city?), and he is one doorkeeper among many. But when the doorkeeper mentions the other doorkeepers, comparing himself to them, he makes clear that each door-keeper is distinct. Moreover, we learn details of the doorkeeper's appearance and of his clothing – the man from the country, however, is never described. We even learn that doorkeeper has fleas in his fur collar. During the long years of waiting, the man from the country focuses more and more on this particular doorkeeper, until he "forgets the other doorkeepers."[27] Any representative of the law is bound to become more and more singular, the more time one spends with such a representative. Kafka's story is, I would argue, as much about the doorkeeper as about the man, and Derrida is correct to refer to "two protagonists."[28] Indeed, the parable begins solely with the doorkeeper: "Before the law stands a door-keeper"[29]; it ends with the doorkeeper stating that he will go and shut the door. While the man from the country waited to enter the universal law, the doorkeeper attended to the particular man. Like the man from the country, the doorkeeper is both universal and particular.

Derrida's essay "Before the Law" ("Devant la loi"), about Kafka's parable "Before the Law," addresses (among many things) the question of the singularity of literature. According to Derrida, literature, insofar as it is literature, can be demarcated and defined (named) but also inherently challenges demarcations and definitions. Literature is not identical with itself. Literature, Derrida argues, unlike "a text of philosophy, science, or history, a text of knowledge or information,"[30] is willing to abandon a name to a state of "not knowing" – as in Kafka's "Before the Law," where one knows "neither *who* nor *what* is the law."[31] Yet what is most important, I would argue, what is unique to literature, what literature is most significantly willing *not* to know, is whether and to what extent it is about a universal or a particular. In literature, as Kafka's text demonstrates, universal and particular cannot even be deciphered – only construed.

---

27 Franz Kafka, "Before the Law," in *Kafka's Selected Stories*, 68–69, 68.
28 Derrida, "Before the Law," 200.
29 Derrida, "Before the Law," 200.
30 Derrida, "Before the Law," 207.
31 Derrida, "Before the Law," 207.

Philosophy trades in universals. In Hegel (or Plato), philosophy attends to particulars, but they are eventually dialectically sublated into universals. Unlike the law, which, as Derrida notes, is not supposed to have a history or require a narrative, philosophy sometimes expresses itself in dialogues or stories – as in Plato or Existentialism or even Hegel's *Bildungsroman* of the unfolding of Spirit. But philosophical narratives are expected to convey something universal, or something about the universal, or even the universal importance of the particular. Philosophy is not supposed to muddle the distinction. This is what literature sometimes does and, I would argue, this is what Kafka frequently undertakes. The last story Kafka wrote, "Josefine, the Singer or the Mouse People" ("Josefine, die Sängerin oder Das Volk der Mäuse"), can be interpreted as studiously muddling the distinctions between universal and particular.

3 The Singularity of Josefine's Universal Singing

Even the unusual must have its limits.
– Kafka, "Blumfeld, an Elderly Bachelor"[32]

In "Josefine, the Singer or the Mouse People," Josefine squeaks or whistles in a way characteristic of the mouse people. She produces sounds universally made; and yet her squeaking or "singing" is captivating. The narrator (who seems to be male) begins his account by relating that anyone who has not heard Josefine "does not know the power of song" and that "there is no one who is not carried away by her singing."[33] This occurs despite the fact that the mouse people are not drawn to music; indeed, they favour "peace and quiet"[34] – they prefer calm silence. And as Kafka notes in "The Silence of the Sirens" ("Das Schweigen der Sirenen"), silence can be a more terrible weapon than song. Since the mouse people are unmusical, it would seem that Josefine's singing is so beautiful that it is difficult to resist, that what rings from her throat has never before been heard, is something only Josefine, "this one individual [...] and no one else,"[35] enables people to hear. This would be the most obvious explanation, states the narrator; but he repudiates it. Were this explanation indeed true, then in the face of Josefine's music one would have the feeling of encountering something extraordi-

---

32 Franz Kafka, "Blumfeld, an Elderly Bachelor" ("Blumfeld, ein älterer Junggeselle"), trans. Tania and James Stern, in *The Complete Stories*, 183–205, 189.
33 Franz Kafka, "Josefine, the Singer or the Mouse People," in *Kafka's Selected Stories*, 94–108.
34 Kafka, "Josefine, the Singer or the Mouse People," 94.
35 Kafka, "Josefine, the Singer or the Mouse People," 95.

nary, yet Josefine's singing is, he alleges, quite ordinary. Indeed, her singing may not even be singing but rather mere squeaking – the squeaking in which almost everyone engages as they go about their daily work. The narrator denies that the sounds Josefine emits are exceptional; consequently, he seeks to account for the effects of her singing, for the crowds it draws, and for its singular achievement – despite its universal quality.

He raises the possibility that Josefine's talent lies in her performance, for she is above all a performer. In order to understand her art, perhaps one must not only hear her but also see her.[36] One may remain critical at a distance, he states, but as soon as one is immediately close to her, one is forced to acknowledge that what Josefine does "really is not just squeaking."[37] But the narrator cannot point to anything singular about Josefine's performances. She does not actually do anything outstanding. What is striking is simply *that* she performs. She stands up and squeaks or sings, inducing her audience to be amazed by what they should not necessarily find amazing – since they all make the same sort of sounds themselves.

Neither does Josefine's personal charisma seem to hold the key. The narrator often depicts her in quite unflattering terms. And although he should not be trusted, of course, and although Josefine has devoted followers, their devotion to her has clear limits. When she demands exemption from other duties, to compensate for the demands of her art, no one supports her. No matter what tact she takes, her demand for release from work is flatly refused. Clearly, Josefine's influence is limited.

Finally, the narrator adduces that Josefine brings people together and lets them dream, temporarily free themselves "from the bonds of daily life."[38] Her concerts permit people to suspend their worries and collect themselves before facing the unending struggles of their lives. The narrator explains that regardless of what one thinks of Josefine's "nothing of a voice," of her "nothing of an achievement,"[39] her singing seeps through the silence and envelops her audience. Through Josefine, the mouse people experience a feeling of community. Her singing is a distraction that encourages them to relax and forget themselves, and to do so together. What the narrator seems to be suggesting is that Josefine is an empty signifier, a placeholder – one that fulfills a crucial function. The power of

---

36 Kafka, "Josefine, the Singer or the Mouse People," 96.
37 Kafka, "Josefine, the Singer or the Mouse People," 96.
38 Kafka, "Josefine, the Singer or the Mouse People," 103.
39 Kafka, "Josefine, the Singer or the Mouse People," 100.

Josefine's singing would seem to lie in its singular effects, which have nothing to do with her actual, universal squeaking.

But if Josefine is only a placeholder, then someone or something would take her place when she disappears. This is a point I would like to stress. In "A Starvation Artist," the public's interest in starvation artists declines, and the artist is eventually replaced by a panther. Josefine, however, is not replaced. She simply disappears and, according to the narrator, will soon be forgotten. If Josefine's squeaking or singing is compelling solely because of the role it fills, however, then someone or something else would subsequently fill this role. If her singing were completely ordinary, significant only because of its effect, then surely something else would emerge to produce the same or a similar effect. This does not occur, however, which suggests that there *is*, indeed, something singular in Josefine's singing.

As noted, Josefine fights to be excused from work, owing to her singing and the effort it requires, but this concession is consistently denied her. As a last resort, she disappears and goes into hiding. The narrator explains that such a strategy cannot work, for the people, "despite appearances to the contrary, can only bestow gifts and never receive them, not even from Josefine."[40] This remark is exceedingly important. It implies that Josefine may have a gift to offer, even if nobody is willing to receive it. And while the German word "Geschenk" does not have the twofold meaning of the English word "gift," which can mean both "present" and "talent," the German word for talent, "Gabe," contains the idea of something being given. Thus, while the narrator denies that there is anything extraordinary in Josefine's singing, he simultaneously suggests that she does indeed have a gift, a particular talent, to give.

Before I further develop this idea of Josefine's gift, I would like briefly to turn to Derrida's discussion of the gift at the beginning of *Given Time: I. Counterfeit Money* [*Donner le temps 1. La fausse monnaie*]. Derrida begins this book by insisting upon the "impossibility" of the gift. He argues that a gift, in order to remain a gift, must avoid economic exchange. The very concept of the gift, he insists, must "defy reciprocity or symmetry."[41] The gift must not circulate, must not be exchanged, must remain "aneconomic." This becomes apparent, Derrida points out, if the receiver immediately reciprocates with something similar; in such a case, there can hardly be said to have been a gift.

---

40 Kafka, "Josefine, the Singer or the Mouse People," 107.
41 Jacques Derrida, *Given Time: I. Counterfeit Money*, trans. Peggy Kamuf, University of Chicago Press, Chicago and London 1992.

It is also difficult to think of there having been a gift if the receiver feels that he or she has thereby contracted a debt, if the receiver consequently feels somehow obligated to the giver. Hence, one could say that it is necessary that the receiver "not *recognize* the gift as gift."[42] When the receiver recognizes the gift, acknowledges it as a gift, he or she "gives back, in the place, let us say, of the thing itself, a symbolic equivalent."[43] In other words, Derrida argues, merely by recognizing the gift as a gift, as being freely given, one gives back to the giver a kind of symbolic currency, which, in a sense, annuls the gift. Moreover, it is not only the receiver but also the giver who must not recognize the gift. Derrida notes that a giver who merely intends to give a gift begins "to pay himself with a symbolic recognition, to praise himself, to approve of himself, to gratify himself, to congratulate himself, to give back to himself symbolically the value of what he thinks he has given or what he is preparing to give."[44] Even an anonymous gift, therefore, would not escape the economic relationship insofar as the giver would feel affirmed through the act of giving. This is the "impossibility or the double bind of the gift."[45] Both receiver and giver must forget the gift in an absolute, instantaneous forgetting.[46]

The concluding words of "Josefine, the Singer" relate that Josefine will soon be forgotten. Josefine's singing, if it is indeed singing and not mere squeaking, if it is indeed a talent, if it is indeed a gift to the people, will not be absolutely and instantaneously forgotten – as is required of Derrida's gift – rather, it will only *soon* be forgotten. But Kafka's story, I would argue, nevertheless, suggests a conception of the gift far more radical than that contained in Derrida's aneconomic, impossible gift. For even if Derrida's givers and receivers must experience a sort of absolute, instantaneous amnesia, Derrida retains a distinction between giver and receiver. Such a distinction is unsettled in "Josefine, the Singer." Indeed, Kafka's story suggests that perhaps the gift truly retains its status as gift only when one cannot be certain who is giving and who is receiving.

The narrator opens his account by stating that Josefine has a love for music, a love she alone knows how to convey – convey to a people who are fundamentally unmusical. Without Josefine, explains the narrator, music will vanish. This suggests both that Josefine is singular in her ability to communicate her love of music, and that she is not actually able to communicate it, since what she com-

---

42 Derrida, *Given Time*, 13.
43 Derrida, *Given Time*, 13.
44 Derrida, *Given Time*, 14.
45 Derrida, *Given Time*, 16.
46 Derrida insists that this forgetting is more extreme than the psychoanalytic notion of repression, for displacing an event into the unconscious is, of course, a way of preserving the event.

municates will not last. The gift she has to give, even if it is only her love for music and not her actual singing, is something that she will take with her when she leaves. It is not clear that Josefine has given the people a gift. It may in fact be the case that it is the people, in allowing Josefine's love of music to infect them (though not permanently) who have given a gift to Josefine. This is what the narrator maintains. He also relates that the people assume a protective attitude towards Josefine; they care for her "the way a father looks after a child who stretches out her little hand."[47] This image clearly suggests that it is Josefine who seeks something from the people. She is their ward, the one who needs their protection, although of course nobody "dares to speak of such things to Josefine"; and yet she believes that she is the one doing the protecting, and even presumes that her singing goes so far as to rescue the people "from grim political or economic situations" and that "if it does not banish misfortune" it at least gives the people "the strength to endure it."[48] Whenever the people receive bad news, Josefine "rises up and cranes her neck and strives to oversee her flock like the shepherd before the storm."[49] The narrator, unsurprisingly, denies that Josefine is anything like a shepherd with a flock; he rejects the idea that she saves the people or even gives them strength. Josefine believes that she protects and fortifies the people; the narrator avers that it is the people who protect and humour her. Who is protector and who is protectee is uncertain. Who is giving and who is receiving remains unresolved.

Even the fact that Josefine is denied any exemption from work could be regarded either as evidence of the ordinariness, the universality, of her squeaking, or as evidence of the extraordinariness, the singularity, of her singing. The narrator claims that the dismissal of Josefine's demand plainly demonstrates that the people realize she is not doing anything special. For the people are fully aware that Josefine would not cease to work if her demand to be excused from it were granted; Josefine is no shirker. What Josefine "strives for is simply the public acknowledgement of her art, an acknowledgement that is unambiguous, that will last for all time, rising far above everything known to this day."[50] That such acknowledgement is steadfastly and universally refused is regarded by the narrator as definitive proof that Josefine's singing is not singular. But if Josefine's concerts are really quite ordinary, and if, as the narrator alleges, she has become known as a singer merely because of supporters who elevate her and her squeak-

---

47 Kafka, "Josefine, the Singer or the Mouse People," 99.
48 Kafka, "Josefine, the Singer or the Mouse People," 99.
49 Kafka, "Josefine, the Singer or the Mouse People," 99.
50 Kafka, "Josefine, the Singer or the Mouse People," 104.

ing above everyone else, then these supporters would likely seek corroboration for their support for Josefine and would back her demand for exemption precisely as a "public acknowledgement." Hence, the fact that the people as a whole categorically refuse Josefine any exemptions could be taken as evidence that her status and fame is the result not of brazen, uncritical fans but of some actual talent. In other words, the blanket refusal to grant Josefine any exemption can be interpreted either as evidence for her having gift or as evidence against it.

At one point, the narrator argues that the very fact that people listen to Josefine should be understood to demonstrate that she is not really worth listening to. It is often the case, he explains, that when the people assemble and Josefine squeaks or sings, the audience is actually preoccupied with more serious matters – matters so serious, he says, that if ever a "true virtuoso of song" were present at such a moment he or she would not be tolerated and the people would "unanimously reject the absurdity of such a performance."[51] In other words, the narrator is asserting that "the very listening to [Josefine] is an argument against her song."[52] Gradually however, his remorseless and inexorable insistence that Josefine does nothing beyond the ordinary leads one to wonder whether the gentleman doth protest too much. At the story's conclusion, the reader still does not know whether Josefine is taking or receiving. It is impossible to untangle her singular singing from universal squeaking.

Secondary sources have generally considered Josefine to be representative of various forms of artists and the story to be concerned with the role of artists.[53] Yet it should be remembered that squeaking is the universal language of the mouse people, to such an extent that not only do many squeak their entire lives without noticing, but that squeaking is "a typical manifestation of life."[54] Thus, this squeaking could represent the speaking of humans, and Josefine someone who gives speeches. Humans speak as they go about their lives, but few imagine that if they were to stand and speak that others would bother to listen. Doubtlessly, Kafka's story can be interpreted as portraying artists who may or may not be underappreciated in their society; yet it can also be interpreted in light of human speechmaking. Clearly, Josefine is not a professional politician, not least as she is never exempted from other work because of her singing/squeaking. The narrator relates that people have lost their lives at Josefine's gatherings, and that

---

51 Kafka, "Josefine, the Singer or the Mouse People," 100.
52 Kafka, "Josefine, the Singer or the Mouse People," 101.
53 For a fascinating discussion of the story in relation to the social, cultural and ideological importance of music, see Nicola Gess's "The Politics of Listening," *Kafka's Selected Stories*, 275–288.
54 Kafka, "Josefine, the Singer or the Mouse People," 95.

her squeaking may even be what attracts the enemy. Perhaps she is an agitator. Given the pervasiveness of agitators during Kafka's lifetime, it is interesting that the story does not clarify whether Josefine is giving something to her audience or receiving something from it.

But Josefine does not have to represent a firebrand. She may simply be someone who gives "talks" and whose talking, in the narrator's view, differs little from what everyone else does. She may also be a writer who gives readings. The narrator begins his account by stating that it seems to him that Josefine "barely exceeds the bounds of ordinary squeaking."[55] In his view, she is someone who has nothing new to say, nothing out of the ordinary to convey. Perhaps Josefine utters platitudes or clichés. Of course, we should not necessary trust the narrator. Indeed, Josefine may be expressing a new form of thinking or a new form of writing, such as literary modernism, that the narrator considers ordinary and unremarkable.

Philosophy frequently goes astray insofar as it generalizes from socio-historical particulars as if they were universals, naively presuming that these (sociological) truths are universal, philosophical ones. Literary works, in contrast, frequently depict eccentric, idiosyncratic, or unusual particulars; even the most bizarre characters or situations can be seen to disclose a universal – including its disintegration or illusory status. Where Kafka's works go further is in their insistence that we cannot necessarily disengage universal and particular, cannot know how, or how much, universal forces constitute us and the particulars of our world. Kafka's works insist that we cannot establish the universals for which philosophy strives and which literature must construe; neither can we isolate its constitutive and constituent particulars. In this way, above all, Kafka's writings are philosophical; in this way they evince their universal quality.

Works Cited

Adorno, Theodor W., *Aesthetic Theory*. Trans. with introduction by Robert Hullot-Kentor (London: Bloomsbury Academic, 2013).

Adorno, Theodor W, "Notes on Kafka," in *Prisms*. Trans. Samuel and Shierry Weber (Cambridge: The MIT Press, 1997), 243–271.

Bourdieu, Pierre, *Distinction: A Social Critique of the Judgement of Taste*. Trans. Richard Nice (Cambridge: Harvard University Press, 1984).

---

55 Kafka, "Josefine, the Singer or the Mouse People," 95.

Bourdieu, Pierre, *Outline of a Theory of Practice*. Trans. Richard Nice (Cambridge: Cambridge University Press, 1977).

Derrida, Jacques, "Before the Law," trans. Avital Ronell and Christine Roulston, in *Acts of Literature*. Ed. Derek Attridge (New York: Routledge, 1992), 181–220.

Derrida, Jacques, *Given Time: I. Counterfeit Money*. Trans. Peggy Kamuf (Chicago and London: University of Chicago Press, 1992).

Dostoyevsky, F., *Notes from the Underground* and *The Double*. Trans. Jessie Coulson (London: Penguin, 1982).

Foucault, Michel, "Prison Talk," in *Power/Knowledge: Selected Interviews and Other Writings, 1972–1977*. Ed. Colin Gordon (New York: Pantheon, 1980).

Gess, Nicola, "The Politics of Listening: The Power of Song in Kafka's 'Josefine, the Singer,'" in *Kafka's Selected Stories: New Translations, Backgrounds and Contexts, Criticism*. Trans. and ed. Stanley Corngold (New York and London: Norton, 2007), 275–288.

Gray, Richard T., Ruth V. Gross, Rolf J. Goebel, and Clayton Koelb, *A Franz Kafka Encyclopedia* (Westport: Greenwood Press, 2005).

Hegel, G.W. F., *Spirit: Chapter Six of Hegel's* Phenomenology of Spirit. Ed. with introduction, notes, and commentary by Daniel E. Shannon. Trans. The Hegel Translation Group (Indianapolis: Hackett, 2001).

Kafka, Franz, *Kafka: The Complete Stories*. Ed. Nahum N. Glatzer (New York: Schocken, 1976).

Kafka, Franz, *Kafka's Selected Stories: New Translations, Backgrounds and Contexts, Criticism*. Trans. and ed. Stanley Corngold. Norton Critical Edition (New York and London: Norton, 2007).

Kafka, Franz, *The Metamorphosis*. Trans. and ed. Stanley Corngold. Norton Critical Edition (New York and London: Norton, 1996).

Kafka, Franz, *The Metamorphosis and Other Stories*. Trans. Joyce Crick (Oxford: Oxford University Press, 2009).

Lacan, Jacques, Écrits: A *Selection*. Trans. Bruce Fink (New York: Norton, 2002).

Liska, Vivian, *When Kafka Says We: Uncommon Communities in German-Jewish Literature* (Bloomington and Indianapolis: Indiana University Press, 2009).

Pirandello, Luigi. *Six Characters in Search of an Author and Other Plays* (London: Penguin, 1996).

Schnitzler, Arthur, *Lieutenant Gustl*. Trans. Richard L. Simon (Los Angeles: Sun & Moon Press, 2000).

Galili Shahar
The Alarm Clock: The Times of Gregor Samsa

1 The Alarms of Time, the Universal

Franz Kafka's story "The Metamorphosis" ("Die Verwandlung") is measured in time. We hear the alarm clock ticking on the chest in Gregor Samsa's room, the clock that measures the times of the story – mechanical time, the time of the family, the time of labor, the time of studies, the musical time, the time of the Messiah. All these definitions of time – its transformations and derivatives, even timeness itself, perhaps, die *Zeitlichkeit*, the being of time, its ecstasies, the awakening of time itself – are written, imprinted, upon Gregor Samsa's body.

It is both the fear of time and the anxieties of not-being-in-time into which Gregor Samsa awakes one morning out of "uneasy dreams." "One morning" he found himself transformed in his bed into an insect.[1] On the same morning, this "one morning," in this time, which is "any time," universal time, the time which repeats itself, the time-structure of repetition, the time of the alarm clock, Samsa awakes. And yet it is morning time, an early hour, the beginning of the day – beginning itself, one could argue – an opening, an hour of creation (a terrible creation) from which he is reborn, thrown into the world in a new, horrifying body – the body of a creature.

This is the *Zeitraum*, the time-space of Gregor Samsa; it is the "empty, homogeneous" realm of time, the time of everyday life, being marked by the clock. The clock is a device, an apparatus of universal time. The universal, that which belongs to all, is being represented (*gezeigt*) in the abstraction, in the repetition, in the sameness of the hour – the time segment of the clock. The representation and the conception (the holding-together) of the universal thus depends on the technical conditions of time, the homogeneity of its segments, their sameness and global validity, being repeated everywhere. Thinking on/of the universal, we argue, should be thus associated with the technical measurement of time, with the "general" work of clock, but also with its alarms – with its calls and raptures.

In this realm of universal time, "one morning," Samsa is reborn: he reappears as a wound – the wound of time. For his reappearance, his transformation into an insect, is the *Ereignis*, that is, an event, a singular moment of revelation,

---

1 Franz Kafka, "The Metamorphosis," trans. Willa and Edwin Muir, in *The Complete Stories*, ed. Nahum N. Glatzer, Schocken Books, New York 1983, 89–139, 89.

an appearance before our eyes. More should be said about the grammar of this event, the awaking before our eyes of something unusual, foreign, singular in the midst of universal time (the time of the alarm clock). The empty space of time, the everyday, signified in this "one morning," is also the moment in which an event transpires.

2 The Work, the Apparatus

Yet the distortions and irregularities of this body – Gregor Samsa, a human, a creature – call for discussion in terms of his/its spaces – the space of family and the minor space of the bourgeois. Here is Samsa's room: four walls, a closed door, the enclosure of his being. One should discuss the boundaries and the margins of this home, the place where Samsa lives, is wounded, and dies. One should explore Samsa's places, the spaces of climbing and of crawling, the thresholds of his realm of being, the paths of withdrawal and the paths of escape.[2] For Samsa dies at-home (*heimlich*) in its deep, uncanny (*un-heimlich*) meaning.

This discussion, however, is about time, and the time of this story is measured by the ticking alarm clock in Samsa's room. The clock signifies mechanical time – the time of the machine that directs and governs the human being and marks his schedule, the "timetable" – the time of work. The clock is one of these machines – the apparatuses, instruments, devices, and tools that Kafka studied during his years as a clerk at the Workmen's Accident Insurance Institute in Prague. In the office and during his official travels to visit factories, workshops, and mines, Kafka learned the secret of the machine, the dialectic of production and destruction, the legal and social complexities of the insurance laws, and how all these influenced the damaged being of the worker. Kafka, in other words, stood before the gates of the law. As a scholar and inspector he explored the intricacies of legal writing and the labyrinths of the law. He met cripples and wounded workers, victims of work accidents, and refugees of the Great War. Without Kafka's experience in these areas of labor and the law, and without his experience in interpreting the writings of the law, one cannot imagine the complexity of his literary creation. Kafka's official writings about machines, accidents, safety measures, and inspection methods for factories should be read as additional prologue to his literature. His fictional work is imprinted with strong

---

2 Gilles Deleuze and Félix Guattari, *Kafka: Toward a Minor Literature* [*Kafka: Pour une littérature mineure*], trans. Dana Polan, University of Minnesota Press, Minneapolis 1986, 16–17.

awareness of the destructive power of machines[3]; likewise, it offers various reflections on the distortions that the human condition suffers in the technical age – the story "In the Penal Colony" ("In der Strafkolonie") being perhaps the best example. Kafka's literature documents the damage caused in a world governed by technological visions and applications. "This remarkable piece of apparatus" of the Penal Colony,[4] like the train, the writing machine, and the telegraph, creates strange and destructive movements, environments of alienation, and meaningless zones of life and death.

In his early story "The Metamorphosis," however, Kafka contends with a minor apparatus, a small mechanical device – a cogwheel, a coil, and a bell – the alarm clock that measures, denotes, and announces the hour.

3 The Creature, the Language (Under the Clock's Sign)

The clock of Kafka's story is a modern device. Various clocks had been produced and used in antiquity, and as early as the fourteenth century time was being measured by mechanical devices. But in the nineteenth century, the century of industry, the century of the train and the steam engine, clocks assumed control over the time of being.[5] Clocks measured the times of work and travel. The time cycles of nature, the seasons, and the phases of the sun retreated and withdrew forever before the new governor. The clock came to govern all realms of being: the town squares, the factories, the train stations, the city halls, the livings rooms, the studios, and the bedrooms. The clock delineates a new measure, a new rhythm, homogeneous and monotonic for the order of all things. It defines a new standard

---

3 Wolf Kittler, "Schreibmaschinen, Sprechmaschinen. Effekte technischer Medien im Werk Franz Kafkas" ("Writing Maching, Speaking Machines. Effects of Technical Media in the Works of Franz Kafka"), in *Franz Kafka: Schriftverkehr* [*Franz Kafka: Correspondence*], eds. Wolf Kittler and Gerhard Neumann, Rombach Verlag, Freiburg 1990, 75–163.
4 Franz Kafka, "In the Penal Colony," trans. Willa and Edwin Muir, in *The Complete Stories*, 140–167, 140.
5 Ulla Merle, "Tempo! Tempo! Die Industrialisierung der Zeit im 19. Jahrhundert" [Tempo! Tempo! The Industrialization of Time in the 19th Century"), in *Uhrzeiten: die Geschichte der Uhr und ihres Gebrauches* [*The Hours of the Day: The History of the Clock and Its Use*], eds. Igor A. Jenzen and Reinhard Glasemann, Historisches Museum Frankfurt, Frankfurt/M. 1989, 161–217.

regulated movement, one of creation and production, and enables a new collective, universal consciousness of existence.[6]

The clock of the nineteenth century was the main carrier of production and travel, trade, and consumption. The hour itself became more economic than it had been previously: clocks measured shorter and more precise segments of time. Time itself, now measured in minutes and seconds, was delineated more finely and accurately than ever. One need not accept the thesis of capitalistic time structure ("time is money")[7] in order to agree that since the nineteenth century clocks have signified the economics of being. Life is now measured, planned, designed, and produced by the universal time of the clock. Like the train, the steam engine, and the telegraph, clocks reconstruct time and space into new dimensions. Being itself turns into a monotonic rhythm.

This drama – the drama of *techne*, the drama of mechanical time, and the rise of new dimensions of being-in-time, a new order of things measured by the clock – is imprinted in the world of Gregor Samsa. He lies in his bed, awoken from uneasy dreams, struggling with the weight of his new body and feeling a pain he had never previously experienced. He feels sad, and the view of raindrops beating on the window "makes him quite melancholy."[8] Samsa complains now about his *Beruf* – his occupation, his call (more should be said about this German word) of being *ein Reisender*, a commercial traveler, an agent who suffers the trials and tribulations of constant travel, including worrying about train connections, eating bad meals, and entering into casual contact with other travelers who never become intimate friends. Samsa is a subject of these time machines that measure and define his being. For the train itself belongs to this world, the world of mechanical time. These are the great clocks hanging above the entrance halls of railway stations as if they were portraits of the new sovereign. In the age of the train, movement itself is faster yet also more precise and detailed. The universal time of the clock is well differentiated: the day is segregated, set apart into hours and minutes. Time itself, however, is never different. What is being measured is the same. The clock signifies the sameness of all things.

This time-space, the universal, mechanical time of travel and labor, is where Gregor Samsa is living. The alarm clock ticking in his bedroom thus hints at

---

6 Gerhard Dohrn-van Rossum, *History of the Hour: Clocks and Modern Temporal Orders* [*Die Geschichte der Stunde. Uhren und moderne Zeitordnungen*], trans. Thomas Dunlap, The University of Chicago Press, Chicago and London 1996, 1–16.

7 Noam Yuran, *What Money Wants: An Economy of Desire*, Stanford University Press, Stanford 2014.

8 Kafka, "The Metamorphosis," 89.

the time schedule of industry and trade, and represents the rational, abstract, global dimension of time. The rhythm of these empty hours is imprinted upon his body – the body of an agent, a traveler, a worker, an employee, who every morning, this "one morning" too, is awoken and thrown into a world of rapid movements, mechanical gestures, and superficial human contacts. This is the world of the train. Like the clock that divides time into equal metered segments, the train breaks and tears the space, the landscapes, into spatial fragments. Like the alarm clock that jolts the world and hurls people from their homes – hurry! hurry! – into the streets and to their offices, to endless movements, so too does the train impose rapid movement on its subjects, the travelers.

Kafka notes the effects of the movement of the train on our observation of the world, the way things appear to us (*das Ereignis*, or "the event"). He writes in his diary:

> Goethe's observations on his travels different from today's because made from a mail-coach, and with the slow changes of the region, develop more simply and can be followed much more easily even by one who does not know those parts of the country. A calm, so-to-speak pastoral form of thinking sets in. Since the country offers itself unscathed in its indigenous character to the passengers in a wagon, and since highways too divide the country much more naturally than the railway lines to which they perhaps stand in the same relationship as do rivers to canals, so too the observer need do no violence to the landscape and he can see systematically without great effort.[9]

In the train era (the technical era) the landscape, the country, and space itself are viewed differently than in Goethe's time, when the mail coach was the main mode of travel. The new movement no longer enables a "pastoral form of thinking"; rather, the world is pictured and written as a violent mode of experience, *ein Erlebnis*, or even, one could argue, a shock. The famous traumatic neurosis, as we know, is partly related to train travel around the turn of the twentieth century. Should one attribute Gregor Samsa's distortions to these travels?

But we are still in Samsa's room, and he is still lying in bed. He has to wake up, for his train is leaving at five o'clock in the morning, and – listen! – the alarm clock is ticking:

> He looked at the alarm clock ticking on the chest. Heavenly father! He thought. It was half-past six o'clock and the hands were quietly moving on, it was even past the half-hour, it was getting on toward a quarter to seven. Had the alarm clock not gone off? From the bed one

---

9 Franz Kafka, diary entry of 29 September 1911, trans. Joseph Kresh, in *Diaries 1910–1923* [*Tagebucher 1910–1923*], ed. Max Brod, Schocken Books, New York 1976, 56.

could see that it had been properly set for four o'clock; of course it must have gone off. Yes, but was it possible to sleep quietly through that ear-splitting noise?[10]

The invention of the mechanical alarm clock has various claimants, some reaching to the seventeenth century. More famous, however, is the one attributed to Levi Hutchins, a watchmaker who lived in the eighteenth century in the town of Concorde, New Hampshire. It is said that his clock was set to ring at one defined hour – four o'clock in the morning.[11] And in Kafka's story? From his bed Gregor Samsa looks at the clock ticking, sees that the alarm was indeed set for four o'clock, and thinks to himself that the clock must have gone off properly. The alarm clock on Samsa's chest indicates the time of Hutchins's clock – the time of invention. However, Samsa did not awaken, although the clock must have gone off at four o'clock, and its noise is supposed to be ear-splitting. Yet Samsa is still in bed and it is already half-past six – indeed, it is moving toward a quarter to seven! Gregor Samsa is late for work, his train having left nearly two hours ago.

The delay, the clock failures, and Gregor Samsa's time inabilities should also be understood in ironic terms as a gesture of resistance. Samsa refuses to wake up, yet he employs the most childish means to stay in bed for another hour and a half.

But "the alarm clock had just struck quarter to seven," and with this "*Schlag*," or hit, at that moment, at that hour, a cautious tap is heard on the door behind the head of his bed: "Gregor, es ist dreiviertel sieben [Gregor, it's quarter to seven]."[12] It is the gentle voice of his mother calling Gregor from behind the door. Gregor cannot answer, however, except in his new voice, a horrible twittering – the voice of a poor animal. This is the vocal drama taking place in Samsa's room, the mechanical sound of the alarm clock, the ticking of its hands, the noise of the bell. Against this we hear the gentle voice of his mother from behind the door, and, in-between, the voice of Gregor himself, a creaturely voice – the tweeting, the cheeping. In the realm of the time-machine, in its shadows, the human

---

10 Kafka, "The Metamorphosis," 90.
11 There is no reference to the invention of the alarm clock in Hutchins's autobiography, which includes an account of his clock-making business during his lifetime. A hint, however, is obtained from his son in the addendum of the book: "One of my father's maxims was, 'Early to bed and early to rise.' Long before sunrise, in summer, he was accustomed to be at work in one of his fields; few men could keep up with him in using the hoe, and his work was not only done quickly but well done. In winter he arose at four o'clock." See Levi Hutchins, *The Autobiography of Levi Hutchins. With a Preface, Notes and Addenda by his Youngest Son* (Private Edition), The Riverside Press, Cambridge 1865, 168.
12 Kafka, "The Metamorphosis," 91.

speaks its creaturely condition – the being of an animal. The clock in Samsa's room thus not only signifies the mechanization of human existence and the creation of the automaton, but also announces the re-turn-of-the-body. This body, creaturely, repulsive, and wounded, hints at certain qualities of resistance. The voices, the noises of Samsa, which remain unnoticed, can be heard as gestures of revolt performed on the stage of a family drama.

But there are other, different voices written, (un-)heard, in Kafka's story: the cry of the mother when she experiences her son's new appearance, the voice of Gregor's sister, the calls of the chief clerk, and the voices of his father, whose cries and noises no longer sound like the voice of a single father. It is perhaps the voice of being-a-father, the sound of the patriarchal order itself, that is being heard – and crushed – in Kafka's story. And, after the father pushes his son back to his room with a strong hit of a stick, as he, Gregor, is wounded and bleeding freely, and the door is slammed behind him – the rest, we hear, is silence.[13] In Kafka's "Metamorphosis," one should hear these voices, the voices of the creaturely body, as being interwoven with the sound of the alarm clock. These are the sounds that exist before the words – and the sounds that return after the silence.

Furthermore: Is not the remnant of the Satyr, the mythical body of the Greek tragedy, half-goat, half-man, whose dance and music signify the birth of tragedy, now being reflected in the physicality of the literary creature in Kafka's story? The return of the creature in Kafka's story signifies a different, archaic time, a slow time that cannot be measured by clocks. Gregor Samsa, however, no longer fills the power and the potential of the creature, namely, the mode of resistance. In his story we find only the leftovers of a strong being, the miserable remnants of a creature. We recall: Samsa is not a wild animal but an insect.

More should be said about the voices in Kafka's story that echo the vocal images of the Jewish body, the unmusical body, the body of the author himself.[14] The unmusical, this figure of thought, signifies in Kafka's world the dissonances and disharmonies of existence, the disorders of desire. And yet the unmusical also recalls a certain sensibility, a way of listening, an attention to the distortion of being. Samsa's unmusical voices can thus be compared with those of the singer Josefine, from Kafka's final story, "Josephine the Singer, or the Mouse Folk" ("Josefine, die Sängerin oder Das Volk der Mäuse"), who does not sing but whistles, and her folk melody is that of the mouse people. Here too a trace can be found of the language of the mouse, the *Mauscheln* language, the pejorative name

---

13 Kafka, "The Metamorphosis," 104–105.
14 Sander Gilmann, "Franz Kafka's Musical Diet," in *Journal of Modern Jewish Studies* 4 (2005): 295–296.

for the Jewish dialect in Germany, which was considered an irregular, distorted body-language. Kafka's remark, in a letter to Max Brod[15] about *Mauscheln* is well-known: he tells Brod first about his disease, tuberculosis, which he names the *Lungenwunde*, the lung-wound, thereby relating the sense of disgust he feels in its treatments; he then turns Karl Kraus's work, which he compares with *Mauscheln*, a Jewish language built on minor gestures, noises and cries. But it is not Kraus alone but rather German-Jewish literature itself that Kafka imagines as a work of *Mauscheln* – an improper creaturely writing. The Jewish writer is identified in Kafka's letter with a poor creature hung between heaven and earth. His back legs are stuck in the Judaism of his fathers, while his front legs search, in vain, for new ground. Out of this impossible situation Jewish writing becomes possible, albeit desperate.

Is this writing, the writing of *Mauscheln*, the creaturely writing of a German Jew, imprinted in Gregor Samsa? This is a possible reading, of course.[16] This time, however, we follow a different thread of interpretation, a different time-line, the time of the alarm clock. On this path I will consider the use of the clock as a metronome that measures the story's rhythm and defines its odd musicality. What is perhaps measured according to this rhythm, the beat, the ticking of the alarm clock, is the violin playing of Gregor's sister that is performed in the living room. Only Gregor likes his sister's playing, as if it were "the unknown nourishment he craved." And so he wonders, "is he an animal, that music has such an effect upon him?"[17] Is musical sensibility perhaps the last sign of humanity that still lives in his body, or is it in fact the real signature of a creaturely being – painful and doomed? We recall that it is the power of music, his sister's performance, that draws him from his room to his last spurt of crawling before he is forced to return to his chamber. There, wounded and hungry, he dies, as the tower clock strikes three in the morning.[18]

Again it is the clock that measures and re-calls the fate of Gregor Samsa. The tower clock that signifies the universal (public) time[19] now echoes the last breath of Kafka's creature. Samsa, who was reborn in the time realm of the alarm clock, dies under the sign of the tower clock, three hours after midnight. Just as he came

---

15 Franz Kafka, *Briefe 1902–1924* [*Letters 1902–1924*], Fischer Taschenbuch Verlag, Frankfurt/M. 1995, 335.

16 Walter H. Sokel, "Kafka as a Jew," in *New Literary History* 30.4 (1999): 837–853.

17 Kafka, "The Metamorphosis," 130.

18 Kafka, "The Metamorphosis," 135.

19 The tower clocks that were placed in the town squares in Europe from the beginning of the nineteenth century replaced the church bells as signifiers of public time. See Merle, "Tempo! Tempo! Die Industrialisierung der Zeit im 19. Jahrhundert," 182–198.

into the world "one morning" (*eines Morgens*), so does he leave it at another morning hour. But at this "one morning," the hour of his birth and death, something principle yet singular is revealed, namely, the event of being. It is morning time, daybreak time, the time between dark and light, night and day, when Samsa appears and disappears. And this is also the time of the story itself that is written in-between the times, in the *difference*. This is the time paradox of Kafka's story: in-between the empty, homogeneous, familiar hours, out of the repetitions of standard, universal time, in the rapture of an endless return, something new, different, and unfamiliar appears – the horrible body of Kafka's literature.

4 Studying, The Time of Childhood

Yet there is a different, additional time that writes itself in Samsa's room – the time of studies (*Studium*) engraved on his writing desk, his *Schreibtisch*. Lying on this desk, there are, as we read at the beginning of the story, a few textile samples.[20] These are the fabrics, the textiles / the texts – the drafts of Kafka's first stories, perhaps? – found on the writing desk of the pitiful protagonist. It is mentioned that Gregor Samsa uses these textiles during his commercial travels; they are examples of his vocation. The writing desk, however, the desk of studies, was used by Samsa during his years as a student at the academy for business and before that, when he was a student at secondary school and also even earlier, when he was a pupil in elementary school.[21] The removal of the writing desk from Samsa's room thus signifies the orientation of writing, the direction of studies, in which time moves back, re-turns in the other direction, to the years of childhood. Studies (and gestures of writing) are intertwined in a complex manner with these zones of childhood and realms of memory, although these realms themselves are already lost in oblivion. Indeed, Kafka's protagonists are often figures of forgetfulness. Yet what is this time-concept of studies, the time being imprinted in these textiles, the "texts" that were left on Samsa's desk? Are they also measured by the clock? Does the empty, circular time of the alarm clock govern also the world of studies, or does a different, archaic direction in time produce inversions of time, delay, and fragmentation? And perhaps there is no time, no "before" and no "after," no past and no future in these textiles, the examples of "writing" that sit on his desk. Possibly the objects on Samsa's desk are objects of exchange. This

---

20 Kafka, "The Metamorphosis," 89.
21 Kafka, "The Metamorphosis," 118.

strange concept of time that is reflected in this writing-desk of Gregor Samsa, the time of condensing (*Verdichtung*), the time of all times being *verdichtet*, poetically condensed, is time of the script.

In Samsa's room one finds a few broken, fragmented signs of the being of a student, a subject lost in the realm of studies, the world of writing, the universe of textiles/texts and scripts. The students in Kafka's world, according to a well-known reading,[22] are doomed to empty, happy travel, or *eine fröhliche leere Fahrt*,[23] in which they sense freedom from the law of time. Samsa, however, abandons his studies and now this miserable creature no longer enjoys this demonic degree of freedom. His travels, we read, are not free and empty; rather, they belong to the realm of duty and vocation; they promise not escape but repetition. Samsa's travels are charged with *Schuld*, a sense of guilt.

And the *Schuld* is measured by the alarm clock that rings and announces both the duties and costs of time. Man, who is a subject in the realm of time, autonomous but occupied, is captured forever in duties, in being-guilt. Escape from these circles of mechanical time, the mechanism of being-thrown-in-the-world (*Geworfenheit*), is a rare possibility, one that few of Kafka's protagonists enjoy and that is no longer possible for Gregor Samsa.

For good reason the story tells about *Schulden* – the family's debts that Gregor took upon himself after his father's ruin.[24] But after the terrible transformation he has experienced and the loss of his job, Gregor feels how the family's debt has turned into guilt. This is how he perceives the wound on his back, a wound caused by one of the apples his father threw at him in his final attempt to escape his room.[25] Thus Gregor must bear not only debt in its commercial sense but also duty and guilt in their theological sense – of having fallen. Gregor Samsa belongs to the community of sons who live and die in this realm, governed by ruined, damaged fathers who in their own falls lead their sons to self-destruction. A similar fate is that of Georg Bendemann's being sentenced to death by his father in Kafka's story "The Judgement" ("Das Urteil"). Each son is condemned in the name of the father and carries the generational burden. In Kafka's unfinished

---

22 Walter Benjamin, "Franz Kafka: On the Tenth Anniversary of His Death" ("Franz Kafka: Zur zehnten Wiederkehr seines Todestages"), in *Illuminations*, ed. Hannah Arendt, trans. Harry Zohn, Harcourt, Brace & World, New York 1968, 111–140; Walter Benjamin, "Franz Kafka: Zur Wiederkehr seines Todestages," in *Benjamin über Kafka. Texte, Briefzeugnisse, Aufzeichnungen* [*Benjamin on Kafka: Texts, Letters and Notes*], Suhrkamp Verlag, Frankfurt/M. 1981, 9–38.
23 Franz Kafka, *Beim Bau der chinesischen Mauer* [*The Great Wall of China*], Fischer Taschenbuch Verlag, Frankfurt/M. 1994, 181.
24 Kafka, "The Metamorphosis," 90.
25 Kafka, "The Metamorphosis," 121–122.

novels this pattern turns cosmic: in short, what the son carries on his back – namely, his guilt – is in fact the universe itself.

5 Not-Yet

The alarm clock ticking on the chest in Gregor Samsa's room signifies profane time, the time of living and working on earth. Samsa lives in this time-space; he feels its surface, having being condemned to crawl on the ground. In this sense he endures the trial; the hard judgment of the fall shapes the human condition – finitude and labor. The being-on-earth that is measured by the alarm clock could not be fully understood without these theological assumptions of the weight of *Schuld*, or debt and guilt, in the design of human subjectivity. How does Kafka contend with these theological assumptions? In his stories the father falls and arises, the son escapes and returns; the women, subjects of desire, are doubled too. It is rather an inversion of the theological assumptions, a difficult irony, in which tradition itself seems to be rewritten against its own path. Samsa's alarm clock also counts these inverted hours – for time seems to go wrong and finally collapses into circles of repetitions.

Did the clock ring? What was it announcing? Or were its hours broken and lost in delays and oblivion? At the beginning of the story the alarm clock does not allow the counting of any special hour, for everything seems to be equally measured into standard, homogenous segments of universal time. In this time-space, in this "one morning," in the timeness of the profane order, in the empty zones of the clock, there is no place for singularity and differences.

And yet, we recall, the alarm clock in Samsa's room signifies one original hour, namely, four o'clock in the morning, the time of beginning, the hour at which all things are called to creation, to return to this world. This hour is measured, recalled with a terrible noise; yet it has passed uneventfully... Gregor Samsa did not awake.

We are thus dealing with this special, singular hour, the time of lost promises and of periods of delay, the time in which Kafka's literary body is being written. It is the time of the story itself that should be understood according to these inversions, not only the period in which Kafka's story was written – those longs weeks of the winter of 1912, the weeks of his desperate exchange of letters with Felice Bauer – but also the time gaps enveloped in the text itself. The literary writing depends on these inversions, suspensions, and distortions of time structures. The poetical moment is of this nature. It embodies a resistance: the resistance to being on time. Meaning, in its literary sense, is reproduced in suspension.

Meaning itself is always and still on its way, and the way is that of the reader, who, like the man from the village standing before the law, always arrives too early or too late. Being before the law is that of coming beforehand, of arriving too early. Yet at the same time his arrival is already late, for he will never be admitted: the entrance, his hour, is past forever. The man from the village arrives not-in-time, and this, we recall, was the guard's answer at the gate of the law in Kafka's story: entrance to the law is allowed, but "not yet" (*jetzt aber nicht*).[26] This is the time digression, the perversion of time that signifies the debt, the guilt, the blessing, and the curse that many of these villagers in Kafka's stories suffer. The country doctor himself is a subject of these time distortions. He is removed from his home at the speed of lightening, and here he stands at night at the gates of a distant village. However, when he wishes to return home, being thrown on to the country road, he lives forever in a different, tremendously slow time. The country doctor's journey comes to a standstill. Who should save him from this journey?

The clock of Kafka's story, the rhythm of his tale, takes place at the extremes. And there, where time is accelerated to a standstill, something is being revealed – the literary matter itself. The alarm clock ticking in Samsa's bedroom signifies the time labyrinths of Kafka's prose. This is how Gregor Samsa is being awakened into the world – he awakens by the sign of the clock. But this awaking, the ecstasy of time, brings time itself to its end.

Thus, in the ticking of the alarm clock, one hears the mechanism, the repetition of work, travel, and trade; one listens to the rhythm of studies and to the timings of childhood and the periods of memory and oblivion. We hear the ecstasy, the noise and the silence of time itself – the time of debts, the time of guilt, the time of judgment, the time that escapes or re-turns to a standstill. In these extremes, in inversions of time, being re-presented in the world of Gregor Samsa, literature reveals itself, I argue. It speaks with suspensions and delays of meaning, in being too early, in being too late, in being "not yet" (*jetzt aber nicht*), but never being on time.

---

26 Franz Kafka, "Vor dem Gesetz" ("Before the Law"), in *Ein Landarzt und andere Drucke zu Lebzeiten* [*A Country Doctor and Other Texts Printed in His Lifetime*], Fischer Taschenbuch Verlag, Frankfurt/M. 1994, 211–212.

6 The Time of the Messiah

And in this time that collapses, the time that is wrong, the time of being late, the time that passed before it was, Kafka's protagonists, and perhaps also his readers, feel this rare impression of singular time that the Talmud relates to the Messiah himself, who sits before the gate and waits to be called into the world – for his time never arrives; his time has already passed.

Works Cited

Benjamin, Walter, "Franz Kafka: On the Tenth Anniversary of His Death," in *Illuminations*. Ed. Hannah Arendt. Trans. Harry Zohn (New York: Harcourt, Brace & World, 1968), 111–140.

Benjamin, Walter, "Franz Kafka: Zur Wiederkehr seines Todestages," in *Benjamin über Kafka. Texte, Briefzeugnisse, Aufzeichnungen* (Frankfurt/M.: Suhrkamp Verlag, 1981), 9–38.

Dohrn-van Rossum, Gerhard, *History of the Hour: Clocks and Modern Temporal Orders*. Trans. Thomas Dunlap (Chicago and London: The University of Chicago Press, 1996).

Deleuze, Gilles, and Félix Guattari, *Kafka: Toward a Minor Literature*. Trans. Dana Polan (Minneapolis: University of Minnesota Press, 1986).

Gilmann, Sander, "Franz Kafka's Musical Diet," in *Journal of Modern Jewish Studies* 4 (2005), 295–296.

Hutchins, Levi, *The Autobiography of Levi Hutchins. With a Preface, Notes and Addenda by his Youngest Son* (Private Edition) (Cambridge: The Riverside Press, 1865).

Kafka, Franz, *Beim Bau der chinesischen Mauer* (Frankfurt/M.: Fischer Taschenbuch Verlag 1994).

Kafka, Franz, *Briefe 1902–1924* (Frankfurt/M.: Fischer Taschenbuch Verlag, 1995).

Kafka, Franz, *The Complete Stories*. Ed. Nahum N. Glatzer (New York: Schocken Books, 1983).

Kafka, Franz, *Diaries 1910–1923*. Ed. Max Brod (New York: Schocken Books, 1976).

Kafka, Franz, *Ein Landarzt und andere Drucke zu Lebzeiten* (Frankfurt/M.: Fischer Taschenbuch Verlag, 1994).

Kittler, Wolf, "Schreibmaschinen, Sprechmaschinen. Effekte technischer Medien im Werk Franz Kafkas," in *Franz Kafka: Schriftverkehr*. Eds. Wolf Kittler and Gerhard Neumann (Freiburg: Rombach Verlag, 1990), 75–163.

Merle, Ulla, "Tempo! Tempo! Die Industrialisierung der Zeit im 19. Jahrhundert," in *Uhrzeiten: die Geschichte der Uhr und ihres Gebrauches*. Eds. Igor A. Jenzen and Reinhard Glasemann (Frankfurt/M.: Historisches Museum Frankfurt, 1989), 161–217.

Sokel, Walter H., "Kafka as a Jew," in *New Literary History* 30.4 (1999): 837–853.

Yuran, Noam, *What Money Wants: An Economy of Desire* (Stanford: Stanford University Press, 2014).

Section 5: **After Kafka**

Shimon Sandbank
Reading Kafka: A Personal Story

The story I would like to unfold here is personal, though I hope its implications are more than that. It is the story of a winding course, of twists and turns; it is a story that is not linear. I always remember T.S. Eliot's wise words: "About any one so great as Shakespeare, it is probable that we can never be right; and if we can never be right, it is better that we should from time to time change our way of being wrong."[1] Kafka, I feel, is great enough for these words to apply to him as well, great enough for us never to be right about him. This is the story of my changing ways of being wrong about him. Yet, being a story, it has a structure, and this structure is circular. It ends at the point where it began, or perhaps not exactly at the same point, for its end cannot but bear the marks of the winding course it has travelled.

The story begins nearly fifty years ago, when I was commissioned by Schocken Publishing House of Tel-Aviv to prepare a Hebrew translation of Kafka's *The Castle* [*Das Schloss*]. I was delighted but also awestruck; until then I had done mainly minor translations, and this new commission posed a formidable challenge: to translate a great novel by a major modern novelist, perhaps the greatest of them all.

I cannot remember how it felt to cope with such a task. As a beginner, both in the field of translation and as university teacher, I went about it with much gusto, perhaps without even carefully reading the novel, and certainly without reading much criticism of it. I remember, however, that in working on the translation and thus being keenly engaged with Kafka's language, what struck me, right from the start, was a recurrent stylistic idiosyncrasy: his way of retreating time and again from what he had just stated. Time and again I found him repudiating, or at least casting doubt on, what he had just affirmed. I wondered if he was basically unsure of what he had to say. He seemed to be using more than one means to express this uncertainty. Often, a sentence would qualify, modify, and finally negate what a previous sentence had stated. For example: "And so that all should know what it was all about, the fight and the victory were repeated once again, or perhaps not repeated at all, but only took place now. The fight did not last long [...] Was it a fight at all?"[2] Such lines seemed to retract what had immediately

---

1 T.S. Eliot, "Shakespeare and the Stoicism of Seneca," in *Selected Essays*, Harcourt, Brace, and Company, New York 1932, 107–120, 107.
2 Franz Kafka, *The Castle*, trans. Willa and Edwin Muir, Secker & Warburg, London 1953, 321–322.

preceded them: in this example, the battle has taken place and is being repeated; then: it is taking place only now; followed by: it does not take long; and finally: is it even a battle? The battle, thus, was both a battle and not a battle.

Similarly, a parenthetical clause would negate a word in the main clause, but the word would then be used again, regardless of the negating clause. For instance: "The receiver gave out a buzz [...] It was as if the hum of countless children's voices – but this hum was not a hum, the echo rather of voices singing at an infinite distance, – as if the hum blended by sheer impossibility into one high but resonant sound."[3] The receiver, that is, gave out a hum; then: it was not a hum; then: the hum blended. More strikingly, an adjective would negate the noun it described, as in the following: "These contradictions had engendered in him the belief that though for the moment K. was wretched and looked down on, yet in an *almost unimaginably distant* future he would excel everybody."[4] The adjectival phrase "almost unimaginably distant" subtly (because it is done so casually) undermines the noun it should be describing: a future "almost unimaginably distant" is hardly a future. Another example: "[...] this last, tiny, vanishing, yes *actually inexistent* hope, is your only one."[5] Here the series of adjectives gradually, almost imperceptibly, shifts from description ("last") to denial of existence ("inexistent"), thereby both affirming and denying hope.

Another relevant device I quickly recognized was the constant use of words of uncertainty, such as "perhaps" and "it seems." German is rich in such adverbs, and Kafka seemed to use them all: *freilich* ("admittedly"), *allerdings* ("though"), *natürlich* ("naturally"), *übrigens* ("incidentally"), *trotzdem* ("nevertheless"), *aber* ("but"), *eigentlich* ("actually"), *doch* ("anyway"), *eher* ("rather"), *oder vielleicht* ("or else"), *von andere Seite her* ("on the other hand"), etc. Another typical characteristic I encountered was the use of hypothetical instead of existential sentences, or logical implication rather than statement of fact. The most famous case in Kafka is from another novel: the first sentence of *The Trial* [*Der Process*] reads, "Someone *must have been* telling lies about Joseph K. [*Jemand musste Josef K. verleumdet haben*]."[6] That is, someone *must* have been telling lies – yet had anyone actually done so? The question is left open, a form of non-committal which I came across repeatedly in my translation. The avoidance of fact in the first sentence of *The Trial* was an anticipation of the indeterminacy that seemed to govern the

---

3 Kafka, *The Castle*, 33 (translation slightly modified).
4 Kafka, *The Castle*, 187 (translation slightly modified; emphasis added).
5 Kafka, *The Castle*, 143 (translation modified; emphasis added).
6 Franz Kafka, *The Trial*, trans. Willa and Edwin Muir, Penguin, Harmondsworth 1972, 7 (emphasis added).

novel as a whole: had someone indeed been telling lies about Josef K.? Is Josef K. guilty – or is he not?

When I arrived at the famous episode in the eighteenth chapter of *The Castle*, where K., unannounced, enters secretary Bürgel's room, what I had come to call Kafka's "cancellation technique" seemed to reach its peak. Bürgel's subsequent speech concerns the possibility given to an applicant to exploit the "nocturnal weakness" of the secretaries to his own advantage. Bürgel discusses this possibility, which "almost never occurs,"[7] in a kind of long interplay of affirmations and negations that can be schematized as follows:

(a) The possibility consists in the applicant's coming unannounced in the middle of the night: that is, there *is* a possibility.

(b) *But* the organization is so foolproof that the applicant receives his summons even before he knows of the whole matter, and thus he can no longer come unannounced: that is, there is *no* possibility.

(c) *But* this refers only to the competent secretary; it remains possible to surprise others in the night: so there *is* a possibility.

d) *But* this would annoy the competent secretary; and would fail also because of the incompetent secretaries' lack of time: in short, there is *no* possibility.

This continues for another dozen or so fluctuations between possibility and non-possibility, to the final paradox: "[...] there are [...] opportunities that are, in a manner of speaking, too great to be made use of, there are things that fail through nothing other than themselves."[8] If up to now affirmation has been followed by negation, or been co-existent with negation, then affirmation now *engenders* negation: possibility, when "too great," must produce its own negation; it must fail through nothing other than itself.

Over time, having begun to teach Kafka and think about him beyond *The Castle*, I came to realize that the same habit of thought, or, rather, habit of doubting his thought, applied to his macro-structures no less than to his micro-structures, to the overall form of his novels no less than to his sentences and paragraphs. I saw that not only in *The Castle* but even more so in *Amerika* and *The Trial*, the overall narrative structure is one of advance and retreat: each encounter that should have advanced the protagonist's course results in its own cancellation and comes to nothing. Take Josef K.: in the course of *The Trial* he tries his luck with the court attendant and the attendant's wife; with his uncle; with the lawyer Huld; with Leni; with the painter Titorelli and with the merchant Block;

---

7 Kafka, *The Castle*, 322.
8 Kafka, *The Castle*, 330 (translation slightly modified).

and with the priest in the cathedral. All these encounters end in failure. In the final encounter, with the priest, who teaches him that "you don't need to accept everything as true, you only have to accept it as necessary,"[9] Josef K. perhaps comes nearest to the truth of the story; but here too it is a truth that eliminates itself: the truth of the story is that it is not necessary to accept it as true...

Reading now what I wrote about this stylistic phenomenon in a number of articles and in my Hebrew book *Derech Ha'Hissus* [*The Way of Wavering*], I find that I more or less consistently avoided touching upon the implications of this stylistic feature for Kafka's general *meaning*, for the world represented in his work. I specifically avoided all metaphysical implications. If Kafka's universe is one of impossibility, as shown in his language, then this did not imply, I thought, that Kafka posited a transcendent world of infinite possibility in recompense.

The Kafka text which I found particularly relevant to this point was "Prometheus," a text which brilliantly destroys, in half a page and through four versions of the story, the meaning that can be attributed to the myth of Prometheus. Kafka's text first presents, in a single sentence, the story's traditional theological interpretation, that of crime and punishment: Prometheus betrays the secrets of the gods to men and is therefore clamped to a rock, where eagles feed on his liver. In Kafka's second version, the theological certainty begins to crumble: Prometheus escapes the pain, by pressing himself into the rock and becoming one with it. Finally, complete withdrawal from meaning takes place: first, everything is forgotten by everybody; then, more decisively, "everyone grows weary of the *meaningless* affair."[10] The text concludes: "There remained the inexplicable mass of rock. The legend tried to explain the inexplicable. As it came out of a substratum of truth it had in turn to end in the inexplicable."[11]

This reduction of myth to the "inexplicable mass of rock" meant, I thought, that one should not try to explain what is inexplicable. I remembered Wittgenstein's dictum: "whereof one cannot speak thereof one must be silent." One could speak about Kafka's semantics, but one had to be silent about his overall meaning. To use Roman Ingarden's terms, only the stratum of meaning units was discussable, not the stratum of represented objects.

Later, I found helpful Wolfgang Iser's discussions of Beckett's prose. In his books *The Act of Reading* and *Prospecting* Iser discusses the effect on the reader of Beckett's sentence structure, which resembles Kafka's but is far more radical

9 Kafka, *The Castle*, 243.
10 Franz Kafka, "Prometheus," trans. Willa and Edwin Muir, in *The Complete Stories*, ed. Nahum N. Glatzer, Schocken Books, New York, 1976, 432 (emphasis added).
11 Kafka, "Prometheus," 432.

in its negativity. Iser writes: "Beckett has devised a sentence structure in which each statement is followed by a negation, which itself is a statement eliciting further negations in an unending process that leads the reader to search for the key, which becomes more and more elusive."[12] As I understand Iser, this search for the "elusive key" is twofold. On one hand, "the reader is forced continually to cancel the meanings he has formed"[13]; on the other hand, it "[shows] us that something is being withheld and [...] [challenges] us to discover what it is."[14] In other words, the reader of Beckett's prose, though continually expected to give up the meanings he has formed, is nevertheless reluctant to forego his search for a final meaning. In my own case, the need to cancel – again and again – the meanings I had formed in reading Kafka had led me to give up the search for a final meaning in his work. I remained convinced that a final meaning was inaccessible, but I felt that it was contrary to one's intuition to reduce Kafka to style, or to the stratum of meaning units. The central secret, what Iser declared was "withheld" from me, "challenged me to discover what it is."

If the first station on my way was largely linguistic, the second was an attempt to move away from language and towards overall meaning. And since language was characterized by negation and incomprehensibility, meaning too was bound to centre on the incomprehensible or transcendent. And the archetype of the transcendent was God. I therefore found the theological approach, whose leading representative was Max Brod, most tenable. In his Postscript to the first edition of *The Castle* Brod had famously claimed that *The Trial* and *The Castle* present two forms of God's revelation – Judgment and Grace. This seemed to me most persuasive: for was not Josef K., in *The Trial*, judged by an unknown power? and did not K., in *The Castle*, pursue unknown Grace?

Yet soon enough I realized that Brod's type of "positive theology" was incompatible with the indeterminacy that I had all along found in Kafka. Kafka's negativity could not be reconciled with Brod's positive categories, for it called for a negative version of theology. Walter Benjamin and Gershom Scholem, though they ridiculed Brod and strongly rejected his approach to Kafka, in fact shared his engagement with transcendence, but – a crucial "but" – in a negative version. For Scholem, as Stéphane MoSès notes, Kafka's work, "[offered] the image of a world bereft of meaning, empty of all divine presence, but where hollow traces still [existed] of the escaped transcendence: unanswered questions, unsolved

---

12 Wolfgang Iser, *The Act of Reading*, Johns Hopkins University Press, Baltimore 1987, 131.

13 Iser, *The Act of Reading*, 223.

14 Wolfgang Iser, *Prospecting: From Reader Response to Literary Anthropology*, Johns Hopkins University Press, Baltimore 1989, 141.

enigmas, whose negativity [indicated] the power exerted over us by the shadow of the dead God."[15] This was much closer to the Kafka I experienced: transcendence was there, but it was an "escaped transcendence," while the world itself was left bereft of meaning. Brod's Judgment and Grace made K.'s fate deceptively meaningful, whereas Scholem and Benjamin, I felt, though differing on certain central points, preserved the meaninglessness of Kafka's "mass of rock."

Benjamin's juxtaposition of *Aggadah* and *Halakhah*, inspired by the Hebrew poet Ch.N. Bialik's essay of that name, which Scholem had translated, was for me an eye-opening image for the relationship between the escaped transcendence and its elusive traces. Kafka's parables, explains Benjamin, have "a similar relationship to doctrine as the Haggadah does to the Halakhah. They are not parables, and yet they do not want to be taken at their face value; they lend themselves to quotations and can be told for purposes of clarification. But do we have the doctrine which Kafka's parables interpret[...]? It does not exist; all we can say is that here and there we have an allusion to it."[16]

In my book *After Kafka*[17] I tried to show that this radical gap between parable and doctrine, or fiction and theme, had influenced major modern writers – Sartre, Beckett, Borges, and Ionesco, among others – but that they had all been unable, or unwilling, to write the radically sceptical type of fiction that was Kafka's great contribution to modern literature. Like Kafka, they created fables to storm the walls of a meaningless existence, around which they let words (as in Beckett) or objects (as in Ionesco) proliferate desperately. Unlike Kafka, however, they stopped short of a final withdrawal from hope.

I continued to read and to puzzle and perhaps to seek an escape from the transcendence that had become an *idée fixe* in Kafka studies. I think this is why the next station on my way was diametrically opposed to the line I have been describing. This was almost a Copernican revolution – transcendence replaced by immanence. The theorists who were responsible for this revolution, Gilles Deleuze and Félix Guattari, meant for their book *Kafka: Toward a Minor Literature* to present a Kafka "freed from his interpreters"[18] – at least, I would add,

---

15 Stéphane Mosès, *The Angel of History*, Stanford University Press, Stanford 2009, 151.

16 Walter Benjamin, "Franz Kafka: On the Tenth Anniversary of His Death" ("Franz Kafka: Zur zehnten Wiederkehr seines Todestages"), in *Illuminations*, ed. Hannah Arendt, trans. Harry Zohn, Harcourt, Brace & World, New York 1968, 111–140, 122.

17 Shimon Sandbank, *After Kafka: The Influence of Kafka's Fiction*, Georgia University Press, Athens 1989.

18 Réda Bensmaïa, Foreword, in Gilles Deleuze and Félix Guattari, *Kafka: Toward a Minor Literature* [*Kafka: Pour une litterature mineure*], trans. Dana Polan, University of Minnesota Press, Minneapolis 1986, xxi.

freed from his interpreters' favourite categories – transcendence and subjective guilt, above all.

I will not go into the details of the theory which accompanies their interpretation of *The Trial*. This theory of what they label "minor literature" is irrelevant to the personal story I am telling. What was important for me was their upside-down reading of *The Trial*. Let me quote a few lines:

> [...] even if the law remains unrecognizable, this is not because it is hidden by its transcendence, but simply because it is always denuded of any interiority: it is always in the office next door, or behind the door [...] (in the first chapter [...] everything happens in the "room next door") [...] it is not the law that is stated because of the demands of a hidden *transcendence*; it is almost the exact opposite: it is the statement, the enunciation, that constructs the law in the name of an *immanent* power of the one who enounces it – the law is confused with that which the guardian utters, and the writings precede the law, rather than being the necessary and derived expression of it.[19]

Deleuze and Guattari are here subverting what until then had been the accepted picture of Kafka's world. The law, they argue, is not a hidden transcendent power whose representatives – judges, secretaries, policemen, painters, priests, etc. – follow its orders and express it. The law, on the contrary, is *immanent* to human society; it is a force of life or desire that operates the social machine from within. The law, far from being the embodiment of a transcendent Law, is a product of all those judges, secretaries, etc., and it is they that project a fictitious image of a trial. In short, "If everything, everyone, is part of justice, if everyone is an auxiliary of justice, from the priest to the little girls, this is not because of the transcendence of the law but because of the immanence of desire."[20]

Deleuze and Guattari have hardly been the only political interpreters of Kafka. Indeed, themes of totalitarianism, political evil, perverted law, bureaucracy, exile, even prophetic anticipation of the fate of Hitler's victims were diagnosed early on by Kafka's critics, and remain to this day the popular connotations of the adjective "Kafkaesque." My own preoccupation with Kafka's language, which had made me deeply convinced that Kafka could not be reduced to any overall meaning, had also left me indifferent to such political and sociological interpretations. This is why Deleuze and Guattari's approach was such a sudden eye-opener for me. It seemed to throw a shocking light on myriad details of the petty, dirty, treacherous world of the novels; in doing so, it ejected all transcend-

---

19 Deleuze and Guattari, *Kafka: Toward a Minor Literature*, 45 (emphasis added).
20 Deleuze and Guattari, *Kafka: Toward a Minor Literature*, 50.

ence from Kafka's horizon, thereby placing the mystery squarely in the midst of human society, perhaps even in the office next door.

But this was not the case for long. For me, Deleuze and Guattari's immanence of the law came to seem completely incompatible with its absolute unreachability in texts like the parable "Before the Law" ("Vor dem Gesetz") or *The Castle*. Soon enough Deleuze and Guattari were replaced in my story by Jacques Derrida. I now see that it must have been my original experience of Kafka, of his cancelling, or deconstructing, himself, that made Derrida's deconstructive method so congenial for me. Although his essay on Kafka's "Before the Law" is over twenty-five years old, Derrida is, to date, the last station in my story. With him the story comes full circle – but with a difference.

It comes full circle because deconstruction seemed especially close to what I had felt from the beginning to be Kafka's own technique, what I had called "cancellation technique." To deconstruct a discourse, as Jonathan Culler explains, is "to show how it undermines the philosophy it asserts, or the hierarchical oppositions on which it relies, by identifying in the text the rhetorical operations that produce the supposed ground of argument, the key concept or premise."[21] This undermining of meaning, the "différance" of meaning, as Derrida terms it, is endless and renders all stable, self-identical knowledge impossible.

I noted that this seemed close to Kafka's technique; but deferral of meaning, as Derrida means it, is governed by language itself, by the play of its signification. In Kafka, however, deferral of meaning is a conscious product of a subjective consciousness, of a constant "presence" of an ever-doubting author. It is Kafka's language, not language as such, that continues doubting and negating its own assumptions and arguments. Kafka's meanings, I felt, are undermined not by language but by Kafka.

As I discovered later, a much-discussed critique of Derrida by Paul de Man centered precisely on this point. De Man, in *Insight and Blindness*, argues against Derrida's reading of Rousseau and claims that the latter, because he deconstructs himself, does not need to be deconstructed. In de Man's view, according to Irene E. Harvey, Rousseau's strength "comes from the fact that he not only knew what he was doing but also indeed exhibited the undecidability that characterizes textuality in general."[22] J. Hillis Miller, in his essay "Deconstructing the Deconstructors," applies this to deconstruction as a whole: " Great works of literature are

21 Jonathan Culler, *On Deconstruction*, Routledge & Kegan Paul, London 1983, 86.
22 Irene E. Harvey, "Doubling the Space of Existence: Exemplarity in Derrida – the Case of Rousseau," in *Deconstruction and Philosophy*, ed. John Sallis, University Of Chicago Press, Chicago 1987, 60–70, 63.

likely to be ahead of their critics. They are there already. They have anticipated explicitly any deconstruction the critic can achieve." The critic's task therefore, he adds, is "to identify an act of deconstruction which has always already, in each case differently, been performed by the text on itself."[23]

This, I realized, is precisely what Kafka's texts do: they do not need to be deconstructed, because they deconstruct themselves and because they *explicitly* anticipate any deconstruction that Derrida – were he to apply his method to Kafka – could achieve.

Were Derrida to apply his method to Kafka: but did he? Derrida's well-known lecture on Kafka, entitled, like its object, "Before the Law," is not an especially good example of his method. Derrida does not deconstruct Kafka's parable the way he deconstructs Rousseau, for instance. Nor does he identify blind spots and contradictions which would undermine Kafka's supposed meaning. Instead, Derrida allegorizes the man from the country, who stands before the gate of the law and does not enter it, into the reader standing before a literary text and finding it inaccessible. As Derrida interprets it, the many guards who follow the first gatekeeper stand for the many deferrals of meaning, or deconstructions, which the reader is called upon to bear. "Before the Law" thus becomes "Before the Text," a manifesto of deconstruction, as opposed to an instance of it.

As such, Derrida's lecture strikes me as a highly sophisticated elaboration of a sentence which Kafka himself includes in the dialogue between Josef K. and the priest, following the parable in the ninth chapter of *The Trial*. Derrida limits his discussion only to the parable, as published by Kafka before he had embedded it in *The Trial*. But in the course of that Talmudic dialogue, the priest says: "I am only showing you the various opinions concerning that point. You must not pay too much attention to them. The scriptures are unalterable and the comments often enough merely express the commentator's despair."[24] The priest, true enough, does not interpret "man from the country versus the Law" as "reader versus text," but he urges the reader Josef K. to realize that the text concerned – that is, the parable "Before the Law" – is inaccessible and uninterpretable. Derrida only inserts the priest's deconstructive counsel into his interpretation of the parable itself.

Derrida's own opinion, thus, is no more than an expression of despair over Kafka's infinitely open parable. As with Kafka's "Prometheus," the dialogue between Josef K. and the priest ends with despair of reaching the truth: "it is not

---

23 J. Hillis Miller, "Deconstructing the Deconstructors," in *Diacritics* 5:2 (1975): 24–31, 31.
24 Kafka, *The Trial*, 239–240 (translation slightly modified).

necessary to accept everything as true, one must only accept it as necessary."[25] All we have, finally, is an endless deferral of the truth. In Benjamin's unforgettable words: "In the stories which Kafka left us, narrative art regains the significance it had in the mouth of Scheherazade: to postpone the future."[26]

Works Cited

Benjamin, Walter, *Illuminations*. Ed. Hannah Arendt. Trans. Harry Zohn (New York: Harcourt, Brace & World, 1968).

Culler, Jonathan, *On Deconstruction* (London: Routledge & Kegan Paul, 1983).

Deleuze, Gilles and Félix Guattari, *Kafka. Toward a Minor Literature*. Trans. Dana Polan (Minneapolis: University of Minnesota Press, 1986).

Derrida, Jacques, "Before the Law," trans. Avital Ronell, in *Kafka and the Contemporary Critical Performance*. Ed. Alan Udoff (Bloomington: University of Indiana Press, 1987), 128–150.

Eliot, T.S., "Shakespeare and the Stoicism of Seneca," in *Selected Essays* (New York: Harcourt, Brace, 1932).

Iser, Wolfgang, *The Act of Reading* (Baltimore: Johns Hopkins University Press, 1987).

Iser, Wolfgang, *Prospecting: From Reader Response to Literary Anthropology* (Baltimore: Johns Hopkins University Press, 1989).

Kafka, Franz, *The Castle*. Trans. Willa and Edwin Muir, with additional material trans. Eithne Wilkins and Ernst Kaiser (London: Secker & Warburg, 1953).

Kafka, Franz, *The Complete Stories*. Ed. Nahum N. Glatzer (New York: Schocken Books, 1976).

Kafka, Franz, *The Trial*. Trans. Willa and Edwin Muir (Harmondsworth: Penguin, 1972).

Miller, J. Hillis, "Deconstructing the Deconstructors," in *Diacritics* 5:2 (1975): 24–31.

Mosès, Stéphane, *The Angel of History* (Stanford: Stanford University Press, 2009).

Sallis, John, ed., *Deconstruction and Philosophy: The Texts of Jacques Derrida* (Chicago: University of Chicago Press, 1987).

Sandbank, Shimon, *After Kafka: The Influence of Kafka's Fiction* (Athens: University of Georgia Press, 1989).

Sandbank, Shimon, *Derech Ha'Hissus* [*The Way of Wavering: Forms of Uncertainty in Kafka*] (in Hebrew) (Tel-Aviv: Hakibbutz Hameuchad Publishers, 1974).

---

25 Kafka, *The Trial*, 243.
26 Benjamin, "Franz Kafka: On the Tenth Anniversary of His Death," 129.

Kata Gellen
Kafka, Pro and Contra: Günther Anders's Holocaust Book

How Jewish was Franz Kafka? How Jewish was his writing? There are no explicit references to Jews or Judaism anywhere in his fictional work, yet so many of the characters, situations, and existential scenarios he depicts seem to allegorize modern Jewish experience. Moreover, there is substantial biographical evidence that Kafka was exposed to Jewish thought and religious practice and that he sustained active interest in such topics as Yiddish, Hebrew, Chasidism, and Zionism. This quandary has been central to much Kafka scholarship, from his earliest critics – including Max Brod, Margarete Susman, and Walter Benjamin – to contemporary biographers, writers, and literary critics.[1] Recent scholarship – such as that of Vivian Liska, Dan Miron, and David Suchoff – has resisted the previously dominant tendency to quantify Kafka's Jewishness, so as to account more subtly for the precise ways in which his writing can be thought of as Jewish.[2]

The philosopher, writer, and activist Günther Anders (1902–1992) was an early contributor to the discourse on Jewish Kafka: he presented a lecture on Kafka in Paris in 1934, and produced two written versions of this study between 1946 and 1952. Nevertheless, in the introduction to a 1984 collection of his essays in which the Kafka essay was republished, Anders made clear that he considered literary criticism, and even literature itself, a luxury in which he and his contemporaries could barely afford to indulge. Indeed, Anders had spent much of his postwar career writing against nuclear proliferation and the dangers of technological modernity, though he did not publish his major treatise on the atomic threat until

---

1 Paul Reitter's review essay offers a good overview of recent criticism, academic and otherwise, on this topic. See Paul Reitter, "Misreading Kafka," in *Jewish Review of Books* (Fall 2010): http://jewishreviewofbooks.com/articles/172/misreading-kafka/.
2 Excellent examples include Vivian Liska, *When Kafka Says We. Uncommon Communities in German-Jewish Literature*, Indiana University Press, Bloomington 2009; Dan Miron, *From Continuity to Contiguity: Toward a New Jewish Literary Thinking*, Stanford University Press, Stanford 2010; and David Suchoff, *Kafka's Jewish Languages: The Hidden Openness of Tradition*, University of Pennsylvania Press, Philadelphia 2012.

I would like to thank Vivian Liska for her kind invitation to participate in this volume, as well as my friends and colleagues Marc Caplan, Doreen Densky, and Ann-Kathrin Pollmann, whose astute comments on drafts of this essay were of inestimable value.

1956.[3] How, then, can one explain his own persistent attention to Kafka, especially in the late 1940s and early 1950s?

It merits noting the forcefulness with which Anders made his claim about the superfluousness of literature in the face of the Holocaust and nuclear catastrophe, twin manifestations of the twentieth century's technocratic "machine world," against which Anders militated. For him, these human tragedies render literary study not only frivolous and impractical, but morally dubious. Of his original 1934 lecture, which he had given in exile, Anders later reflected:

> That's how Kafkaesque our situation back then was. And one could think that it must have actually been "difficile" for the likes of us not to write about Kafka. However he who is forced to live a Kafkaesque life does not read Kafka and does not write about Kafka. Even K. would not, under these circumstances, have read Kafka. We had more urgent matters to attend to.[4]

Anders dismisses the idea of a simple connection between the experiences Kafka depicts (marginalization, powerlessness, suffering) and the motivation to study his literary works. Without denying that Jewish exiles in the 1930s might have found points of identification with Kafka's characters, Anders argues that this alone could not have motivated them. As for his own exilic work on Kafka, he claims that the French academy sought a lecture on Kafka and that he needed money: Kafka was thus "useful" as a source of income.[5] This, Anders suggests, and not the plight of Josef K. or Gregor Samsa, is *real* existential angst.

Nevertheless, Anders continued to engage with Kafka quite intensively during his years in New York (1936–1950), though he distanced himself from the scholarly academic discourse on the writer. He writes about this period in the 1984 introduction, and notes, rather dismissively, that there was at the time already an overabundance of scholarship – over 11,000 works – on Kafka.

> I have not read a single one of these 11,000 secondary texts – [...] because I would find it inappropriate to dawdle away our time sifting through wagons of German literary philology in this age of ours, where the main concern is to combat the onset of certain catastrophe.[6]

---

3 This work was published as *Die Antiquiertheit des Menschen. Band I: Über die Seele im Zeitalter der zweiten industriellen Revolution* [*The Outdatedness of Human Beings. Volume 1. On the Soul in the Era of the Second Industrial Revolution*], C. H. Beck, Munich 1956.
4 Günther Anders, "Einleitung" ("Introduction"), in *Mensch ohne Welt. Schriften zur Kunst und Literatur* [*Human Being Without World: Writings on Art and Literature*], C. H. Beck, Munich 1984, XI–XLIV, XXXIII. See also XXXVIII. Unless otherwise indicated, translations are my own.
5 Anders, "Einleitung," XXXIII–IV.
6 Anders, "Einleitung," XXXVIII.

When standing before the greatest ethical and political crisis of the modern age, one did not waste time reading (much less writing) esoteric tombs on Kafka – or at least one should not have. And yet during these years this is precisely what Anders did, more than once. I explain this apparent contradiction by arguing that, for Anders, writing about Kafka was a means to another end. This is true not only in the mundane sense that Anders himself acknowledges – earning a bit of money when resources were scarce – but in the deeper sense that writing about Kafka was a means for Anders to channel thoughts about both the coordinated mass annihilation of European Jewry and postwar German society's insincere relationship to its crimes. Anders's Kafka book is his reckoning with the Holocaust.

The hidden thesis of Anders's 1951 book, *Kafka, Pro und Contra. Die Proceß-Unterlagen* [*Kafka, Pro and Contra: The Trial Documents*],[7] takes the form of a moral judgment. Anders believes that Kafka, often taken as the exemplar of Jewish suffering, in fact absolves Germans of their responsibility for this suffering. Thus, critics who think that Kafka somehow predicted the plight of the Jews under Nazi rule and exemplified the condition of the victimized Jew have inverted the true meaning and implications of his writing. Their arguments are not only historically untenable on the grounds that they render Kafka into a prophet of doom; they are also a misreading of power relations in Kafka's work. Anders makes the somewhat radical claim that Kafka, who is generally thought to have given voice to the weak, the oppressed, and the victimized, is actually doing major psychological and moral work to liberate a generation of Nazi sympathizers from their guilt. According to Anders, Kafka offers them a painless distraction from their crimes, in the form of a morally neutral and spiritually edifying "Kunstbewunderung,"[8] or appreciation of artistic mastery. While Anders is ostensibly critiquing Kafka's readers and not the author himself, my analysis will show that Anders in fact holds Kafka responsible for a moral and religious system that enables this kind of facile absolution.

Anders's claims about postwar Kafka reception are inextricable from his ideas about Kafka's supposedly universal (but actually Christian) perspective and his conviction that Kafka represents the position of oppressor rather than oppressed. By attributing this viewpoint to Kafka, Anders can argue that Kafka's works become available for postwar Germans to absolve themselves of a guilt they

---

7 The book was translated into English simply as *Franz Kafka*. See Günther Anders, *Franz Kafka*, trans. A. Steer and A. K. Thorlby, Bowes & Bowes, London 1960. Since Anders's ambivalence toward Kafka is a crucial aspect of my argument, I refer to this work as *Kafka, Pro and Contra*.
8 Anders, "Einleitung," XXXIX.

possess but do not properly feel or acknowledge. Anders wishes to hold Kafka morally responsible for this. Anders claims that Kafka in some sense stands for (which is not to say *stands with*) the "winner," and that this allegiance ultimately enables the unholy marriage between a suffering Jew and criminal Germans. Without denying that Kafka also appeals to Jews struggling to understand twentieth-century Jewish experience, Anders claims that Kafka, who presented a world in which guilt and punishment are uncoupled, also allows Germans to sidestep their collective guilt for Nazi crimes. According to Anders, this is not a distortion or misreading of Kafka, though it might be a misappropriation, perhaps even an ethically unsound reading. Kafka's German readers do not betray him; rather, Kafka betrays the weakling or "loser" at the center of his literary universe, and Anders feels compelled to identify this act of treason and to pronounce judgment, to be *pro* or *contra*. Indeed, his book is laden with anger, resentment, and grievance, much of which is directed against Kafka and reflects a discernible vengefulness. It is not only Anders's final judgment, but also this intensity of undigested and unresolved affect that make his Kafka study legible as a Holocaust book. Thus Anders's account of Kafka tells us less about Jewish suffering than about German guilt during and after the Nazi era.

1 Franz Kafka: Universal and Particular

The complex history of Anders's work *Kafka, Pro and Contra* has been further colored by Anders's own somewhat polemical and mythologizing statements about it. Anders delivered a lecture on Kafka at the Institut d'Études Germaniques in 1934, during his Parisian exile. Among the (future) luminaries in attendance were Walter Benjamin, who wrote his essay on Kafka the same year in Paris, and Hannah Arendt, who was married to Anders at the time. Ten years later, now an émigré in New York, Anders revised the lecture for *Commentary*, a magazine recently founded and published by the American Jewish Committee. The essay appeared, in English translation, as "Kafka: Ritual Without Religion: *The Modern Intellectual's Shamefaced Atheism*," in the December 1949 issue.[9] Anders had written a prefatory note in New York in 1946, which was published by the German press C. H. Beck, in 1951, alongside a significantly expanded German version of

---

9 See Günther Anders, "Kafka: Ritual Without Religion: *The Modern Intellectual's Shamefaced Atheism*," in *Commentary* (December 1949): 560–569. As Anders explains in the 1984 introduction to *Mensch ohne Welt*, excerpts from the first part had also been published in the West German literary magazine *Die Neue Rundschau* in April 1947. See Anders, "Einleitung," XXXVI.

the essay. The essay was republished, with a new introduction, in Anders's 1984 collection *Mensch ohne Welt: Schriften zur Kunst und Literatur* (also published by Beck).

Though the text of the original lecture has been lost, the extant versions and prefaces suggest that the central tension in the argument remained the same over five decades. On the one hand, Anders wants to treat Kafka as an abstract thinker – of metaphysics, aesthetics, and religion; on the other hand, he insists on the Jewishness of Kafka's writing and experience, which signify their cultural and social specificity. Anders's Kafka is caught between the universal and the particular, a point illustrated and exemplified by the fact that Anders's central (universalizing) thesis about Kafka's "religiosity without religion"[10] co-exists with a series of (particularizing) Jewish readings of Kafka's works. Anders resolves this apparent contradiction by arguing that while Judaism has no role, so to speak, in Kafka's "theology" – which he identifies as a typically modern "shamefaced atheism" – it is nonetheless an important aspect of Kafka's cultural and social experience, and thus essential to the interpretation of individual literary works by Kafka. To rephrase this in somewhat schematic terms, in Kafka the problem of group belonging (identity, affiliation, exclusion, alienation) is *Jewish*, whereas the theological problem (guilt, redemption, punishment, sacrifice) is not.

This "division of labor" is both convenient and plausible, and Anders's readings of Kafka's works largely bear it out. He argues that Kafka's view of guilt is decidedly non-Jewish, since it is based in a conception of original sin and redemption. According to Anders, this is a Christian notion of guilt that is assumed to be universal, and it is what allows Kafka to be a modern *homo religiosus*: someone for whom the absence of God results in a nonetheless rigid commitment to ritual, officialdom, protocol, and punctiliousness, albeit bereft of any higher purpose or meaning. Anders argues that nineteenth-century secularism and atheism amount to a "history of shame-faced atheism," by which he means a rejection of specific religions but a continuation of their ethos, "religiosity without religion,"[11] exemplified by such writers as Nietzsche and Kafka. For Anders, the topics that fall under the rubric of "religiosity without religion" – which include reflections on public life, bureaucracy, the impenetrability of the law, inexorable guilt, and

---

10 Günther Anders, *Kafka, Pro und Contra. Die Prozeß-Unterlagen*, C. H. Beck, Munich 1963 [1951]: 76 (my translation). At times I will quote from the English-language essay that preceded both the German publication (from 1949) and the book's English translation (from 1960), though the latter, as its translators note, is more an adaptation than a translation (see Anders, *Franz Kafka*, 7). Here, and in some other instances, I provide my own translations.
11 Anders, *Kafka, Pro und Contra*, 71, 76.

punishment without cause – have nothing to do with Jewishness. Rather, they relate to a secular universalist theology that derives from Christian thought and tradition, and they are inflected neither by Kafka's experience as a Jew nor by his ideas about Judaism.

Where, then, does Kafka's Jewishness lie? For Anders, there are two major Jewish questions in Kafka; these questions are pervasive and significant, yet not "religious":

> few statements can be advanced about Kafka with more certainty than the statement that his religiosity has no direct connection with the Jewish religion. Wherever he dealt with the Jewish question, he either formulated the position of the Jew in the world or that of the de-Judaized Jew confronting the "Jewish Jew."[12]

These two aspects of contemporary Jewish experience – the Jew's ineluctable status as outsider and the post-Enlightenment encounter between traditional and modern Jews – are central to Anders's "Jewish readings" of Kafka. For instance, Anders argues that Kafka's story "Der Riesenmaulwurf" ("The Giant Mole") stages a textual battle between the "orthodox [E]astern European Jew and the cultured Jew who only tenuously belongs to Judaism."[13] Anders convincingly draws out the condescension and misguidedness of the Western secular narrator's apologetic defense of the pious teacher's earnest and unpretentious academic treatise. This brief reading evinces a nuanced understanding of Kafka's ambivalence towards various aspects of Jewish social existence (assimilation, Yiddish, Zionism). Anders is clearly alert both to the prejudices and misconceptions that Kafka thematizes and to those to which Kafka himself falls victim.

If the reading of "The Giant Mole" exemplifies the second main Jewish topos in Kafka's work ("the de-Judaized Jew confronting the 'Jewish Jew'"), then Anders's reading of the fragment "Forschungen eines Hundes" ("Investigation of a Dog") illustrates the first (the inescapability of non-belonging as a Jew), though the two topoi in fact converge in his analysis. Anders sees Kafka himself as the narrator: caught between "the bourgeois European Jews from whom he descends" and the "the [E]astern Jews, who really did live as a nation [Volk]," he is a "pariah twice over, caught between two groups of Jews, neither of which can ever be 'his people.'"[14] This "double dog-life" offers insight into competing models of Jewish

---

12 Anders, "Kafka: Ritual Without Religion," 568 (text slightly modified). This passage, taken from the English version of the essay that preceded the book's German publication, is simply omitted from the book's English translation, along with many other important passages.
13 Anders, *Franz Kafka*, 93.
14 Anders, *Franz Kafka*, 19.

existence, but actual affiliation with neither. The dog's narration amounts to an explanatory lamentation on the "ambiguity of non-belonging,"[15] which Anders associates primarily though not exclusively with Kafka's own Jewish experience.

These are insightful readings,[16] yet also highly particularizing: they imply that the significance of Jewishness in Kafka's works derives from experience rather than concepts, that it represents a reaction to a specific lived situation rather than a theological position, and that it is historically contingent rather than timeless. There is Jewishness in Kafka's works, but no Judaism. He is a *homo religiosus*, Anders claims: he belongs to a Western Christian-cum-secular tradition of "shamefaced atheism," and even views and experiences Judaism from this perspective. Kafka, in short, is a Jewish outsider *and* an outsider to Judaism.

Whether Anders's "division of labor" implies a normative judgment is unclear. Is there an intellectual hierarchy at work here, in which Kafka's Jewishness must remain of local interest whereas his religiosity is granted universal significance? Is Anders attempting to "save" Kafka from mere particularism and "elevate" him to a position of universal importance – i.e., to rescue him from his own Jewishness? It would not be surprising if some of these sentiments and intentions were at play, given the intellectual milieu in which Anders was writing. In the following section, I present an overview of this scene and its stakes, and then return to Anders's Kafka study to show how it both engages with and transcends this debate about the status of Kafka's writing. For Anders, Kafka's Jewish particularism is not something from which Kafka needs to be "saved," since, per Anders's analysis, it can co-exist with his Christian theology – though this particularism does reflect a fundamental detachment from Jewish sensibility that Anders finds alienating and potentially treacherous.

---

15 Anders, *Kafka, Pro und Contra*, 18–19.
16 Somewhat less plausibly, Anders's comments on Kafka's "Josefine, die Sängerin oder das Volk der Mäuse" ("Josephine the Singer, or the Mouse People") are meant to prove his explicit (though encoded) rejection of Jewish theology. Josephine is read as a religious leader who cannot in fact hold the attention of the people and who will fade into history: the Jewish people will live on (i.e., their social existence matters), but the Jewish religion is irrelevant. As Anders puts it, "How little Kafka conceived of his writings in the spirit of Jewish theology is evident from the beautiful [...] story Josephine, in which he clearly represents [the] Jewish religion as an incident in the history of the Jewish people" (see Anders, *Franz Kafka*, 92).

2 Seeing the World Through Christian Eyes: Anders's Critique of Kafka

In June 1947, William Phillips, co-founder of the *Partisan Review*, published a review article, in the newly launched magazine *Commentary*, of a translation of Kafka stories and a volume of critical essays on Kafka.[17] Phillips's remarks about the essay collection constitute a scathing critique of their particularism. For Phillips, Kafka's great achievement is his capacity "to maintain a kind of permanent crisis, which loads each particular experience with the sum of all experience."[18] The error of nearly all the essays in the volume, he argues, is that they "ride some personal notion or some half-baked thesis":

> [T]he theoreticians present us with a variety of "interpretations," all plugging some extreme view of Kafka's work and all canceling each other out. Perhaps the oldest distortion is Max Brod's attempt – in a kind of Zionist Emersonianism – to squeeze a Jewish oversoul out of Kafka. Less sectarian and more fashionable, however, is the Protestant non-denominational view taken by a number of critics who have transferred Kafka into a pure theologian. On the secular side, there are a number of "social" approaches, some of which argue that Kafka's fiction was basically a protest against the injustices of modern society, while others berate Kafka for his reactionary and "escapist" attitudes.[19]

Phillips continues in this vein: all these efforts to appropriate Kafka for a particular religion, cause, or ideology misconstrue the main strength of Kafka's writing, which is to reflect the universal in the particular. According to Phillips, the search for alternative particular encodings in Kafka's works renders them provincial and flat.

Two months later, in the August 1947 issue, the Viennese writer Friedrich Torberg published a sharp critique of Phillips's review. Torberg was living in New York at the time, working as a translator, journalist, and critic. His mentor, Max Brod, who also wrote a response to Anders's book, had been integral to the publication of Torberg's first novel. Torberg did not hold back in his retort to Phillips:

> There seems to be in this country a general critical tendency to discard Brod's insistence on Kafka's Jewishness as a kind of sectarian queerness, and it seems particularly outspoken

---

17 Hannah Arendt was also a member of the "New York Intellectuals" and had written for *Commentary* within its first year of publication. Anders and Arendt, both students of Martin Heidegger, were married from 1929 to 1937.
18 William Phillips, "*The Great Wall of China*, by Franz Kafka; and *The Kafka Problem*, edited by Angel Flores," in *Commentary* (June 1947): 594–596, 595.
19 Phillips, "*The Great Wall of China*," 596.

among Jewish critics – obviously as part and parcel of that glorious Jewish attitude which refuses to look at a problem, be it ever so Jewish, from a "merely" Jewish standpoint. This Jewish standpoint, if rightly understood, might easily be the most reliable graduator of any spiritual or cultural situation, and there is nothing "mere" to it but, on the contrary, quite a catholicity.[20]

Torberg's statement is, first, a provocative accusation of Jewish self-hatred: he regards Phillips's insistence that Jewish writers transcend Jewish issues as a charge of Jewish particularism. Torberg's critique is moreover a remarkable intervention in the Kafka debate: he argues not only that it is unnecessary to choose between the particular and the universal when it comes to Kafka, but that it may well be that Kafka's Jewishness – that aspect of his person and writing which is taken to be most local, personal, contingent, and particular – is in fact the best measure of his universalism (what Torberg cleverly refers to as his "catholicity"). Torberg adds, "As a matter of fact, I believe that if something is 'good for the Jews,' it is usually good for all others, too; but then, it could be that this is just a personal notion and a half-baked thesis of mine."[21] Rather than set aside Kafka's Judaism and thereby attempt to stand above or outside of it – as if this were the only way to grasp his universality – Torberg insists that Jewish concerns are in fact universal concerns. Thus, by identifying with Kafka's "Jewish standpoint," one can grasp the universalism of his writing.

Torberg's rhetoric and positioning are crucial to understanding Anders's conflicted relationship to Kafka: the overt concern with particularism versus universality; the question of perspective, i.e., seeing and judging matters "as a Jew" or "universally"; the thinly veiled accusations of self-hatred and treason. Indeed, this miniature postwar New York Kafka debate provides the context for Anders's central claim about Kafka, to which I have alluded: namely, that Kafka views Judaism from a Christian perspective. Thus, Anders writes:

> It is quite misleading to interpret Kafka as carrying on the tradition of Jewish faith or theology. But at the same time it is partly as a result of his Jewishness, through the fact of his being a Jew, and as a Jew socially an outsider, that he comes to feel "sinful" and "in need of salvation." He judges his position as a Jew from a Christian perspective. He is not a Jewish theologian but a Christianizing theologian of Jewish existence.[22]

---

20 Friedrich Torberg, "Kafka the Jew," in *Commentary* (August 1947): http://www.commentary-magazine.com/article/kafka-the-jew/.
21 Torberg, "Kafka the Jew."
22 Anders, *Franz Kafka* 91–92; translation slightly modified.

Anders's "particularizing" readings of Kafka – he detects aspects of modern Jewish experience encoded in Kafka's stories – are in fact central to his understanding of Kafka as a universal *homo religiosus*. Anders does *not* think that Kafka's Jewishness can simply be set aside in order to discover the universal aspects of his thinking and writing. Nor does he believe that there is any Jewish theology in Kafka's religiosity (the "shamefaced atheism"), which for Anders is the source of Kafka's universalism. He asserts, instead, that Kafka stands outside of Judaism, and that this standing outside is at once the archetypical expression of Kafka's Jewishness *and* what precludes him from truly adhering to Judaism. Moreover, this positioning is what gives Kafka a decidedly Christian view of Judaism. This relates to Torberg's notion of Kafka's Jewishness *constituting* his universalism (or catholicity), but Anders is far more skeptical than Torberg about how neatly Judaism, Christianity, and universalism fit together in Kafka's oeuvre.

What exactly does Anders mean when he states that Kafka looks at his being a Jew with Christian eyes? He argues that this is more than just a preoccupation with guilt, redemption, punishment, and sacrifice. Indeed, Kafka sees the Jew's outsiderhood through a Christian lens, i.e., Kafka reads a socio-cultural condition theologically. For Kafka, according to Anders, the "expulsion from Paradise" is an "eternal condition" from which we cannot be redeemed in this world, and this produces a "frozen striving for redemption."[23] Anders considers this notion decidedly Christian for at least two reasons: first, because the existential situation of unshakeable guilt reflects an internalization of the idea of original sin; and second, because Kafka's insistence on non-belonging *to the Jewish people* is fundamentally non-Judaic. For instance, Anders invokes Abraham's covenant on behalf of the Jewish people to suggest that Judaism is founded on an idea of (Jewish) inclusivity, such that, theologically speaking, the Jewish religion emphasizes the belonging and inclusion of Jews, not the exclusion of non-Jews.[24] Without disputing Kafka's feelings of outsiderhood as a fact of social experience, Anders contends that Kafka Christianizes this condition by expressing the need to be redeemed from a state of permanent exclusion.[25]

Significantly, it is precisely those aspects of Kafka's writing that supposedly reflect a Christian perspective that Anders painstakingly distanced himself from in his own personal efforts at Jewish self-fashioning. In his 1978 essay "Mein Judentum" ("My Judaism") Anders identifies the essence of his identification as a Jew in his rejection of the doctrine of original sin and the imperative to correct

---

23 Anders, "Kafka: Ritual Without Religion," 567.
24 Anders, "Kafka: Ritual Without Religion," 568.
25 See Anders, *Kafka, Pro und Contra*, 93–94.

the Christian misunderstanding of Jewish chosenness. Two passages from this essay are particularly revealing. The first is an anecdote from his schoolboy days, in which Anders answers the question of when he first felt himself to be Jewish. Asked by another child about redemption and sin, the young Anders already then refuses to accept the state of affairs that the Christian child takes as given – namely, that we are all born into sin, that we are awaiting redemption, and that Christ is the redeemer. He states quite explicitly that "being a Jew" ("ein Jude sein") took on a certain significance at this point: it meant a firm rejection of the guilt internalized by Christians and imposed by them onto Jews.[26] Anders thus asserts that even he, whose Jewish upbringing was significantly less traditional and observant than Kafka's, feels an innate disconnect from the doctrine of original sin. His unwillingness to internalize inescapable guilt and participate in a "frozen striving for redemption" is the foundation of Anders's self-understanding as a Jew, whereas Kafka's whole oeuvre struggles with guilt and redemption. Anders's own Judaism is rooted in a few essential beliefs and convictions that are contradicted by Kafka's writing.

The second aspect of Anders's self-description as a Jew that sheds light on his critique of Kafka concerns his understanding of Jewish election, which also relates to the matter of inclusion and exclusion.[27] He explains that much anti-Semitism derives from misunderstandings of this idea, which in facts stems from a rather commonplace and uncontroversial passage in the Bible: the Jews were "chosen" in the sense that they had a "unique reciprocal covenant" with their God; they could worship no other God, and God could "choose" no other people. Yet there were other groups who had their own gods, perhaps with the same covenant as the Jews; this is the concept of henotheism, according to which a monotheistic group does not necessarily deny the existence of other deities that might be worshipped by other groups. During this "*'henotheisitic' epoch of Judaism,*" monotheism did not mean that there was only one God in an absolute sense, but rather that each people had its own "tribal god" and was potentially "chosen" by that God. The problem, Anders explains, arose when other groups, i.e., non-Jews, adopted the Old Testament and transformed the God of the Jews into the God of all people. This led non-Jews to believe that the Jews were asserting an arrogant

---

26 Günther Anders, "Mein Judentum," in *Das Günther Anders Lesebuch* [*The Günther Anders Reader*], ed. Bernhard Lassahn, Diogenes, Zurich 1984, 234–251, 235–236.
27 My claim is that there are two theological ideas – one relating to original sin, the other relating to Jewish election – that are crucial for Anders's own Judaism and for his critique of Kafka. There are additional social, historical, and cultural dimensions of his Jewishness that he describes in "My Judaism."

and exclusionary claim that only they were the chosen people of the one true God, a misevaluation which fostered centuries of resentment and hatred. Thus, according to Anders, the problem of Jewish election exists only for non-Jews who misunderstand the henotheistic period as simply monotheistic and who misconstrue Jewish claims to chosenness as universal rather than private. Anders feels a "Jewish duty" to clarify this misunderstanding about Jewish election to his Christian readers.[28]

Anders's well-intentioned but unorthodox interpretation of Jewish election appears to stem from distaste for the concept of chosenness. His explanation reflects a left-wing universalism that relativizes this idea. And yet it also invokes and advances the rhetoric of inside and outside, and treats his Jewish perspective as privileged. For Anders, it is natural – and forgivable – that his Christian readers would misconstrue the idea of Jewish election; as a Jew, he is uniquely poised and morally compelled to clarify the matter.[29] Anders thus reaffirms, this time through his own ability and need to see the world from a Jewish perspective, the outsider position of the Jew. Indeed, he thoroughly embraces and participates in this brand of Jewish outsiderhood: the Jew stands outside, according to Anders, but he stands outside *together with other Jews*, and this confers certain benefits and enables certain insights. The privilege of this outsider position is what allows and obligates Anders to help bring about religious harmony and understanding.

In Anders's view, Kafka is fundamentally alienated from Judaism: he adopts a Christian perspective on original sin and Jewish chosenness. This is what makes him a "double pariah" not only in the sense that Anders explicitly intends – belonging fully to neither Eastern nor Western Jewry – but also in the sense that he experiences exclusion as a Jew (Eastern *and* Western), and then again on account of his Christianizing perspective.[30] This actually makes him a triple pariah, though Anders does not himself state this. To claim that Kafka looks at his being a Jew with Christian eyes is a highly personal charge: Kafka accepts original sin and the endless striving for redemption, the rejection of which lies at the heart of Anders's own definition of his Judaism.[31] Though he empathizes

---

28 This is a paraphrase of Anders's argument (see Anders, "Mein Judentum," 245–246).

29 Anders, "Mein Judentum," 245–246.

30 Anders, *Kafka, Pro und Contra*, 18.

31 Anders's argument seems theologically flawed. After all, the endless striving for redemption belongs more to Judaism than Christianity, where the savior has already come and saved the souls of his followers. Anders seems aware of this objection, and responds with a preemptive but unsubstantiated claim: "The paradox of Jewish messianism (which might be said always to have rejected any Messiah appearing in the real world as a false Messiah) has nothing in common with the paradox of Kafka's ideal of redemption, devoid as it is of a definite goal" (see Anders, *Franz*

with Kafka's Jewish suffering, he cannot accept Kafka's fundamentally non-Judaic worldview. Indeed, this is so insidious that it kindles suspicions of treason. Anders is not simply confused, alienated, and disappointed by Kafka; he feels, as a Jewish writer and thinker, a deep sense of betrayal.

3 Writing for the Perpetrators: Anders Sharpens His Critique

Though Anders's ambivalence toward Kafka had been openly declared by 1951 via the title of his book about Kafka, it became most explicit in the Kafka section of the 1984 introduction to his essay collection *Mensch ohne Welt*, the tone and content of which oscillate between reverence and dismissal. Anders states that while re-reading Kafka's works in preparation for the publication of his essay in *Commentary*, he had been caught between "*Bewunderung und Abneigung*," or "admiration and aversion." He explains that, on the one hand, he felt that he had established a quite accurate reading of Kafka's religiosity, a reading "whose sharp and polemical tone and content stood out in the generally fashionable, pseudo-religious as well as pseudo-political, murmurings about Kafka."[32] (To support this assessment, Anders mentions several important thinkers, including Ernst Bloch and Georg Lukács, who had praised his essay.[33]) On the other hand, he realized that the human catastrophes of the time – including the Holocaust and the bombing of Hiroshima – had rendered literary study, and even literature itself, a luxury. Anders's ambivalence plays out not only on the level of Kafka criticism, or literary criticism in general, and its relationship to moral and political crisis, but also in his own "personal" relationship to Kafka. Indeed, it is here that Anders identifies the matter of original sin as having stood at the core of his resistance to Kafka:

> Since the (very belated) moment I realized that without the concept of original sin all of European culture would have been impossible, I have been outraged by the injustice of this concept. I have always rejected as presumptuous the meaningless and worthless demand that I, without awareness of sin or guilt of any kind (let alone an inherited one), should feel guilty, even savor the feeling of guilt – which many took as further proof of my guilt. He who

---

Kafka, 91). Even if this were a valid interpretation of Jewish messianism, Kafka's striving without a goal is unlike Christian striving, the point of which is the return of Christ.
32 Anders, "Einleitung," XXXVI.
33 Anders, "Einleitung," XXXVI–VII.

defends himself as non-guilty, insists even on his innocence, supposedly makes himself more guilty, for example of "self-righteousness." To me, as opposed to Kafka, this was all absolutely unacceptable. To confess guilt, to go so far as to take pleasure in the confession of guilt – I was profoundly resistant to this while writing my Kafka essay.[34]

Anders is not merely skeptical of the authors of those 11,000-plus books on Kafka. He is, at some level, angry with – or at least disapproving of – Kafka himself for having provided fodder for this industry. Echoes of the story about the school-boy from "Mein Judentum" resonate in the preceding quotation: Anders suspects that Kafka would have readily submitted to the Christian boy's accusations and assumed the guilt ascribed to him. For Anders, such an action amounts to a kind of Jewish treason – felt all the more acutely because Kafka not only accepts Christian guilt, but takes pleasure in it.

Traces of Anders's feeling of betrayal are present in the versions first published in English, in 1949, and in German, in 1951; however, it is most explicit in the 1984 introduction. Here Anders argues that Kafka does not in fact write for the weak, the victimized, the disenfranchised, the underdog, the Jew – the "loser sons," as the literary scholar and cultural critic Avital Ronell has memorably called them – but for the winners, the authorities, the fathers, the Christians, the postwar Germans – the "Eichmannsöhne und -enkel" ("the sons and grandsons of Eichmann"), to use a phrase Anders employs in "Mein Judentum" and elsewhere.[35] Anders's response to Kafka's supposed treason is decidedly vengeful: it involves not only a gesture of disavowal and expropriation, but also a literary and ethical subversion that strikes at the heart of Kafka's writing. By claiming that Kafka falls on the side of winners rather than losers, Anders reverses the power dynamic that seems to undergird Kafka's moral universe, thereby rendering him a far less sympathetic writer than he is generally taken to be. While other Kafka critics of the day – existentialists, atheists, Jews, Germans, Austrians, Czechs, etc. – were desperately trying to claim Kafka as theirs, Anders seemed eager to disavow him.

My reading is closely tied to Max Brod's critique of Anders's essay. Brod asserts that Anders misconstrues this power dynamic in Kafka, in that Anders mistakenly thinks that Kafka validates rather than criticizes those who exert authority, ascribe guilt, and exact punishment. By ignoring "that which is positive and active in [Kafka] that exists alongside the negative" – in particular Kafka's capacity for belief in a higher power – and missing Kafka's irony, the

---

34 Anders, "Einleitung," XXXIII.
35 Anders, "Mein Judentum," 235.

point of which is to expose and reject these arbitrary abuses of power, Anders, according to Brod, comes to the absurd conclusion that "Kafka was an anticipatory fascist."[36] This conclusion *would* be absurd, were it an accurate description of Anders's position. It seems unlikely that Anders believed that Kafka displays a proto-fascist ideology. (It is similarly doubtful that Brod sincerely thought this about Anders.) However, Anders does declare Kafka guilty of a kind of treason – against the Jew, the weakling, the loser – which lends some credence to Brod's admittedly exaggerated charges. Without ascribing to Kafka the invidious position that Brod claims it does, Anders's characterization of Kafka's failed or absent Judaism undermines the attitudes toward power and submission generally associated with Kafka's writings.

The following passage from *Kafka, Pro and Contra* effectively illustrates Anders's critique:

> In his own complicated but consistent way, then, Kafka is a realist; he shows what the world looks like from the outside. [...] The possibility that the newcomer might be right in suspecting that customs are in fact decrees, that the rationalist might in fact have an insight into *truth*, is an idea which Kafka never expresses. For him the newcomer is *always* wrong, on principle, for in a way Kafka sees the problem of the alien, the newcomer, the Jew, *through the eyes of those who do not accept the alien*.[37]

Anders is attempting to paraphrase the perspective that Kafka represents, not the belief that underlies this perspective, which is neither Anders's nor Kafka's. Brod misreads Anders: he thinks Anders is claiming that Kafka *agrees* with this perspective, and thus thinks that Anders attributes deep malice and even fascist inclination to Kafka. However, Anders is not claiming that the stranger is wrong to question authority, or that Kafka believes this: after all, the only one who possesses the "truth," even in Anders's account, is the stranger. But he is saying that Kafka only ever represents this position – the one according to which "the alien, the newcomer, the Jew" never finds acceptance or validation. According to Anders, Kafka writes the story of the loser, but from the perspective of the winner.

Anders's reading does not quite attribute fascist attitudes to Kafka, and yet it is accusatory. Brod discerned this without having found the proper expression for it. If Kafka truly represents the perspective of the winner, even in a story about the plight of a loser, where does this leave the loser? If Kafka fails to give voice to the views and beliefs of the weakling, even if the reader senses that this weak-

---

36 Max Brod, "Ermordung einer Puppe namen Franz Kafka" ("Murder of a Puppet Named Franz Kafka"), in Über Franz Kafka [*On Franz Kafka*], Fischer, Frankfurt/M. 1985: 375–387, 382, and 385.
37 Anders, *Franz Kafka*, 28 (italics added to reflect the original).

ling is indeed the bearer of truth, then it would seem that Kafka has abandoned the very ones who most need him. To depict every situation "through the eyes of those who do not accept the alien" is to forsake all the aliens who seem to occupy the moral center of his stories and garner the reader's attention, sympathy, and support. This is the charge Anders levels against Kafka: not proto-fascism, but abandonment – of the weaklings, the sons, the servants, the Jews. As he notes in the 1984 introduction, "if in this work I persuaded myself that I had discovered an *enemy* in Kafka, this was because every inclination to servility and assimilation rubbed me the wrong way."[38] This is the closest Anders comes to a confession: he thinks that Kafka champions – or at least takes some degree of pleasure in – weakness and submission, and Anders finds this intellectually and morally repellant. He is determined to show that there are dire and dramatic consequences to Kafka's "Christian worldview" – not just for Kafka, but for his readers and above all for his "loser sons," who are left with nothing. It is *supposed* to hurt to think that Kafka has forsaken his weaklings, his strangers, his Jews. This, it should be noted, is why Brod is so upset in his rejoinder to Anders's essay.

According to Anders, Kafka adopts a Christian perspective on Jewish matters. This move by Kafka not only estranges Anders, but also results in a shift of narrative and figural allegiance away from the loser: the winner is validated, not in the sense that he is on the side of truth and right, but in the sense that the story belongs to him. Thus, Kafka's fiction presents heroes, not anti-heroes; the weak are left with nothing, not even narrative perspective. The final, arguably most extreme step in Anders's critique occurs in the final paragraph of the Kafka section of the 1984 introduction, which, as noted, teems with hostility and arrogance towards literary critics and even Kafka himself. Anders attempts to explain the postwar German resurgence of interest in Kafka in a way that indirectly but undoubtedly blames Kafka for making himself available to a society of guilty Germans who have consistently failed to take responsibility for their complicity in Nazi crimes:

> The interest that Jews have taken in Kafka's representation of Jewish existence is of course completely legitimate. In contrast, what requires explanation is the fervent curiosity that broke out among Germans after 1950. Those who were guilty of and complicit in the excessive crimes of the Hitler regime, who knew very well what they had done and yet were not only not charged with or punished for anything, but rather, with few exceptions, continued to live in a self-satisfied and smug manner – they were presumably thankful to have been supplied with an *antipodal* figure.[39]

---

38 Anders, "Einleitung," XXXII.
39 Anders, "Einleitung," XXXIX.

Anders suggests there was a perfect fit between postwar Germans – who were aware of their guilt but were neither charged nor punished for their crimes – and a character like Josef K., in *Der Proceß* [*The Trial*], who is not guilty but is nevertheless accused and convicted of unknown crimes. Such characters, according to Anders, provide a kind of moral-psychological absolution for guilty Germans: "*The deification of Kafka once again erased the fact that his family of millions had been killed.* And if he is made famous, then primarily not as a writer, but rather as someone who provides a figure that, though *not guilty, nevertheless gets punished.*"[40] For Anders, Kafka's "counter-figure" offers a convenient escape from causal thinking about guilt and punishment, which is precisely what postwar Germans were seeking, given that their guilt had gone unpunished. By praising and deifying Kafka – not for his literary talent, but for creating this figure of moral absence – they find a means to erase their own crimes. Kafka thus enables postwar Germans to acknowledge their guilt without having to face any consequences for it, such as suffering or loss. This is the precise opposite of how things work in Kafka's fictions, where there are consequences regardless of culpability, but in both situations guilt and punishment are uncoupled and exist in an unpredictable relationship.

Anders concludes the Kafka section of the 1984 introduction – his last word, so to speak, on the author – by claiming that this moral-psychological "Kafka epidemic" (the "Kafka-Seuche," as he terms it) was most pronounced not necessarily among the most ideologically committed and criminal Nazis, but among the far more numerous group of fellow travelers. This epidemic, he notes, "arguably broke out in particular among those Germans who had participated halfheartedly and who wished to prove – also to themselves – that they could accept, at least in the form of literature, the guilt ascribed to them by the victors, and thereby work through their remorse in the form of artistic admiration."[41] According to Anders, Kafka upsets the moral order, enabling everyday Germans to cover over their crimes against the Jewish people with literary appreciation. He enables a generation of complicit Germans to sidestep their guilt by offering up "artistic appreciation" ("Kunstbewunderung") as a valueless substitute for and distraction from ethical behavior. (Incidentally, this reading sheds light on Anders's suspiciousness of German literary study, or *Germanistik*.)

Anders thus performs a radical reversal of the received wisdom about Kafka. Rather than give voice to the weakling, the victim, the Jew, Kafka actually offers a generation of Nazi fellow travelers a free pass, liberating them from their guilt not

---

40 Anders, "Einleitung," XXXIX. Emphasis in original.
41 Anders, "Einleitung," XXXIX.

through actual atonement but through a quick aesthetic fix. Kafka is thus deified not because he is a suffering Jew (though presumably this adds a useful note of piety and solemnity to the Nazi sympathizers' interest in him), but because he presents a world in which punishment is uncoupled from crime. If there are people who suffer the consequences of transgression without having transgressed, so the thinking goes, then there must be people who transgress without suffering any consequences. By depicting a situation of moral chaos, Kafka makes himself available to soothe the collective conscience of the "sons and grandsons of Eichmann" that populate postwar Germany and facilitate their false and facile efforts to come to terms with the past.

The arguments about Kafka's appeal to a postwar German audience are thus closely tied to Anders's claims about Kafka's supposedly universal but actually Christian perspective on guilt and his idea that Kafka tells the story of the loser from the perspective of the winner. His Christian "winner" perspective makes him appealing to and worthy of admiration among Germans, especially guilty ones. It is only because Kafka embraces a Christian worldview that he can be such a feel-good source of wonder to guilty Germans, which means not that Kafka is responsible for or had somehow predicted the Holocaust, but that he is part of the reason why postwar Germans continue to shirk responsibility for it. Thus, by identifying the heart of Anders's critique in his claim about Kafka's Jewish treason, we begin to understand Anders's peculiar conclusion that Kafka helps complicit postwar Germans forget their guilt, or gives them license to ignore it.

4 Conclusion: On Not Forgiving Kafka

There is much to object to in Anders's critique of Kafka. As a psychologistic reading of literature, it is not especially convincing: can matters of personal conscience and responsibility really be projected onto fictional characters in the way that Anders assumes, and will such projection achieve for the reader the kind of moral cleansing that Anders suggests? It is far from clear that literature works this way for any individual reader, much less for a (national) body of readers. As an ethical reading, Anders's critique likewise misses the mark: as Brod notes, the fact that Kafka presents a world in which guilt and punishment are unlinked does not mean that he approves of such a world or is a moral nihilist. Kafka presents a modern existential condition; he does not validate it, and his fictions in fact leave much room for moral deliberation. Moreover, as concerns literary form, Anders's reading seems simplistic: a detailed analysis of Kafka's rhetoric and narrative strategies would reveal that he never really chooses sides, and thus he cannot be accused of betraying his weaklings, servants, and Jews. He channels winners and losers, Jews and Christians, fathers and sons, often in close succession or even simultaneously. Kafka represents the world not simply from multiple perspectives, but from perspectives embedded within other perspectives; similarly, he never levels absolute judgment, be it *pro* or *contra*. It is senseless to argue that he writes from one position and against another, for Kafka's work often evidences multiple shifts in perspective, reversals in voice, and acts of ventriloquism. This is true even within some of the short texts.[42] Finally, the emotional charge of Anders's commentary arouses suspicion: can someone so clearly driven by anger, resentment, and a sense of betrayal really be trusted to read Kafka fairly?[43] Anders seems eager – even fixated – to punish Kafka for having betrayed the principle belief at the heart of Anders's own identification as a Jew, namely, the rejection of original sin. But why should Kafka have felt Jewish in precisely the same way as Anders? Indeed, Kafka surely could never have written an essay entitled "My Judaism" (or, for that matter, "My Jewishness"), given his ambivalence and exasperation over these issues. It is only because Anders identifies so closely with Kafka that he can feel so betrayed when it turns out that Kafka's sense of Jewishness lies elsewhere than his own. Anders's deeply personal and idiosyncratic vendetta against Kafka casts suspicion on his interpretive motives.

And yet there is also an important point that speaks for Anders's critique: it posits a meaningful connection between Kafka and the Holocaust without subscribing to the "Kafka-as-oracle-of-doom position," as the literary critic Paul Reitter has termed it.[44] Rather than claim that suffering and loss in Kafka have pre-

---

42 See, for example, Avital Ronell on the "corruption" of perspective in Kafka's *Brief an den Vater* [*Letter to the Father*], in Avital Ronell, *Loser Sons: Politics and Authority*, University of Illinois Press, Urbana 2012, 118.

43 Ronell serves as a counter-model to Anders, for she discerns precisely the same problem in Kafka (a siding with authority, a delight in submission), yet her response is earnest and straightforward. Ronell cites the "noble and fruitful feeling" that accompanies Kafka's sense of domination by the father and notes that she is uneasy about this "miniscule supplement of profit when accounting for the losses" (Ronell, *Loser Sons*, 127):

> the way Kafka aligns disruptive allegations within the frame of description makes one slow down and crawl under newly oppressive spaces. I would not be forced to crouch and strain in this way if our letter writer had not included-excluded the parenthetical bit about the noble feeling and fruitfulness, perverting an otherwise perfectly tranquil-seeming semantic field, shaking it up so as to expose uneven valences and intrusive tropes of encounter. (Ronell, *Loser Sons*, 128)

Ronell registers with dismay and distaste the very thing that Anders registers with thinly concealed anger and resentment, namely the pleasure Kafka takes in being a "loser."

44 Reitter, "Misreading Kafka."

dictive value, which always implies, implausibly, that he had somehow divined future catastrophes and that the Holocaust could be predicted, Anders suggests that literary expression can have a psychological *use value* for Kafka's postwar German readers. He does not analyze Kafka's works in order to explain an event that Kafka could not have anticipated. This alone puts Anders a step ahead of most readings that suggest a link between Kafka and the Holocaust. Rather, he looks at a contemporary phenomenon – the resurgence of interest in Kafka in postwar Germany – and tries to explain it as a matter of reception. According to Anders, suffering and loss in Kafka do not enable us to see the future; instead, they help us understand how a later generation of readers might have reacted to the reality that their undeniable guilt had gone unpunished. Even if this is a misreading of Kafka for the reasons outlined above, it is nonetheless a productive and revealing one vis-à-vis the society that Anders is critiquing.

First, regardless of whether Kafka can actually perform this work of collective postwar German absolution, the diagnosis itself is important and largely accurate. Kafka may not provide the solution to the moral problems of German guilt, but Anders has correctly identified the issue. He warns against substituting aesthetics for ethics; such substitution is why he worries that Kafka, in upsetting the moral order according to which guilt and punishment exist in a predictable causal relationship, has opened the door for *Kunstbewunderung* to fill the void of ethics. Anders seems keenly aware of the ease with which postwar Germans could let ideals of culture, art, and education stand for (and in the way of) a sincere reckoning with their moral failings. Indeed, he suspects that this is precisely what has motivated their exaggerated interest in Kafka. Let us not be fooled by superficial or self-serving philo-semitism, he seems to say. Let us not believe that a widespread social pathology has been cured simply because postwar Germans have elevated a Jew to the status of a literary god – a Jew, by the way, who can be deified thusly only because he himself died before he could become a victim of the Nazis. Regardless of whether Anders is correct about why postwar Germans read Kafka (and assuming, contra Anders, that Kafka is indeed free of any culpability for this possible misappropriation), he is right to admonish them for any possible attempt to transfigure literary appreciation into moral defense.

Second, Anders perceptively draws attention to the problem of mass complicity under the Nazis, a topic which Hannah Arendt had already written about in 1945[45] and which would be a cornerstone of Anders's only other work on Nazi crimes and the Holocaust. In the latter work – an open letter to the son of

---

45 Hannah Arendt, "Organized Guilt and Universal Responsibility," in *Essays in Understanding, 1930–1954*, ed. Jerome Kahn, Schocken Books, New York 1994, 121–132.

Adolf Eichmann, entitled *Wir Eichmannsöhne: Offener Brief an Klaus Eichmann* [*We Sons of Eichmann: Open Letter to Klaus Eichmann*], from 1964[46] – Anders acknowledges the centrality of Arendt's concept of organized guilt to his thinking about postwar Germany. Arendt had developed this concept as a means to describe a totalizing politics in which everyone is guilty but no one can be held accountable. However, whereas Arendt's theory is descriptive, Anders's is prescriptive: he believes in the possibility for personal moral behavior despite the assembly-line character of modern life, in which individuals perform localized tasks and shirk responsibility for the end results of the "totalizing machine" – results that include such catastrophes as the Holocaust and the bombings of Hiroshima and Nagasaki.[47] The mental abdication of responsibility leads Anders to dub postwar Germany and Austria an "Eichmann world" ("Eichmannwelt") inhabited by "Eichmann sons" ("Eichmannsöhne").[48] Understanding the central claims about responsibility and moral action that Anders advances in the open letter sheds light on his critique of Kafka from thirteen years earlier, even before that critique had been fully elaborated in the 1984 introduction to *Mensch ohne Welt*. Moreover, it helps show that Anders's Kafka book had always – or at least since 1951[49] – been an attempt to expose and explain postwar German society's failure to take responsibility for its Nazi past. It is a Holocaust book not because it accounts for the source of Nazi atrocities, but because it accounts for and reflects upon their disturbing afterlife. Anders's *Kafka, Pro and Contra* is thus an important intervention in the debates about responsibility and culpability under the

---

46 Günther Anders, *Wir Eichmannsöhne. Offener Brief an Klaus Eichmann*, C. H. Beck, Munich 2002.

47 Anders, *Wir Eichmannsöhne*, 81–82.

48 Anders, *Wir Eichmannsöhne*, 58. See also Ann-Kathrin Pollmann, "Ein offener Brief an Eichmanns Söhne. Günther Anders schreibt Klaus Eichmann" ("An Open Letter to Eichmann's Sons. Günther Anders Writes Klaus Eichmann"), in *Interessen um Eichmann: israelische Justiz, deutsche Strafverfolgung und alte Kameradschaften* [*Concerning Eichmann: Israeli Justice, German Law Enforcement and Old Comraderies*], ed. Werner Renz. Campus Verlag, Frankfurt/M. 2012, 241–258. As Pollmann argues, for Anders postwar Germany is an "Eichmann world" ("Eichmannwelt"), a society thoroughly in the grips of the legacy of National Socialism. Anders addresses and takes up the fates of "significant individuals" – e.g., Eichmann's son, or the pilot of the airplane from which the atom bomb was dropped on Hiroshima – who enable an articulation of broad complicity in mass annihilation. Anders does not simply condemn this "Eichmann world," but seeks to show how the catastrophes of World War II created new kinds of guilt and demanded new measures for atonement.

49 It is possible that this dimension of the text also goes further back, but nothing definitive is known about the content of the 1934 lecture. Ann-Kathrin Pollmann has searched in vain for lecture notes or a transcript.

Nazis, especially as it presents an early diagnosis of widespread moral failing that survived the defeat of the Third Reich.

In a curious way, it is the Holocaust that saves Anders's Kafka book. As suggested earlier, his readings, though astute and quite intelligent at times, are nonetheless psychologically unconvincing, morally simplistic, insufficiently attentive to literary form and rhetoric, and too laden with affect to be considered neutral or objective criticism. We should read Anders less for his literary insights than for his account of postwar Germany's lingering Nazi problem; for him, the enthusiastic reception of Kafka is merely a symptom of this problem. Anders does not blame Kafka for the Nazi genocide against the Jews, nor does he praise Kafka for having some sort of prescient vision of this horror. Instead, he evaluates the guilt of a society of "Eichmen" ("Eichmänner") and blames Kafka for unwittingly helping them to assuage this guilt.

By reading Anders's Kafka study as a book on the afterlife of the Holocaust in postwar Germany one comes to understand why his critique of Kafka grows sharper, not milder, over time. From 1951 to 1984, Anders seems to have become angrier and more resentful toward Kafka and to have formulated the charge of betrayal in increasingly direct and harsh terms. This development makes sense only if his book is meant not simply as a reading of Kafka but as an explanation of a postwar German pathology that Kafka's writing allegedly exacerbates. If the evasion of moral responsibility for Nazi crimes was acute in 1951, it was even worse in 1984. The longer Kafka enables this evasion, the more guilty he becomes of betraying his Jewishness. This is why Anders articulates the disturbing implications of his original assessment of Kafka so explicitly in the final publication of the essay. It is also why Anders cannot simply forgive Kafka. Time does not heal this wound. Indeed, the effects of Kafka's ostensible treason – that he takes a Christian view on the world and that he tells the story of the loser from the perspective of the winner – become more pronounced and far-reaching over time. This also explains why Anders's reading of Kafka remained essentially unchanged from 1934 to 1984, even as his sense of its power as a tool of societal diagnosis further solidified.

Even if Anders would agree that Kafka, sixty years after his death in 1924, cannot possibly be blamed for the misuse of his writings by morally compromised Nazi collaborators in the decades after World War II, he would probably be unwilling to pardon him for his supposed acts of betrayal on ethical grounds. Anders holds that people must be held responsible not only for their actions and words, but also for the consequences of these actions and words. This is the essence of the practical ethics he puts forth in *We Sons of Eichmann* and elsewhere. Moral behavior, in his view, involves projecting beyond one's particular place in the world and addressing one's role in the totalizing "world machine." This requires acts of imagination through which we will finally learn to assume responsibility for our behavior and choices.[50] Thus, to excuse Kafka for inadvertently facilitating a process of facile self-absolution for guilty Germans would constitute an abdication of moral responsibility.

And yet it is not the case that Anders's belief system affords no possibility for forgiveness. A central point of his letter to Klaus Eichmann – a letter which fell upon deaf ears – is that Anders is willing to forgive him for having consistently supported his father, but only on a double condition: Klaus Eichmann must publicly renounce this position now that his father has been condemned and hanged, and he must join the fight against nuclear proliferation. This is not Christian forgiveness; rather, it is a forgiveness that hangs together with Anders's moral pragmatism: forgiving someone, since it involves sanctioning or at least overlooking immoral behavior, can be justified only when past wrongdoings can be redressed via future good deeds – a kind of practical, this-worldly repentance. It is only the living, one must assume, who can be forgiven, since they remain capable of reforming themselves for moral action and preventing future catastrophe. Klaus Eichmann did not accept Anders's suggestion for repentance. Kafka, however, was never even offered the chance. He died before he could prove himself worthy of forgiveness for an offense for which only Anders thought to condemn him.

Ironically, Anders transforms Kafka from a prophet into an agent of historical delusion, from someone who sees into someone who prevents others from seeing. Nonetheless, in the process Kafka also shifts once again from the particular to the universal. His Jewishness is not merely of local interest, relevant only for Jews, but something that relates to a large segment of postwar German society. Anders is speaking from both sides of his mouth: he is deriding and dismissing literary study as a senseless luxury, yet is also explaining the extremely damaging effects of a certain phenomenon in literary reception. He wishes to expose Kafka's supposed universalism as actually Christian and to reveal Kafka's betrayal of his fellow Jews, and yet he makes a remarkably convincing case for using Kafka as a cipher by which to understand the general phenomenon of postwar German guilt, and maybe even the universal problem of literature and critique.

---

50 Anders, *Wir Eichmannsöhne*, 34–35.

Works Cited

Anders, Günther, "Einleitung," in *Mensch ohne Welt. Schriften zur Kunst und Literatur* (Munich: C. H. Beck, 1984), XI–XLIV.

Anders, Günther, *Franz Kafka*. Trans. A. Steer and A. K. Thorlby (London: Bowes & Bowes, 1960).

Anders, Günther, *Kafka, Pro und Contra. Die Prozeß-Unterlagen* (Munich: C. H. Beck, 1963).

Anders, Günther, "Kafka: Ritual Without Religion: *The Modern Intellectual's Shamefaced Atheism*," in *Commentary* (December 1949): 560–569.

Anders, Günther, "Mein Judentum," in *Das Günther Anders Lesebuch*. Ed. Bernhard Lassahn (Zurich: Diogenes, 1984): 234–251.

Arendt, Hannah, "Organized Guilt and Universal Responsibility," in *Essays in Understanding, 1930–1954*. Ed. Jerome Kahn (New York: Schocken Books, 1994), 121–132.

Brod, Max, "Ermordung einer Puppe namens Franz Kafka," in *Über Franz Kafka* (Frankfurt/M.: Fischer, 1985), 375–387.

Phillips, William, "*The Great Wall of China*, by Franz Kafka; and *The Kafka Problem*, edited by Angel Flores," in *Commentary* (June 1947): 594–596.

Pollmann, Ann-Kathrin, "Ein offener Brief an Eichmanns Söhne. Günther Anders schreibt Klaus Eichmann," in *Interessen um Eichmann: israelische Justiz, deutsche Strafverfolgung und alte Kameradschaften*. Ed. Werner Renz (Frankfurt/M.: Campus Verlag, 2012), 241–258.

Reitter, Paul, "Misreading Kafka," in *Jewish Review of Books* (Fall 2010), http://jewishreviewofbooks.com/articles/172/misreading-kafka/, 7 May 2015.

Ronell, Avital, *Loser Sons: Politics and Authority* (Urbana: University of Illinois Press, 2012).

Torberg, Friedrich, "Kafka the Jew," in *Commentary* (August 1947), http://www.commentarymagazine.com/article/kafka-the-jew/, 7 May 2015.

Birgit R. Erdle
Dis/Placing Thought: Franz Kafka and Hannah Arendt

1 The Grounds of Reality

The position in which thought finds itself after 1945 forces Hannah Arendt to leave the realm of philosophy and turn to literature. Only there does she encounter the question preoccupying her. In her "Preface: The Gap Between Past and Future," which precedes the essays of her 1961 volume *Between Past and Future*, the moment in which she moves into a reading of Kafka is rooted in an experience that refers to the relation between thought and reality: "reality has become opaque for the light of thought."[1] For Arendt, the present Now in which she writes and thinks is marked by the fact that thinking and reality are no longer linked with one another. Thought does not withstand the shock of reality. Therefore, thinking – "no longer bound to incident as the circle remains bound to its focus" – risks "either [...] becom[ing] altogether meaningless" or relying on truths that have been passed down, "old verities which have lost all concrete relevance."[2] Through the quote from René Char's *Feuillets à Hypnos* [*Leaves of Hypnos*] that introduces her essay – "*Notre héritage n'est précédé d'aucun testament* – 'our inheritance was left to us by no testament'"[3] – Arendt's reflections on the divergence of thinking and reality are temporally and logically connected back to the time of the resistance and to the realization of the abyss into which the grounds of reality, *der Boden der Tatsachen*, have changed, as she writes in an earlier text.

So it is the wish to describe this particular situation in exact terms that leads Arendt to Kafka. She reads Kafka's text – an account from the series of the "He" pieces from 1920[4] – as a "parable." In this term, she follows the word's etymological traces of meaning (*para*, next to, and *ballein*, to throw) and describes the text as a kind of missile of rays, which sheds light on the hidden inner structure of occurrences. It is precisely in this image that she sees the singularity of Kafka's

---

1 Hannah Arendt, "Preface: The Gap Between Past and Future," in *Between Past and Future. Eight Exercises in Political Thought*, Penguin Books, New York 2006, 3–16, 6.
2 Arendt, "Preface: The Gap Between Past and Future," 6.
3 Arendt, "Preface: The Gap Between Past and Future," 3.
4 Franz Kafka, *Tagebücher* [*Diaries*], eds. Hans-Gerd Koch, Michael Müller and Malcolm Pasley, Fischer Taschenbuch Verlag, Frankfurt/M. 2002, 851–852.

literature. These rays of light, "thrown alongside and around the incident [...] do not illuminate its outward appearance but possess the power of X rays to lay bare its inner structure that, in our case, consists of the hidden processes of the mind."[5]

Kafka's text constructs a thought-image in which a man, "he," is caught between two antagonistic forces: "The scene is a battleground on which the forces of the past and the future clash with each other; between them we find the man whom Kafka calls 'he,' who, if he wants to stand his ground at all, must give battle to both forces."[6] Arendt emphasizes that the time currents of the past and the future collide as antagonistic forces only because "he" is already there: "the fact that there is a fight at all seems due to the presence of the man."[7] The term "presence" here emerges in its spatial connotation. Arendt's commentary moves back and forth between "the human being" and the "he," the pronoun that occurs in Kafka's text; this oscillation thereby signals how the contradiction between the universal and the singular in her reading is at once opened up and settled. "Seen from the viewpoint of man," she notes, time is not a continuum; rather, it is precisely "at the point where 'he' stands,"[8] broken or cracked open. In the course of Arendt's reading, her formulation of "the point where 'he' stands" – in which the place available to "him" has shrunk to an extreme minimum, to a point on a line – translates itself into the "standpoint," addressing the capacity of judgment: "'his' standpoint is not the present as we usually understand it but rather a gap in time which 'his' constant fighting, 'his' making a stand against past and future keeps in existence."[9] Thus, Arendt's interpretation introduces the figure of speech of the "ground under one's feet" [*Boden unter den Füßen*] and links it to a reflection on temporality by reading it as an "insertion in time": "Only because man is inserted into time and only to the extent that he stands his ground does the flow of indifferent time break up into tenses."[10] For Arendt, it is precisely this insertion, this point of rupture in the indifferent flow of time, that marks the beginning of a beginning, as she writes with recourse to Augustinus.

Kafka's "he," in its third-person singular form, appears as a pronoun that designates a person who can jump out of the line of battle only in dreams. In this sense, one can claim that the form of grammatical speech in Kafka's text enacts

---

5 Arendt, "Preface: The Gap Between Past and Future," 6–7.
6 Arendt, "Preface: The Gap Between Past and Future," 10.
7 Arendt, "Preface: The Gap Between Past and Future," 10.
8 Arendt, "Preface: The Gap Between Past and Future," 10.
9 Arendt, "Preface: The Gap Between Past and Future," 10.
10 Arendt, "Preface: The Gap Between Past and Future," 10.

the tension, or perhaps even the conflict, between the singular and the universal: the "he" in Kafka at once opens and limits generalization; it does not mediate between the singular and the universal. Arendt, however, wishes to develop a generally valid metaphor for the activity of thinking via her insertion of and commentary on Kafka's text. She searches for a metaphor that allows her to think the activity of thinking in such a way that it is bound to and remains anchored in the present – "rooted in the present."[11] Thus, she is concerned with a thinking that remains embedded in "human time"[12] and does not surrender to "the old dream which Western metaphysics has dreamed from Parmenides to Hegel of a timeless, spaceless, suprasensuous realm as the proper region of thought."[13] Arendt brings the jump of which Kafka's "he" "at least" dreams, namely, that "some time in an unguarded moment – and this would require a night darker than any night has ever been yet – he will jump out of the fighting line,"[14] into accord with the jump that thought makes from human time into the timeless sphere of metaphysics, as passed on in the Western history of philosophy.

For Arendt, Kafka's "he" has barely enough room to stand, because Kafka clings to the traditional image that presents time as a straight line.[15] She replaces the figure of the line with a parallelogram. According to her argument, this form comes into being due to the mere fact that the "he" is imprisoned in the flow of time: "The insertion of man, as he breaks up the continuum, cannot but cause the forces to deflect, however lightly, from their original direction."[16] This tiny deflection of powers allows something spatial, an angle, to appear, and so the geometric metaphor changes: the line becomes a plane. Or in Arendt's words: the interval, the gap where "he" stands, becomes something like a parallelogram of forces. Yet what is decisive for the genesis of this metaphor of the activity of thinking, which Arendt gleans from her reading of Kafka, is that now the point where the forces collide becomes the origin of a third figure: namely, a diagonal line. Exactly inverting the two forces that meet in the point, this diagonal force would be limited from its point of origin but infinite with regard to its end. The movement of thinking expressed in this image would thus have a determined direction through past and future, yet at the same time it would not be completable. Arendt

---

11 Arendt, "Preface: The Gap Between Past and Future," 12.
12 Arendt, "Preface: The Gap Between Past and Future," 11.
13 Arendt, "Preface: The Gap Between Past and Future," 11.
14 Arendt, "Preface: The Gap Between Past and Future," 7.
15 See Arendt's notes and comments on different conceptions of temporality in her *Denktagebuch. 1950–1973* [*Thinking Diary. 1950–1973*], eds. Ursula Ludz and Ingeborg Nordmann, Piper, Münich and Zürich 2002.
16 Arendt, "Preface: The Gap Between Past and Future," 11.

describes the figure constituted in this way as a "small non-time-space in the very heart of time,"[17] which cannot be passed on but must be constantly reinvented. According to this thought-image, then, it is the activity of thinking itself that forges a narrow path of non-time in the time-space of the mortal human.

Thus, we see that the attempt to open the battlefield outlined by Kafka characterizes the direction that Arendt's reading of Kafka takes. However, citing an insertion from Kafka's text, Arendt emphasizes that "this is only theoretically so"[18] – *so [...] aber nur teoretisch ist.*[19] According to Arendt, it is more likely that "he" – unable to find the diagonal – perishes from fatigue, "aware only of the existence of this gap in time which, as long as he lives, is the ground on which he must stand, though it seems to be a battlefield and not a home."[20] Moreover, Arendt clarifies that her aim is to confront "the contemporary conditions of thought" with the help of a metaphor. She emphasizes that her claims apply only to mental phenomena, in other words, to thought in time, and cannot be transposed to historical or biographical time. But fragments from the ruinous landscape of biographical and historical time can be touched and sheltered by thought and memory and saved into the (previously noted) "small non-time-space in the very heart of time."

2 Survival and the Temporality of Thought

In her reading of Kafka's text, Arendt is concerned with the interconnection of thought and experience. She thus faces an epistemological question: namely, interrogating the possibility of the recognition – and more generally the acknowledgment – of facts,[21] a question that Arendt confronted not only due to her own experience of persecution, but also because of the knowledge she possessed after 1943, and, later, because of her work for the committee for Jewish Cultural Reconstruction, an organization founded in 1947. Arendt repeatedly cites the recourse to terms, categories, and patterns of explanation that have been handed down,

---

17 Arendt, "Preface: The Gap Between Past and Future," 13.
18 Arendt, "Preface: The Gap Between Past and Future," 12.
19 Kafka, *Tagebücher*, 852.
20 Arendt, "Preface: The Gap Between Past and Future," 12.
21 See Nicolas Berg, *Der Holocaust und die westdeutschen Historiker. Erforschung und Erinnerung* (Göttingen: Wallstein, 2003), 471; edited and shortened English version: Nicolas Berg, *The Holocaust and the West German Historians: Historical Interpretation and Autobiographical Memory*, ed. and trans. Joel Golb, The University of Wisconsin Press, Madison 2015.

including those of philosophy and historiography, as ways that allow us to evade this actuality. How we may understand the figure of speech of the "ground under one's feet," which belongs to the register of long-established idiomatic formulations, as a palimpsest in Arendt's reading of Kafka, emerges when we consult one of Arendt's earlier texts, the "Dedication to Karl Jaspers" ("Zueignung an Karl Jaspers"), written in 1947. There, she speaks of the grounds of reality [*dem "Boden der Tatsachen, wie er sich mir darstellt"*][22] and remarks: "In Auschwitz, the factual territory opened up an abyss into which everyone is drawn who attempts after the fact to stand on that territory."[23] Thus, if one must leave the grounds of reality so as not to disappear into the gaping abyss and not to accept "the world created by those facts as necessary and indestructible,"[24] then how can thought nevertheless expose itself to this actuality, that is, not turn away from it, not negate it? Arendt's conception of the "world" at this point suggests that she is concerned with a universal referentiality of thought. Indeed, for Arendt, as we have seen from her reading of Kafka in "Preface: The Gap Between Past and Future," the universal is not situated beyond time. Yet one may note a universalizing gesture in the "Dedication to Karl Jaspers," a gesture that passes through the term of the "singular." If the grounds of reality have become an abyss, then the space that one enters to gain distance from this abyss is, in Arendt's view, an empty space. In this empty space, she remarks, there would be neither people nor nations, and thus no national belonging, but only "individuals."[25] In Arendt's argument, these individuals [*Einzelne*[26]] are translated into "survivors"[27] [*Überlebende*[28]], in order to lead to the term "human beings"[29] [*Menschen*[30]].

22 Hannah Arendt, "Zueignung an Karl Jaspers," in *Sechs Essays* [*Six Essays*], Lambert Schneider, Heidelberg 1948, 5–10, 6. In the English translation, the passage reads, "I speak here only of factual matters as I see them." See Hannah Arendt, "Dedication to Karl Jaspers," in *Essays in Understanding, 1930–1954*, ed. Jerome Kohn, trans. Robert and Rita Kimber, Harcourt Brace Jovanovich, New York 1994, 212–216, 213.

23 Arendt, "Dedication to Karl Jaspers," 215. In the original German, the passage reads, "In Auschwitz hat sich der Boden der Tatsachen in einen Abgrund verwandelt, in den jeder hineingezogen wird, der nachträglich versucht, sich auf ihn zu stellen." Arendt, "Zueignung an Karl Jaspers," 9.

24 Arendt, "Dedication to Karl Jaspers," 213.

25 Arendt, "Dedication to Karl Jaspers," 215.

26 Arendt, "Zueignung an Karl Jaspers," 9.

27 Arendt, "Dedication to Karl Jaspers," 215.

28 Arendt, "Zueignung an Karl Jaspers," 10.

29 Arendt, "Dedication to Karl Jaspers," 216.

30 Arendt, "Zueignung an Karl Jaspers," 10.

But the figure of speech of the "ground under one's feet," bound to the reading of Kafka's "he," also migrates into a text written much later, namely, "Where Are We When We Think?" the fourth chapter of Arendt's posthumously published volume *The Life of the Mind*. In this chapter, it is not only the reflection on the requirements of thought after the Shoah that is at stake; rather, the question bound with this problematic has broadened into one about the temporality of thought. In other words, it is a matter of discovering "where the thinking ego is located in time and whether its relentless activity can be temporally determined."[31] The context of the argument in which Arendt's reading of Kafka is now embedded has come uncoupled from the question about the inheritance, the testament, the legacy, conveyed in her essay "The Gap Between Past and Future" through the citation from René Char's *Feuillets à Hypnos*. Arendt refers to Kafka's text as a poetic analysis, thereby highlighting the knowledge of literature and of the literary process that constitutes such knowledge: "he" "analyzes poetically our 'inner state' in regard to time, of which we are aware when we have withdrawn from the appearances."[32] Even if the impossible task of understanding what occurred is not foregrounded here, the situation of the "he," who is caught between the forces of the past and future and must battle both "if he wants to stand his ground at all,"[33] is described in almost the same words as in the essay written nearly a decade earlier. As is the case in the earlier essay, Arendt's way of reading the Kafka text describes the present as a "battleground." And she adds, "This battleground for Kafka is the metaphor for man's home on earth."[34] If a universalizing gesture is undeniable in this formulation, which transforms Kafka's "he" into an "Everyman," then Arendt's commentary in the following sentences again restricts this generalization, by adapting the pronominal form: "seen from the viewpoint of man, at each single moment inserted and caught in the middle between *his* past and *his* future, both aimed at the one who is creating his present, the battleground is an in-between, an extended Now on which he spends his life."[35] Thus, Arendt's rhetoric vacillates between, on one hand, generalization – "the insertion of a fighting presence,"[36] in which "he" has suddenly disappeared from the scene – and, on the other hand, concretization: "Only insofar as he thinks [...] does man – a 'He,' as Kafka so rightly calls him, and not

31 Hannah Arendt, *The Life of the Mind. 1: Thinking. 2: Willing*, Harcourt Brace Jovanovich, San Diego, New York, and London 1978, 202.
32 Arendt, *The Life of the Mind*, 202.
33 Arendt, *The Life of the Mind*, 203.
34 Arendt, *The Life of the Mind*, 205.
35 Arendt, *The Life of the Mind*, 205.
36 Arendt, *The Life of the Mind*, 208.

a 'somebody' – in the full actuality of his concrete being, live in this gap between past and future."[37]

In the recurring reading of Kafka's text that Arendt offers in *The Life of the Mind*, the category of the "temporality of thought" mediates as question between the singular and the universal. The movement of thought that Arendt initiates here positions Kafka's thought-image in line with the respective philosophical concepts of Nietzsche, Heidegger, and Kant, yet it still attributes to Kafka's text a specific reference ("the fable's realism"[38]) to reality. This may stem from the radical way in which Kafka's language displays both the desperate situation of the "He" and resists translation into general terms. The experience of losing all ground, which Arendt expresses in her "Dedication to Karl Jaspers" and which characterizes her reading of Kafka in "Preface: The Gap Between Past and Future," is re-written in the chapter "Where Are We When We Think?" in such a way as to foreground other questions and motives: namely, the question of books' survival,[39] the project of dismantling metaphysics and the inherited categories of philosophy,[40] and the turn towards a fragmented past, from which perhaps only pieces can be saved.[41] If what is at stake in Arendt's question about the place of the thinking I in time is the term of a form of thought that remains embedded in "human time,"[42] removed from the old dream "which Western metaphysics has dreamed," then the desperate position of the "he" in Kafka's text, as Vivian Liska emphasizes, would hardly be solvable by repeating this old dream.[43] According to Liska's interpretation, Kafka's desperation consists in the fact "that, beyond the realm of the theoretical, he is defeated and stifled by *both*," by past and future:

---

37 Arendt, *The Life of the Mind*, 210.

38 Arendt, *The Life of the Mind*, 203.

39 Arendt, *The Life of the Mind*, 210.

40 Arendt, *The Life of the Mind*, 212.

41 Arendt, *The Life of the Mind*, 212. At this point in Arendt's text, the structure of literary quotes inserted into the discursive language of her philosophical argumentation thickens. In addition to a fragment from Shakespeare's *The Tempest* (I, 2), which recurs throughout her writings, she cites a passage from W.H. Auden's 1937 poem "As I Walked Out One Evening," which takes up again the connection to the dead: "'O plunge your hands in water, / Plunge them in up to the wrist; / Stare, stare in the basin / And wonder what you've missed.//'The glacier knocks in the cupboard, / The desert sighs in the bed, / And the crack in the tea-cup opens / A lane to the land of the dead...'" Arendt, *The Life of the Mind*, 212–213.

42 Arendt, "Preface: The Gap Between Past and Future," 11.

43 Vivian Liska, "The Gap between Hannah Arendt and Franz Kafka," in *arcadia. Internationale Zeitschrift für Literaturwissenschaft / International Journal of Literary Studies* 38.2 (2003): 329–333, 332.

"What he is searching for, what would truly redeem him, seems to happen some-where else entirely – somewhere else than in theory."[44]

3 Kafka's "He" and "We": Beyond the Dualism of the Singular and the Universal

One of Kafka's diary entries from 1910 shows how discussion of the "he" in Kafka's literature both plays out the tension between the singular and the universal and translates the static aspect of this dualism into a flexible, dynamic structure. The "ground under one's feet," the figure of speech that underlies the notion of the present as battlefield, as Arendt develops it in her interpretation of the Kafka text of 1920, is explicitly evoked in the diary entry: "he has only as much ground as his two feet take up, only as much of a hold as his two hands encompass, so much the less, therefore, than the trapeze artist in a variety show, who still has a safety net hung up for him below."[45] The space in the world accorded to this single subject refers to his body by corresponding precisely with its measurements.

Thus, Kafka here takes up the figure of speech of the "ground under one's feet" in such a way that the space allotted "him" has shrunk to the dimensions of "his" feet. The deictic form that occurs in the second sentence of the diary entry already makes clear, however, that this does not describe a general "human condition: "But forgetting is not the right word here. The memory of this man has suffered as little as his imagination."[46] A complex system of relations between "he," "we," "man," and "human" begins in the following sentence, a system that discloses the relation between the designated individual and the collective: "But they just cannot move mountains; the man stands once and for all outside our people, outside our humanity."[47] Moreover, a reflection on figures of temporality

---

44 Liska, "The Gap between Hannah Arendt and Franz Kafka," 331.
45 Franz Kafka, *The Diaries of Franz Kafka, 1910–1913*, ed. Max Brod, trans. Joseph Kresh, Secker & Warburg, London 1948, 26–27. The German original reads, "er hat nur soviel Boden als seine zwei Füße brauchen, nur soviel Halt als seine zwei Hände bedecken, also um soviel weniger als der Trapezkünstler im Varieté, für den sie unten noch ein Fangnetz aufgehängt haben." Kafka, *Tagebücher*, 118.
46 Kafka, *The Diaries of Franz Kafka, 1910–1913*, 26. ("Aber Vergessen ist hier kein richtiges Wort. Das Gedächtnis dieses Mannes hat ebensowenig gelitten als seine Einbildungskraft." Kafka, *Tagebücher*, 118.)
47 Kafka, *The Diaries of Franz Kafka, 1910–1913*, 26. ("Das Gedächtnis dieses Mannes hat ebensowenig gelitten als seine Einbildungskraft. Aber Berge können sie eben nicht versetzen; der

develops from the opposition of the singular subject, who stands "outside our people," "outside our humanity," on one hand, and "[us] others," on the other. Outside – this term also refers to the exclusion from past and future. As we have seen, the text refuses the possibility of deducing the radical and irrevocable position of this *outside* from the two categories of forgetting and of memory, and it does so already in the first sentence ("But forgetting is not the right word here"). So it is not a problem of forgetting that leads to the fact that this one nameless person has neither a future nor a past, that he owns "only the moment," "the everlasting moment of torment which is followed by no glimpse of a moment of recovery" [*der immer fortgesetzte Augenblick der Plage, dem kein Funken eines Augenblicks der Erhöhung folgt*].[48] The temporality that takes shape in this passage is one of continued moments; the duality and dynamic of the relation between continuity and moment has collapsed in the scene described.

The text opposes the individual, whom it introduces as "this man," to a collective *we*, from whose perspective and with whose voice it argues or recounts. Where the one who stands outside finds footing on the plane only to the degree that the plane corresponds with the undersides of his feet and hands, those who belong to the collective *we* are held by their past and future: "We others, we, indeed, are held in our past and future" [*Uns andere uns hält ja unsere Vergangenheit und Zukunft*].[49] But this hold is not described as a static prop. Rather, it is presented in the image of a floating balance, which relates size and weight – size of the future and weight of the past – to one another: "We pass almost all our leisure and how much of our work in letting them bob up and down in balance. Whatever advantage the future has in size, the past compensates for in weight, and at their end the two are indeed no longer distinguishable."[50]

Past and future have turned unnoticeably from a mooring into a burden. To keep them in balance apparently requires much time, attention, and strength. At their ends, past and future are indistinguishable – "earliest youth later becomes

---

Mann steht nun einmal außerhalb unseres Volkes, außerhalb unserer Menschheit." Kafka, *Tagebücher*, 118.)

48 Kafka, *The Diaries of Franz Kafka, 1910–1913*, 26; Kafka, *Tagebücher*, 118. The obvious difference in meaning that exists here between the word "recovery" (*Erholung*) in the English translation of the diary entry of 1948 and the word "*Erhöhung*" (exaltation) in the German-language critical edition of 2002 can perhaps be traced to a misreading of the original manuscript version.

49 Kafka, *The Diaries of Franz Kafka, 1910–1913*, 27; Kafka, *Tagebücher*, 118.

50 Kafka, *The Diaries of Franz Kafka, 1910–1913*, 27. ("[F]ast allen unseren Müßiggang und wie viel von unserem Beruf verbringen wir damit, sie im Gleichgewicht auf und abschweben zu lassen. Was die Zukunft an Umfang voraus hat, ersetzt die Vergangenheit an Gewicht und an ihrem Ende sind ja die beiden nicht mehr zu unterscheiden." Kafka, *Tagebücher*, 118.)

distinct, as the future is, and the end of the future is really already experienced in all our sighs, and thus becomes the past."[51] Therefore, the idea that past and future can be differentiated does not hold, and it is exactly this impossibility that prevents either from assuming the shape of a circle that closes. Yet it is not this little gap which is decisive in developing the imagery over the course of the text but rather the relation between center and periphery. "So this circle along whose rim we move almost closes. Well, this circle indeed belongs to us, but belongs to us only so long as we keep to it."[52] Instantly, within one sentence, both power relations and spatial relations have turned nearly into their opposite. The subjects and the "we" referred to in the text occupy not the center of the circle but its rim, and what promised to provide support, upon which one could rely, to which one could hold, has revealed itself to be something that must be held in turn – a task nearly impossible to fulfill, or one that seems, at any rate, excruciatingly difficult. In the next phrase, the perspective – that is to say, the spatial relations – again change completely because of a tiny misstep: "if we move to the side just once, in any chance forgetting of self, in some distraction, some fright, some astonishment, some fatigue, we have already lost it [the circle] into space."[53] The image of losing the circle, which is actually a rim, into space – an almost unavoidable loss if one lives and thinks – outlines the real place of the subject or subjects.

This image of the relationship between past and future, which the text develops here as a thought-figure of time, is a geometrical image. Similarly to the "He" text from 1920, it presents a status report, a structural image, a linear ruling, in which the graphic, circle, point, line, plane emerge. This geometrical image stands in opposition to that metaphor of time designating a condition beyond or before this loss, namely, the metaphor of the "tide of the times": "until now we had our noses stuck into the tide of the times, now we step back, former swimmers, present walkers, and are lost."[54] The historical metaphor of the "tide of

---

51 Kafka, *The Diaries of Franz Kafka, 1910–1913*, 27. ("[F]rüheste Jugend wird später hell wie die Zukunft ist und das Ende der Zukunft ist mit allen unsern Seufzern eigentlich schon erfahren und Vergangenheit." Kafka, *Tagebücher*, 118–119.)

52 Kafka, *The Diaries of Franz Kafka, 1910–1913*, 27. ("So schließt sich fast dieser Kreis, an dessen Rand wir entlanggehn. Nun dieser Kreis gehört uns ja, gehört uns aber nur solange als wir ihn halten." Kafka, *Tagebücher*, 119.)

53 Kafka, *The Diaries of Franz Kafka, 1910–1913*, 27. ("[R]ücken wir nur einmal zur Seite, in irgendeiner Selbstvergessenheit, in einer Zerstreuung einem Schrecken, einem Erstaunen, einer Ermüdung, schon haben wir ihn in den Raum hinein verloren." Kafka, *Tagebücher*, 119.)

54 Kafka, *The Diaries of Franz Kafka, 1910–1913*, 27. ("[W]ir hatten bisher unsere Nase im Strom der Zeiten stecken, jetzt treten wir zurück, gewesene Schwimmer, gegenwärtige Spaziergänger und sind verloren." Kafka, *Tagebücher*, 119.)

the times," of swimming "with the tide" or "against it," was entirely common in Kafka's discursive environment. In the figure of the "former swimmers," Kafka literalizes the metaphor; he exposes its figurative center.

Yet the sentence concluding this text brings into play another category, namely, that of the law: "We are outside the law, no one knows it and yet everyone treats us accordingly."[55] Caused by a tiny oversight or by a moment of awe or fright, a constellation has been produced by the end of the text, a constellation similar to the one at the beginning of the account but not identical: a position *outside* – but now in regards to the law, that is to say, the sphere of the law and/ or religious teachings, and not, as in the beginning, in relation to "our people" or "our humanity."

In contrast to the beginning of the account ("But forgetting is not the right word here. [...] the man stands once and for all outside"), this loss of the circle is not without prerequisites; rather, it emerges from a process that is tied back to the world of the social, of leisure time and profession. If, at the beginning of the tale, an opposition between the nameless individual and a collective speaking in the first-person plural ("our people," "our humanity") is decisive, then at the end it is the opposition of this "we," "lost" and unprotected by the law, and a collective that consists of "everyone." "Everyone": on one hand, the features of mass man or of the average man are delineated there; on the other hand, this means every individual, without exception.

We could read the conversion of the constellation and positions as an allusion to the reality that any identification with an ethnic group (majority or minority) as well as any identification with a universal humanity offers no protection against the threat of falling into an *outside* of the law. Kafka shows the *time of this being lost* as present. "Present walkers": Kafka presents them at once as iconic figures of modernity and as lost beings, no longer supported by past and future, no longer belonging to the flow of history, no longer protected by the law. So one could say that Kafka's diary entries address two forms of the present: first, the continuous grammatical present tense in which the "we" speaks; and second, the present of the *now*, which forms on the surface of the first by producing a past at the same time ("*now* we step back, former swimmers, present walkers, and are lost"). This *now* corresponds with the *extended Now*, as Arendt terms it in her reading of Kafka (referring to "the one who is creating his present, the battle-

---

55 Kafka, *The Diaries of Franz Kafka, 1910–1913*, 27. ("Wir sind außerhalb des Gesetzes, keiner weiß es und doch behandelt uns jeder danach." Kafka, *Tagebücher*, 119.)

ground is an in-between, an extended Now on which he spends his life"⁵⁶) – but at the same time, as we see, it is starkly different.

At this point, where literature and philosophy encounter one another anew, the following question arises: can we read the tension or the opposition between the singular and the universal, negotiated in Kafka's two texts and in Arendt's commentary, as a conflict between, on one hand, what is singular in Jewish experience and, on the other, what is universal in any reflection on the place of thinking and writing? Kafka's "he" in the diary entry from 1910, who owns nothing but the instant ("he has only the moment"), corresponds entirely with a passage from a letter that Kafka wrote to Milena Jesenská in November 1920: "to exaggerate, not one second of calm has been granted me; nothing has been granted me, everything must be earned, not only the present and future, but the past as well – something which is, perhaps, given every human being – this too must be earned, and this probably entails the hardest work of all."⁵⁷ Similar to the passage from this letter, in the 1910 account Kafka thematizes how the individual of whom he speaks here is refused the present of any time, of the future, the present, and past time. We could interpret the correspondence of the two formulations – one from Kafka's journal; the other from his correspondence – as evincing the specific situation of Western Jewish time. This time is measured in seconds.

Kafka's description of events in the public space of Prague in November 1920 testifies to how this conception of time is bound up with the issue of enmity: "I've been spending every afternoon outside on the streets, wallowing in anti-Semitic hate."⁵⁸ The experience of threat and the signs of the crisis or weakness of public space, worsened by war and processes of nationalization, illuminate after the fact the vulnerability that manifests itself in this diary entry of 1910.

Another diary entry, from the same year, similarly pulls the place of writing into the constellation evoked by the account. The expression "hold on," *festhalten*, institutes a link between the scene described in the text and the following

56 Arendt, *The Life of the Mind*, 205.
57 Franz Kafka, *Letters to Milena*, trans. Philip Boehm, Schocken Books, New York 1990, 217. ("[...] das bedeutet, übertrieben ausgedrückt, daß mir keine ruhige Sekunde geschenkt ist, [...] alles muß erworben werden, nicht nur die Gegenwart und Zukunft, auch noch die Vergangenheit, etwas das doch jeder Mensch vielleicht mitbekommen hat, auch das muß erworben werden, das ist vielleicht die schwerste Arbeit." Franz Kafka, *Briefe an Milena. Erweiterte und neu geordnete Ausgabe*, eds. Jürgen Born and Michael Müller, Fischer, Frankfurt/M. 1986, 294.)
58 Kafka, *Letters to Milena*, 212–213. ("Die ganzen Nachmittage bin ich jetzt auf den Gassen und bade im Judenhaß." Kafka, *Briefe an Milena*, 288. See also page 295 and the letter of 30 May 1920 (page 26), in which Kafka speaks about the precarious position of the Jews and the threat and intimidations against them.)

sentence: "December 16. I won't give up the diary again. I must hold on here, it is the only place I can."[59] The dating inscribes a mark in time, which is held in place by the strategic conception of the diaries, in which the diary pages become an open experimental space for writing.

Works Cited

Arendt, Hannah, "Dedication to Karl Jaspers," trans. Robert and Rita Kimber, in *Essays in Understanding, 1930–1954*. Ed. Jerome Kohn (New York: Harcourt Brace Jovanovich, 1994) 212–216.

Arendt, Hannah, *Denktagebuch. 1950–1973*. Eds. Ursula Ludz and Ingeborg Nordmann (Munich and Zürich: Piper, 2002).

Arendt, Hannah, *Essays in Understanding, 1930–1954* (New York: Harcourt Brace Jovanovich, 1994).

Arendt, Hannah, *The Life of the Mind. 1: Thinking. 2: Willing* (San Diego, New York, and London: Harcourt Brace Jovanovich, 1978).

Arendt, Hannah, "Preface: The Gap Between Past and Future," in Hannah Arendt, *Between Past and Future. Eight Exercises in Political Thought* (New York: Penguin Books, 2006), 3–16.

Arendt, Hannah, *Sechs Essays* (Heidelberg: Lambert Schneider, 1948).

Arendt, Hannah, "Zueignung an Karl Jaspers," in *Sechs Essays* (Heidelberg: Lambert Schneider, 1948), 5–10.

Berg, Nicolas, *Der Holocaust und die westdeutschen Historiker. Erforschung und Erinnerung* (Göttingen: Wallstein, 2003).

Berg, Nicolas, *The Holocaust and the West German Historians: Historical Interpretation and Autobiographical Memory*. Ed. and trans. Joel Golb (Madison: The University of Wisconsin Press, 2015).

Kafka, Franz, *Briefe an Milena. Erweiterte und neu geordnete Ausgabe*. Eds. Jürgen Born and Michael Müller (Frankfurt/M.: Fischer, 1986).

Kafka, Franz, *The Diaries of Franz Kafka, 1910–1913*. Ed. Max Brod. Trans. Joseph Kresh (London: Secker & Warburg, 1948).

Kafka, Franz, *Letters to Milena*. Trans. Philip Boehm (New York: Schocken Books, 1990).

Kafka, Franz, *Tagebücher*. Eds. Hans-Gerd Koch, Michael Müller, and Malcolm Pasley (Frankfurt/M.: Fischer Taschenbuch Verlag, 2002)

Kafka, Franz, *Tagebücher. Apparatband*. Eds. Hans-Gerd Koch, Michael Müller, and Malcolm Pasley (Frankfurt/M.: Fischer Taschenbuch Verlag, 2002).

Liska, Vivian, "The Gap between Hannah Arendt and Franz Kafka," in *arcadia. Internationale Zeitschrift ffi Literaturwissenschaft / International Journal of Literary Studies* 38.2 (2003): 329–333.

---

59 Kafka, *The Diaries of Franz Kafka, 1910–1913*, 33. ("Ich werde das Tagebuch nicht mehr verlassen. Hier muss ich mich festhalten, denn nur hier kann ich es." Kafka, *Tagebücher*, 131.)

Notes on Contributors

Michal Ben-Naftali is a writer, a translator, and a lecturer at Tel Aviv University; an editor of the series "The French" for Hakibutz Hameuchad Publishing House and "Après Coup: For Hebraic Aesthetics" for Resling Publishing House. Amongst her books: *Chronicle of Separation* (2000) (translated into English, Fordham University Press, 2015), *The Visitation of Hannah Arendt* (2006), and *Spirit* (2012). Her novel *The Teacher* will be published by the end of 2015. Her translations include *Derrida Reads Shakespeare* (2007), *Nadja* by André Breton (2008), *Le livre à venir – an anthology* by Maurice Blanchot, and *Tales of Love* by Julia Kristeva. She received the Prime Minister's Prize for Hebrew Writers in 2007 and Ha'Aretz's prize for best literary essay in 2008.

Arthur Cools is Associate Professor in Contemporary Philosophy and Aesthetics at the University of Antwerp. He is the author of *Langage et subjectivité. Vers une approche du différend entre Maurice Blanchot et Emmanuel Lévinas* (2007) and co-editor of *The Locus of Tragedy* (2008) and *Metaphors in Modern and Contemporary Philosophy* (2013). His work concentrates on the field of contemporary French philosophy, with particular interest in the question of singularity in relation to subjectivity and the interplay between philosophy and literature.

Stanley Corngold is Professor Emeritus of German and Comparative Literature at Princeton University and a Fellow of the American Academy of Arts and Sciences. He has published widely on modern German writers (e.g., Dilthey, Nietzsche, Musil, Kraus, Mann, Benjamin, Adorno, among others) but for the most part has been translating and writing on the work of Franz Kafka. In 2009, with Benno Wagner and Jack Greenberg, Corngold edited, with commentary, *Franz Kafka: The Office Writings*. In 2010, as a Fellow of the American Academy in Berlin, he published (with Benno Wagner) *Franz Kafka: The Ghosts in the Machine* and edited (with Ruth V. Gross) a collection of essays titled *Kafka for the 21st Century*. Since then he has edited and translated Goethe's *The Sufferings of Young Werther* and a Modern Library edition of Kafka's *The Metamorphosis*. He is currently writing an intellectual biography of the philosopher Walter Kaufmann.

Birgit R. Erdle holds the DAAD Walter Benjamin Chair at the Hebrew University of Jerusalem. She has been a Visiting Professor at the Fritz Bauer Institute at Goethe University Frankfurt/Main (Gastprofessur zur Erforschung des Holocaust und der deutsch-jüdischen Geschichte), the Technical University of Berlin, the University of Vienna, and Emory University. Her research focuses on German-Jewish literature and intellectual history, correspondences between literature and philosophy in modernity, post-history of National Socialism and the Shoah, relationships between memory, materiality, and knowledge, and the epistemology of time in literature and theory. Her recent publications include *Literarische Epistemologie der Zeit. Lektüren zu*

Kant, Kleist, Heine und Kafka (2015) and *Theorien über Judenhass – eine Denkgeschichte. Kommentierte Quellenedition 1781–1931*, co-edited with Werner Konitzer (2015).

Rodolphe Gasché is SUNY Distinguished Professor & Eugenio Donato Professor of Comparative Literature at the State University of New York at Buffalo. His latest book-length studies include *The Stelliferous Fold. Toward a Virtual Law of Literature's Self-Formation* (Fordham, 2011); *Georges Bataille: Phenomenology and Phantasmatology* (Stanford University Press, 2012), and *Geophilosophy: On Gilles Deleuze and Félix Guattari's* What is Philosophy? (Northwestern University Press, 2014). A new book, *Deconstruction, Its Force, Its Violence*, will be forthcoming from SUNY Press at the end of 2015.

Kata Gellen is Assistant Professor of German at Duke University. She is currently completing a manuscript entitled *Kafka and Noise: The Discovery of Cinematic Sound in Literary Modernism.* In a second project, she will explore the Eastern European German-Jewish novel as a modernist form. She has published articles on various topics in German literary modernism, German-Jewish writing, and Weimar Cinema in such journals as *Germanic Review, Modernism/Modernity,* and *The Journal of Austrian Literature.* The authors she works on include Franz Kafka, Joseph Roth, Soma Morgenstern, Robert Musil, and Elias Canetti.

Anna Glazova received her PhD in Comparative Literature and German Studies at Northwestern University. Her dissertation focused on the role of citation in the poetry of Osip Mandelstam and Paul Celan. She has held a postdoctoral fellowship at Cornell University and taught at Johns Hopkins University, as well as at the Goethe-Universität in Frankfurt-am-Main. Her most recent appointment was as Visiting Scholar at Rutgers University. She has published articles on Paul Celan, Osip Mandelstam, Franz Kafka, and Walter Benjamin and co-edited a volume of essays, "Messianic Thought Outside Theology" (Fordham, 2014).

Vivian Liska is Professor of German Literature and the director of the Institute of Jewish Studies at the University of Antwerp. She is also permanent Distinguished Visiting Professor at the Hebrew University of Jerusalem and a member of the visiting staff of New York University. Her academic work focuses on German literature, literary theory, German-Jewish thought, and Modernist literature and poetry after 1945. She is the editor of the book series "Perspectives on Jewish Texts and Contexts" (De Gruyter, Berlin), the *Yearbook of the Society for European-Jewish Literature* (with A. Bodenheimer), and *Arcadia. International Journal of Literary Studies* (with V. Biti). Her most important recent books are *Giorgio Agambens leererMessianismus*; *When Kafka Says We. Uncommon Communities in German-Jewish Literature*; and *Fremde Gemeinschaft. Deutsch-jüdische Literatur der Moderne.*

Lorraine Markotic is Associate Professor in the Department of Philosophy at the University of Calgary. She has published articles and book chapters on Lou Andreas-Salomé, Ingeborg

Bachmann, Marlen Haushofer, Ruth Klüger, Nietzsche, Adorno, Freud, Heidegger, Lacan, Iriga-ray, Kristeva, and Badiou. Her publications have appeared in *Hypatia, symplokē, New Nietzsche Studies, German Life and Letters, Modern Austrian Literature, American Imago, Seminar, Paragraph, Nietzsche-Studien, Modern Drama,* and *Deutsche Zeitschrift für Philosophie.*

Brendan Moran is Associate Professor of Philosophy (and Affiliate Associate Professor of German) at the University of Calgary. His publications include *Wild Unforgettable Philosophy in Early Works by Walter Benjamin* and, co-edited with Carlo Salzani, *Philosophy and Kafka* and *Towards the Critique of Violence: Walter Benjamin and Giorgio Agamben.* He has published articles on Benjamin, Agamben, Kafka, Heidegger, Levinas, and Salomo Friedlaender, and recently completed a study titled *Philosophy as Renegade: Benjamin's "Kafkan" Politics.*

Jean-Michel Rabaté, Professor of English and Comparative Literature at the University of Pennsylvania since 1992, co-editor of the *Journal of Modern Literature,* is a co-founder and senior curator of Slought Foundation, Philadelphia, an arts institution promoting conversations in visual culture. Since 2008, member of the American Academy of Arts and Sciences. Rabaté has published more than 35 books and collections of essays. Recent titles include *Handbook of Modernism Studies* (Blackwell, 2013), *Crimes of the Future* (Bloomsbury, 2014), *The Cambridge Introduction to Literature and Psychoanalysis* (Cambridge University Press, 2014), and *1922: Culture, Politics and Literature* (Cambridge University Press, 2015). Forthcoming are *The Pathos of Distance* (Bloomsbury), *Think, Pig! Beckett at the Limit of the Human* (Fordham), and the edited volume *After Derrida* (Cambridge University Press).

Søren Rosendal is a PhD scholar at the University of Aarhus in Denmark. His thesis (working title *Hegelian Tensions*) is a reading of Hegel that focuses on the ambivalent or contradictory structures of Hegel's logic. From these structures the goal is to outline a minimal ontology of tensions, especially as regards freedom and cognition. Besides work in German idealism his research also focuses on French structuralism, philosophy of nature, and literature. He has presented at various international conferences and is currently working on an extended article on the ideology of possibility (publication forthcoming).

Shimon Sandbank is Emeritus Professor of English and Comparative Literature at the Hebrew University of Jerusalem, where he held the Katherine Cornell Chair of Comparative Literature. He has published books and articles on connections between Hebrew poetry and the European tradition, theory of translation and Kafka (*After Kafka: The Influence of Kafka's Fiction* (1989)). His Hebrew translations of English and German literature include Chaucer's *Canterbury Tales,* Shakespeare's *Sonnets* and *Richard II,* Kafka's *The Castle* and *Description of a Struggle,* Brecht's *Mother Courage,* and collections of poems by Goethe, Hoelderlin, Celan, Yeats, Hopkins, and many others. Sandbank is the recipient of the Israel Prize for literary translation (1996).

Eli Schonfeld is a Berkowitz Fellow at New York University School of Law, specializing in phenomenology and modern Jewish thought. His first book, *The Wonder of Subjectivity: A Reading of Levinas' Philosophy* (Resling, 2007) interprets Levinas from a metaphysical point of view, stressing the importance of the question of God and the question of the soul in his philosophy. He is currently completing a work on the phenomenology of consolation in philosophy and Jewish thought.

Galili Shahar is Professor of Comparative Literature and German Studies and serves as the head of the Minerva Institute for German History at Tel Aviv University. His field of research and teaching includes German, Jewish, and Hebrew literature and thought.

David Suchoff received his PhD in Comparative Literature from the University of California at Berkeley and is Professor of English at Colby College. He is author of *Kafka's Jewish Languages: The Hidden Openness of Tradition* (2012), and *Critical Theory and the Novel* (1994). He has translated and written the Introductions to Alain Finkielkraut's *The Imaginary Jew* and *The Wisdom of Love*, and Hermann Levin Goldschmidt's *The Legacy of German Jewry* (2007), Introduction co-written with Willi Goetschel; his translation from the Yiddish, *Listen and Believe: The Ghetto Reportage of Peretz Opoczynski and Joseph Zelkowicz*, will appear with Yale University Press in 2015. A new essay, "Kafka's Openings and Beckett's Cage," is forthcoming from *The Germanic Review*.

Arnaud Villani, scholar of classics and philosophy. His work is divided between: (1) poetry (poems, translation of poetry, theoretical articles; an unpublished book: *Poetry, as Step Beyond Phenomenology*); (2) Philology (collaboration with André Sauge on the philology of Heidegger; with Heinz Wismann on pre-Socratic philosophy: *Before Philosophy* (unpublished); translations and commentary on *Poem* by Parmenides: *Parménide or Denomination*, preface by Gilbert Romeyer-Dherbey (Hermann, 2011), and *Parmenides in five concepts* (Sils-Maria, 2013); and (3) philosophy: *Précis of Naked Philosophy* (Nu (e) 2002), *Small Metaphysical Meditations on Life and Death* (Hermann, 2008), and *Short Treatise on Nothing* (Hermann, 2009). He maintained a correspondence with Gilles Deleuze and devoted three books to him: *The Wasp and the Orchid* (Belin, 1999), *The Vocabulary of Gilles Deleuze* (Noésis, 2003) (with R. Sasso), and *Logic of Gilles Deleuze* (Hermann, 2012). His study on Kafka, *Kafka, Man in Free Fall*, will be published shortly.

Name Index